The History of Crime and Criminal Justice Series

David R. Johnson and Jeffrey S. Adler, Series Editors

Murder in America
A History

Roger Lane

Ohio State University Press
Columbus

Library of Congress Cataloging-in-Publication Data

Lane, Roger.
    Murder in America : a history / Roger Lane.
        p.   cm. — (History of crime and criminal justice series)
    Includes bibliographical references and index.
    ISBN 0-8142-0732-4 (alk. paper). — ISBN 0-8142-0733-2 (pbk. : alk. paper)
    1. Murder—United States—History.   I. Title.   II. Series.
HV6524.L36   1997
364.15′23′0973—dc21   96-39626
                                                                                          CIP

Cover design by Gore Studio.
Type set in Adobe Garamond by G&S Typesetters, Inc.
Printed by Thomson-Shore, Inc.

9   8   7   6   5   4   3   2   1

For Maggie and Mike, who grew up with it,
Joanna, who signed on,
and, of course, for Marjorie

Contents

Acknowledgments

Many people contributed to this book, at many levels. Three editors at Ohio State University Press, who suggested the project, are among the more obvious. The enthusiasm of Charlotte Dihoff made a great difference, especially toward the end. Jeffrey Adler was a perceptive and supportive critic. Above all, David Johnson, an old friend, was an indispensable guide this time around, answering a barrage of electronic questions with patience and wit.

Any book of this kind relies on the scholarly work of others as well as myself. Most of the authors listed in the Select Bibliography are owed a debt, and many of them, such as Ted Robert Gurr and Julie Johnson-McGrath, are longtime associates and correspondents. Two people read the manuscript with especial care. Randolph Roth, years ago, inspired me with his nonviolent approach to the study of violence, and more recently shared a number of useful suggestions. And Eric Monkkenon, as he has before, continually supplied specific information, bibliography, and ideas before reviewing the final draft.

Some time ago Amanda Crane, Lydia Martin, and Dr. Eric Pollack did much research on early twentieth-century homicides in Philadelphia that never saw the light until now. More recently, Tara Steeley performed a range of duties as research assistant with efficiency and good cheer. Ken Cooper did the table, with accomplished ease. Copy-editor Sheila Berg did her job with hawk-eyed vigilance and great speed.

Robert Collins, in the name of his father, Benjamin R. Collins, furnished much of the needed support. Haverford College was helpful as always; I want especially to thank former provost Bruce Partridge, Dorcas Allen, Sharon Nangle, the entire staff at McGill Library, and all of my colleagues in the history department, including John Spielman, who has just retired.

I owe a special debt to my large and lively family, above all to my closest critics, Joanna and Marjorie, who had the most to endure, and, in many ways, to contribute.

Introduction

The Historian as Detective

This book is a history of criminal homicide, or murder, in America. Murder is one of the two most common forms of intentional homicide, defined simply as the killing of one human being by another; the other is war. The third, capital punishment, is linked to both; death may be decreed either for failing to kill when a society demands it or for killing when a society forbids it. All three forms are linked in other, sometimes surprising ways. But while war has been a main—perhaps the main—subject of traditional history, historians have only newly turned their attention to criminal homicide.

As fact of life and death, object of horror and curiosity, subject of epic and myth, murder of course goes back as far as we can dig; Cain's slaying of his brother, Abel, is central to the biblical account of human genesis, and the bones of prehistoric men and women show clear evidence of homicide, even cannibalism. But while the subject is older than history itself, what is new is serious historical investigation of murder, and the legal response to it, as a means of understanding social behavior.

In fact historians have simply added a new layer of questions to those that have long been asked by ordinary citizens, theologians, and scholarly experts of all kinds. Many of the old questions endure simply because they are always fresh, or cannot be answered with certainty; and some of the old answers endure simply because they work. But historical detective work has provided some surprises, as careful analysis of the who, what, how, and when of homicide in earlier times has often challenged the conventional wisdom, clearing some of the usual suspects

and pointing to others. At the same time, the nature of the clues left by
past events has left much unanswered, often unanswerable, confirming
what every reader knows: that much about murder remains a mystery.

One of the ways in which the study of murder fits into the study of
history is that writing history is really a form of detective work. The
object for both detectives and historians is to reconstruct a version of
some past event or events as accurately as possible, to make a convincing story out of whatever clues have been left behind. A good historian,
or detective, needs imagination, logic, and experience to make the case,
but ultimately it must be based on the evidence—whether interviews,
fingerprints, official documents, private papers, or physical remains.
And while good clues make a tight case, some can be read in more than
one way, and scattered, ambiguous, or absent clues leave us with mysteries difficult or impossible to crack.

But while professional historians are often mystery fans, there are
differences between writing the social history of homicide and solving
a crime, some of which may be seen through a look at two of the best-
known murder cases in American history. The killings of Abby and
Andrew Borden in Fall River, Massachusetts, on the Thursday morning
of August 4, 1892, held the title "Most Famous Murder Case in American History" for a little over a hundred years, until the Los Angeles
knifing deaths of Nicole Brown Simpson and Ronald Goldman on the
Sunday evening of June 12, 1994. Despite differences in these cases
almost as great as the century and continent that divide them, there
is no secret to why they seized our imaginations. Both involved two
victims; both were exceptionally bloody events, the Bordens savagely
chopped up, apparently by an ax, Simpson and Goldman by a knife.
The accused killers in both cases were close relatives, the Bordens'
daughter, Simpson's ex-husband; both defendants were seen as objects
of sympathy, unlikely villains universally and semiaffectionately known
not by their full names but as "Lizzie" and "O.J."

But above all, both cases presented strong elements of mystery: the
timing was tight, no weapons or bloody clothes were found, the prosecution's expert witnesses were tripped up by the defense. And while
millions believed that the accused were guilty, millions more, and more
important all of the jurors, could not believe that two middle-aged

people with spotless public reputations could commit such acts of apparently senseless brutality.

The central question in both cases, as in most brought to trial, was simply *who,* with other questions—how, why, and where—treated as secondary and the answers, such as "he was jealous" or "in the bedroom, with an edged instrument, around 8 A.M.," used simply as part of the evidence pointing to the specific identity of the killer. But for the historian, *who* in this sense—answerable in terms of individual identity—is rarely the central issue. Sometimes it is possible to reinvestigate ancient murder mysteries, to stretch the "true crime" genre back decades or even centuries, to suggest who might have killed the Bordens or even the "little princes in the tower," two young heirs to the British throne who disappeared sometime in 1483. But for a social history of homicide in general, it is not the exceptional cases but the typical ones that are most interesting, those that reveal the most about the times and places in which they occurred. And in most cases there is rarely any doubt about who committed the crimes. The more important question is rather *why,* as applied to both the accused and the legal outcome of the case.

For a time, during the nineteenth century and part of the twentieth, there was an attempt to answer the more general *why* about the act itself in terms of the individual *who.* As part of an attempt to establish a new science of criminology, to explain the causes of crime in general and homicide in particular, researchers turned to the more established science of biology, later to psychology. Criminal behavior was "deviant," or different, by definition—which suggested that criminals were, too; that is, the shape of their heads, or their intelligence quotients, or their genetic makeup was different from that of ordinary law-abiding people. But this has proved an investigative dead end; while biology has some bearing on the subject of violence—most obviously, males, especially young males, behave more violently than women, for example—it has so far proved almost impossible to distinguish killers or other criminals from others of the same age and sex in terms of their internal chemistry or the wiring of their brains, and absolutely impossible to predict that any given individual will or will not commit a given crime.

That is in fact perhaps the one conclusion shared by those who have investigated the subject not through science but through religion, philosophy, and the arts. The issue that has always made murder a major theme of the world's great literature—not only the Bible and our own Western *Oedipus, Hamlet,* and *Macbeth* but also the great epics of many peoples across the globe—is again not who but why. The simple identity of a killer is rarely a question, and never as important as the reasons underlying the act; the exploration of homicide is at this level part of the ongoing effort to understand and explain the nature of our common humanity. The key word is "common": it is assumed that to understand murder is to understand ourselves, in that we all share at least the capacity to destroy ourselves and each other.

This book shares that basic assumption. But beyond that no history is able, as history, to explore the deeper questions of responsibility and morality any more than it can those of individual identity.

The historical record, then, with its often incomplete or absent clues, does not allow us to search everywhere the imagination reaches. But it suggests its own versions of the questions who? and why? Sometimes historians can unearth much about an individual act and probe its significance; certainly we can add up and speculate about the meaning of many thousands of acts spread over centuries, and the social and legal reactions to them. One key question, as among contemporary sociologists and criminologists, is thus, how many? This and the other questions that grow out of it are not then individual but collective and social—to ask *who* means "what kinds of people" commit homicide, to ask *why* means "what kinds of conditions" or "motives" have driven them. Given the uniquely historical dimension, the next obvious set of questions is comparative: in terms of who does what to whom, how often and why, and what then is likely to follow, how does the modern United States compare to seventeenth-century Massachusetts, the slave South, or the western frontier? How have homicide and the reactions to it changed over time, and why?

The ultimate purpose of all these questions about murder is to find out more about the societies in which it has occurred. And to compare different times and places is to suggest the kinds of conditions that drive murder rates up and down among different groups.

The answers are not always fully satisfactory. The most obvious of historical questions, to begin with, is, how much higher (or lower) are today's murder rates than those of one or two or three hundred years ago? But despite its simplicity, this is a question that the historical record cannot answer with any precision.

It is never easy to measure the extent of any illegal activity. Even in the most vigilant of modern jurisdictions there is a "dark figure" representing the unknown and unknowable number of acts that are never discovered, or reported. The job of measuring gets harder when the search is extended back into times and places in which assault, for example, or prostitution were so common, or so fully tolerated, that no records were kept of how much or how many. Things get even more complicated when some acts are declared criminal at one time but not another: cockfighting, selling horse meat, carrying a weapon without a license.

Murder is in fact the easiest of crimes to trace through time: always taken seriously, almost always subject to law, never common enough to be completely tolerated or overlooked. The legal disposition of murder cases is—usually—a matter of record, wherever records have survived. And while there is a dark figure for wholly undiscovered homicide, as for all crimes, the number is rarely large: exotic or hard-to-detect ways of murdering people are not often found in the real world, in which dead victims are usually identified and so are the majority of killers. But even murder presents problems of comparison across time.

In the United States today the procedure for counting the "murder rate" for any jurisdiction is a standard one. A coroner's inquest or medical examiner determines that a given death is a homicide; the number of such homicides is tallied for a full year; the total number of people in the population, calculated from the census, is then divided into the number of homicides, and the result is expressed as a rate per 100,000. In Louisiana, for example, the rate for 1993 was 20.3 killings per 100,000 residents, in Maine 1.6, across the United States as a whole 9.5. But it is usually impossible to make the same calculations for times past.

First, there are sometimes no official or trustworthy figures at all, or figures that are not easily comparable to others. The best available may not count deaths directly. More usual are court records of several kinds, each representing a different stage in the legal process: homicide indictments, trials, convictions, finally executions, with the numbers shrinking each time the process moves farther away from the original act of homicide.

Problems of legal or social definition also cloud the count. Abortions, in the past, have sometimes been classified as homicide; so have fatal automobile accidents. And not all people were always counted, or counted in the same way, in all jurisdictions; it is sometimes unclear whether official records were kept of the murders of slaves, say, whether by other slaves or by whites, or the victims of formal duels at one end of the social scale or lynchings at the other. And as another kind of complication, since calculating a murder "rate" involves division, its relative accuracy depends not only on the numerator—number of homicides—but also on the denominator—size of the population. And while in the modern United States the denominator is based on a reasonably reliable census, that kind of count is not always available, and for some times and places the size of the population is no more than an educated guess.

In the end, finally, any kind of numerical statement about the history of homicide must be cast as a statistical generalization, meaning that it is "mostly" or "typically" true, but not always. If, for example, it is statistically accurate to say that most homicides have been committed by males, especially young males, most especially poor young males, it should be noted that O. J. Simpson belongs in only one of these three categories, Lizzie Borden in none.

And yet despite all of these problems, it is still possible to make at least rough numerical comparisons across time. Given the numbers, the wider purpose of the investigation is to find out more about the societies that produced them. And the numbers are only one set of historical clues, always used together with others. It is not only the rate and nature of criminal homicide but the way it is treated in law and in custom that helps reveal what a given society fears and what it does not, its economic or psychological tensions, the value it places on human life, perhaps the different kinds of values it places on different kinds of human life.

The historical evidence is not always tidy; it does not fit easily into any kind of box—such as those currently labeled politically "right" or "left"—and sometimes the attempt to solve the mystery of what happened in the past generates new mysteries of its own. But the potential results are worth the effort. The richest, strongest nation in the world, we have scandalously high rates of murder, higher than those of any other country in the West, or among the prospering free societies of the Pacific Rim. Fear of criminal violence plagues the United States today, driving much of our politics, our patterns of settlement, the relations among our races and social classes. But these rates have varied greatly over the centuries, generations, even shorter spans of time. We have not always been so fearful, nor have our citizens always led the Western world in homicides. One purpose here is to trace the origins of both developments.

Two sets of questions, then, run throughout this book; both of them require that the story of homicide be set firmly inside the wider history of America, with all its different regions and peoples. The first examines how, and how well, the justice system has worked in dealing with homicide and other capital crimes. Who has run the system, historically, and for what ends? How efficiently has it detected murder, and how fairly has it dealt with murder suspects? How does legal theory compare with actual practice? What kinds of killings have been most harshly punished, what kinds tolerated, even applauded?

The other set of questions concerns the social or historical conditions that drive the number of homicides up or down. These questions in turn include a number of others that will be treated, as fully as possible, in the context of the specific time and place covered in each of the chapters that follow. Many (not all) of them are the familiar ones of contemporary debate. Does the historical record suggest that murder rates rise as the result of geographic change, of migration from country to city? How much results from changes in the family or the justice system, from obsession in the media? What are the respective roles of economic change, of widespread gun ownership, of the frontier experience, Indian fighting, slavery, and social class, of regional or racial differences and conflicts?

But if these questions are (mostly) familiar, the evidence from history suggests some unfamiliar answers, beginning with the experience of the preimperial England that shaped our basic legal procedures and sent our first permanent white settlers.

I

The British Background

The story of murder by and among the Europeans who peopled what is now the United States begins centuries before the first settlers arrived from England. Packed with the rest of the history that these men and women carried with them in their heads was their experience with criminal homicide, not only laws and legal procedures but moral attitudes and social expectations as well. All of these had been developing over several centuries, and form the background and baseline for the history of murder in America. This chapter, and our story, begins in the thirteenth and fourteenth centuries, then jumps to the seventeenth century, to the England from which the first colonists came. There are holes in the story: some of the evidence is indirect; some elements remain mysterious. But the outline is clear, and it is at least possible to sketch some of the legal, political, and social conditions that helped to shape it.

I

The sketch begins in the late Middle Ages because before then there is almost no evidence at all. While assassinations and murder among royal and aristocratic families had long rivaled warfare as subjects of song and story, the criminal behavior of ordinary people did not attract much

---

The major sources used in this and later chapters, together with citations for quotations, can be found in the Select Bibliography at the end of the book.

notice from the tiny literate elite who wrote narrative chronicles for posterity. The records of the Kingdom of England are the earliest to allow any systematic attempt to describe specific rates and routine cases, but even there the trail cannot be traced beyond the thirteenth century.

What makes it possible at all is that England, although not yet of first rank in power, was in comparison with its contemporaries remarkably well governed. An important part of that government was the machinery of criminal justice. And it is the records of the legal system that have allowed two ingenious historians, Barbara Hanawalt and James Givens, to supply at least rough answers to several questions: What was the medieval murder rate? Who, typically, were the killers and their victims, and why? What were the kinds of homicide that most concerned law and society, and why?

What makes the English legal records important, and nearly unique, is that by the High Middle Ages ordinary crime had become official business. In much of the Western world, as earlier in England itself, routine offenses were not then the business of the state. Among the Germanic tribes who once overran Europe, assault and even murder were considered matters for the injured individuals or families to settle among themselves, either by killings in revenge or through the payment of wergild, or blood money, as compensation for lives taken. Criminal justice was later taken over by feudal overlords or other local authorities. But in England keeping domestic order and providing the rule of law more broadly had in England become a royal responsibility.

In an age of generally decentralized authority, minor crimes were still left to local lords, or the church, to handle according to their own rules. But while most medieval men and women worked the land and rarely journeyed far, the exceptions were important. Three kinds of travelers crisscrossed the king's highways: those on church business, those on political business, and those simply on business, all moving often between London, the one great city of perhaps 35,000 or 50,000 inhabitants, and a number of smaller market towns. All of these people wanted security while on the road. They looked not to the local barons whose land they crossed—and who sometimes threatened rather than protected them—but to the central government. For these travelers there were obvious advantages to having a standard set of rules and legal procedures, a "common law," for the kingdom as a whole. And even for those who did not travel much, the king's courts were generally thought more fair and rational than those run by local oligarchs.

From the royal perspective, too, there was an advantage in defining crimes not as simply the business of perpetrator and victim, or perhaps their families, allies, and friends, but as acts that concerned or injured the whole society. Since the society was personified by the monarch, a criminal act was then officially a kind of personal insult to him, or "breach of the king's peace," to be punished as such. In the continual medieval battle between local and central authority, it was a major victory for the king over the local aristocrats to establish that all major crimes, or felonies, the common law offenses such as larceny, burglary, robbery, rape, and murder, must be tried in royal courts. Prestige and power flowed to anyone who could effectively deliver justice. So did money; the court system was a rich source of fines, fees, and forfeitures.

But the system of criminal justice was not wholly dominated by the king. The Roman Catholic church had established the principle that its own officials, if tried in royal courts, could only be punished by the church itself. This exemption, "benefit of clergy," applied to thousands of people in the Middle Ages, not just parish priests, bishops, monks, and nuns but a host of minor clergymen, wandering friars, and university students, who were not punished physically but made to do penance, at worst losing their positions in the church. Church and barons, too, shared in the business of lawmaking by dominating the parliament. The Magna Carta, or Great Charter, of 1215 not only confirmed the parliamentary right to consent to new laws but also established that the king, too, was subject to them. Above all he could not, acting alone, punish any powerful parliamentary nobleman; such noblemen were subject only to the "judgment of their peers," meaning that they could be tried only before the whole House of Lords.

Those lower in the social scale also shared both rights and duties under the evolving system of criminal justice. While several layers of royal officials were concerned, every free male inhabitant was a potential agent of law enforcement, responsible for reporting and investigating criminal behavior, and catching and passing judgment on suspected criminals. It was a system that probably worked best in dealing with homicide, which ranked in official importance second only to treason—and in fact was in some cases classified as a form of treason.

The key unit in local government was the county, whose main officer was the sheriff, chosen by the king from among local landed families. The sheriff in turn chose deputies, bailiffs, and constables to help him administer the smaller units into which each county was subdivided, including towns or vills. In addition, at the county level, those local aristocrats who qualified as "knights" elected from their own ranks four coroners who served as royal agents to investigate all violent or suspicious deaths for evidence of murder or suicide. Three times a year traveling royal judges held court at the county jail, disposing of those felons who had been identified since their last visit.

None of these officials except the judges were paid regular salaries, and all of them had a number of duties not directly related to the investigation and punishment of crime. There was no real equivalent of police, detectives, or regular patrol, the closest thing being the night watch that was ordered, in walled towns, to look out for fire or other kinds of trouble. Real responsibility for law enforcement did not rest, then, with what were at most a few dozen part-time officials in the counties, but rather with the ordinary free men of the realm, whose active cooperation was required at every level.

A suspected murderer was always accused through a formal legal document, usually an indictment. The two most common procedures began with the men of the neighborhood in which the victim was found. If a murderous robbery, for example, was actually witnessed in progress by a man plowing nearby, responsibility began right there; anyone unable personally to stop the killing was supposed to raise a "hue and cry," calling on all other members of the town or vill to form a posse and chase the killer. If successful, they then turned their catch over to the sheriff, who called on a local grand jury to review what they knew of the case and swear out an indictment.

A mystery, in contrast, such as a stranger's remains found in the marsh or a bloodied widow in her hut, brought on the coroner. He then called a jury of inquest, consisting of free men from the nearby vills. In their presence he measured the wounds, noted the condition of the corpse, and called on them to declare a cause of death: suicide, accident, or murder. If it was officially declared a homicide, the same inquest jury was then asked to name, or indict, a suspect or suspects on the basis of their local knowledge. In about 20 percent of cases no suspect could be identified and the case remained officially a mystery. In the remaining 80 percent, bailiff or sheriff was ordered to make an arrest, if the killer named had not already been caught by the posse raised through the hue and cry.

There were two other legal routes to court. In one, a criminal already in custody might become a "king's approver," confessing to the crime and naming accomplices, perhaps persuaded by an earnest clergyman but more often, it seems, by a sheriff applying some of the ugly arsenal of torture routinely used in the Middle Ages. With luck the accomplices named were then arrested. In a second procedure, already rare by the thirteenth century, a private person, perhaps the wife or other relative of the victim, might bypass the procedure of indictment by a jury and bring an "appeal," or suit, directly to court, naming an alleged killer.

Both approvers and appealers put themselves at some risk. In theory, and if they were male and healthy, any other male they named as murderer might challenge them to a duel, usually to the death. This brutal legal shortcut was not based on the simpleminded premise that might makes right. In an age when religious belief governed much behavior, the idea was rather that a duel was an indirect appeal to the judgment of heaven, which would grant victory to whoever was telling the truth. But the Catholic church had never fully endorsed the notion that God was, in effect, on the side of the bigger and uglier party to a fight, and by the thirteenth century the secular authorities were also committed to more rational procedures. Judicial duels were then rarely allowed. But even without a duel the tables might turn; if the accused was eventually declared not guilty, the accuser might be fined or even hanged.

Apart from the duel, there were two other ways for an indicted killer to escape trial. One of these was legal, although rare. If a shrewd felon, perhaps a minor clergyman, managed to escape into a church, he might claim sanctuary; armed pursuers were not allowed into this consecrated ground to lay violent hands on anyone. If, further, the fugitive was able to hole up and hold out for forty days and nights, living on bad bread and tainted water, he might claim the right to escape trial if he swore after that time to "abjure the realm," that is, to leave England entirely, an echo of the ancient punishment of banishment. Given the minimal machinery of enforcement, it is not clear how many of the handful who took advantage of this loophole actually sailed off and stayed away for life; some simply used the abjure device as a thin cover for escape. And

escape, pure and simple, was very common indeed; it was hard in an
era of poor roads and communications to track down anyone who fled
the county. And although it was also hard for an escaped killer to make
a new life, given a society in which land and jobs were usually inherited
or entered only through tightly guarded trade associations, it was not
wholly impossible. The penalty for failure to show up for trial was to be
declared an "out-law"—a man who, being outside the law, could be
killed by anyone, at any time, with full legal blessing. But in fact a very
large proportion, perhaps 40 percent, of indicted murderers skipped
trial; and many of these joined roving bands of outlaws.

2

Whatever the outcome of trials, the records of inquests and indictments
have provided historians with their first glimpse of how many murders
were committed. The rate cannot be determined as nearly as modern
rates, not only for the usual reasons involving the undetected and undetectable dark figure for murder itself but also because of uncertainties
about population sizes. While it is possible with some confidence to
count the number of homicide indictments for a given county over a
series of years, to calculate these per 100,000 population requires that
we have a figure for the number of people in the county. And with no
real census available since the late eleventh century, any population estimate for the thirteenth or fourteenth century is no better than an
educated guess. But whatever the precise rate, it is clear at least that it
was surprisingly, even astonishingly, high.

The current rate of homicide in the United States, calculated on the
basis of a "body count" of victims, is officially somewhere between 9
and 10 per 100,000 people each year. In modern England it is only a
tiny fraction of that—often less than 1 per 100,000. But estimates for
the medieval counties, calculated on the basis of indictments (which are
considerably lower, on average, than actual body counts), give an average of well over 20 per 100,000. Even far more conservative estimates
are high in comparative terms, with rates in the more peaceful places,
in quiet years, comparable to those of the modern United States, or ten
times those of Great Britain.

The reason these figures are surprising is that most of the popular
theories used to explain violent behavior in the modern United States

simply do not apply to medieval England. The English population was then overwhelmingly rural, most of it living in small communities. Utter dependence on local agriculture and the weather and the continual threat of famine helped shape a fearfully conservative outlook in matters social and economic. The medieval English, like virtually all peoples before the modern era, struggled to follow the wisdom of their elders as best they could recall it. Insistently they condemned innovation in all things and tried to live by what we would call tradition. Their ethnic mix was relatively simple and by that date cause of little serious tension. Only perhaps 15 percent of the people lived in towns. The great majority were peasants, serfs, or free tenants of feudal landlords or of Roman Catholic monasteries or bishops. The church itself enjoyed an essentially unchallenged monopoly.

High rates of homicide then cannot be explained in terms of the availability of firearms, which had not yet been invented. Nor did they typically result from the dangers and tensions of life in the big city; there were no big cities, as London was then no larger than, say, modern Kokomo, Indiana, and it seems in fact that rates in London were lower than in most rural areas. The medieval English did not suffer from rootlessness or from failure to respect religion or other traditional values. Neither did they experience the shock of cultural conflict. They were surely capable, like virtually all peoples, of hostility based on racial, religious, and ethnic difference. But by our standards, at least, they were a remarkably homogeneous people who rarely encountered others much different from themselves. The Crusades against Arab Muslims having sputtered out, for practical purposes, a century or so earlier, even the king's warriors—and these were relatively peaceful times—mostly fought long-familiar foes, the French and Scots, in equally familiar fashion. And yet there were clearly sources of tension and conflict in that society which led a large number of people to violate the most solemn laws of church, state, and community by committing murder.

3

The official documents provide clues not only to the rate of murderous violence, but also through the who, where, and when, to its causes. Here again the record is not always clear; an indictment is in form a short story, with only the barest information. "On the 3d day before

Michaelmas, in the 2d Year of the Reign of King Edward," it might read, "John Smith quarreled with Henry Brown about a penny, outside of Smith's shop, and Smith and William Jones then beat Henry about the head with staves until his skull cracked and he died forthwith." But on analysis even these minimal accounts provide significant information about the people accused, those they killed, and the nature of their fatal encounters. Hanawalt and Givens have studied different counties, at somewhat different times, asking somewhat different questions. And although it gives a false sense of precision to provide detailed rather than approximate percentages, the patterns they find are roughly compatible.

In some ways these patterns resemble those found in most other times and places. Homicide was a matter of the warm months, typically, of the twilight and evening hours of the traditional Sunday or day of leisure. It was an overwhelmingly male phenomenon; more than 90 percent of accused killers were men, and although ages were not specified, the majority seem to have been young and vigorous. Most victims, too, more than 80 percent, were male. They were more likely to be poor men, peasants or laborers, than knighted landlords or merchants. The evidence for social class is part of another familiar pattern: the medieval English tended to murder people much like themselves. At least three-fourths of these killings involved men or women who were probably at least acquainted with each other, often neighbors or people from the same or nearby villages.

But in other ways the patterns of reported medieval homicides are different from those of later times. The three most striking are (1) the low percentage of killings among family members (even apart from infanticides, to be considered below); (2) the high proportion committed by two or more killers acting together; and (3) the high proportion of murders committed in the course of robbery.

The first finding is truly extraordinary. In samples of some thousands of reported thirteenth- and fourteenth-century homicides, only between perhaps 2 and 8 percent occurred within nuclear families. This is a range radically lower than that in the modern West: in the United States today, despite a sharp drop-off over the past generation in the number of annual murder cases involving family as both killers and accused, the proportion is about 12 percent; and in Great Britain, about 50 percent.

Two possible explanations point in different directions. On the one hand, it may be simply that the emotional temperature within medieval families was low. Marriage, only recently made a sacrament by the church, was primarily a property arrangement. Both romantic love and its all-too-frequent complement sexual jealousy were then relatively unimportant; the ties that bound were still loose and informal, easily cut or shifted if the parties, or at least the husbands, felt confined. On the other hand, men and women in an agricultural society needed each other for survival. The household was the basic economic unit of the society, and to work as a unit it needed spouses and children to do complementary specialized tasks, traditionally done by one gender and not the other, from plowing the fields to making clothes. This need, coupled with an emphasis on heredity in both property and status, might create a kind of practical bond that in time became emotional and stressed the interests of family against the world in ways that made internal violence unthinkable.

But it may be that both explanations miss the real point. The figures for domestic violence, expressed as rates per 100,000, are not really low as compared with those for modern Britain. The fact that they represent a small percentage of all reported cases just reinforces the most basic conclusion: homicide in general was then rampant, with the sheer number of other kinds of cases dwarfing those that occurred within families. Medieval England was simply a violent society, for a number of different reasons, political, social, and cultural.

The king, first, legally required that every healthy man in the realm, excluding clergy, must be ready to fight. Males of the aristocratic or landlord class, all over Europe, were distinguished from commoners by being made knights. The elaborate exercises in armored horsemanship required to qualify for knighthood had long reinforced the reality that to be a member of the governing class was to be a member of the fighting class. In England the kings had extended the requirement that all men should bear arms downward into the villages, where competitions in archery and other martial arts were held to assure that the inhabitants would be ready to serve their sovereign if called.

And if few were called in this cause, many were ready to fight in others. Royal government and the rule of law, if relatively stronger than earlier, were still resented and resisted. If thirteenth- and fourteenth-century England seems peaceful in comparison, or from a distance, at the time and on the ground its high politics was riddled with violence and assassination. In 1265, King Edward I had to fight to win back his father's crown from a group of barons who were holding it in a kind of trust, and a long generation later, in 1320, his own son Edward II was deposed by the Parliament; accused formally of breaches of law and informally of sodomy, the former king's captivity was soon cut short in gruesome fashion, by a poker thrust up his rectum.

In this atmosphere tradition and training combined to exalt the direct settlement of disputes; to appeal to the king's courts was dangerous for his political opponents, and perhaps branded as cowardice even among his friends. Great nobles kept crews of bullying retainers to overawe the countryside they considered their rightful turf, sometimes intimidating royal judges and sheriffs, as when Sir William Bradshaw brought sixty armed men to court to keep Cecilia le Boteler from appealing against him. The use of arms was a way of life at the highest levels, central to virtually all masculine recreation, from hunting deer and boar to war games that pitted knights against each other in violent jousting that proved for some losers as fatal as the real thing.

At lower social levels, too, weapons were always at hand. In addition to the bows and arrows kept stashed by royal edict, medieval men and indeed women routinely carried knives—forks were not yet used—to cut their bread and meat. In an agricultural society the most common of tools, hoes and axes, scythes and threshing hooks, could easily be turned to lethal work. And for ordinary villagers or townsmen, as for aristocratic warriors, the settlement of quarrels by peaceful legal means often failed to work, although for different reasons.

The formal ways of resolving conflict in the Middle Ages were either through politics, broadly defined, or through the courts. Differences might be heard before a town or village council, or the meeting of an occupational guild; those with unsettled grievances could appeal for help to some superior, a landlord for example. People might also go to a court run by a local magnate, since only the major felonies were reserved for royal justice. There is evidence that this system worked fairly well for those with local influence and prestige: few indictments accused members of the village elite of going outside the law by murdering those further down the social scale, simply because they did not have to, since they had ways of bending law to their will. But it cost money to go to court, where poorer men had little influence, and they had reason to fear that the whole system was run by men who had little sympathy for them—a set of reasons that help explain why the poor are often more prone to violent behavior than the rich. Murder was typically an affair among neighbors, and although there was surely a history of bad blood behind it, in many cases the actual event, as in other times and places, tended to result spontaneously from simple arguments rather than from well-thought-out motives of revenge, greed, or domestic jealousy. It is hard, from the brief stories on the record, to tell just what the fights were about, but it is clear that the parties were people with short tempers and often long histories of petty friction over boundary lines, uneven tasks, strayed animals, or refusals to go along with guild or village decisions. There were, in theory, deliberate ways of dealing with these sore issues. But the quickest one was the one too often chosen. And if John raised his hoe against William, brothers or friends, always nearby, were likely to join in, and the result was often a fracas that ended with a single victim and several killers.

The fact that a fight tended so often to pull in others ready to pile on reflects the second striking characteristic of medieval homicide: the high proportion of multiple indictments. One study of the thirteenth century shows that in roughly two cases out of three accused killers acted in company with one or more accomplices. What this characteristically collective aggression reflects is the characteristically collective nature of medieval economic and social life.

One hallmark of village agriculture was the blurred and sometimes contested line between public and private. Much of the acreage used by villagers belonged, by custom, to the entire community—woodlands for gathering fuel and hunting rabbits, wells and streams as sources of water. Small plots were wholly owned by individual families, who raised beans and chickens just back of the cottage. But the bigger fields, given over to the great grasses, wheat or rye, barley or oats, although divided into privately owned strips, were plowed by communal teams, with the major decisions as to what and when to seed and harvest made collectively. In town, too, economic life was tightly regulated. Small enterprise was the rule, but individual artisans, skilled shoemakers or tailors, had to belong to shops run by a master according to collective rules set by guild or association, rules that limited the number of employees, set maximum wages and hours, and dictated standards of workmanship.

At every social level, too, medieval men and women lived not only their economic but their personal lives in the company of, and under the eye of, other people. Individualism was not prized in the abstract, and privacy was rare in practice. Peasants lived in crowded one-room cottages, working, eating, and making love elbow to elbow with family and, on really cold nights, livestock. Even the greatest houses lacked truly private rooms, with doors and locks; owners, spouses, children, servants, visitors, retainers, and dogs continually jostled each other through the arches. Very little was done alone—including, it seems, murder.

If the medieval British were used to living and working in company and making decisions collectively, continual closeness was then a source of tension as well as cooperation. It is hard to find just what accounted for fluctuations, over time, in the annual rates. Such usual suspects as war and political turmoil do not seem to have had much direct impact. But it does seem that economic conditions were important, as measured at bedrock by the price of bread. Bread was by far the leading source of calories, and hunger has always been at best a source of hair-trigger irritation and at worst a source of desperation. Besides hunger at the poorest levels, crop failure affected everyone on up through the medieval hierarchy. Barons and bishops with shrinking rent rolls were frustrated by shrinking ambitions and lifestyles, while their retainers who lost lands or jobs might take to the woods and highways as robbers.

The third noteworthy pattern among medieval homicides is in fact the high proportion that occurred as the result of robbery. Since robbery, unlike impulsive fights, typically occurred in lonely places or in the dark and since roving robbers were less likely to be known locally than quarrelsome villagers or townsmen, a large part of the 20 percent of known killings that wholly mystified coroners' juries was surely the work of robbers. The indictments that specify robbery as motive range from perhaps 10 up to 25 percent. Some of these were the work of desperate loners, but more, in keeping with the finding about accomplices in general, were committed by confederate bands, some of them casual, some clearly organized as professional thieves and killers.

Ballads sang (although rarely) of gallant outlaws such as Robin Hood, but there is no evidence that these men gave anything to the poor. And in fact, although they sometimes robbed and killed merchants on the highways, they had no wish to tangle with the rich and well protected. They tended to operate from poor rural areas, where population was thin, law enforcement weak, and deep woods offered places to hide. Their victims, overwhelmingly, were ordinary people, often attacked in their own homes, with little to offer but food, perhaps some cloth or a few pence. Otherwise outlaws were distinguished mostly by their savagery, by their willingness to kill women and children or any possible witnesses to their crimes.

4

The third major set of clues about medieval homicide comes from the courts, and suggests something of social attitudes toward it. Evidence, as above, about rates and patterns is mostly from indictments, the first stage of the legal process. It is the next two stages, trials and sentences, that tell what medieval Englishmen thought about these rates and patterns and what they did or hoped to do about them.

The trial was held before a royal judge in the course of one of his several yearly visits. The accused was brought out from jail—no bail was allowed in cases of homicide—to face a jury. The trial jury was made up of twelve to twenty-four free men who lived in the vicinity where the crime had been committed. It might in fact include some of those who had sat in on the same case in its earlier stages, as members of the inquest or indictment juries; it might even include men who had answered a hue and cry and helped catch the accused. Above all, in direct contrast to modern legal practice, they were not supposed to be wholly open-minded or ignorant of the case. Their job in practice combined those of a modern jury and of witnesses. The trial itself featured little or no new testimony but rather consisted of mutual consultation among men who usually knew both victim and accused, their local reputations, perhaps their families, and had already done their investigating. They were then supposed to arrive at a unanimous verdict, achieved quickly at that stage, often in a matter of minutes, and tell it to the judge.

But there are strong clues to the attitudes of ordinary Englishmen in the gap between the black letter law and what happened in actual operation. The law in some ways represented the ideal of absolute justice, the hope for certainty reflected, for example, in prayers that God would indicate the truth through the judicial duel, or oaths, or other direct appeals to His judgment. But in practice criminal justice was a political system in which a number of different opinions, constituencies, and pressures were represented. The results were then often a compromise among the formal demands of the state, the interests of the officials who administered the law, and the attitudes of the ordinary free male inhabitants of the realm who made up the juries.

The king's interest in criminal matters was driven in large part by simple greed; all convicted felons were hanged, usually within hours of sentencing, at most a couple of days, and all their goods were as quickly forfeited to the Crown. As a result state officials, paid in fees and shares, had on the one hand an interest not only in detecting but also in convicting as many killers as possible. But in some cases, on the other hand, they were afraid of powerful local landlords or outlaws protected by them, or open to bribery; throughout the Middle Ages, clerical sermons, parliamentary petitions, and popular songs all complained of favoritism and corruption among those charged with administering the law. Since, too, all but the judges were county residents, they were also subject to local pressures and attitudes that sometimes conflicted with the king's interest. Fear and bribery might affect jurors in the same way. They, too, were local folks, normally closer in social rank to the ordinary villagers or townsmen who were brought to trial than to knightly sheriffs or coroners. And after their participation in a given case was over, they had to go back and live among, perhaps answer to, the people in their neighborhoods.

One striking illustration of the way in which all of these filters shaped the law in practice was the treatment of infanticide. The killing of infants was a crime in medieval England, which in defining homicide made no distinctions about the age or sex of victims, or indeed the motives of killers. But it had not always been a crime; in the Roman Empire a head of household had the absolute right to dispose of any newborn child unwanted because of its physical defects, its sex, or simply the burden of its care and feeding. In early medieval villages, too, skewed sex ratios—as many as three males to every two females— strongly suggest that at least in famine times, as in much of the modern non-Western world, female infants were often strangled or left to die. It was one of the long slow campaigns of the Catholic church to curb this practice through insistence on the equality of all souls. It was very long and slow in reaching conservative countrymen, in Latin *pagani,* or pagans, who resisted for centuries. Only by the High Middle Ages, in

England, had it largely succeeded, as evidenced less by the law than by the fact that the rural ratio of males to females was not unusual.

But success was not total; there are reports that fourteenth-century parents did sacrifice newborns when crop failure pushed them to this last resort. Most significant is that these and similar deaths simply did not reach the courts. Among some five thousand fourteenth-century homicide cases culled from courts and coroners, the leading historian, Barbara Hanawalt, has found just three involving newborns. In terms of actual acts of homicide, by the standards of an earlier time (or, as will be shown, a later one), this is an extremely low figure. The records in all three cases are murky; at least two of the babies were drowned, it seems, one by a person unknown. It is suggestive that no parent was directly accused and no one was convicted in any of the incidents.

It is hard not to conclude that these escapes from hanging were no accident. On the presumption that infanticide is almost always an act of desperation, committed by the poorest and most distraught parents, no one had any interest in pursuing them. The king had nothing to gain from confiscating their miserable belongings. More important, a jury of neighbors perhaps recalled a distant time when their actions did not violate village custom, and surely had some sympathy for their plight. In an age of high infant mortality it was hard to tell homicide from accident in any case. The men of the village, then, exercised their discretion at the very first stage of the criminal process by simply failing to indict.

Nothing in law, tradition, or experience suggests that hanging was in principle abhorrent to these medieval Englishmen. There was no recorded objection to the death penalty as such. Execution had been a traditional punishment in both the Roman Empire and among the Germanic tribes of pre-Christian Europe, although among the Germans it was reserved for cowards or traitors rather than for ordinary murderers. By the thirteenth century the formal purpose of the death penalty was twofold. One was revenge; clerical legal scholars cited the Book of Noah: "Whoso sheddeth man's blood, by man shall his blood be shed." The other was the protection of society, or deterrence.

But the legal code of the thirteenth and fourteenth centuries went well beyond revenge, or "an eye for an eye," in calling for death in all felony cases, of which homicide accounted for only about one in five.

Royal greed, as suggested above, was one reason for this. And it was the king and the parliamentary elite who defined the social interests that got most support from the written law. The most serious crime in the code was treason; the punishment involved dragging a convict behind a cart to the gallows. The offense included not only spying for an enemy but counterfeiting, the right to stamp coins being a royal monopoly. The protection of the social hierarchy more broadly is suggested by the fact that the killing of one's lord or master was defined, with the obvious support of those who ran the Parliament, as "petit treason," subject to the same penalty. And so, finally, was the killing by a wife of her husband, the difference being that the penalty for a woman convicted of treason was, uniquely, death by fire.

The law itself allowed for mitigating circumstances. Death was the penalty for all convicted of committing a common law felony of any kind, "with felonious intent," whether the specific offense was stealing clothes or butchering widows. Purely accidental homicides, done "without felonious intent"—those in later centuries classed as "excusable"—were not subject to legal penalty. And it was recognized that those under the age of twelve, the "age of reason" as defined by the Catholic church, were not fully capable of forming intent. Neither were the insane. Young or clearly crazy defendants, then, although declared guilty, were pardoned immediately. Otherwise the judge had little discretion; guilty or not guilty were the only possible verdicts, and these were in the hands of the jury.

Those at the top of the social hierarchy expressed their attitudes toward crime directly, in part through the legal code, in part through well-recorded actions, in part through written chronicles, petitions, and complaints to king and Parliament. The king himself was willing, in his own interest, sometimes to excuse criminal behavior: strong, aggressive felons might be saved from the noose if they agreed to serve for a term in the royal army, a practice not always popular with his other subjects. Powerful magnates, for similar reasons, might provide protection for outlaw bands that did some of their political dirty work; their own retainers did their share of bullying as well. Rival magnates, traveling merchants, and clergymen all complained loudly about these bands, who threatened them directly. But the attitudes of ordinary people about ordinary crimes were not usually recorded so conveniently, and must be inferred from the decisions of trial jurors.

Thirteenth-century jurors were used to death in all its forms. Roughly half their children died as infants, on average, and in the absence of any useful treatment for trauma and little for infection fatal accident was a routine event. The death penalty was advertised purposefully, with executions as public events held on busy crossroads, the bodies of victims left to swing and rot as reminders of what it meant to defy the king's law.

But if these medieval men were used to death, they do not seem to have been brutalized into indifference to it. The threat of hanging hung heavily in the minds of all those involved in executing the law. And even apart from the special case of infanticide, jurors were not eager to inflict death; in practice they registered their opinions about crimes in general and the various kinds of homicide in particular through the rate at which they convicted or acquitted those accused of them.

Routine violence, even fatal violence, did not shock jurors into demanding retribution. Those actually tried for homicide, as opposed to those who escaped detection entirely or fled into outlawry, were overwhelmingly men, sometimes women, who lived nearby; the whole system was arranged so that their reputations were already known to the jurors. So, importantly, were the accuseds' families or friends, if any, who would remain neighbors, possibly angry or vengeful if verdicts went against a son or brother. The conviction rate for all kinds of crime was quite low: during nearly half a century, in a study of eight counties, more than two-thirds of those indicted were acquitted. Most striking, the rate for homicide conviction was the lowest for any offense that accounted for a significant number of cases—a little over 12 percent. Property crimes were clearly more worrisome than violent ones, by this measure, with a little over 30 percent of accused burglars and robbers convicted, 22 percent of simply larcenous thieves. It is especially significant that nearly two-thirds of all indicted clergymen were convicted, a rate many times that for laity. The explanation is simply that jurors knew that as a result of benefit of clergy these men would be, at worst, defrocked and made to do penance, and so felt free to call them guilty as they saw it.

If the law made no distinctions either about the degree of the offense or among persons, the jurors clearly did. Ordinary fights were common events; most men had seen or done their share. In many cases of what in modern law would be manslaughter, only a lucky blow, given or taken, separated winners and losers; in others, victims were notoriously quarrelsome or aggressive people, or killers had acted in self-defense. Jurors were tolerant in such cases. With no alternative to hanging but a not guilty verdict, not guilty it was.

This was a clear evasion of the law. Beginning in the thirteenth century (and continuing ever after), the common law doctrine of self-defense was defined quite narrowly. It was in the interest of the king's power and purse that conflict should be resolved by his courts, not by the parties involved. Homicides were justifiable on grounds of self-defense only if the killer had exhausted all other options. He was supposed to give ground; indeed it was in a later formulation "his duty to retreat" in the face of a persistent aggressor. Only with his back to the wall, quite literally, was a man legally justified in standing his ground and killing to save his life. But here again, the law said one thing and jurors another.

However tolerant of their peers, jurors, like merchants and clergymen, feared and certainly hated robbers and outlaws, strangers to the village. In contrast, they almost never convicted sisters or uncles or other family members who abetted or sheltered relatives after the fact; although in law these were accessories to murder, the ties of blood were honored through acquitting them of all guilt.

Not only as accomplices in family cases but as principals as well, women were treated differently from men. Medieval attitudes toward women and women's behavior were complex. Females under indictment for murder were often active agents, who wielded knives and even swords. But they were acquitted more often than men for these and indeed all other kinds of crime, whatever the sex of their victims. And if most killings resulted from fights and fighting in general was widely tolerated, men who killed women were not. Medieval males had relatively little reason to fear domestic violence, but the rate of conviction for this and other homicidal attacks on females was significantly higher than that for men who killed men.

5

Three hundred years later, in dealing with homicide as with other crime, seventeenth-century England still kept most of its medieval forms and institutions. One major legal change had occurred since the fourteenth century: homicide was graded into degrees of guilt, not simply in terms of the fatal act itself but also in terms of the intent, the mens rea, of the killer. "Murder" itself by then required premeditation, or "malice aforethought," and a murderer was denied the right either to receive a royal pardon or to plead benefit of clergy. To kill an officer of justice, such as a sheriff, while carrying out his duties was also ruled unpardonable. Other kinds of culpable homicide, typically the result of "a sudden occasion," such as a fight, were downgraded to "manslaughter. " Otherwise legal procedures remained much as before, from hue and cry or inquest on through indictment and trial, with, normally, hanging following conviction. But the political, economic, and social context of homicidal behavior had changed radically, and so had its level.

What separates England of the early modern era from its medieval predecessor were two great movements that were transforming the whole of Europe, and with it the world. One was the narrowing of the globe symbolized by Columbus's voyage to the New World in 1492, the other the Protestant Reformation inspired by Martin Luther's challenge to the Roman Catholic church beginning in 1517.

Both of these events greatly multiplied the potential for homicide in the form of war. It was in this era that Europeans not only circled the planet but also began to conquer it, greatly expanding the international market economy, establishing military outposts in Southeast Asia, helping to transform western Africa into a great slave market, subjugating and exterminating much of the population of the South American continent and beginning to probe north. At the same time the religious revolution created wholly new reasons for Europeans to hate each other. The rival dynastic and economic ambitions of the great states were now greatly complicated by a wholly different and uniquely fierce set of motives: the clash of Catholics and a variety of mutually hostile new Protestants, sometimes within states, sometimes between them.

England, still a relatively small nation on the fringes of this troubled world, experienced all of this turmoil on its own scale. While it is at least possible to imagine the island in the Middle Ages as tranquil and tradition-bound, the early modern era was obviously unsettled. As foreign trade grew more important, the sixteenth century witnessed a sharp disruption in traditional village agriculture as more goods and animals were made and raised for export. A long-term and massive shift from growing grain for food to raising sheep for wool threw former peasants off their land, creating a major crisis of unemployment, swelling the population of London especially, and reviving, for the first time since the Roman Empire, the sense that a whole society might suffer from overpopulation.

As foreign trade moved all around the world, English seamen and merchants challenged the larger Atlantic powers, France and especially Spain. Economic rivalry was aggravated by religious difference, with England by the middle of the sixteenth century a Protestant state, defying the imperial Spanish crusade for a reunited Catholic Europe. And to a degree never known before, foreign and religious issues were reflected in domestic politics.

England's Tudor monarchs had come to power through civil war, their claim to the throne shaky at its base. And when Henry VIII in 1534 declared that he, not the pope, was now head of the English church he opened a whole new era of mutual suspicion between sovereign and subject. As Henry was succeeded by his son Edward and daughters Mary and Elizabeth, the official state religion shifted from Protestant to Catholic and back again. With church and state closely entwined, savage warfare engulfing the European continent, and Spain thought to be plotting on behalf of Catholic pretenders to the throne, to be of the wrong religion was something close to treason.

The Tudor fear of assassination and religious difference verged at times on paranoia. Heretics, in the sixteenth century, were burned at the stake. Treason, brought to secret Star Chamber courts without the protections offered by jury trials or public proceedings, was punished with an official savagery unknown in the late Middle Ages. The ancient instruction that women traitors were to be burned seems merciful in the new context, as men, while still alive, were to have their genitals cut off and bowels burned, then their heads severed and bodies cut in quarters to be spiked and displayed in public places. The number of these vicious public spectacles as well as ordinary hangings reached an all-time high in the century following Henry's breach with Rome.

Yet somehow in the midst of all this official brutality the rate of ordinary private homicide fell off dramatically, as compared with the rates of the late Middle Ages. The extent of this decline is impossible to measure closely. The survival of official documents depends on the unpredictable whims of man and nature, changing bureaucratic rules and storage systems, fire and rot. In England, as it happens, it is far harder to gather evidence about ordinary crime for the sixteenth century and most of the seventeenth than for the fourteenth; only three counties have criminal records for any significant number of years, the cases available for survey numbering only in the hundreds, rather than thousands. For these counties, too, as for the Middle Ages, population figures are only guesses. But the most informed estimates for the homicide rates in Essex, Sussex, and Hertfordshire, measured by indictments, are 7, 14, and 16 per 100,000, respectively, during 1559 and 1603, rates so far below those of two and three centuries earlier that there can be no mistaking the trend.

The patterns of homicide, too, while hard to see at this distance, confirm the differences in rates. In early modern as in medieval England, not surprisingly, most killings resulted from impulsive male quarrels, probably among acquaintances. But proportionally far more occurred within families—something between 13 and 18 percent at a minimum, which indirectly suggests proportionally fewer robbery murders, or killings by strangers. The dark figure for undetected or unindicted murders was probably lower for the later period than the earlier. A greater zeal for prosecuting is shown above all in the number of cases brought for infanticide, which, largely ignored in the Middle Ages, now amounted to about 20 percent of all homicide indictments. Many of those accused were unwed mothers; to make the case against them easier to prove to jurors, who often found it hard to decide whether a given infant was born dead or killed afterward, it was specifically made a capital offense, in 1624, to "conceal the death of a bastard child," whatever the cause, by attempting to hide its body.

This apparent concern for the fate of newborns might be used as evidence for one possible explanation for falling murder rates. It has been argued that there was a slow trend, stretching all across Europe over many centuries, toward more civil, humane behavior, reflected in everything from improved table manners to less aggressive personal behavior. Fewer homicides and a lower threshold of tolerance for them would both result from this emotional shift. But such a humanitarian trend, if it existed, is impossible to see in the gruesome reign of Henry VIII and his successors. The statute making it a crime to conceal the death of an illegitimate newborn was designed after all to make it easier to hang young women, and reflects not greater humanity but the

zealous prosecution of sexual sin. And if Englishmen were not murdering each other as often as earlier, they were finding other ways of killing
off those they feared and hated. One of the by-products of religious
zealotry and radical insecurity in early modern Europe was the persecution of people, usually but not always lone women, accused of prac-
ticing witchcraft; literally hundreds of thousands were burned to death
for this alleged crime. And while England was spared the worst of this
misogynist hysteria, witchcraft was defined as a capital crime beginning
in 1542, and in some times and places more people were accused of
this than ordinary homicide, their bodies added to the grim totals piled
up by official executioners in this era.

A better explanation, then, for the falling murder rate is simply that
the Tudor-Stuart state, however troubled, was far stronger and better
able to impose the rule of law than its medieval predecessors. The
growth of state power was then felt both high and low, at both levels
cutting into the kind of disorder and desperation that led to homicide.

At the higher level, early modern England was no longer troubled by
private war among great nobles, or by their potential defiance of royal
law. The great and powerful were more likely to be found, with Sir
Walter Raleigh, dancing, writing sonnets, and currying favor in the
court of Queen Elizabeth than supporting small armies of retainers,
sheltering outlaws, or bullying the countryside. And the state had much
for ambitious and warlike men to do, both on land and on sea, and in
effect exploited aggression by exporting it outside of the kingdom. Raleigh himself participated in the conquest of Catholic Ireland, a notably
ugly war involving the slaughter of women and children, as well as the
exploration of North America. English seamen were beginning to de-
velop a reputation as the world's most daring. Not only Russia and
India but the New World offered whole new theaters of adventure. Naval officers and pirates, often hard to tell apart, terrorized much of the
Spanish Caribbean.

Back home, in the countryside, the rule of law and the habit of turning to the courts rather than to personal confrontation to settle disputes
had strengthened over the centuries. One clue pointing to the declining
murder rate and to the fuller use of the law is that homicide indictments, once 1 in 5 of all brought to royal justice in the counties, had
dropped to 1 in 20, 40, even 50, as less serious crimes were prosecuted
more often. Lower courts were busy as well. One historian has even

argued that the number of witchcraft prosecutions may be interpreted as evidence that early modern villagers were using the official system, however cruelly, as an alternative to homicide as a means of dealing with the tensions and hostilities that plagued their communities.

In dealing with felonies of all kinds, Tudor and Stuart juries were more willing to convict than their ancestors, acquitting only about half of all those brought before them. But ordinary crime, including murder, was still not a major concern among those who made or administered the law. In many cases, as earlier, jurors committed "pious perjury" by knowingly freeing people who, while guilty, did not in their opinion deserve to die. Only a small proportion even of those convicted, perhaps 1 in 5 or even 1 in 10, were actually sent to the gallows, as the old loopholes, pleas and pardons, were widened even further, notably the plea of benefit of clergy. While this had originally been an escape limited to those who had taken holy orders, by the early modern era, in a Protestant state, it was extended to all who could prove that they could read and write. Proof of literacy could be used, one time only, to escape the gallows; offenders were simply branded on the thumb. In a highly class-conscious society such people were thought more socially useful than illiterates. But while still a minority, they were a growing proportion of the male population, and that they were in effect given one free ticket to commit a serious crime suggests that punishing such crime was not a high social priority.

There was some concern, among the literate class, about the "rogues and beggars" who infested the highways, a recognition that former soldiers and peasants driven off the land in hard times might turn to violence. Firearms became a concern for the first time; a few murders, still less than 10 percent, were being committed with guns, and a series of laws beginning in 1541 forbade their use by ordinary nonaristocratic civilians. But there was no real equivalent of the medieval fear of organized robber bands or gangs. The church, in an era of religious tension, was worried not about violence but about heresy and sin; the new law about illegitimacy and infanticide was one product. The state worried about invasion from abroad and treason at home.

High rates of homicide in medieval England had resulted in part from social tolerance, in part from official weakness. The violent settlement of disputes was accepted among men at every social level, and among the knightly class it was encouraged, even honored. And the state provided neither workable methods of settling chronic disputes among neighbors nor effective protection against murderous robbers.

Early modern England, too, was a sometimes fearfully cruel society, full of mutual hostilities and suspicions, and many of its people had good reason to leave it for a new world. But the state had grown strong enough to curb most aristocratic violence and outlawry, and by providing more effective courts and law enforcement had driven down the number of ordinary homicides from the peaks reached in earlier centuries. If the fear of violence played an important role in the decisions of those émigrés who sailed west across the Atlantic, it was not murder that concerned them but rather the very real possibility of foreign, civil, or religious warfare.

2

The Colonial Era, 1607–1776

The first permanent English settlements in North America were the Virginia and Massachusetts Bay colonies, founded early in the seventeenth century. Over the following generations the dominant white inhabitants of these and later colonies began to establish a distinctively American identity. But history does not move in straight or simple lines; the "American" experience was complicated, differing radically across time, among settlements, and above all among the different peoples whose lives shaped and were shaped by it. And while the colonists cut their formal political ties with the British Empire in 1776, they could not so easily abandon the British experience that had formed them. From beginning to end, the history of the American colonies was framed by the concerns that had founded them: finding their place in the international market economy at a time of severe religious and political differences in Europe and within England itself.

Both developments had several lasting results. British North America was from very early on a place where three races from three continents were entangled in ways that ensured the continual threat of murderous violence. Settlement required displacing and periodically fighting the original Indian inhabitants. The fact that all the territory from Maine to Georgia was in effect a string of imperial outposts, challenged by Catholic French rivals to the north and Spanish to the south, meant that these native warriors often found powerful European allies, making wars frequent and peace unstable. Meanwhile many of the American goods most valuable in international trade were increasingly produced by slaves, originally kidnapped from Africa. The use of reluctant slave labor, complicated by racial tension, generated fears and threats inside many of the colonies at least as great as and more continuous than those from the outside.

Amid all this menace, maintaining civil order was a matter of the highest importance to those who ran the American colonies. Violence of many kinds was inevitable, but homicidal conflict among white settlers could not be tolerated as it was in medieval or even early modern England. Being English, the governing class codified its authority in rules of law and established systems of criminal justice. Being American, facing wholly new conditions and challenges, they did things differently. Within each colony and certainly across each of the three regions—the South, New England, and the Middle Colonies—the activities thought to threaten the social order, the workings of the justice system, and the use of capital punishment varied distinctively with the local mixture of race, religion, and economic structure. So did the murder rate. But across the whole of the English New World, the ultimate and paradoxical result was a society both more and less violent than the mother country's.

I

Virginia, the first English colony, was the first to encounter several wholly New World problems. Its early leaders took for granted a world in which the system of justice, among other things, was based on town or village community, acceptance of hierarchy and tradition, and the rule of a landed aristocracy drawing rents from a dependent peasantry. But those expectations were severely eroded by the cultural clashes, economic geography, and labor problems of actual settlement, specifically the relations with Native Americans, the loss of village or community tradition, and the wholly novel institution of chattel slavery based on race.

The merchants of the Virginia Company who financed the pioneering voyage to Jamestown in 1607 and the captains who commanded it hoped first to strike it rich like earlier European adventurers in South America and Asia. The Spanish had found gold in Hispaniola, and rich but vulnerable empires to conquer in Mexico and the Andes. Their own fellow countrymen, traveling to Russia, the Near East, and India, had landed their ships, asked the nearest inhabitants to "take us to your leader," won an audience with representatives of the local state and the merchant community, displayed their arms and wares, and begun to trade. But none of this worked in English North America.

There was no gold to be mined, or rich civilization to exploit. The leaders of the Virginia settlement were experienced men of affairs, but they were not cultural anthropologists, and it took them many years to fully understand that the woodland Indians had no territorial state, as they understood the concept, no merchants, and made nothing worth money in the international market. If the Virginia Company was to make a profit for its sponsoring investors, then, the English settlers would have to dig in, literally, and make or grow their own products of value. This in turn meant that instead of a trading post, Virginia must become, and be governed as, a territorial state.

The Spanish in Latin America had made this transition easily enough, not only claiming but actually ruling virtually all of the territory they found useful. The natives they encountered had been easily dominated, some of them already used to centuries of imperial rule, all of them demoralized and decimated by disease and culture shock. Many were worked as slaves, the rest allowed to live in and run their own dependent states, all of them treated as actual or potential converts to Roman Catholic Christianity. This was the only example known when the English landed in "Virginia," which, on parchment signed by the distant king of England, stretched all the way from its Atlantic coastline to the Pacific. To convert this into a territorial state would require that the peoples already living there be subjected to English government, including the English systems of criminal law and justice, which in turn depended on established Christian belief.

King James decreed at the outset that these natives should be treated kindly, as his co-subjects, and the Church of England hoped to bring them into the Anglican fold. But the possibility of making this Virginia a state on the Spanish model was thwarted by the resistance of the native inhabitants, who did not easily bend to English law and government. What happened in practice is neatly summarized in the story of the Chesapeake "princess" Pocahontas.

Whatever distant sachems decreed in theory, the hungry, ignorant Englishmen who landed at Jamestown soon clashed with the Chesapeake tribesmen loosely governed by the chieftain Powhatan. There was enough mutual dependence—the invaders needing food, the curious

Indians intrigued by cloth and metal goods and hoping to use the invaders against other tribes—so that hostilities stopped short of mutual
annihilation. The famous encounter between Captain John Smith and
one of the chieftain's many daughters ("princess" was the English version) seems to have been part of a diplomatic show of strength. And in
the first decade of settlement there were some signs that the two groups
might fit together, as individual Chesapeakes came to live and work in
the English encampment at Jamestown and some English fled hunger
and misery into the surrounding native villages.

But sporadic warfare continued—in part inspired by episodic acts
of murder between Indians and whites, who shared no common law.
Among the eastern Indians, as among the Germanic ancestors of the
settlers, murder was treated as an offense against the victim's family,
rather than the society as a whole, to be settled with the killer and his
family, ideally by a payment, next by surrender or execution of the of-
fender, or failing these, through blood feud. When the people involved
were of different cultures, in an atmosphere full of often tragic misunderstanding, it was hard to draw the line between the sanctioned homicides, or wars, that followed from policy decisions on either side and
the unsanctioned homicides that followed from impulsive individual
acts of anger or fear. Both groups, in either case, took revenge, or hostages. And it was as part of an attempt to free English hostages that
Pocahontas, long familiar to the English as a playful visitor cartwheeling
through the Jamestown market, was kidnapped in 1613.

The princess, then a teenager, was treated well, and while in loose
captivity herself captivated the leading settler, Sir John Rolphe. Sir
John's intentions were honorable but illegal, not because of the difference in race but religion; as a pagan Pocahontas was not eligible for the
Anglican sacrament of marriage. Rolphe, however, saw this problem as
opportunity. His lovelorn obsession with a maiden "to whom my best
thoughts are, and have a long time bin so intangled, and inthralled in
so intricate a laborinth, that I was even awearied to unwinde myself
thereout" was in fact God's way of "pulling me by the eare, and crying,
why dost thou not indevor to make her a Christian?" Pocahontas was
in fact duly converted, baptized, and married. Her father and the English governor saw this alliance as a device common to both cultures, a
signal for peace between their nations, perhaps eventual union. Lady

Rolphe, a bright and gifted linguist, went on to entrance the royal court on a visit to London in 1616.

But events took a tragic turn when Pocahontas died on the return voyage. Her father followed shortly, and within a few years, in 1622, her uncle broke the uneasy biracial peace with a surprise attack against the Virginia settlement that killed nearly 350 people, roughly a third of the white population.

Of the several crucial elements in this story, the Christian baptism on which it turns is one of the most unusual. While the Roman Catholic church had many centuries of experience in converting preliterate peoples, including the Saxon ancestors of the English themselves, the official British Anglican church had none. No Protestants could match either the inherent drama and color of Catholic liturgy or the zealous missionary devotion of monastic orders like the Jesuits. For Protestants, conversion required the need to understand the Bible, ideally to read it, and to accept such difficult theological doctrines as predestination. As a result, few North American natives, then or later, followed the example of Pocahontas in adopting English religion. And given the official connection between state and church, to remain stubbornly pagan was in white eyes to remain something like "outlaws," beyond the normal protections of law and government.

Far more typical than Pocahontas's life was her death. American natives had no acquired immunities to many common European diseases; Lady Rolphe died of a lung ailment, hundreds of thousands of others of smallpox, measles, and pneumonia. There are many reasons why the English invaders were able to drive back the original inhabitants of Virginia and other colonies. But sheer military superiority was not one of them; if the musket was more powerful than the bow, the margin was not great, and native warriors had many other advantages. More important was native disunity, the way in which united white forces were able to exploit ancient enmities, always to find allies against whatever tribe was slated next for conquest. But the most important English allies may have been the invisible microbes that moved inland ahead of them, destroying whole villages, leaving empty spaces, fatally weakening the ability to resist.

The great massacre of 1622 was no more than a defiant gesture. The Virginians regrouped and retaliated, crushing serious opposition. Any hope of achieving the kind of biracial society and government symbolized by the Pocahontas story was then lost. In Virginia, as in other later colonies, the Indians acquired a reputation as incurably treacherous, potentially murderous outsiders. And because they remained outsiders, the official boundaries of Virginia did not define a single territorial state, like England itself. Instead, there were several systems of law and government, one dominant, the others subordinate.

In this Virginia set an example for the rest of British North America. A few native servants, slaves, or Christian converts lived inside the white world, clearly subject to colonial law, and seem to have been treated, in normal times, much like others of the same status. But differences of language and culture made their positions tense, and in wartime they might be subject to hostility up to and including massacre. The rest of the native population, living in tribes or settlements in varying states of dependence, was left to do justice to each other as they saw fit. But when there was conflict with whites, certainly when encounters on lonely farms, trails, or taverns erupted into bloody violence, the dominant colonial law took precedence.

Three early murder cases may be taken as typical. In 1638 four white men, indentured servants escaping from their masters in Plymouth Colony, fled along the trail to Providence. Along the way they encountered a Narragansett; poor and desperate, fully aware that natives were often used to track white fugitives, they robbed and murdered him. For this they were condemned to death, and three of them were hanged. The next year, in New Haven, the leader of the Quillipieck accused one of his tribe of murdering Abraham Finch and turned him over to the white authorities; Nepaupuck first denied the accusation but was convicted on the testimony of his cousin, finally confessed, asked to die, and was beheaded. Three years after that, in Maryland, when John Elkin confessed to killing an Indian "commonly called the king of Yowocomco," the jury refused to convict, on the ground that a pagan was "outside the king's peace"; the governor rejected the verdict and impaneled two more juries, both of which found self-defense, until at last a fourth trial, more to his liking, found Elkin guilty of manslaughter.

These incidents were relatively rare in the early years, when most interracial killings occurred during wars. But all parties knew that the two forms of homicide were related, and all the above cases illustrate the politics that often dominated the treatment of white-Indian murder. The two New England cases occurred within a year of the 1637 Pequot War, in which Connecticut and Massachusetts forces combined to quash a rebellious tribe. Both white and Indian authorities, then and later, were acutely aware that individual acts of murder, if not treated in ways seen as just on both sides, could lead to escalating hostilities. In Maryland, as elsewhere, ordinary settlers tended to be hostile to "strange" and potentially dangerous people who held desirable land. Higher authorities, however, had geopolitical and economic interests not well shared by the average colonist; the Indians were potential allies against the French, for example, and trapped beaver and marten for favored politicians to forward for trade in Europe.

As the colonies grew and settlement moved west, the early patterns were duplicated. Ordinary settlers and Indians had, literally, little use for each other, and expansion created friction, sometimes bloodshed, especially over claims to land. But both sides were policed by their leadership, whose needs were more complicated. The result was complex: several systems of criminal law and procedure, in practice run by the needs of politics more than ideals of justice. But there was no question, after the very earliest years, either about merging all into one or about which was supreme. Indians accused of murdering whites were usually turned over to be tried in white courts; when whites were accused of murdering tribal Indians, the authorities sometimes arranged for monetary compensation, as a de facto admission of guilt, or at least responsibility, but whites were never surrendered to Indian justice.

And if the native people created unanticipated problems in Virginia, so did the local soil and climate. The economic geography and human ecology of the Chesapeake region made important changes in the balance between individual and state power, changes reflected in the system of criminal justice. Above all, the problem of labor supply was met by adding a third race, the African, to the two already in place. That this addition was based on naked force, and attended with continual fear of violence, had results of enormous importance to the future of criminal justice in America.

While white Virginians were soon forced to trade their dreams of quick exploitation for the harder job of growing or making their own products to sell abroad, they still thought in terms of making a killing. That is, they might grow exotic things, flax, for example, silkworms, or wine grapes. Only after many failed experiments did they reluctantly conclude that, among those that would actually flourish in the soil along the Chesapeake, only the stinking weed tobacco had any commercial value. And once the bitter native leaf smoked by Pocahontas and her people was replaced by a better variety introduced by her husband, John Rolphe, Virginians were able at last to establish an agricultural economy.

But tobacco was a crop unlike any the English had known, and it helped create a society unlike any they had known. The plant itself notoriously exhausted the soil, so that planters continually had to move on to new fields. Luckily for them the Chesapeake region, across the bay in Maryland as well as in Virginia itself, was honeycombed with tidal creeks and rivers. This, and the virtual extinction of the local Indians, made it easy to pole upstream a mile or two every few years, carve out a new plot, and still float hogsheads of packed leaves down to the bay for shipment to addicts back in England. But what was fortunate for individual colonists was a nightmare for colonial administrators.

The settlement was governed at first by the private Virginia Company, under a charter granted by King James. In the earliest years, the settlers, disoriented and often hungry, faced a great green jungle, full of strange creatures and equally strange people. Their appointed captains, as dazed as they, had none of the authority that came with centuries of settled rule, symbolized by all the pomp and majesty of the state back in England. To win obedience they had few weapons but fear, and invoked all the authority of the death penalty not only against the starving madman who boiled and ate his wife but also against political opponents and a variety of petty violations of social order. This policy, extremely unpopular and hard to enforce, gave way as the colony moved toward establishing English institutions under the kind of constitutional government familiar at home, a mixture of hereditary right, appointment, and election.

When in 1624, after the Indian massacre, the king canceled the company charter and took over direct responsibility, the change made little difference on this side of the Atlantic. Chief executive of the central government was still a governor, now chosen by the king. He in turn appointed an advisory council, roughly equivalent to the House of Lords back home, which acted as one branch of the colonial lawmaking body. The other branch, created in 1619, was the House of Burgesses, elected, like the House of Commons, by the "planters" or landholders in the local counties, or towns. Governor, councillors, and burgesses would then make the laws; appointed judges, county sheriffs, and local juries would administer them.

But there were in fact no "towns" outside of Jamestown. More important, there were no real villages. In Virginia, like most later colonies, land was not worked in common or shared by peasants, usually renters, living close together in the traditional English fashion. Instead, given the immense amounts of unsettled land available on the North American continent, it was typically owned outright, in what by European standards were huge amounts; in Virginia the usual unit was fifty acres, and many planters held thousands. And since planters continually moved out and away from each other as tobacco land wore out, there were no real communities. This in turn had profound implications for criminal justice.

In England the whole system of criminal justice had rested on the men of the neighborhood, who formed posses, captured felons through the hue and cry, investigated violent deaths through the inquest system, served on grand and trial juries, and made decisions on the basis of long-standing custom and tradition. But there was no long-standing custom and tradition in this new world. The authority of all colonial governments was almost continually challenged, as they had to confront new situations and invent novel solutions just when the government back in England, through much of the middle seventeenth century, was in crisis, even civil war. It was hard for governors, sheriffs, and judges to win obedience. It was hard, to begin with, to find neighbors. And once found, the independent planters of this turbulent early society were not easy to deal with.

One key reason for their sense of independence, and for the turbulence of the society, was that so many of them owned guns. In England, and in Europe generally, the ownership of firearms, often the right to hunt game, was legally restricted to an elite. But from very early in British North America the official need for an armed militia to deal with natives or Frenchmen made owning a musket a civic duty. On isolated farms, too, the presence of meaty big game combined with fears of bears, wolves, and lurking Indians to assure that planters knew how to shoot. And this new and characteristically American phenomenon, a man on a lonely farm with a gun, made law enforcement hard. Courts and governors sometimes challenged the land titles of men like these, and sent sheriffs out with legal papers; the warrants came back from the frontier with notations such as "not executed by reason of a gun" or "defendant swore that he would shoot me if I touched any of his estates."

But the most important effect of weakened law enforcement on the early Chesapeake frontier was that it opened the door to African slavery.

The story of slavery begins with the fact that tobacco is a demanding crop, each plant requiring painstaking attention throughout the growing season. To make a profit took hard work; to get rich took extra labor. No free whites in Virginia would do this for mere wages, given the opportunities to farm their own land. Neither would the Indians. While English law allowed for war captives, especially pagans, to do forced labor, the natives of North America, unlike those to the south, were not used to regular agricultural work, and most resisted coercion to the point of death. The search for tobacco hands then led back to the British Isles, where economic developments had created a big potential labor pool.

To deal with all those "rogues and beggars" on the highways to London, men thrown out of work by the disruption of village agriculture in response to the new international market, the authorities in the sixteenth century had created a new class, "indentured servants." Under new Poor Laws these men could sell themselves, or be forced to do so, for a term of four or seven years. While they were supposed to be treated much like a master's children, allowed to go to church, perhaps taught to write, they got no pay but their keep. Thousands of them came to Virginia in the first generation alone, whether as volunteers or as alternative to jail or poorhouse. From the landowner's point of view their labor was critical and the pay ideal. But there were two problems: their death rate and their behavior.

Especially in the brutal early years, the death rate among these poor and exploited young men was appalling; around 1620 it approached 80 percent annually, a truly shocking figure, higher even than in London during the plague, the result of malaria and typhoid combined with overwork, malnutrition, and general ill-treatment. Planters, however, continued to import new ones, who arrived fresh and ignorant off the boat. From their point of view, again, the problem was less those who died—replaceable free of charge—than those who survived to fill out their terms. Virginia law required that these servants, overwhelmingly young men of the poorest classes, be given fifty acres of land when their terms of indenture ended. These often swampy plots were rarely enough to make them into substantial farmers, certainly not family men (there were very few white women about). But they were free now, away from their masters' control, and in this new world this whole class of not-very-responsible young bachelors often had guns and played important roles in local power struggles.

The first Africans imported to Virginia seem to have arrived as indentures like these, rather than slaves. English law did not then allow for hereditary or even lifelong slavery. But in the Chesapeake colonies, where outlying planters tended to be a law unto themselves, it was easy to cheat these black pagans, who spoke no English, knew no law, and had no idea of when, if ever, their terms were up. Some of them, in these early years, were relatively well treated, freed, and became part of the society. But more, in practice, were kept in bondage for long years, even for life. Over the years practice became custom, and custom, law. In 1664 the legislature of Maryland took the final step, decreeing not only that all "negroes" were to be slaves for life but that the children of all female slaves were also to be slaves, ensuring that those with known African ancestry were doomed to serve forever.

In earlier years it did not pay planters to buy servants at high prices, because the death rate was so high. But by the late seventeenth century it made economic sense to buy slaves for life, and their children for eternity, instead of white indentures for a few years. And this economic logic was bolstered by a major social and political development. In 1676–77 Virginia was wracked by the civil war known as Bacon's Rebellion, which had begun, like many colonial wars, with murder: an Indian raid on Nathaniel Bacon's isolated plantation which killed his overseer. Accusing the governor of coddling the "darling Indians," Bacon led a revolt against the authorities in which poor and angry young indentures and former indentures, some of them black men with guns, played an important part. Once they were put down, the advantages of slavery over indenture were clear to the colony's governing class. Poor free men were a menace to the established political order; lifetime slaves could be shut out of politics entirely.

But the fatal step into racial slavery, followed with enthusiasm in the new Carolina colonies and spreading north as well, had enormous consequences for both black and white southerners.

The West Africans imported into the colonial South came mostly from societies of considerable sophistication, with some similarities to the English. They were used to patriarchal authority and to village government, run by male elders, with more direct power to punish murder, for example, than among the Native Americans. They were also used to war and to relatively benign forms of enslavement for the losers. But daily life in the west of Africa seems to have been generally peaceful, with little physical aggression among members of the same community; nothing had prepared these men and women for the new kind of bondage they encountered when kidnapped for sale to Europeans, certainly not for the routine brutalities they encountered during the voyage across the Atlantic or on arrival in Virginia. They did not take to it easily, or without resistance.

The English themselves had to feel their way into the new situation. Since hereditary slavery was without precedent in common law, its features had to be invented on the spot. And if the labor system was to be based on the involuntary service of imported Africans, sullen if not violent, the whole society must rest on the constant use or threat of force.

In this context the low incidence of murder along the Chesapeake through most of the seventeenth century is in many ways surprising. Given political, social, and racial tension, the enormous death rate of the early years, and the callous exploitation of servants and then slaves, the population must have been hardened to illegal violence. But the ruling authorities never tolerated it officially, and were serious about their responsibility to protect the lives of whites of every status, as well as others who fell under their jurisdiction.

Doubtless on the fringes there were cases of undetected murder, their actual number a mystery, but it does not seem large. North Carolina made it a crime to bury a servant without notice, much like concealing the death of a bastard child, to protect the most helpless victims of mistreatment. There is just a single recorded case, in Virginia, of the opposite kind of killing, or petit treason, in which one Matthews, a servant, turned on and murdered his master. In Maryland, to match that, John Dandy in 1657 killed a servant boy, Henry Gouge, and threw the body in a creek to hide it, a crime for which his peers condemned him to hang. In all of the others brought to trial, the parties were social equals, generally of low status: family members, fellow servants, blacks, or Indians.

Most important, there were very few such trials at all. Although the records for Virginia are not fully complete, just ten cases are known before 1660 in all the Chesapeake region. As compared with the English rate, late in the previous century, this seems very low. The conviction rate, in contrast, was comparatively high—eight of the ten were found guilty—and so was the rate of execution, as at least three, possibly four, of these killers were hanged. Taking the two colonies together, there were comparatively far fewer legal executions than in the mother country, a total of eight, with homicide accounting for less than half, the others being for buggery, rape, larceny, and piracy.

Two patterns, then, emerged in the early South. Within the clearly settled areas, murder was not a major threat to social order. But given the insecurities of a new society, when it occurred it was taken seriously, certainly among white colonists. Conviction rates for homicide were far higher than in the old country, whoever did it and to whom. It is hard to know what was happening on the wilder fringes. Meanwhile, tribal Indians remained a genuine if decreasing threat outside of the society and enslaved blacks a growing threat within it, both groups regarded with resentment and fear and dealt with according to laws that applied to them alone.

2

Massachusetts, during these early years the model for New England as Virginia was for the South, faced many of the same New World problems and dealt with some of them in similar ways. But some issues of law and social order were treated very differently. Whereas Virginia owed its settlement to the first of the European changes of the era, the development of an international market economy, Massachusetts was founded as a result of the second, the Protestant religious revolution. While the social and labor systems of the New England colonies were less radically different from the Old World model than those to the south, the New England authorities, unlike those in Virginia, had ideological objections to the English state and church. As extreme Protestants, or Puritans, they were convinced that their settlements were a kind of Godly experiment in right living, that "the eyes of the world" were upon them. And so they insisted on establishing their communities, and law codes, on a different and stricter biblical foundation.

Relations with the Indians, first, ran roughly parallel to the experience along the Chesapeake. The natives of New England, even before white settlement, were hit even harder by smallpox and other Old World microbes than those to the south, and so offered less armed resistance. The Puritans, too, put more energy into attempts at education and conversion than their Anglican brethren, earnestly sending a number of souls to Harvard College with sometimes bizarre results; the only one to graduate died of illness within a year. Some Puritans, too, like Roger Williams of Rhode Island, attempted to treat the natives with Christian justice. But the number of "praying Indians" remained small, and relations were marked with mutual suspicion punctuated with savage warfare.

As in the South, then, two systems of justice developed within the New England colonies, one for the whites and those who lived in white settlements, one for tribal Indians. Again in cases of homicide across this line, the fate of accused killers was a matter for political negotiation, with Indians sometimes handed over to white justice, but whites never to Indian justice. The New Englanders insisted, in fact, that any killing of a white was murder and should be tried in their courts, in their language; refusing to recognize legitimate resistance against Christians by pagans, they made no exception even in wartime. And it was a murder, specifically native hostility to the dominance of white law in a homicide case, that sparked the biggest war in New England history.

During the early 1670s Metacom, chief of the Wampanoags (known to whites as King Philip), deeply resentful of the slow invasion of Indian lands, joined with several other tribes in an effort to resist the whites. An elderly praying Indian, Sassamonn, once an interpreter and ally of the Plymouth colonists, renounced his baptism to join these disaffected natives as a respected adviser to Metacom. Then, in 1674, the old man again changed his mind, was accepted back into the Christian fold, and informed the white governor that his people were secretly plotting armed rebellion. In January 1675 his body was found under the ice of Assawompsett Pond, victim of an execution as traitor to his people. A native eyewitness accused three Wampanoags; the three were captured, tried in a white court that June, and hanged within days. Days later guerrilla war broke out all over New England, led in the west by the Nipmuc chieftain Matoonas, whose own son, too, had been hanged for the murder of an Englishman.

King Philip's War raged for over a year, with the Indians, as was their custom, both fighting white troops and slaughtering men, women, and children found in isolated settlements, dismembering and mutilating their bodies and displaying the pieces on poles. The colonists retaliated with almost equal savagery, until in August 1676 "Philip," exhausted and hiding in a Rhode Island swamp, was betrayed by a follower and shot dead by an Indian ally of the New Englanders. Pieces of him were hung from four trees, as warning; the bounty paid for his head, with an irony that seems to have escaped the Bible-reading Puritans, was thirty pieces of coin.

But while Metacom's death effectively ended the war, more than half the colonial settlements had been attacked, with over one-tenth of the white males killed. And if the coastal natives were effectively wiped out, white New England was more than ever convinced of the need to guard against murderous Indians on their northern and western frontiers.

Although the threat of outside warfare never faded, the New England colonies were plagued far less by internal weakness than were those to the south. The Puritan leadership of Massachusetts and the several smaller colonies that bordered or split off from it were resolved above all to maintain Godly communities. Without a single staple crop like tobacco to pull them apart geographically, they were able for generations to defy the fact that they were surrounded by fertile lands unclaimed by any Christian and hold the population together in villages. They engaged in communal agriculture much like an ideal version of that practiced by their medieval ancestors, dividing some of the land, sharing the rest, making key decisions in council, governed by leaders elected by householders and viewed as well as "Elected," or destined to salvation, by the Lord Himself.

While the New Englanders used indentured English servants and, later, African slaves, neither group played as large a role as in the South. With no one labor-intensive crop to sell abroad, they had less need to exploit large numbers of unskilled workers. They were reluctant, too, to admit either rowdy bachelors or pagan Africans into their largely closed societies, unless employed by and under the care of watchfully paternal householders. After a brief "starving time," as in Virginia, their new lands, too, carefully tended, helped make them as physically healthy and long-lived as any people on the planet, far less liable to cycles of want and violent desperation than the peasants of Europe. At the same time, with little movable wealth and few allowed to live outside communal boundaries, they offered virtually no opportunities for bandits or outlaws.

Murder, then, as ordinarily defined, was even less a threat to social order in seventeenth-century New England than along the Chesapeake. Tight neighborly vigilance assured that even fewer cases went undetected, and the New England justice system, even more than those to the south, took seriously its responsibility for the lives of social inferiors. Again, as in medieval England, Maryland, and Virginia, most of the seventeen homicide cases tried before 1660 involved social equals: neighbors, family, companions in a tavern, fellow Indians. Only two involved a wife killing a husband, none an Indian, black, or servant killing an authority figure. In 1644, in Massachusetts, one "Cornish's wife" was hanged—not burned, as under English law—for stabbing her husband to death and, with the help of an adulterous accomplice, sinking the body in a canoe; while in 1658, in Connecticut, Goodwife Boston was acquitted of poisoning. On the other side, five masters were tried for murdering servants; three whites, in the single Plymouth case described earlier, for killing an Indian.

A related feature of New England justice was its severity. There was no tolerance for impulsive homicide, or fatal fighting. The majority of cases—as in the contemporary South, but unlike earlier in England—resulted in guilty verdicts, and when the legal charge was specifically "murder"—with no room for the possibility of accident or manslaughter—every one of the accused was hanged. A total, then, in the first two generations, of seven men and four women were sent to the gallows, and one Indian was beheaded.

Ordinary homicide, then, was both rare and quickly quashed in these colonies. The real threat to social peace, as viewed by the Puritan authorities, was very different. During the first two generations, when the English state back home was wracked by political turmoil and civil war, the little New England colonies were effectively free of supervision from across the sea. Basing their legal code in many cases explicitly on the Bible, rather than the inherited common law, they essentially followed the Old Testament by eliminating capital punishment for theft—property crime was no real threat in any case. Murder and treason were still hanging offenses, although as noted in the case of Cornish's wife, above, the more barbarous forms of execution were eliminated. But what most concerned both the law codes and the justice systems in practice was sin and its sometime wellspring in religious dissent.

Massachusetts, by far the biggest of these colonies, hanged three murderers before 1660. In a mild echo of the hysteria in contemporary Europe, the authorities also hanged two witches, both of them, as usual in such cases, highly unpopular women, tried as the result of accusations by neighboring villagers. The contemporary English, by midcentury, were painfully learning to outgrow extreme penalties for religious dissent, but Massachusetts decreed banishment for several religious offenders and then the hanging of four Quakers in 1658—including a woman, Mary Dyer—who refused to go away when ordered and returned persistently to preach their heretical doctrines. But what really distinguished local justice was the 1644 trial and execution of Mary Latham and James Britton for the biblical sin of adultery. Three years earlier, in an even more striking case, an "ignorant and blockish lad," William Hackett, "was found in buggery with a cow, upon the Lord's day." Just before he, too, was led to the gallows, his sexual partner, the heifer, was slaughtered in front of his eyes, as prescribed in Leviticus 20:15.

The conflation of sin with crime also accounted for the severity with which the authorities pursued infanticide. This is a crime that historically was mostly ignored, and the justice systems of truly violent times and places have rarely wasted time and resources on it. But seventeenth-century America, in part as a result of its self-appointed contest with the Catholic world, inherited the late Tudor and Stuart preoccupation with morality of all kinds, from swearing on the Lord's Day to acting badly in church. Pregnancy outside of wedlock was clear evidence of sexual sin, fornication, and perhaps adultery. And to murder a bastard child was to violate at least two and perhaps more of the Ten Commandments.

Those accused of this crime were almost always poor unmarried women, often servants, wretched souls who posed no physical threat to the social order and scarcely inspired imitators. But fully four of the seventeen early homicide cases in New England (and some in the South) involved infanticide; every one was found guilty, and all but the one who died in jail were hanged. What inspired this unique record was, in Puritan eyes, the opportunity it opened to educate the community in morality, indeed theology. Every one of the women accused confessed her guilt, admitted the sin, and gave the presiding clergyman at the gallows the occasion to deliver and later print an "execution sermon," a form of address not confined to New England but carried there to its most solemn heights.

Death in any form was an opportunity to teach moral lessons, and even little children were thrust into its face, held up kicking and screaming in front of open coffins, so that they could smell it and be reminded that the world was not long with them. And if ordinary death was an opportunity, an execution was especially prized.

Capital punishment in New England as in Old was a form of theater, a set of rituals, guaranteed to draw a crowd, performed on a platform high enough for many to see. Convicted sinner and hangman shared the stage with a clergyman, there to symbolize that human justice had divine sanction, in some places to perform last rites or hear a confession and say something to the crowd. For the devout, hanging a penitent was a very different matter from exhibiting the gibbeted pieces of a traitor, pirate, or other murderous disturber of the king's peace. The message was not the simple one that defiance of authority carries a terrible penalty but that we are all potential sinners. In detailing the story of the crime, the life that led to sin, the minister reminded the crowd that God had so far spared them through His "restraining grace," but this was surely a time to examine one's soul. At the same time it is never too late; the one in the noose, if truly contrite, may yet have been saved: no one knows how and why He shows His mercy.

All legal hangings in New England were accompanied by the execution sermon, and most by public confession: there were many sinners but not many atheists in that age, and few were defiant to the end. But those convicted of infanticide were the ideal subjects for this ultimate drama, reminders to all New England that however threatened by warfare from without, the real threat to Godly community came from inside the society, indeed inside the soul.

That was precisely the issue in the most famous series of capital cases in American colonial history, which began in the Salem, Massachusetts, kitchen of the Reverend Samuel Parris, in the spring of 1692, where a group of teenage girls were excited by some experiments with the occult led by a West Indian slave, Tituba. Some of them began to act hysterically; their elders suspected witchcraft, the Devil's work, and Tituba, under questioning by village magistrates, confessed and pointed to five other agents of Satan. The girls themselves named still more, and the governor appointed a special court that proceeded under English rules specific to such cases. With the normal rules of evidence greatly relaxed, the teenagers' nightmarish visions of Sarah Goode and others appearing to torture them—sometimes in the open court, although invisible to the adult spectators—were accepted as valid evidence. So was much neighborhood gossip about dire events and coincidences. As some bewildered villagers confessed, under great legal and emotional pressure, they were welcomed back into God's fold, purged of Satanic possession usually at the price of accusing still others. As the net widened, none who refused to plead guilty were spared, and over the course of the summer and fall nineteen men and women were hanged, while one stubborn old man, Giles Corey, elected to be pressed to death under heavy weights, taking advantage of the English law that allowed such brave or mad souls to save their goods from confiscation by the state.

With over one hundred suspects awaiting trial that winter, many all across the province were growing queasy about the whole proceeding, and the clergy took the lead, after searching their own souls, in calling a halt. The Reverend Increase Mather declared that "spectral evidence" was suspect, possibly even a devilish device to convict the innocent, and the governor disbanded the court and freed all prisoners.

Historically the Salem episode was triply unique for America, given the great numbers involved, the special court, above all the social standing of accused and accusers. There are many layers of explanation for what happened in Salem Village. Some villagers may have been playing with the occult; many and perhaps all of the girls were surely seized with a form of hysteria. As usual, too, in witchcraft cases, there was a history of community gossip and feuding behind it. What is most unusual is that in this criminal case the accusers were typically from the wrong side of town, the losers in earlier arguments about the choice of ministers, for example, above all those left behind by the movement toward a more modern commercial economy; the victims were typically from what had been the winning side, those who were prospering with change until blindsided by the accusations and hanged in infamy.

The governor's order to halt the proceedings in any case marked a turning point in several ways. North American prosecutions for witchcraft had always been few, by European standards; after 1693 they nearly stopped entirely. And as the heat of religious tension was already giving way, all over the Western world, to the cool rationality of the eighteenth-century Enlightenment, the nature and concerns of criminal justice shifted all across the British colonies.

3

As they moved into the later seventeenth century and then the eighteenth, the number of New England and southern colonies grew and were joined by the Middle Colonies, New York, Pennsylvania, New Jersey, and Delaware. All were connected through the imperial government at home, a growing power on the world scene, and some common American features. Over time their systems of justice, too, in dealing with settlers of European descent, developed along roughly parallel lines. The dominant movement was toward more rational and in some ways more humane ways of treating offenses of all kinds, notably capital crimes, although neither reason nor humanity was clearly triumphant. But persistent differences remained, as no two colonies were quite alike. Above all, the special status of Africans, slave and even free, set them apart from each other and from the home country.

The royal charters that established each of the North American colonies generally provided that the governor had the power to enact law, with the approval of an elected assembly, so long as the results were "not contrary to the laws of England." Until about 1660 turmoil at home prevented any real oversight. After that king and ministers tightened the reins some, notably over the New England settlements, which had been for practical purposes independent states. But as England became a leading player in world trade, the British interest was almost exclusively confined to economic matters. With a few exceptions—Massachusetts was no longer allowed to hang Quakers once a royal governor was appointed—each colony was free to make criminal law and define capital offenses as it chose. What pulled their justice systems together was, then, less a common authority than common origins and experience.

The American experience made colonial government and justice more democratic than the English. Ideology was partly responsible for this; Puritans and other Protestants were theologically opposed to the notion of hereditary wisdom or virtue, used to electing church officers of many kinds. Geography was even more important: the king was far away, almost no titled nobles crossed the Atlantic, and above all land was abundant. In England the privilege of political participation, the right to sit on juries as well as to vote, was reserved for men who owned land of some worth, about one man in five. Across the colonies, the same landowning qualification was usually met by a majority of adult white males. But this democratic potential was rarely exercised in practice. The majority was still steeped in ideas of class and hierarchy and almost always chose leaders from among the richest and most respectable. As at home, then, colonial justice systems rested on local male landholders and amateur officials under the direction of a confident elite.

The men who first made and administered colonial justice, whether along the Chesapeake or in New England, were typically landholding gentlemen who had served back home as justices of the peace in their counties. English justices, or magistrates, by the seventeenth century, had become the key officials in enforcing criminal law. Across the county officials responsible to them replaced grand juries in officially reporting that crimes had occurred, grand jurors serving now only to issue indictments. Justices decided minor cases in their own neighborhoods, and when gathered all together as a county court of sessions, they in turn replaced the medieval traveling royal judges in hearing felony cases. Roughly the same system was adopted in all of the North American colonies, with appropriate variations.

Except in New England, unique in having real towns or villages, the key unit of government was still the county. County magistrates, increasingly elected, directed the activities of coroners, jurors, constables, or sheriffs, and in towns the nightly patrols of watchmen. Except for the sheriff, all of these men were amateurs, typically reluctant to serve, paid at best by fees; constables and watch usually had to be drafted. Outside of New England the enforcement of most law was typically careless and weak, easily evaded at least by determined felons willing to desert their communities and run. But in part for this very reason, colonial authorities were serious about reinforcing the lessons of social order whenever possible.

Especially in the earliest years, magistrates were in charge of the colonial trial process as judges just as firmly as they were in charge of the society as planters or merchants. Court day, especially in thinly settled southern or mid-Atlantic counties, was a major event: court time was theater, full of small tragedies, paybacks, sparks for gossip. With so many people gathered together it was a time for politicking, hawking goods, and racing horses. A good time, too, to remind all those gathered what justice was about: to impose order, from the top down, on a naturally disorderly society. And about murder and other capital cases they were truly vigilant, as in the seventeenth century: Bradley Chapin, a leading historian, has insisted that "it is safe to say that no suspicious death went unexamined," with special attention paid to the corpses of infants and servants.

Virtually all homicide cases began when someone reported an odd or violent death to a magistrate, who then called the coroner to hold a jury of inquest. The coroner, often a teamster, reported back to the magistrate and then hauled the body off for burial. As in England, if the inquest jury named a suspect not already captured through the hue and cry, a magistrate issued a warrant for arrest by sheriff or constable, followed by jail where available, grand jury indictment, and jury trial. But there were significant differences in colonial practice.

The reasons for this were many. The early settlers could not duplicate the Byzantine complexities of the English court system, the tangled inheritance of centuries, and had no wish to: they were not lawyers and in some colonies passed laws forbidding lawyers. At the same time they lived in an age when the exercise of arbitrary authority was under attack all over the English-speaking world: one issue settled in the civil wars at home was elimination of secret or Star Chamber proceedings run by servants of the Crown. And so, while by modern standards criminal proceedings in America as well as in England were heavily stacked against defendants in capital cases, the trend was toward easing the odds.

The trend was apparent in small ways and large. Legal forms such as the grand jury indictment were greatly simplified at every stage, written in plain English rather than Latin. Felons were often allowed to learn the nature of the charges against them in time to prepare for trial, and in some cases bail was allowed even in capital cases. More striking was the elimination of torture—at least on the books—as a legal tactic by the state. While for theological as well as legal reasons the ideal case resulted in confession, the pressures were religious and social rather than physical, as torture was specifically made illegal in New England and soon abandoned everywhere in dealing with ordinary white felons.

The more cruel and unusual punishments, too, were largely eliminated. The case of old Giles Corey, the convicted witch who sought to save his goods for his heirs instead of the Crown by undergoing "peine forte et dure," was a rare one; colonials rarely enforced the forfeiture of a felon's property. There is only a single known case in which the traditional penalty for petit treason was ordered against a white convict: Catherine Bevan of Pennsylvania, having conspired with a lover, her servant, to poison her elderly husband in 1731, was burned at the stake. Even after convictions for high treason, such as followed a 1690 uprising against strict new English control over New York, while the dread sentence was read, requiring among other things that "their Bowells be taken out and they being alive burnt before their faces," the rebellious Colonel Jacob Leisler was in fact simply hanged. All capital cases were treated with the utmost solemnity. In Massachusetts, typically, in the early years, the governor, deputy governor, and upper house of the colonial legislature acted collectively as judges, the lower house as jurors; almost always and everywhere no British subject was sent to the gallows without a trial before the highest court in the colony. Such trials were relatively rare, too, because colonial legislatures generally followed the early New England colonies in greatly reducing the number of crimes punishable by death.

This trend was an especially striking departure from the practice in England. In the mother country, especially during the eighteenth century, Parliament greatly multiplied the number of property crimes subject to hanging, the total eventually reaching past three hundred, in an utterly futile attempt to terrify wrongdoers into mending their ways. In the American colonies, in contrast, murder and treason were the only universally capital crimes, although some others were listed in most codes.

The difference in practice was equally sharp. Only a few habitual offenders paid for robbery and burglary at the end of a rope, and by the eighteenth century rape was the only sexual offense that carried any risk of death. Morality was still a concern, from Georgia to New Hampshire, and those who disrespected religious teachings faced fines, shamings, the whip, or stocks. But while adultery and sodomy remained hanging offenses on the books, there were few or no prosecutions.

One strong sign of a growing humanitarian sentiment, on both sides of the Atlantic, was a decline in prosecutions for infanticide. In Massachusetts, always a bastion of Protestant morality, the rate of indictments in the late seventeenth century ran over twice that for Middlesex County, which includes sinful London, where illegitimacy was far higher in fact. But the rate in both places dropped fast, and by the 1770s they had moved quite close together. While the American colonies generally adopted the early seventeenth-century English law that made it a crime to "conceal the death of bastard child," the statute was always unpopular with juries, who found many ways of evading both that and the common law prohibition. Of the seventy-one cases of both kinds brought in Massachusetts, which led all of North America, only twenty-six resulted in conviction, just two after 1740, with executions dropping in rough proportion.

Like their medieval predecessors, colonial juries in these and other cases generally decided matters on the basis of their own moral calculus, freeing women more often than men, being more tolerant of killings committed in fights than in robberies. By the later eighteenth century they often won the right, still denied in England, to judge matters of law as well as of fact. Their roles differed from the original in part because, given the nature of dispersed settlement, only in New England could anyone count on a jury of neighbors familiar with the accused. Increasingly the town constables or county sheriffs responsible for rounding up juries simply chose them by lot. They were in any case rarely called except in capital trials; the great majority of accused felons, usually poor and young, sometimes strangers, chose to plead guilty and throw themselves on the paternal mercies of magistrates rather than submit to the hard-eyed scrutiny of local landowners.

A growing American difference in capital and some other trials was that a new office, a public prosecutor, unknown in England, took over one side of the case in many colonies. Defendants in turn were allowed legal counsel, again unlike England, at least on points of law and sometimes as full advocates—although the right to a lawyer did not include the power to pay for or otherwise guarantee one, and while some attorneys volunteered to help in death cases, the typically young, poor, and ill-educated defendants were usually on their own.

Otherwise, practice followed tradition. A trial began with arraignment, within at most a few weeks after a grand jury's finding, where the indictment was read to the defendant. If he pleaded not guilty, by far the most common in death cases, twelve jurors were then called, with the defendant having the right to challenge. Once all were in place, the prosecutor gave an opening address, outlining the case and presenting sworn witnesses, with the defendant, rarely his lawyer, given a chance to cross-examine. The Crown then might present virtually any sort of evidence, including statements made by or taken from the accused; defendants were rarely given the same latitude. Following testimony, and sometimes physical evidence, the defendant had a chance to make a statement in reply; the prosecution responded to that. Finally, the judge turned the case over to the jury after some instructions on points of law.

The forms might be elaborate or casual, the evidence thick or thin, but the trial was always short—not as short as in the Middle Ages, when the jurors already knew all about the principals and the issue, but a day or so at most. The jurors, busy men, were often far from home, and if they felt the need to leave the courtroom at all, to deliberate in secret, they were in no mood to quarrel with the New York law that required that they meet "without Meat, Drink, or Candle light" until they returned a verdict—a rule that only a court order could loosen. In capital cases, far more often than in others, the usual verdict was not guilty. And even when guilt was found, most defendants, again as in the Middle Ages (but not the colonial seventeenth century), were spared the next stage.

The most usual escape from the noose was through the ancient plea of benefit of clergy, by the eighteenth century stretched long past its already thin medieval rationale in England, and even farther in the colonies. Commonly invoked after sentence in all but rape, murder, and treason cases—it worked for manslaughter—the required Bible reading was reduced to a few lines from Psalm 51 ("the neck verse"), beginning "Have mercy on me O God, according to thy loving kindness." Virtually anyone unable to plead insanity, a rarer alternative, could manage to memorize the formula; by the early eighteenth century women were eligible to cop the plea, and in Virginia, as the ultimate absurdity, even slaves. Those who did, for first offenses, were branded on the thumb and let go.

Benefit of clergy in England may have persisted, as much else, as frozen irrational tradition, but here it requires another explanation. The colonists were deeply hostile to inherited Roman Catholic forms, sometimes to Anglican ones, but even New Englanders occasionally allowed the ancient plea. And when "clergy" was not available, functional substitutes were: many were pardoned, others let off with cropped ears or striped backs. The reasons for all this lenience lie in the paradoxical nature of the colonial society and economy.

British North America was full of the raw ingredients for homicidal violence. Ethnic diversity was the rule, with Anglo-Saxon Anglicans a minority almost everywhere. Most New Englanders still dissented from the established church back home; the conquered Dutch, in New York, stubbornly refused to cooperate with the local authorities. The Middle Colonies and the southern backcountry filled with Scots-Irish immigrants bitterly resentful of the English Crown, and a few Jews and Catholics joined a long stream of Protestant refugees from France and Germany. While by the eighteenth century the tight bonds that held together the traditional village communities of New England began to break down, Boston, Philadelphia, and especially New York were becoming truly polyglot capitals, doubling in size every few decades.

The men at the very top of this potentially volatile and often brutal society were used to physical violence; most served in the militia, many actually fought against French or Indians, some were accustomed to physically "correcting" servants or apprentices, virtually all beat or spanked stubborn children—all these forms of punishment were thought a man's duty, not to be evaded through excessive softness. Meanwhile, the British authorities continually pumped single young criminals into the bottom of the white social pyramid. Beginning in the eighteenth century "transportation" to the colonies replaced hanging as the most common sentence for felony, and tens of thousands were shipped across the sea as indentured servants, joining the other more nearly voluntary emigrants.

But the overriding characteristic of the American colonies was widespread abundance and economic growth, not loss of lands and chronic unemployment but widespread ownership and chronic labor shortage. There was little reason for desperation, no room for any class of professional criminals. And the confident, prosperous men who ran colonial justice systems, while used to and tolerant of some kinds of violence, were not worried about felonious crime of any kind.

Certainly ordinary homicide seemed no threat. Although the records allow no careful description of most killings, some things are clear. As compared to the Middle Ages, robbery murder, especially involving whole bands of outlaws, was quite rare. The growing individualism of American society meant that the overwhelming majority of homicides were committed by men, and often women, as evidence of their growing independence, acting alone. Two other American characteristics dramatically cut the number of homicidal quarrels over land and labor. One is that Americans were farmers, rather than peasants, whose land was typically held in "fee simple"—that is, owned outright, with no communal obligations and restrictions. That meant they worked alone, or with family or slave labor, rather than communally, and so, unlike medieval peasants, did not continually squabble about whose turn it was to lend a plow or herd the cattle. Second and equally important, the court system was widely available to free men and heavily used in those areas, like early New England, where village closeness and community obligations made for friction.

Other than infanticides, then, murder and manslaughter typically involved quarrelsome fellow servants, artisans, laborers, or small farmers, sometimes spouses. Surprisingly few involved the still clumsy firearms of the period, despite their wide availability. Capital punishment would deprive father, master, or colony of useful hands; better, then, to send a criminal back to work, if not truly penitent at least mutilated; a common sentence was to extend or impose a number of years of indentured labor.

The statistics, while fragmentary, show clearly that the murder rate among white colonials was comparatively low, executions lower yet, and both dropping over time. Strict Massachusetts juries convicted in capital cases at a relatively high rate, a little over 60 percent, but there were only 232 convictions for homicide of any kind in the whole century between 1673 and 1774; by the last generation this was far less than 1 per 100,000 annually. In Pennsylvania, which had the longest list of capital offenses in any colony, there were 170 death sentences, but only ninety-two convicts, or roughly one a year, were actually executed, a little less than half for murder or infanticide, with habitual burglars a close second. In the small and proverbially disorderly colony of North Carolina, finally, where only about a quarter to a third of accused killers were convicted, there were only 67 capital verdicts, 20 for murder, and (given the state of the records) just two men are actually known to have been hung.

But in North Carolina, indeed all over the colonies, there was another kind of problem.

4

If the men on top of white colonial society did not doubt their ability to handle violent behavior on the bottom of it, they had also to deal with other people wholly outside and below it. The same labor shortage that made life relatively good, and lives valuable, among even the poorest whites, made it economic to import larger numbers of African slaves. A growing slave trade was a part of the international market seized early by merchant shippers in Great Britain and its American colonies. And as slavery spread in law and fact, the need to control black behavior became a daily and continuous fact of life in the South, and sometimes, in the North as well, inspired fear and even hysteria.

The earliest generations were the most brutal in the history of North American slavery, an institution still new to both races, As the traffic kept swelling through most of the eighteenth century, large numbers of raw Africans had to be taught some rudimentary English and trained in the needed agricultural skills by men who themselves had little experience in managing slave labor. The fact that the newcomers were pagan compounded the fact that they were black, a color long identified with fear and evil in all Indo-European languages, with their black "moods," "magic," "hearts," and "futures." English racism had helped make slavery possible—there are no famous love stories, like that of John Rolfe and Pocahontas, in the early history of black-white contact—and it continued to strain all relations. Faced with a range of African reactions from simple misunderstanding to fierce resistance, early slaveholders, with no more sophisticated techniques in their arsenals, were quick to resort to brute force and the whip.

But the other side of brute force was fear; centuries before the Romans had recognized that "as many slaves, so many enemies." Virtually all the leading men in the South owned slaves by the early eighteenth century; slaves were the very basis of their wealth and influence. That their laborers had to be forced to work each day, often sullen if not mutinous, deeply colored the way in which they saw their world and used their institutions of law and control. And what was true of Maryland and Virginia was even more true of South Carolina and Georgia, smaller colonies settled after black slavery had been made legal. Free men would simply not work semitropical crops like rice and indigo, grown in malarial lowlands with high death rates, and in the coastal areas black slaves soon outnumbered white planters, with relatively few small white farmers to even the balance.

One fear was of group flight and even rebellion. In practice the danger was not great; Africans from many tribes, of many languages, were rarely able to plot together in number. But the fear was not wholly unreasonable. To the south of Georgia was Florida, claimed by the traditional Spanish enemy, and to the west almost everywhere were Indians, many of them hostile, who could and sometimes did shelter and even help arm runaway slaves. South Carolina deliberately used slave troopers in its Indian wars, hoping to divide and conquer by intensifying hatred between the two groups. While some allied tribes owned slaves of their own, others used their woodland skills to chase down runaways. Following the Stono Revolt in 1739, when several dozen Africans killed some whites and evaded the militia while striking out for freedom in Florida, the authorities paid a handsome £2,000 in bounty money to native trackers who returned the fugitives dead or alive.

But while white fear of mass revolt was never far from the surface, the most basic need was to deal with the daily confrontations and acts of defiance, the routine resistance that, if not put down, would undermine the whole social and economic system. The first line of defense was the owner himself. Virginia in 1669 essentially declared that the master's rules had the force of law, meaning that whatever short of murder he defined as "crime" on his own property could be punished by him as he saw fit. The whip was the usual instrument for punishing "obstinacy"—indeed it became the very symbol of slavery—but shackles and mutilation were also common, and so long as the intention was "correction," the master could not be prosecuted, even if a slave died of "violent means."

But as slavery was compounded by racism, and became a caste system that defined the line not only between owner and slave but also between all blacks and all whites, the whole official machinery of law enforcement was needed to uphold it. In the 1680s the Virginia assembly made it a crime for any slave to "lift a hand" against any Christian; by the early eighteenth century every southern colony had created in effect a whole series of separate laws, "slave codes," to govern their human property.

The alternative to these codes, given the degree of white fear and hostility, was purely vigilante justice, beatings and even killings outside the law. In practice the fact that a slave was valuable property was the best defense against maiming or murder. A key and largely successful provision of slave codes, designed to assure that those accused of felony would be brought to court and not simply lynched, was that if a slave was condemned to death the colony itself would compensate the master, at fair market value, for the loss. The law presumed first that no owner would deliberately destroy his own property and second that he would insist on formal proceedings if one of his blacks stole something from a nearby farm or assaulted a neighbor.

The Virginia code, as matured by 1705 and widely imitated, called for patrols of whites to check on Africans traveling outside their plantations without special passes or assembling in number; small plots, and rumors of plots, involving escape and revenge were enough to keep patrollers busy and slaves nervous. The code also created a separate court system to try slave crime, although administered by the same justices of the peace who ran the usual county courts. Rules of law were in fact observed, but the rules were unique. The two most important were that no black could testify against any white and that in capital cases— in powerful contrast to the usual proceedings—no juries were allowed.

The rule of law was stressed by Virginians themselves as essential to justifying slavery to themselves and others. And whites, accordingly, were sometimes prosecuted for the murder of blacks, although the records tell little about why these incidents were chosen for action. In one

Virginia case, in 1716, a woman who had secretly buried a dead African was accused of murder by a coroner's inquest; the governor, in urging the case forward, justified the action in almost medieval terms: "At the same time the slave is the master's property he is likewise the King's subject." And when in 1739 two white men—one an overseer, neither an owner—whipped a black to death "in a most cruel and barbarous manner," the two were actually hanged. But there could be no more than these spasmodic convictions since slave testimony could not be used; in practice anything a master did was beyond punishment if not committed in the presence of other whites hostile enough to insist on prosecution.

Justice ran in only one direction: blacks could not accuse whites of crime. Being property themselves, legally they had no property to be stolen by anyone of any color. African women could not, in law, be raped: no such crime was defined or prosecuted. But the special courts were not wholly sham affairs; white Virginians insisted on the essential fairness of the institution. Many accused slaves were declared not guilty, roughly a third, whether in cases of property crime, rape, or murder. Slaveholding justices, too, sympathetic at least to the owner, often allowed benefit of clergy to the guilty. But given their original purpose, to deter crime by making slaves "affrighted," they were supposed to be harsh. And the numbers tell a stark story.

Although Virginia's slave population grew rapidly, by the time of the American Revolution it had not reached much past 40 percent of the whole. This minority had relatively few opportunities to commit property crimes off the plantation—the only ones for which in practice they were ever tried in court. Many of those guilty of felonious violence on the owner's plantation, especially against other slaves, were "sold to Georgia," often a death sentence in itself, without any formal proceedings. Still others were lynched, or shot by pursuers, again leaving no trace in the record. The historian Philip Schwartz believes it impossible to tell how many, in these early years, were killed in this fashion. And yet a careful but incomplete tally of Virginia sentences during eighty years of the eighteenth century finds, after excluding known pardons, that some 555 slaves were sentenced to death, a number that dwarfs the count, for all races, anywhere to the North. During the same years, just 77 free people are known to have been hanged in the same province. At

the level of capital punishment, clearly, the criminal courts of the Old
Dominion were working far harder to keep control over blacks than to
deliver justice among whites

The crimes that inspired this terrible record reflect white concerns
better than black actions. Crimes against property, as in many colonies,
accounted for the majority. Acts of stealth and darkness, such as arson,
given its deadly potential, and burglary, or breaking into private places
at night, were much scarier than, for example, rustling hogs out of the
woods. Some 155 slaves were accused of murder and attempted murder, 109 convicted. They were tried and often hanged for killing other
slaves—that is, destroying property—although doubtless far more of
these escaped formal trials than those who murdered whites.

Not one master in Virginia is known to have been murdered by a
slave before 1740; the number of verified white victims of black homicide during the eighty-year stretch of the century, most of them not
masters but other free men, is just twenty-four; a careful maximum
estimate ranges between sixty-four and eighty, meaning that probably
fewer than one black-white killing occurred, on average, in any year.
But these rare events inspired a disproportionate terror. Late in the century, especially, fear of poisoning, secret and undetectable, perhaps accompanied by African spells, administered by trusted servants, in a
master's own home, preoccupied white minds to an especially irrational
degree. And when in 1747 "Eve," of Orange County, was convicted of
petit treason for poisoning Peter Montague, her master, she was given
the full medieval sentence: drawn to the stake in a hurdle and there
burned alive.

This fear of blackness, difference, mystery, and paganism in fact per-
vaded the American colonies, north as well as south. The fearsome
events in Salem had begun with a black woman's kitchen witchery. In
most places, as in Virginia, special restrictions governed not only slaves
but freed people of African descent. These men and women were no
longer slaves, but they were still black, objects of racism. They were also
special objects of suspicion, when thoughts of insurrection were in the
air, simply because of their relative sophistication and ability to travel
freely, although there was no actual example of any joint conspiracy
between them and their enslaved fellows. Everywhere they were denied
full equality in law; in the South, like slaves, they could not testify

against whites in criminal cases; even the New England colonies forbade them from joining the militia—that is, learning to use guns. Gathered increasingly in towns, often along the waterfront and poorer neighborhoods that boasted what little there was of an underworld of prostitution, robbery, and alehouse violence, free blacks everywhere contributed disproportionately to the annals of colonial crime. And in fact the most dramatic examples both of slave revolt and of white hysteria occurred not in the rural South but in New York City.

New York's slaves in the early eighteenth century were scattered about the city as gardeners, servants, porters, and longshoremen, numbering a little less than 20 percent of a uniquely polyglot and often mutually suspicious population. All colonial cities, wooden and crowded, were nervous about arson. And one night in the summer of 1712, two dozen blacks fired a building and killed nine whites, shooting at others who came to put out the blaze, and fled. Angry New Yorkers hunted them out; some were shot, others slit their own throats. Those captured were tried, under provisions of a slave code much like Virginia's. But while the usual forms of law were followed, the usual punishments were not: thirteen were hanged, one was left to die, in chains, of thirst, four were burned to death—one of these over a slow fire lasting most of a day—and one was broken on a wheel.

This episode, almost uniquely, was in fact a real plot, with real victims. A generation later, in 1741, matters were not so clear. Real fires were set in the most conspicuous places—the fort, the barracks, the governor's mansion and chapel—and much of the city fled in fear. With no real clues, panicked authorities turned to the usual suspects and found an imaginative young white woman, Mary Burton, servant in a tavern where stolen goods were fenced, who told them that her master and mistress had conspired with black customers, free and slave, to set New York afire and slaughter its white inhabitants. With an audience in the form of a special court, Burton kept coming up with more names; Africans condemned to the stake gasped out still others. There was that year a war with Spain, and the Papists were accused as well; the court was convinced that an itinerant dancing master, John Ury, was actually engaged in the plot as a Spanish priest in disguise. By the time the metastasizing proceedings were halted, with Burton's credibility and the jails both strained past capacity, four whites and thirteen blacks had been hanged, eighteen others—all black—burned to death. Those still in jail, several dozen in all, were then "sold to Georgia" and other places of exile, as the final victims of "the Great Negro Conspiracy."

In British North America, then, through the seventeenth century and most of the eighteenth, both the incidence of homicide and the use of capital punishment present a number of paradoxes. In an age in which physical brutality was an accepted part of life, all thirteen colonies were full of the preconditions of violence, peopled often by alien white immigrants and convicts, in frequent conflict with hostile natives, built in large part on the unwilling labor of fearsome Africans. But as unparalleled levels of prosperity, generally full employment, and rapid growth absorbed all internal problems, the murder rate among and between white colonials was low and growing lower. Largely self-governing in criminal matters, the colonists used capital punishment far less, and for different offenses, than the authorities at home.

In effect, both their aggressiveness and their fears were directed down and out. They often felt surrounded by enemy Indians and their European allies and by blacks, free and slave, who amounted to fully one-fifth of the non-Indian population by the time of the American Revolution. In law as well as in practice, the dominant white population then developed three different systems of justice, one for each of the three races.

All of this was challenged, however—the prosperity, the race relations, above all the self-government—as toward the close of the eighteenth century relations with imperial England moved into crisis.

3

The American Revolution and the Early Republic, 1776–1829

The American nation proclaimed in 1776 captured attention by defying the world's greatest imperial power. But the success and prestige of the new American Republic depended not only on its unexpected military victory but also on the ideals that it stood for. The rational principles of the late eighteenth-century Enlightenment were reflected in the Declaration of Independence and in the constitutions and laws of the new federal and state governments. While continued growth in area, wealth, and population was still the essential basis of national self-confidence between the 1770s and the 1820s, a reputation for rational, humane innovation was one of the things that Americans were most proud of, and the rest of the Western world most curious about. New ways of thinking about and dealing with crime and punishment were high on the list.

But the Revolution did not affect all Americans equally. The very ways in which it was fought, at the same time humanely and inhumanely, reflected the fact that there were great differences not only among the red, white, and black peoples who lived in the new nation and its territories but among its geographic sections as well. The old threefold division was replaced by a new one: as the Middle Colonies mostly joined the "North," or "East," the pulls between North and South now centered on a growing "West." And as the nation moved away from its hopeful revolutionary origins, the applause of foreign admirers was muted, and patriotic pride chastened, by continuing problems of race, above all slavery, which carried over from its colonial origins. These in turn continued and in some ways widened the gap among regions, a gap measured by, among other things, differing murder rates and different ways of dealing with several kinds of homicides.

I

The political quarrel that led to revolution broke out shortly after a long series of wars culminated in a combined Anglo-American victory over the French in 1763, which finally drove those persistent rivals off the continent. The British, with a huge new empire to administer, not only in Canada but also across the globe, tried to tighten control and raise taxes in the thirteen colonies. The colonists resisted not simply through petitions, pamphlets, and resolutions but through direct action. Direct action, on both sides of the Atlantic, was a traditional form of political protest, especially among those who had no right to vote—the great majority in England—or were frustrated, like many colonials, by decisions made by high or faraway authorities. Americans throughout the eighteenth century had rioted over the "impressment," in effect kidnapping, of sailors in port towns to serve in the royal navy, over the export of food in times of shortage and high prices, over the enforcement of unpopular customs taxes. These riots were not nonviolent: they destroyed property, and British officials, especially native colonials acting in defiance of the communities they were raised in, were sometimes tarred and feathered—and scraping tar off the genitals, later, was a painful process. But while their houses were often burned, they themselves were almost never killed, certainly not deliberately. In contrast to similar incidents in London, for example, the number of casualties was kept low in part because there was no army to call on; in most mob actions it is the rioters, not the forces of law and order, who suffer most. But the low incidence of lethal violence among whites may also be explained more simply as not in the colonial tradition.

While mob action was mostly urban, the most violent encounters involved men from the frontier, often ethnic Scots-Irish, with political and other grievances against dominant easterners. And the issues tended directly or indirectly to involve the Indians. In 1763, when western Pennsylvanians believed that Quaker policies were denying them protection from attack, an armed band known as the Paxton Boys marched east. Murdering peaceful "praying Indians" in villages along the way, they were turned back from Philadelphia only by Benjamin Franklin's adroit diplomacy.

America's first organized vigilantes, the South Carolina Regulators of 1767–69, were more notable for their restraint. Partly because of a war with the Cherokee, the backcountry of that province was left with no organized law enforcement and plagued by outlaws. Bands of felons, mostly poor white war veterans, attracted escaped slaves and other fugitives from the law and organized an intercolonial trade in stolen horses. The term "vigilante" applies simply to those who take the law into their own hands; these Carolinians, mostly local property owners, accused the outlaws of rape, kidnapping, and torture in addition to theft and proposed to "regulate" matters on their own. Holding extralegal trials in the absence of official courts, they sentenced captives to flogging, banishment, and forced service on the Regulators' own plantations—but not death. The outlaws were crushed, and the Regulators almost as quickly disbanded when the provincial government provided district courts and sheriffs for the area.

Two years later, the most lethal revolt in colonial history occurred in neighboring North Carolina, where again the backcountry was in turmoil. Leading frontiersmen there, too, proposed to "regulate" their own affairs, although the issue was not outlawry but the misbehavior of corrupt sheriffs and other agents sent out from the capital. The frontier was grossly underrepresented in the colonial assembly, and without legitimate ways to protest defiant Regulators took to burning the barns and beating the bodies of offending officials. The royal governor finally led an eastern militia west to counter these loosely organized guerrillas. The two sides drew up facing lines near Alamance Creek, in May 1771, insulting each other but not firing until the governor gave the order; eastern artillery won the day after a loss of nearly twenty men on both sides. Two days later a prisoner was executed by a military court as an "Out Law." The next month twelve more were tried for treason by a special court; all were found guilty and six were hanged—triple the known total who suffered capital punishment for ordinary crime in the entire previous history of the province. The rest were reprieved, at the governor's own request.

But this episode only underlined the fact that American colonists, during the entire period between 1763 and 1775, while continually defying the agents of royal authority, were extremely reluctant to take their lives. As in earlier episodes, those who objected to new taxes and other imperial policies burned houses and trashed furniture, lit bonfires, threw garbage, laid on tar and feathers; the only tactical innovation was pioneered by patriots, disguised as Indians, who peacefully dumped imported India goods into cold harbor waters at the Boston Tea Party.

There were almost as many reasons to resent and even hate imperial authority as there were Americans: fear that the Anglican religion would be established everywhere, ethnic resentments of the English, the hunger to swarm across the Appalachians. But one of them was the sometimes ugly behavior of imperial troopers, redcoats, newly stationed in towns like Boston. Rudyard Kipling, himself an imperialist, nonetheless observed that "single men in barracks don't grow into plaster saints." Eighteenth-century British soldiers, poor and hungry, who had often "volunteered" just a jump ahead of the hangman, were not the best of neighbors. Boston's own young men, like young townies everywhere, were loosely organized in gangs, proud of their "ownership" of certain corners, taverns, or women; the new guys in town, swaggering in their uniforms, were a threat to all of them. And when the friction got too hot, it was the British who fired, and killed.

On the cold winter night of March 5, 1770, following several days of tense encounters, a big crowd, mostly young men and boys, pinned eight redcoats and their Irish captain, Thomas Preston, against the wall of the Customs House, center and symbol of imperial rule. Yelling insults and waving sticks, throwing stones and snowballs, they dared the Brits to shoot. One threw a club; it hit a soldier. A single shot rang out immediately; then, after a pause of about six seconds, a whole round of shots—without Preston's order. A number of townsmen were hit in this Boston Massacre, five of them mortally, including the escaped slave Crispus Attucks, traditionally counted the first victim of the American Revolution. The crowd fell silent; Preston screamed at his panicked troops, lined them up, and marched them off, without pursuit or retaliation. The royal governor quieted the city with the promise that the troopers would stand trial for murder.

On this issue the leaders of colonial dissent sided with the governor. Whatever else they stood for, they were insistent on their traditional "Rights as Englishmen." Their objection to tightened British rule was precisely that it threatened these rights; it was their side, in resisting arbitrary imperial action, that upheld the memory of the Magna Carta, the English Bill of Rights won in the previous century, the very principle of the rule of law. At a time when the British government threatened to try patriot leaders in special courts back in England, trial by jury was symbolically and rhetorically central to the American cause. And so Preston and his men were duly indicted by a Boston grand jury, and after many delays were tried that September, with their defense led not by a British official but by a patriot leader, John Adams, later president of the United States.

Radicals hoped for a conviction. But Adams took great care, in challenging jurors, to strike those with strong anti-British leanings, carefully eliminating residents of the city of Boston itself. And even prosecution witnesses admitted that the scene that night was chaotic and threatening. Adams summed up the law: if the men were endangered, they had the right to fire in self-defense; if provoked, although not endangered, they had at worst committed manslaughter. One jury acquitted Preston—who had neither ordered shots nor fired them. Another found six of the soldiers innocent, the other two guilty only of manslaughter. In a final irony, these pleaded benefit of clergy and were let go with branded thumbs. The rule of law and the practice of restraint both triumphed.

The war that began at the bridge in Concord on April 19, 1775, as the American Revolution finally turned to arms, was conducted (outside of Indian country) with the same obedience to rules and lack of atrocities that had marked the conflict up to then. It was, being war, violent and bloody by definition, and since it was in effect a civil war—John Adams once estimated that a third of the colonial population remained loyal to the British and another third took no sides—it was full of potential betrayals and tensions. The American armies, full of short-termers and fierce individualists, were hard to discipline: in Philadelphia, between 1776 and 1781, courts-martial or civilian courts ordered three men shot and six hanged for spying, desertion, or treason, one of them on order of General Benedict Arnold, just months before he turned his coat and became the most famous traitor in American history. But through all of this, political opponents of the Revolution, while some were stripped of their property, all were harassed, and many were exiled, rarely had reason to fear for their lives—in powerful contrast to the losers in the French Revolution, a few years later, who were drowned, butchered, and guillotined by the tens of thousands.

And it was less the conduct of war than the hopes for its results that marked the Revolution, as between the opening of hostilities and July 1776, when independence was finally declared, the patriot cause was transformed in a way that had enormous significance for the proposed new nation. For over a decade the colonials had been insisting only on their Rights as Englishmen, demanding no more than what was allowed the natives of the British Isles themselves. But now they were no longer to be "Englishmen" but citizens of "America." And Thomas Jefferson's famous Declaration of Independence was addressed to what we would now call world opinion, and based not on the rights of Englishmen but "the Rights of Man," partly as an appeal for foreign support. Thomas Paine, newly arrived from England, sounded the same call in declaring, "The cause of America is in a great measure the cause of all mankind." And the call was answered by the young men of the eighteenth-century Enlightenment, the Marquis de Lafayette, Kasimir Pulaski, and Thaddeus Kosciuszko, come to fight for what America meant to them.

The new nation could not be grounded on the same base as those in the Old World: the polyglot Americans shared no common ancestry, history, or religion, not even a unique language of their own. This country could be based only on its principles—the proud new principles of freedom, reason, and natural rights. Up to the Revolution, leading Americans had been embarrassed by the way in which their provincial institutions only roughly and incompletely mirrored the English originals. Now it could be seen, to the accompaniment of Enlightened European applause, that the very ways in which the New World differed from the Old—its simplicity, its closeness to raw nature, its lack (outside of New England) of any strong state support for religion, the absence of a true hereditary aristocracy—were not faults but virtues. Even before the Revolution was over, the former colonies, now states, began to act on these principles, and over the next several decades to transform their societies.

2

For the native Indians, however, the American Revolution and its aftermath was a disaster.

From the viewpoint of the great imperial powers, England and France (generally allied with a fading Spain), eastern North America had always been a minor theater in their many seventeenth- and eighteenth-century wars. But these conflicts loomed large among the white settlers of French Canada and the thirteen British colonies. And they were of life-and-death importance to original natives. Throughout the colonial era the British were able to hold their own in large part through alliance with the powerful Iroquois Confederacy. From the beginning, the inland Iroquois, by far the strongest and most diplomatically sophisticated of the eastern tribes, had stood aloof from the early contests between the English settlers and the natives of the New England and Chesapeake coasts. Their scouts and warriors were later crucial to the Anglo-American side in King William's War, Queen Anne's War, King George's War and ultimately the French and Indian War of 1756–63. In the final Peace of Paris, the French were at last driven off the continent and Canada awarded to Britain. But this very success led to tragedy.

One issue in the Anglo-American political argument that followed the military victory was of crucial importance to the Iroquois. More than other natives they had come to understand the difference between white and Indian conceptions of landownership: whites owned land not tribally or communally but individually, not just to hunt over, or to use and move on, but to farm and fence, permanently, keeping all others off. The colonists, long pent up on the coast by French and Indians, were eager for land across the mountains: Indian territory. The British were not so enthusiastic; in the larger imperial scheme the white colonies were sources of much trouble and little profit while the Indians had proved as loyal as their fur trade was valuable. The imperial authorities then casually drew a line, on a map in London, across what they imagined was the crest of the Appalachians, and forbade their white subjects to cross it. And when the quarrel among the white men led to war, for this and other reasons, the Iroquois and others rightly judged that the land-hungry Americans were a bigger threat to their way of life than the faraway king, and chose to side with the redcoats.

By the late eighteenth century in Europe, uniformed armies had developed civilized rules about the difference between friend and foe, soldier and civilian, the legitimate or "necessary" homicide of formal warfare and wanton murder. But no such rules were followed in the murky conflicts, far from the more famous actions, that raged among the Iroquois, the Americans, and their respective native allies beginning in 1775. And when Thomas Jefferson complained to the world, in the 1776 Declaration of Independence, that the king's Indians were a merciless people whose "known rule of warfare is an undistinguished destruction of all ages, sexes, and conditions," he was telling less than half of a complex story.

The relations between whites and Indians on the margins of settlement had long been tangled, as they traded, sometimes intermarried, and fought. Both groups mingled and borrowed from each other, iron tools, moccasins and muskets, the techniques of woodland ambush, the collecting of human scalps. The English had always complained that by their standards acts of war were hard to tell from simple murder: hostilities were not announced by formal letter but by surprise raids, often on isolated settlements or cabins, with families kidnapped or butchered before they had a chance to learn the reasons why. But their own tactics often involved the destruction and uprooting of whole native villages, the extermination of peoples. And along the northern and western borderland, the American Revolution was fought with a ferocity by then traditional.

Although the Iroquois were most important, all the eastern Indians were drawn in. Neutrality was impossible, and hard choices had to made by every tribe, even village, as well as by each individual among the many half-breeds, or métis, who had for generations interpreted and counseled among the natives and the white authorities. George Washington's blue-uniformed "continentals" did not fight out west, but some redcoats did, together with state militiamen on short terms, hard to tell from buckskinned white guerrillas, including many in the southern backcountry loyal to the Crown. There were few pitched battles among this kaleidoscope of opponents—that was not the frontier way—but many killings, much treachery, and acts of atrocity and revenge. Most important was the disintegration of tribal organization through flight and forced migration, the destruction of villages and crops.

Triumph for the new United States, completed by a 1781 victory on the faraway coast of Virginia, was a crushing defeat, a turning point, for the woodland Indians. Long since outgunned and outnumbered, their only hope had been the alliance with Britain. Now the peace ceded all the British land east of the Mississippi to the victors. Under the law of the new United States, Indian tribes were considered "nations," of a sort, but within the boundaries and ultimately under the control of the larger American nation. And over the next forty years, several American governments, scarcely in control of their own advancing frontiersmen, made a number of treaties with the actual inhabitants, guaranteeing tribal boundaries "as long as grass grows and water runs," only to break them soon after.

While some serious fighting and the usual murderous raids and retaliations accompanied the white onrush, the outcome was not in doubt. For three decades the British in Canada and the Spanish in Florida teased nearby natives with promises of aid, and the great chieftain Tecumseh rallied natives of all tribes to join together against the Americans. But Tecumseh was killed in a cavalry charge early in the Anglo-American War of 1812. And the end was reached when Britain and the United States made a final peace, in 1815, and the Spanish sold Florida four years later.

As all hope of violent resistance died, then, the biggest of the remaining contested lands was the several million acres belonging to the Five Civilized Tribes of the Southeast. And their traditional leaders, the Cherokee, tried another tactic in their effort to hold on. After generations of contact with white culture and with the encouragement of politicians like Thomas Jefferson and a host of Christian missionaries, they decided not to resist but to adopt white institutions, learning to read and write, approving a form of government modeled after the Constitution of the United States, carving out independent farms, many of them worked by black slaves.

One of the two critical issues, they recognized, was homicide. And what their leaders, many of them métis, in effect proposed to do was to enact in a single generation what it had taken Anglo-Saxons centuries of evolution to accomplish. A promise to end the age-old practice of infanticide, killing unwanted babies, was perhaps only a bone thrown to Christian missionaries, and not really enforced. More serious was the direct assault on "the law of blood," the traditional insistence that any homicide must be revenged by the victim's clan. The Cherokee, like the ancient Angles and Saxons, did not recognize any distinction between murder and manslaughter, indeed between murder and accident. Generations of alliances and battles with whites had turned on this tradition. And although it was not very different in practice from the way of their fierce Scots-Irish neighbors, the Cherokee began slowly to change it to meet white standards.

Beginning in the late eighteenth century a tribal council declared that revenge should be sought only when killings had been done "with malice aforethought." Shortly after, a kind of police force, the Lighthouse Regulators, was established, whose members were supposed to be exempted from revenge if they should arrest a killer. But these innovations were resisted by many traditionalists.

One typical case arose in May 1802, a time of peace, when a drunken Cherokee visited an outlying plantation, threw a baby into the fire, and then "killed a young woman with a Mattuck, splitting therewith her face from her forehead to the chin. . . . [T]he Man of the House . . . took his gun, loaded her with nails, for want of Bullets, and shot the Indian dead." Worried authorities on both sides agreed that the Cherokee was at fault—but the tribal elders claimed no power to restrain the man's family from further killing. Just months later, another tribal council pushed harder, and when a white man, Barefoot Runion, accidentally killed a tribesman named Goose, the elders forbade retaliation. When Goose's uncle defied them and slaughtered Runion's family, the council, trying to prevent war, arrested the killer, who was tried in a white court, pleaded in vain that he had killed only as a sacred duty, and was sentenced to hang.

The Cherokee complained that their attempts to deal with interracial homicide were not matched on the other side, where the peacekeeping efforts of governors and generals, like those of royal officials earlier, were canceled by American legal procedures: frontier jurors simply refused to convict their fellows of killing Indians. But given the imbalance of power, it was the Cherokee who were forced to change. The next step, suggested by the white authorities, was another echo of ancient Germanic law: the clan of any homicide victim was urged to accept money, perhaps $100 to $200, instead of blood, a solution only grudgingly accepted, beginning in 1803, as it left the unavenged spirits of the dead still restless.

But in the end, all of these reforms proved useless. If homicide was one of the two biggest issues between Cherokees and whites, the bigger one was land, and on that the whites could not be satisfied. In 1829 the state of Georgia, whose citizens especially hungered for their rich cotton plantations, declared the Cherokee's constitution and laws null and void, insisting at the same time that all Indians accused of crime be tried in state courts but that no Indian jurors or testimony be allowed. President Andrew Jackson and the Congress of the United States sided with Georgia and ordered the whole tribe removed west of the Mississippi.

Since the days of John Rolfe, many white Americans had admired or sympathized with the Indians. During the eighteenth century, Europeans had romanticized them as "noble savages," and once they posed no real threat, Thomas Jefferson, Tecumseh's nemesis General William Henry Harrison, and Andrew Jackson himself found much to praise in their sometime foes. Jackson, the most famous Indian fighter of them all, even adopted a three-year-old boy found clinging to his dead mother after one of his own battles with the Creek. The Cherokee found support, during the 1820s and 1830s, in the Supreme Court of the United States, which declared in 1832 that they had full authority over their own lands. But the decision was ignored, and in 1838 the whole of the tribe was forced on a long, deadly march to the dry lands of Oklahoma, an epic later known as the Trail of Tears.

Under the new American Republic, then, as under the Province of Virginia two centuries earlier, there were several ways of dealing with native and interracial homicide. Indians who killed Indians on tribal land were ignored by the white authorities. Those living outside tribal lands were fully subject to white law. Otherwise whites who killed Indians were tried by whites, and generally freed; Indians who killed whites were surrendered to white courts, at peril of war, to confirm their legally inferior status.

3

But while the Native Americans suffered massacre and defeat throughout the Revolution and its aftermath, humanitarianism was flourishing within the new American nation, with an important impact on ways of dealing with crime and criminals.

The nation was born at a time of great revolutionary optimism, when Benjamin Franklin, having taken a ride in the new "balloon," believed that all wars might be abolished: it was now possible to drop bombs from the air, a tactic so unthinkably barbaric that no one would adopt it. The new American Republic, having shaken off the rule of kings and aristocrats, would lead the way to a new era: dozens of movements, hundred of societies, sprang up to improve education, eliminate drinking, help the poor, heal the sick. And as part of this broader movement the Americans would reform and rethink the traditional ways of dealing with crime and criminals. Having begun their Revolution by insisting on their English rights, they enshrined some of them in bills of right, most famously the first ten amendments to the federal Constitution, adopted in 1789, collectively known as the Bill of Rights.

The first of these amendments guaranteed freedom of speech, press, and religion, issues in the war just over. The second, inspired by the conduct of the Minutemen who at Lexington and Concord had been instantly ready to challenge the British when called, ensured the long colonial habit of widespread gun ownership: "A well-regulated Militia, being necessary to the security of a free State, the right of the people to keep and bear arms shall not be infringed." But nearly half of the amendments dealt specifically with criminal procedure and were designed to protect accused criminals from high-handed state action in ways that proudly and formally confirmed the ways in which the Americans had already differed from English practice, and in some ways pushed beyond.

These procedural guarantees included the need for warrants to carry on searches in private homes, the need for grand jury indictments in all capital cases, protection against double jeopardy—that is, not being tried twice for the same crime, as had occasionally been ordered by royal officials—and the right not to be a witness against oneself (to prevent confessions via torture). While the original concept of a jury literally of "neighbors" had long been lost in mobile America, the right to a speedy trial in the state or district of the alleged crime was guaranteed, to prevent—as the British had threatened in the case of some patriots—removal to distant or hostile jurisdictions. A defendant also had the right to be informed of all charges in writing, to subpoena defense witnesses, to have "the Assistance of Counsel," and not to pay "excessive bail."

The several states in the new Republic separately added their own provisions designed to protect defendants. Those indicted for murder were now generally allowed to testify in their own behalf, if they so chose. And the laws of evidence were carefully and formally elaborated with a care that went well beyond English precedents, with elaborate rules to keep hearsay testimony out of court, for example, and strict guidelines to be followed literally, at every stage, on pain of having convictions overturned on appeal to higher courts. But beyond these procedural rights, the most characteristic demand of the early republican era was that no one should suffer "cruel or unusual punishments."

The first American law codes and constitutions were written at a time when enlightened thinkers were much influenced by the criminal theories of the Italian Cesare Beccaria and English reformers such as Jeremy Bentham and John Howard. What all these men wanted was to codify the law, that is, to put it in writing and so out of the hands of quirky or arbitrary judges, to get rid of the old and outworn, to make criminal law a part of a broader social policy. All law should be subject to the test of reason: the issue was not how old was the precedent or tradition but whether it made sense. And punishment, above all, should not be an end in itself, a form of revenge, as in the most ancient of theories. The idea was increasingly that crime was not the result of original sin, or a naturally weak or corrupted will, but of social circumstances, bad company, bad families, above all—as seemed obvious to anyone who saw the kind of people usually brought to court—of poverty and ignorance. It was still rational, then, to think of punishment as a deterrent to weak wills who might otherwise be tempted into antisocial behavior. But more than that, ideally, it should have the humane end of reforming the criminal so that he might return, purged of his misdeeds, as a useful member of the society.

During and immediately after the Revolution, most American states got rid of such traditional irrationalities as benefit of clergy. They did away as well with whippings, brandings, cut ears and slit nostrils, and such obviously "cruel"—and in America always "unusual"—means of capital punishment as burning and butchering. The law of treason, in the federal Constitution, was defined to include only making war on the United States or aiding its enemies: eliminating the common law capital offenses of petit treason, such as murdering a husband or master, counterfeiting coin, or killing a government official.

Most states, too, in codifying their laws, proudly drew a contrast with contemporary England by limiting the death penalty to a few crimes only, including treason, murder, and sometimes rape or certain kinds of arson. Pennsylvania, most democratic of the new states, formally eliminated capital punishment for robbery, burglary, and sodomy in 1790. But this, typically, only ratified earlier practice; few men had ever hanged for the first two, none for the last. More striking was an innovation: the offense of homicide, earlier split between "murder" and "manslaughter," was further subdivided in 1794. Murder "in the first degree" was a crime committed willfully, with premeditation, or as part of another felony, such as robbery or rape. Murder "in the second degree" was, like manslaughter, defined as the result of a sudden or impulsive passion, although unlike manslaughter the fatal action was actually intended to kill. Only "first-degree" killers were to hang.

But with benefit of clergy codified out of existence and the various forms of maiming branded as "cruel and unusual," what was now required for most forms of murder, and indeed other offenses, was a new and "enlightened" form of punishment. Here again Quaker Pennsylvania led the way, with the establishment of Walnut Street Prison in 1790.

The few "prisons" that had existed earlier were places of "horrid gloom" like the copper mines of Simsbury, Connecticut, converted for penal use just before the Revolution, where shackled felons spent their time shivering under the perpetual drip of the cave walls. This worked, at best, as the grimmest kind of deterrence, with the bonus, it was hoped, that prisoners would do useful work. Those at Simsbury made metal; in other places offenders spent their nights in jail and their days slaving in irons, along the roads, as a form of public humiliation.

But in a more enlightened time this kind of imprisonment was condemned as doing nothing to reform those who suffered under it. Walnut Street, in contrast, was supposed to be a place where offenders would be locked in solitary confinement, still at work—work being good for both body and soul—living under harsh conditions, but with plenty of time, alone, to think about and repent for the crimes that had brought them there. The Walnut Street Prison was in fact not well designed for this kind of reformation, but it served as forerunner to the penitentiary system that followed it, after decades of planning and public agitation.

The first four true penitentiaries were built between 1819 and 1829 in Auburn and Ossining (Sing-Sing), New York, and in Pittsburgh and

Philadelphia, Pennsylvania. They were designed to encourage the kind of "penitence" from which the name was taken. In New York, inmates worked together by day and went to lone cells at night; in Pennsylvania they stayed solitary all day, the better to enforce the rule, in both states, of absolute silence among inmates, who were supposed to be isolated from the bad company that had helped bring them to this sad place. Bibles were provided, to help, it was thought, in the process of individual meditation and reformation. Hard labor and the strictest of lockstep routines were also thought to be antidotes to the irregular habits, bad family upbringing, and sheer laziness that helped cause crime.

These giant structures, with their massive walls, turrets, and huge gates, ironically reminded visitors of the Middle Ages; Eastern State, now in ruins, is still an awesomely gloomy sight. But they were in fact carefully designed and forward-looking testaments to the wealth and reforming optimism of the postrevolutionary generation. So was the simple act of incarcerating hundreds of inmates, who, despite all efforts, never really paid for their own upkeep through hard labor. Only a nation as rich as the United States—or those mostly northern and western states who adopted penitentiaries—could afford to support so many able-bodied men outside of the workforce. But the new approach was the envy of the Western world, whose own reformers could only theorize about the ideas that the Americans actually made into stone, mortar, and system and which drew admiring visitors from Alexis de Tocqueville to Charles Dickens to see what they had wrought.

4

One reason for the optimism behind the early penitentiary movement was that violent crime in the early American Republic, notably murder, inspired little worry among contemporaries then—and little interest among historians since. Richmond, Virginia, offers a good example. A frontier town of just 1,000 souls in 1784, it had grown by 1820 to over 12,000 permanent residents, the political, financial, and commercial capital of the South's biggest state, full of the potential tensions posed by a population composed of casual travelers, slaves, free blacks, and settled whites. There were some hangings and some homicides, but in the course of the entire thirty-seven years not one hanging for homicide.

Among the explanations for low murder rates in this period was the end, with independence, of the British practice of shipping felons to America. Not only was the whole class of indentured servants virtually eliminated, but, as the result of almost continual warfare in Europe, until after the defeat of Napoleon in 1815, there was no mass immigration of any kind. As in the colonial era, the new United States was rich and growing, with a marked need for labor and little long-term unemployment among its young men.

But a funny thing happened to murder in the young Republic: although of little concern in real life, it became of enormous concern to the imagination, an object of fascination, of romance, for the first time associated with *mystery*. During the course of the later eighteenth century, all over the Western world, the Enlightenment's stress on human rationality gave way, perhaps as reaction, to an emphasis on the deeper, less definable, wilder aspects of our human nature. This romantic movement—which would last for generations—was no less humane than the Enlightenment, but it was far more complex. It helped inspire both a new mass interest in religion and a middle-class delight in secular courtship and love. But it also reached down into another level of the soul, the one that shivered not only with passion but with horror.

The late eighteenth century was the age that in Europe produced the first "Gothic" literature, with all of its attendant sound effects, from the soft rustle of skirts and bodices through heavy breathing on to the clanking of chains and the shrieking of ghosts. And it was just at this juncture that the American novel was born, the very first, *The Power of Sympathy*, published in 1789 by William Hill Brown, dealing with murder, love, and suicide, themes that have never since gone out of style.

The murder novel was neither the first nor the only literary form to deal with these subjects. In New England, from seventeenth-century beginnings, the ritual of the gallows had included the obligatory execution sermon, immediately printed for the benefit of those potential sinners who had not heard it on the spot. But the original tightly governed village communities of the region were loosened over time. And so, too, with time the nature and appeal of gallows literature gradually shifted away from exclusively clerical themes toward others with more sensational appeal. Packed into pamphlets with the sermons were, increasingly, narrative accounts of trials, the confessions or dying statements of the condemned, even poems about them—often hard to tell from a kind of boasting about colorful lives of sin and crime, not always elevated material for impressionable young people or servants. By the end of the American Revolution, a newer and even more subversive note was sounded, loudly: the historian Daniel Cohen notes that "virtually all of the most popular crime pamphlets published in the early republic dealt with alleged miscarriages of justice," meaning both that established authority was wrong and that if murder was involved the crime remained unsolved, its elements mysterious.

The most popular cases, as ever since, were not of course those involving the dreary procession of poor and desperate people who were normally accused of homicide but those that featured more romantic and especially erotic subjects, betrayed wives or mistresses, seductive courtesans, virgins led astray. One of them inspired dozens of accounts, including *A Deed of Horror! Trial of Jason Fairbanks . . . for the Murder of . . . His Sweetheart!!!* published in August 1801.

Fairbanks was a respectable youth from Dedham, Massachusetts, who had long been involved with Elizabeth Fales, daughter of a prosperous local family. But the courtship had resulted in neither marriage nor engagement; her parents presented "obstacles," perhaps related to his having no job, his incipient tuberculosis (favorite romantic disease), his partly crippled right arm. On Sunday, May 17, the two agreed to meet in a thicket of birches near her house on the following afternoon to reach "a final determination."

Both of them seemed their usual selves that day, Betsy preparing for their tryst by reading an English novel about the tragic deaths of two young lovers. That afternoon, from the birch grove, nearby friends heard laughter—or maybe cries. About three o'clock Jason burst into the Fales household, carrying a knife, covered with blood, to tell her mother and sister that Betsy had killed herself and that he—with wounds to prove it—had tried to follow her. Rushing to the spot, they found the young woman suffering from multiple cuts all over her torso and a slit throat that allowed her only a few strangled gasps before she expired at their feet.

At the inquest, a coroner's jury named Jason, weak from illness and loss of blood, only as an "accessory" to her death, suggesting suicide. But in August he was charged with murder before the supreme judicial court, and his weeklong trial was a sensation. The prosecution painted him as an "idle, pampered, lustful young man" who had played with the younger Betsy's heart; the defense painted Betsy herself as having been corrupted by tales of romantic self-destruction. For readers, even more than for those in the courtroom, where speculation was not allowed as actual evidence, there were many mysteries within the central mystery: Had Jason actually tried to kill himself? What were the "obstacles" to marriage? Had he betrayed his sweetheart and boasted to his friends? Was she pregnant? How had she gotten slashed on the back? How could a sickly young man with a weak and shrunken arm overpower a strong and healthy farm girl of eighteen?

Twelve jurors deliberated all day August 7; at eight o'clock the next morning they declared Fairbanks guilty of murder. On Thursday, September 10, two companies of cavalry and Dedham's own militia escorted him through a thunderstorm from jail in Boston to the town common; ten thousand spectators were there to watch him hang. Many of them, grieving for his lost youth, together with thousands more readers, later, of the published accounts, were still not convinced that the mysteries had been solved.

During the same time, too, romance came to shroud or exonerate an entirely different kind of homicide: killings committed in the name of "honor." In the course of the Revolution, provincial Americans had been exposed, often for the first time, to the manners and mores of aristocratic French and British officers, who made formal dueling a fashion. By that time, a century and a half after the fictional Three Musketeers, the weapons of choice were not rapiers but special pistols, and an elaborate etiquette had developed. An insult, real or fancied, was met with a challenge; the challenger had the right to name the weapons, place, and conditions of the encounter; all matters were negotiated among trusted seconds of the two parties involved. These associates also supervised the occasion itself. Typically, but not always, the antagonists stood with backs to each other, counted off ten paces, and at a signal turned and fired, if sometimes only in the air, honor being satisfied simply by the demonstrated courage to go through the ritual.

The fact that proper forms were observed was perhaps not fully satisfying to those shot dead in the process. But while dueling was everywhere illegal, and all participants in fatal encounters clearly guilty of first-degree murder as either principals or accessories, the law was in many places simply ignored; in the army and navy, where the practice flowered especially, there was not a single case of court-martial.

For a brief time dueling was practiced both north and south: indeed, the most famous duel in American history was fought by Alexander Hamilton and Aaron Burr, two residents of New York State, meeting in New Jersey. The long-standing political antagonism between the former treasury secretary and the incumbent vice president of the United States, both former revolutionary officers, had embittered Burr's failed candidacy for governor in the spring of 1803. The loser blamed defeat on statements and rumors fueled by his old enemy, and sent a letter of challenge. Hamilton not only disapproved of dueling on principle but two years before had watched his eldest son, Philip, die in agony, in his own home, after having been shot on "the field of honor." But however reluctant, he had no way out within the rules of his time, place, and class. On the morning of July 11, after arranging his affairs, he and his seconds rowed across the Hudson to the same traditional spot, on Weehawken Heights, where Philip had gone, carrying the same borrowed pistols. At the signal, Hamilton shot into the air; Burr did not.

The outcry over this killing was intense, and Aaron Burr, after some delay, was indicted for murder both in New York and in New Jersey and had to flee in secrecy. The charges were later forgotten; more important than what happened to Burr was what happened to dueling itself—from then on not only condemned in theory but prosecuted in practice, it virtually disappeared in the North.

Its death was hastened by the fact that from the beginning, and certainly by the nineteenth century, leaders in New England and the North had consistently challenged the traditional, external code of honor in the name of the newer, internal concept of dignity. The difference between the two, as analyzed by social scientists, is that between two different conceptions of the relation between individual and society. "Honor" is a matter of reputation, as judged by the community; a person's worth is what it appears to be, to outside observers. "Dignity" is a matter of the soul; a person's worth cannot be judged from the outside, but only by the individual conscience—a doctrine long encouraged by Protestant ministers—or by God himself: all of us must eventually stand before Him wholly alone, and the opinions of others will matter not. An insult, then, to a "man of honor" must be answered publicly; a "man of dignity" may ignore the same insult, as not touching his inner worth. It is the same lesson taught by generations of mothers: "Sticks and stones may break my bones, but names can never hurt me." Of course, even men of dignity if injured in some real way may sue for assault, or libel: New Englanders, more than southerners, were notorious for taking quarrels to court.

Dignity, with its emphasis on self-control, discipline, and delayed gratification, was well suited to the conduct of life in an increasingly commercial and capitalist North, and to a polyglot society in which people of other religions and ethnic groups could not be expected to share the same standards of conduct and propriety. Honor, in contrast, continued to flourish in the more ethnically homogeneous white South, where all of a man's peers—blacks and other social inferiors did not count—were assumed to hold the same values and where, at least as important, the need to maintain personal dominance over slaves was a daily battle and the slightest insult could not be tolerated.

After 1803, then, for many decades, the "code duello," or code of honor, was almost exclusively identified with the South. At the simplest level it involved nothing more than the ancient insistence that a real man could neither ignore an insult nor back down from a challenge in public. Here the mores of the backcountry Scots-Irish needed no overlay of French ritual. No quarter was given or taken; European travelers to Georgia or Tennessee brought back gory accounts of the number of men whose ears or noses had been bitten off, or eyes gouged out, in tavern brawls. These fights, if conducted "fairly," were considered a form of purely private recreation, carried on without official interference from the few extant officials of law enforcement. In Richmond, during its frontier stage, there were no prosecutions for assault; it was not done to call the sheriff. The combatants were kept out of court only by the fortunate fact that it is hard for adult human beings to kill each other with no more than fists, feet, and teeth.

But when weapons were involved, the casualties could mount. Tennessee's own General Andrew Jackson, for example, emerged unscathed from two wars with the British and several with the Indians, but he was not so lucky in dealing with his fellow white southerners. While honor was satisfied by deliberately or accidentally missed shots in some early encounters, he killed at least one young hotshot who had insulted his wife, and was himself severely injured in several duels (or brawls), formal and informal. And the fact that his legendary temper was fueled by continual pain from old wounds and bits of lead still lodged in various parts of his body was no bar, in 1828, to his landslide election to the presidency of the United States.

5

But even more fundamental than the concept of honor in explaining southern violence was the fact of slavery, and the legal and personal habits and tensions that came with it. For those interested in the abolition of slavery, the revolutionary and early national periods were a time first of hope and then of disappointment. In the midst of the war for independence, the supreme judicial court of Massachusetts boldly eliminated the institution at a stroke, ruling that it was self-evidently incompatible with the Enlightened battle cry of "natural rights." Other northern states were slower, mindful of the property rights of owners, but within a few years all provided for at least gradual emancipation. In the South, too, abolition societies sprang up, and all of the famous generation of Founding Virginians, including Jefferson, James Madison, and George Washington, recorded their opposition to slavery at least in theory. Many individual blacks were freed during and just after the war, some in recognition of military service, others at least in part because of unfavorable conditions in the international market, where tobacco prices were depressed.

But while it was not hard to free slaves in northern areas where they were relatively few and slave codes light, it was not so easy in the South. There, especially in coastal neighborhoods, Africans and their descendants were often a majority of the population, their unpaid labor crucial to the economy, their trade value often worth more than plantation land itself. And in the Constitutional Convention of 1787, the opposition of the Deep South states prevented the Founding Fathers from abolishing the institution outright and put off the end of the infamous and deadly international trade until 1808 at the earliest.

One salve to the white conscience was that the nature of slavery had in general improved over the eighteenth century. Even before the Revolution a "Great Awakening" had brought Christian missionaries to the quarters, and as the generations passed Africans became African Americans, and they and their masters came increasingly to share each other's language and beliefs. It grew generally harder then (although never impossible) to treat slaves as less than human. The humane principles of the Enlightenment combined with revolutionary idealism to soften law and practice in Virginia, where, although rape might still result in legal castration, "cruel and unusual" forms of capital punishment were outlawed for all peoples. Masters and overseers, too, were in 1788 made liable for charges of manslaughter if "correcting" a slave resulted in death, and over the years several prosecutions resulted.

But none of this was emancipation. Thomas Jefferson, as usual, put one prime reason most memorably: "We have a wolf by the ears." White southerners simply feared black revenge—that is, murder—should they let go. Virginia typically came to forbid freeing individual slaves unless they were sent out of state and provided for; it was impossible for the races to live together, Jefferson argued, given implacable prejudice on the white side, and on the other "ten thousand recollections of the injuries they have sustained."

During the 1790s these fears were aggravated by the great slave revolt in Santo Domingo, which before resulting in the independent state of Haiti gave life to fears of widespread black-white murder. And during the same decade, Eli Whitney's cotton gin helped create a new and valuable cash crop that made black labor more profitable than ever, decisively ending both the postrevolutionary depression in the South and any hope that slavery would be willingly abolished.

Over the next several decades, as cotton land expanded beyond Georgia and South Carolina into the rich bottomlands of Alabama, Mississippi, and the newly acquired territories of Florida and Louisiana, Virginia's economy was revived in part by its ability to sell its human capital south and west. In fact no other sector of the American economy boomed as loudly during the early nineteenth century, fixing slavery more firmly than ever.

At the same time there were continual reminders that this form of property was uniquely dangerous. Echoes of Santo Domingo never faded, revived by the discovery of large-scale black conspiracies organized in 1800 by Gabriel Prosser, near Richmond, and in 1822 by Denmark Vesey, in Charleston. And on August 13, 1831, a charismatic, educated slave preacher named Nat Turner got a mystic sign from the color of the sun that the time for his band of confederates was come.

At two o'clock on the morning of the twenty-second, six of them moved in to murder three white men, a woman, and a child on the Joseph Travis farm; over the course of the next forty hours they picked up several dozen more slaves, many armed and mounted, and moved across the countryside, slaughtering about sixty whites—sparing some nonslaveholding poor folks—until they were met and put down by U.S. troopers, the state militia, and assorted volunteers.

While this insurrection was the only one in the history of the Republic to push beyond plotting into action, it drove the South wild with fear. Turner's captured band were quickly executed, but he himself disappeared; no one knew how big the plot was, or where he was, and in an atmosphere full of rumor far more blacks were put to death after panicky proceedings than whites were killed originally. Matters quieted, some, only after Turner was found in a nearby swamp, on October 30, and tried and hanged on November 11.

But while fears of insurrection dominated white imaginations in periodic waves, what really dominated the lives of owners and overseers was the daily grind of getting work out of the unwilling. The whip was not only a private but sometimes a public, legal weapon, as planters turned to the law and whipping post to deal with petty slave thieves and runaways, or simply proud men and women who would not bend to their orders. And for the truly dangerous, or stubborn, above the whip still hung the noose.

The mildly humane changes of the revolutionary era are reflected in the records of capital punishment in the Commonwealth of Virginia. Far fewer slaves than earlier were hanged for committing property crimes, just 13 percent. Another 13 percent were sentenced for "insurrection"—mostly the Prosser and Turner affairs. The vast majority, then, were judged guilty of serious crimes against the person, with first-degree murder accounting for 40 percent of the total. But while executions overall were in decline, in proportion to population, the grand total, after 1784, some 626 men and women, was still enormous and far in excess of that for free whites; all of the 20 sent to the gallows in Richmond between 1784 and 1820, for example, were black slaves.

But at the same time white southerners themselves paid for the system in many ways beyond their continual edginess. Jefferson commented that the absolute ownership of other human beings encouraged self-indulgence of many kinds, including the instant gratification of passing temper. A woman observing southern child raising from the outside noted that "the nurse . . . often fosters in her bosom a little Nero"; another, an insider, noted ironically that the system produced "slaves to passion." Both observations were confirmed in fact by the behavior of two such passionate Neros, Jefferson's own nephews, Lilburne and Isham Lewis, of Livingston County, Kentucky.

Late on a Sunday, December 15, 1811, a young house servant, George, accidentally broke a pitcher belonging to Lilburne's dead wife, Lucy. The drunken master, with his brother's help, then decided to teach all hands a lesson by herding the other slaves into a kitchen cabin, bolting the door, and proceeding, with an ax, to dismember the terrified boy while he was still alive. His remains were burned in a fireplace, a long process that Lilburne enlivened with passionate lectures about the duty of obedience; to complete the Gothic scene, cabin and chimney collapsed that night in an earthquake. The incident was uncovered shortly after, when a neighbor found his dog chewing on George's head, and Lilburne and then Isham were indicted by their horrified peers for murder in the first degree. Since the only other eyewitnesses were black, and so legally unable to testify in court, conviction was by no means certain, but Lilburne, his reputation and "honor" fouled beyond repair, ended the suspense in April by committing suicide in the local graveyard.

Lewis's murderous insanity shocked the local justice system into taking action, but southerners were normally more tolerant. In Kentucky the maximum penalty for manslaughter, by far the most common form of homicide and for practical purposes the only sentence that Lilburne risked, was then just six years, less than that for horse theft, breaking and entering, and a dozen other offenses. And in impoverished South Carolina, at the same time, the collective jitteriness about keeping the slaves in order was a great strain on the state's ramshackle system of law enforcement. Conditions, and local opinion, greatly favored white defendants in murder cases, whatever the color of victims: only a little over a third of those presented to grand juries resulted in conviction, and as many melted away with escapes beforehand or pardons and the plea of benefit of clergy afterward. Archaic and neglected, the historian Michael Hindus notes, "white justice . . . was largely a private affair, and one not taken too seriously," meaning often that courts were by-passed in favor of private vengeance, fights and duels.

The promise of revolutionary reform, then, was unevenly distributed across the new nation. Relatively low and apparently dropping levels of homicide in more populous areas sparked optimism about new methods of treating crime. But much of this was offset by unknowable but clearly higher rates among whites, slaves, and Indians in the South and especially the Southwest. There was hope in the crucial fact that despite bitterly partisan politics, fueled among other things by wars declared and undeclared, enemies foreign and domestic, the officeholders of the early Republic established the crucial habit of surrendering their seats when voted out, and purely political assassination was almost unknown. And yet when in 1829 Andrew Jackson, Indian fighter, slave owner, brawler and duelist, was inaugurated as the seventh president of the United States and a great mob of celebrants nearly destroyed the interior of the White House, it was hard to deny that the nation was capable of dangerous violence and applauded some of its forms.

4

The Antebellum Decades and the Civil War, 1829–1865

The years between the election of President Jackson and the Civil War were a time both of enormous growth and of mounting tension. American cities in the East and Midwest grew at a rate unmatched before or since, swelled by the first beginnings of the urban industrial revolution and more immediately by the first great waves of immigration from Europe. To the south, the boom in King Cotton, richest of American exports, continued across the Mississippi Valley into the newly annexed state of Texas. Toward the end of the period the long westward movement reached a climax when, just as the United States filled out its continental borders as a result of a war with neighboring Mexico, thousands of Americans rushed to the Pacific in search of gold in California.

But all three kinds of growth posed problems in terms of murderous disorder. Middle-class Americans in the antebellum years were more aware of murder, in fancy and in fact, than in any previous time, sometimes fascinated, sometimes fearful. Many of them, full of romantic idealism, hoped to make the Republic a more orderly and peaceful society; Christian reformers worked toward a new millennium, free of criminal violence and the social problems associated with it. But in the real world, for many reasons, the promising start of the 1830s and early 1840s turned bleak as the homicide rate rose markedly, and these antebellum years turned out, ironically, to be the most disorderly and bloodiest in our history.

Sheer newness, heavy immigration, and crowding created some of this bloodshed, sobering earlier optimism as the decades passed. But more important than any of these was the fact that growth led directly to an increasingly violent national confrontation over the ancient curse of slavery, resolved only through the ultimate violence of a massive civil war.

I

Murder, as a subject, continued central to the romantic movement in literature, which reached its peak in the midcentury years. One height was scaled by Edgar Allan Poe, who not only embellished the older Gothic tradition but also invented the detective story, another genre that has not yet run its course. But in basing his famous Parisian "Mystery of Marie Roget" on the true case of New York's Mary Rogers, apparent victim of a botched abortion, Poe was merely one of many. This was an age in which the oldest form of crime literature, the execution sermon, simply disappeared under a wave of newer ones: poems, songs, and trial pamphlets, popular newspaper and then magazine coverage, and a host of murder novels typically, if often fancifully, based on already notorious real incidents.

This wave of blood in print was driven by the fact that the American reading public, proportionately the biggest in the world, was an enormous source of profit to writers and publishers who knew how to exploit it. As the number of those living in "urban" places multiplied more than five times between 1830 and 1860, reaching well over six million, two crucial discoveries were made almost simultaneously. First, it was not necessary to market newspapers through expensive yearly subscriptions; in 1831 the first "penny paper," the Boston *Times,* designed to sell by the issue, inspired imitators all over the country. A second truth, even more enduring, was that nothing on the streets sold better than sex and violence.

One way of exploiting the interest in crime was by sending a reporter each day to the local magistrates' courts, to write a regular column about the little tragedies and comedies that brought people to the dock—hungry young mothers, drunken Irishmen full of fanciful tales delivered in brogue. But nothing beat a juicy murder. Of the ideal ingredients, blood and sex were common enough, but mystery and, perhaps above all, a victim or an accused of at least respectable status were not so easily found. Still, if nothing sensational was happening in Cincinnati at the moment, with a little creative embellishment Philadelphia, Boston, and certainly New York could be counted on to provide something for eager readers.

James Gordon Bennett, one of the giants of American journalism, founded the New York *Herald* in May 1835 on just $500 in working capital. After surviving a fire and finding a racy style suitable for life in the big city, he hit full stride the following April when a young prostitute named Helen Jewett was found axed to death in a brothel one morning, and not far away a cloak belonging to Richard Robinson, a client from the previous night.

Between them the two typified the kind of young people who were flocking to the Big City, and now read its papers. "Helen Jewett," originally from Maine, had arrived with the more prosaic name Dorcas Dorrance: the *Herald* described hers as a life of sin, yes, but also refinement and glamour, green dresses, rich patrons, a taste for Lord Byron's poetry. Robinson, a clerk just nineteen years old, was the classic young man on the make, a type that could also be read in two ways. And in the two months between murder and trial's end, reporters observed, embroidered, and invented a host of gossipy details about high life and low, judge, jurors, lawyers, and spectators. The *Herald* originally described the accused as "a villain too black a die for mortal" but when the rival New York *Sun* declared him guilty, changed its mind, insisting in contrast on his injured innocence. And it was Bennett who won in the end, when the verdict freed his "client"—who had helped in the meantime to triple his circulation.

Crime literature of all kinds benefited from continual improvements in technology, notably the ability to reproduce illustrations cheaply and, through the rotary steam press, a dramatic fall in the cost of publishing pamphlets. The *National Police Gazette,* a nickel weekly founded in 1845, took advantage of both in covering a notorious Boston case that conveniently occurred that very fall, and sounded some echoes of the earlier Robinson-Jewett affair.

Albert J. Tirrell was a married "gentleman" of Weymouth, Massachusetts, who in the spring of 1845 was indicted for adultery with an unnamed "paramour," perhaps as a device—not unusual—to get him to return quietly to his young wife and daughter. While still under this cloud, on October 22 he checked Maria A. Bickford into a Boston lodging house of dubious reputation. The following Monday morning, the twenty-seventh, Bickford was found with her jugular vein and windpipe completely severed, her bed set afire, her hair partially burned and face charred and blackened.

Several papers printed the next day's inquest testimony almost verbatim. A bloodied razor, man's clothing, and a letter from "A.J.T." to "M.A.B." were found in the room; witnesses testified that Tirrell was about the place at least much of the night and that at 5:30 A.M. a young man of his description, referring breathlessly to "a little difficulty," had rented a horse to ride to Weymouth. On this basis, the coroner's jury concluded that Bickford had been murdered by her lover.

That he had disappeared allowed the press to fill in its own details. Probably the most accurate version of Bickford's life was supplied by her estranged husband, who described her as a small town girl seduced by the big city into deserting him for a life as prostitute. But nothing stopped the papers from inventing Bickfords of their own and casting her, according to their various versions of mid-Victorian sexual fantasies, as either an innocent victim of a villain's lust or a home-breaking sexual predator. The *National Police Gazette* supplied an erotic drawing in which a mustachioed Tirrell, in formal dress, slashed a Bickford draped backward on a bed, her billowing hair conveniently falling around a huge expanse of white bosom. And the first novel, *Julia Bicknell: or, Love and Murder! Founded on a Recent Domestic Tragedy,* came out within a week of Tirrell's capture in the Gulf of Mexico, December 5, on a vessel bound for New Orleans.

The trial, in March, was a vivid illustration of the way in which American procedures had changed since the colonial era, when the courtroom was dominated by the judge, the office of prosecutor was a new American invention, and in felony cases defense counsel was only partially and reluctantly admitted. The Constitution had since guaranteed the right to an attorney; in Massachusetts, as in many states, each county had a public prosecutor; and by the 1840s a major capital trial was viewed by spectators (and readers) as a duel of wits and rhetoric between two sides, with judge serving merely as referee.

Tirrell's case was argued by three men, headed by the flamboyant Senator Rufus Choate, leading advocate of the day. His summation— by then a traditional highlight—took six and a half hours, enough time, in an earlier day, for several whole murder trials. In the course of

provoking "reasonable doubt," his first argument was that Bickford—
in his version, of course the seductress—had slashed her own throat.
This theory did not easily fit with the physical evidence, above all the
burning bed. But for that he had an alternative, truly novel and ingenious hypothesis: his client had suffered from "somnambulism" since
boyhood and had perhaps killed the accursed woman in his sleep, under
the control of a kind of nightmare. In the peroration that followed he
noted that "in old Rome . . . it was always the practice to bestow a civic
wreath on him who saved a citizen's life." "Do your duty today," he told
the jurors, "and you may earn that wreath."

The jurors took only two hours to find Tirrell not guilty of the murder. They earned, as a result, not wreaths of honor but at best mixed
reviews from the nation's press. Sentimental outpourings on behalf
of Tirrell, his widowed mother, and his restored young family were
matched by much indignation as the villain went free. The old, simple
morality of the execution sermon was by then long dead, as readers got
no single message at all. Much of the literature of homicide now suggested that what had once been clear was now mysterious, and further
that the justice system was not only sometimes mistaken but even corrupt. In the democratic atmosphere of the Age of Jackson, the penny
papers often vied with each other in casting criminal trials as contests
of the rich against the respectable working class. Ten years before, while
the *Herald* had hinted that some rich patron of Helen Jewett had conspired to pin the crime on young Richard Robinson, the *Sun* had denounced the accused as a well-connected wastrel who had managed to
buy his way out of trouble with the help of a $1,500 defense team. And
in Tirrell's case it was hard to deny that money bought ingenuity, as
"somnambulism" swept the East Coast as a fashionable defense.

2

But "somnambulism" and indeed innocence were not the only arguments used by his defense to save Albert Tirrell from the gallows: one
of his lawyers, in open court, directly attacked the death penalty itself.
And even more strongly than the celebrity given trial attorneys and the
sentimental fascination with selected defendants in murder cases, the
humane side of the romantic era was represented by the movement to

amend or even halt the practice of capital punishment. This was actually a many-sided movement, based on several rather different but not incompatible approaches to criminal reform.

The first of these was based on the needs of a changing economic system. Especially in the North and East, the rapid growth of an urban commercial economy was dependent on rational, predictable behavior, rules made and followed, contracts reliably executed. All of this behavior, which we have come to call middle class, in turn required a new kind of working class. Farmers were used to working hard but unevenly, with each day or season bringing its change and long slack periods between harvest and planting. American farmers, too, typically owned their own land and were used to working independently, unlike peasants, without coordinating their labor with anyone else. But now employers required people who could tell time, work ten or twelve hours a day, six days a week, all year round, meanwhile placidly taking directions from supervisors and cooperating with their peers in the office or factory.

The need for this new kind of cooperative, tractable workforce was one reason—by no means the only one—for the powerful support given many of the reform movements that flourished especially during the 1830s and 1840s. The penitentiary movement, still growing, depended in part on the faith that character could be reformed and virtue taught through insistence on strict clockwork routines. Beginning in the late 1820s, a powerful temperance movement promoted moderation in the use of liquor—early Americans drank heavily and often—with real success. By the 1830s reformers were calling for total abstinence; by the 1840s, legal abolition. Several northern and western state laws in fact decreed absolute prohibition.

The movement appealed strongly to businessmen. While occasional binges did little harm on the farm, and a man who drunkenly chopped up the chicken coop was a problem only to himself, his family, and perhaps the chickens, lurching intoxication in factory or office could be a disastrous disruption of cooperative routines. And one of the most important tasks of the new urban police forces, which first appeared in the 1830s and 1840s, was to enforce the new temperance laws, if not shutting down all traffic, then restricting it to adults, in licensed places, during approved hours—and of course arresting drunks. From the

1820s through the 1840s, all of these reforms resulted, one historian has estimated, in more than halving the average per capita consumption of alcohol.

The public school system, too, was created in the same era: Pennsylvania was the first state to provide for tax-supported education open to all in 1834, with others following shortly. The issue was neither literacy nor numeracy; Americans had always learned somehow to read, write, and figure, and led the world already. But as the great Massachusetts educator Horace Mann insisted, the very fact of mass democracy demanded a responsible, orderly population. Discipline was an obsession in these early schools, and learning to sit still, take turns, mind the teacher, hold your water, and listen for the bell was perfect training for later work in a factory or office. In 1841 one cotton manufacturer testified that those employees with public school educations indeed had better morals, "were more orderly and respectful in their deportment, and more ready to comply with the . . . regulations of an establishment."

The same logic, the same search for order and discipline that helped the public school movement called at the same time for the abolition of public hanging. The simplest argument was that hanging was simply "cruel" punishment—and the very fact that it was fairly "unusual" made it more so. With the exception perhaps of sheriffs in slave country, there were no truly experienced hangmen in the United States, no one who could guarantee a quickly broken neck. Given the "short drop" then practiced, without expert placement of the knot the victim often jerked violently about for eight or twelve minutes, spinning in the air, his contorted face and antics horrifying—or worse, delighting— the ten or twenty thousand who often gathered to watch him strangle. But it was not the tortured victim but those unruly spectators who most concerned those worried about public order.

The old Puritan ideal, in which gallows rituals were intended to inspire introspection and repentance, was clearly dead. Indeed death itself, for the middle class, was becoming increasingly distasteful: instead of looking it straight in the face, those who could afford it were finding others, a whole new class of professionals, to "undertake" the often messy business of washing and clothing corpses and preparing them for burial. In this atmosphere, observers agreed, public hangings were simply lewd spectacles whose supposed moral lesson often backfired. If any elevated sentiment was aroused, it was sympathy for the condemned. The "deterrence" argument might apply to the punishment itself but surely not to the sight of it. In England, the nation that led the European world in hangings, American reformers were well aware that pickpockets notoriously worked the crowds come to see other pickpockets die. And here as there the public "gallows tree" seemed only to encourage drunken, disorderly, unseemly behavior in the masses.

And so Pennsylvania in 1834 decreed that state hangings should henceforth be held privately, inside jail or prison walls, attended only by sheriff, family, a handful of witnesses, and a doctor, a move that quickly spread across the North and East.

But the move to make capital punishment a more private matter was by no means the ultimate reform. And the rationale behind it, to make a more orderly society of America's untidy young democracy, was only one of the four that drove contemporary reform. And the other three reforming rationales did not aim to make hanging more acceptable but to abolish it outright. One of them was based on the continuing Enlightened belief in the superiority of America's republican institutions, a second on romantic humanitarianism. Third and newest was a profound religious reawakening, which began in the 1820s and continued, with pauses, to make waves over the next three decades. Together they combined to make an attack on the death penalty the center of a fundamental debate about human nature itself.

The medieval case for capital punishment had been based in part on the Old Testament, added to the even older demand for simple retribution. Some thinkers of the rational Enlightenment contributed more sophisticated theories of deterrence, while for many conservatives simple tradition was argument enough. None of these arguments, ancient or modern, was now safe from attack.

Those who argued for American superiority, first, were not interested in tradition but progress. Progress had already been made in the revolutionary generation by generally limiting the death penalty to murder, then subdividing that into first and second degrees, excusing those who had killed in fits of anger, perhaps under the influence of drink. More recently the old finding of "not guilty by reason of insanity" was clarified; under the "M'Naghten Rule," borrowed from England beginning in 1843: those who qualified were "laboring under such a defect of reason, from disease of the mind," that either they literally did not know what they were doing at the time of the crime or they could not know right from wrong. Now many reformers believed that all murder, all crime, was the result of such external influences, some sort of physical or moral disease—Albert Tirrell's somnambulism, perhaps, was an example—and so it was time to get rid of the ultimate penalty altogether.

The case specifically against deterrence was led by Edward Livingston, the Enlightened jurist who wrote the legal code of Louisiana and hoped to influence other states. Abstract ideas, such as fear of death, had no effect on the minds of criminals, in contrast to the kind of behavioral change demanded by the penitentiary. And with the help of reformers in England, Livingston used a battery of statistics—among the first times this key weapon in the arsenal of social science was tested in the field—to show that hanging had in fact no impact on the crime rate and that murders often occurred immediately after executions for murder. Brutal sights naturally brutalized those who saw them, violating our natural moral sense. And for the state itself to endorse legal homicide could only encourage disrespect for life, and so illegal homicide. Benjamin Rush had put it neatly, during the revolutionary era: "Murder is propagated by hangings for murder." The old Puritan notion that the eyes of the world were upon us, finally, was as powerful for this generation as it had been for Rush, and Livingston's most fervent appeal to lawmakers was that the United States was still the world's only true republic and should take the lead in showing the way to the future. To do the right thing was, then, not only a patriotic duty but would be a blessing to all mankind.

The romantic contribution to rational appeals like Livingston's was its stress on our common humanity. Across the Atlantic, giants like Charles Dickens and Victor Hugo were writing fiction that explored the hearts and minds of criminals from the inside; so in America were men as different as the ardent southerner William Gilmore Simms and the Quaker abolitionist John Greenleaf Whittier. Their work suggested that even those who commit homicide have feelings like ours—Albert Tirrell as son, husband, and father—and that an injury to any of us is an injury to all. The fear felt by those under sentence is our fear, and the experience of those actually hanged, their breeches all wet and beshitted from loss of control over bladder and bowels, is an affront to human dignity.

In full agreement with these sentiments, finally, the preachers of the Second Great Awakening used them to overturn the traditional theology that had dominated American religion from the beginnings. In an earlier time, the prevailing Calvinist Protestantism had stressed the doctrines of original sin and predestination. All are sinful, no one can possibly earn or deserve salvation by their own efforts. God determines those whom He will "elect" to salvation long before birth; in what amounts to something like a divine lottery, these, a minority or remnant, are winners; the rest, losers. But in the second quarter of the nineteenth century, the new interpretation stressed that Man was made in God's image, that human nature was naturally innocent, like a child's, and if properly nurtured all of us are perfectible. God loves us all—so should we. There are, then, no losers, not even among the more obviously miserable of His Creation.

Sentiments like these helped inspire the temperance movement to reform drunkards, Dorothea Dix's campaign to improve conditions among the insane, the years of work put in by the old war hero Samuel Gridley Howe to reach the soul of Laura Bridgeman, a child born deaf, dumb, and blind. The continued spread of the penitentiary movement was testament to a faith that even hardened criminals could be redeemed. And of course the ultimate criminals, and victims, were those condemned to death before the natural process of repentance and redemption could run its course.

For this new religious left the very model of progress had been that from Old Testament to New, or as they interpreted it, from a stress on God's vengeance to Christ's love. God's famous words to Noah, the medieval justification for the death penalty, "Whoso sheddeth Man's blood, by Man shall his blood be shed," might be interpreted not as an order but simply as a prophecy. And to cite the Old Testament selectively was to overlook the death penalty it commanded elsewhere for adultery, blasphemy, even gathering sticks on the Sabbath.

Some combination of these arguments made sense to governors and lawmakers in many states. Through the 1830s and early 1840s, Tennessee, Alabama, and Mississippi made hanging no longer mandatory but, at the jury's discretion, optional even after first-degree verdicts in murder cases, a practice that quickly spread to other states. Capital punishment itself survived close votes in Pennsylvania, New Hampshire, and New York. The widely copied Maine Law of 1837 decreed that at least a year must pass before a convicted felon could be executed, and then only after issuance of a written death warrant from the governor. And finally the new state of Michigan, in 1846, abolished hanging altogether.

But even as Michigan was followed by Wisconsin the next year, and by Rhode Island in 1852, the movement had already passed its peak. Conservative clergymen and lawyers had of course rallied, adding to their older arguments the idea that the very dignity of human life cited by their opponents demanded an awesome penalty for those who took it. Most discouraging was the result of a popular referendum in the state of New Hampshire, with Vermont perhaps the least murderous state in the Union, a place of deeply religious, settled communities where conflict was handled by set rules and the Protestant sense of dignity had long triumphed over the sense of honor. And in this peaceful state, in the summer of 1844, as an adulterous young farmer convicted of strangling his wife lay in jail awaiting execution, the death penalty was put to a popular referendum; the result was nearly 2 to 1 in favor of keeping it.

But more important than either abstract argument or popular sentiment in defeating reform was the concrete reality that things were simply not working as hoped. It was growing harder to deny, first, that the penitentiary movement was not living up to its promise, that in actual operation prison was no more than a dismal place that had no redeeming effect on its inmates. Even more disheartening was overwhelming evidence that, after more than half a century of criminal law reform, the nation's murder rate was higher than ever and that for several reasons disorder threatened to tear the whole society apart.

3

The changing character of American cities in the antebellum decades, above all their increasing disorder, was most dramatically shown by the adoption of regular salaried police. Americans had long resisted the kind of authority—perhaps "French," certainly autocratic—represented by such officers. The English before them had feared a "standing army" in peacetime, and the new United States had inherited the idea that providing muscle to the government might threaten individual liberties. For centuries a few rotating night watchmen had been patrol enough, looking above all for fire, sometimes answering calls to break up fights. Arrests were made by these watchmen, or coroners, sometimes by ordinary citizens on the spot. Otherwise people went to court to get warrants against others who had stolen from or injured them, bringing constables or sheriffs along, for a fee, to supply the needed strong arms and authority. But beginning in the 1830s, the citizens first of Boston, then New York, then major cities from east to west, abandoned their reservations and put regular salaried officers on the street.

As in London, which had pioneered in police patrol beginning in 1829, the new police were expected to fill a number of municipal needs. But in the United States virtually all of the early police departments were founded to deal with one specific problem: mob riot. During the single year 1834 a mob of teamsters, wholly without official interference, burned down an Ursuline convent just outside of Boston, sending nuns and pupils fleeing into the night; Philadelphia and Baltimore witnessed major race riots; and New York mayoral elections brought clashes between Jacksonian Democrats and the new Whig party that pushed the city close to anarchy. As over three days of street fighting escalated into gunfire, the Whigs had just broken into an arsenal, threatening a bloodbath, when order was restored.

One immediate reason for all this violence was the onset of a commercial depression. But there were deeper reasons, rooted in the shifting nature of urban populations and economies, why not only the frequency but also the very nature of riot was changing.

Throughout the colonial period direct action had been a quasi-tolerated tactic of the politically powerless, and in the revolutionary era played an honored role in patriot victory. Led usually by community notables, mobs had often destroyed property but rarely harmed people, and were seen, at least ideally, as the outraged expression of a united community, vented on traitors or outsiders. But increasingly riots in the new Republic were directed not at limited or political targets but at groups, defined in terms of religion, race, or class, by members of other groups, typically young men from the "lower orders." They were not well controlled, they were intended to hurt, and sometimes they killed.

In an earlier generation, when the basic economic unit of towns from

Portland to Baltimore was still the household, the violent potential in their young male populations was restrained by built-in social controls. Indentured servants and apprentices lived in the master's household, were treated legally as his children or wards, and worked under careful discipline. However rowdy on recognized holidays, they still responded when the reins were pulled tight. Habits of obedience and deference ran all through colonial society: even the furious crowds who had witnessed the Boston Massacre had responded dutifully when their leaders told them to stay quiet and trust in the law.

But indentured servitude essentially died after the Revolution, and apprenticeship decayed. Bigger economic enterprises meant impersonal labor relations, with employers and employees no longer under the same roof. There were few organized forms of male recreation in antebellum cities, no ball clubs, no parks, no spectator sports. Young men left to themselves have always organized themselves into gangs, strutting like peacocks and fighting like roosters. Sometimes they joined and transformed existing institutions. Volunteer fire companies, observers noted, increasingly turned their traditional competition to be first and most conspicuous when the bells rang into more direct action, battling each other instead of the fire. Others joined political clubhouses; their elders had jobs for tough young men who could vote early and often and keep rivals away from the polls. Still others, like New York's Highbinders and Forty Thieves, operated as criminal gangs with no cover at all. And none of them deferred to their betters: when Henry Lambert, one of New York's leading businessmen, returned from a wedding one June night in 1825 his carriage was hit by a stone; crossing the street, expecting that he and his aristocratic party would awe the young assailants, they were instead tripped and taunted, and Lambert was beaten to death by drunken members of the Spring Street Fencibles.

And as the nineteenth century progressed, such aggression by and among young men was intensified by the equally elemental hostility among ethnic groups. While colonial and early republican America had been made up of diverse peoples, virtually all but blacks and Indians had been of northern European Protestant descent. But the year 1815 marked the fall of Napoleon on the other side of the ocean and the end of the War of 1812 on this, opening the gates to long pent-up European immigration. Germans came in number, as did the English, but the most notorious and violent of the newcomers were the Catholic Irish.

Anti-Catholicism was a long Anglo-American tradition, and anti-Catholic parades and ceremonies were part of the urban ritual year. Through the colonial period all this had been carried on in the absence of live opposition, as the French and Spanish, in peacetime, remained safely out of reach. But once the Irish began to arrive, they not only fought back but transformed the very nature of urban street warfare. Persecuted for centuries by their Anglo-Saxon Protestant rulers, the Irish had a long tradition of hostility to official authority. Together with their ethnic cousins and bitterest enemies, the "Scots-Irish" Presbyterians or "Orangemen" of Ulster, they drank whiskey even more heavily than the early Americans drank rum. And they fought more seriously, replacing fists and feet with clubs and bricks, escalating the relatively harmless battles of earlier years into murderous affrays.

Developments in New York showed the way. Traditionally the most polyglot of American cites, and by the 1820s the biggest, it was the first to attract the Irish in number. New Yorkers had often found reason to riot in earlier years, whether as political protest or simply as entertainment. But deaths resulted when in 1799 local Orangemen had the ill wit to mount an anti-Catholic parade on St. Patrick's Day, and again when in 1806 a gang of Highbinders tried to storm a Catholic church.

In a nation still unused to dealing with diversity, in New York as everywhere the ethnic thread shot through all the other occasions of mob disorder. Labor disputes, tavern riots, and attacks on brothels all rose dramatically in number and intensity over the first three decades of the century. Many of them were essentially ethnic conflicts in disguise, as blacks, native whites, and Catholic and Protestant Irish tended to congregate in specific occupations and neighborhoods and battled over control of their own jobs and turf. Political parties, too, divided along ethnic lines, as the labels "Jacksonian" and "Whig" thinly disguised older quarrels during the great Election Riot of 1834.

Much of the ferocity of the Irish, in particular, was born of desperation. Unlike the Scots-Irish they arrived typically as wholly impoverished peasants, unable to buy land or even move out of their port of entry, stuck in the city without skills. Their very presence as a pool of unskilled labor, ready to hire out at the lowest wages, threatened all the Protestant journeymen and artisans a little further up the occupational scale. And they themselves were for parallel reasons especially hostile to the African Americans, those nearest to them on the same metaphorical ladder.

The African Americans had been there first; that many were skilled workers and small businessmen only intensified jealousies among poor whites of all groups. But most blacks were stuck in unskilled labor, back work along docks and ditches, in direct competition with Irish immigrants. Black New Yorkers themselves repeatedly rioted against visiting "blackbirders," or agents sent to catch and return fugitive slaves. Still, they were more often targets than aggressors, up and down the East Coast, as their own growing community institutions, theaters, schools, above all churches, were continually harassed. Only months after the Election Riot in New York, in July 1834 thousands of white New Yorkers, at first set off by meetings to discuss the abolition of slavery, rioted over several days, destroying businesses, a schoolhouse, and St. Phillip's African Episcopal Church in an all-out effort whose object seemed to be nothing less, according to the historian Paul Gilje, than "to purge the city" of the black presence. The riot was quieted only when a thousand militiamen answered an emergency call and were issued live ammunition with orders to volley across barricades into the crowd.

But the militia was a blunt and untrustworthy weapon: citizen volunteers, sometimes sympathetic to rioters, they were under the control of a possibly hostile governor rather than local authorities. The underpaid and undermanned night watch, traditionally a refuge for the old and weak, had been a joke since Shakespeare's time. And as towns became cities, personal authority in the old manner no longer worked. In Boston, Mayor Josiah Quincy had been able, in July 1825, to put down a series of attacks on the brothels of Ann Street by personally leading a kind of posse of truckmen to arrest the rioters; ten years later, Mayor Theodore Lyman vainly begged with a surging mob on Broad Street which not only nearly lynched William Lloyd Garrison, editor of the abolitionist *Liberator,* destroying the presses, but also roughed up the mayor himself and stormed his office in the process. And in June 1837, after it took eight hundred state cavalry to put down a street battle sparked when a group of volunteer fire companies bumped into an Irish funeral, the city fathers had finally had enough.

Mayor Samuel Eliot then ringingly declared that while riot was understandable in despotic countries, it was not tolerable in the American Republic, where every individual shared in government through the vote. An aldermanic committee was critical of the Irish, but as good businessmen they insisted that in a free country with high wages and a chronic shortage of labor their neighbors must learn to tolerate them. And all agreed both that the volunteer fire companies must be replaced by less combative professionals and that Boston needed a professional police force to deal with "the lawlessly violent."

And so, in May 1838, the first police were assigned to regular patrol, charged with seeking out trouble before it got out of hand, with reinforcements in reserve to answer riot call or other emergencies.

During the 1840s and 1850s all major American cities followed Boston in authorizing professional police, and a few funded professional firemen. But the worst was yet to come. Propelled by powerful social, political, and technological developments, riots grew continually bigger and more intense, and a thin line of municipal employees was little more help than a glass of water in a house fire—when not actually acting more like a stream of kerosene.

The new men did prove useful in many ways. The eyes and ears of the city while on patrol, they performed a range of functions from lighting street lamps and unsnarling traffic to harassing drunks. They made arrests when called, sometimes broke up fights. Man for man they were usually bigger and healthier than any opponents, but not always as battle ready; Americans were reluctant to put them into uniform, and resistance was led by the cops themselves, who found it easy to take off their badges and slip into friendly saloons when the weather on patrol was too hot, too cold, or perhaps somewhere in between. In this and other ways they were much like members of the urban gangs they were often called to confront. Although Boston insisted that they be married taxpayers, many in other cities were simply strong young men who had nothing to sell but their muscles.

Unlike the London bobbies—civil servants, charged with being polite, careful to avoid controversy—these early police were wholly untrained, in most cities patronage employees, at election time the strong arms of the party in power. Depending on the political winds of the moment, they were alternatively supposed to enforce or ignore a host of laws against drinking, gambling, and whoring that were widely unpopular in their own class and neighborhoods; there was more money in ignorance than in outrage. They could count on no automatic respect for

The Law in cities full of clashing values and peoples. They had then to establish their personal authority through sheer toughness, on the spot. It was not enough: in the 1840s and 1850s, nothing was or could have been enough.

All city life in those years was dominated by a great surge in immigration, as what had been a growing stream became a flood. Some 180,000 newcomers to the United States had come officially in the thirteen years between 1819 and 1831, 893,000 between 1832 and 1844. Then, between 1845 and 1857, the number soared fourfold to 3,600,000. During and after the Hungry Forties many were Germans of all classes, others from elsewhere on the Continent. But above all the newcomers were Irish, who in 1844 had begun to see their basic crop turn black and slimy from a new potato blight; the resulting Great Famine, over the next several years, forced millions either to starve or to flee. Suffering from malnutrition, tuberculosis, and then cholera, arriving sometimes nearly naked—the average life expectancy off the boat was under fourteen years—these people were far more desperate than any whites that had come before them. And their arrival in waves simply swamped all institutions of charity and police.

Reformers to then had had some success in making northeastern America a more orderly place, drying up the drinking habit, improving education, providing places of refuge and hope—at least in theory—for the miserable and criminal. But the Irish had little interest in temperance, and the Germans imported a new drink, lager beer, which swept the country. Catholics everywhere resisted a public school education that in practice stressed moral training out of the King James Bible. And the effect of this flood of peasants on the urban economy was to push crime and misery to new heights.

During the 1840s, with the use of stationary steam engines, factories were able for the first time to move away from rural sites along waterfalls, until then their only power sources, and into the cities. And in time the existence of a big pool of wholly unskilled urban labor would enable these steam-powered factories to create a true urban industrial revolution. But with the movement just beginning, that time had not yet come. The city still needed mostly skilled workers, artisans or "mechanics." Outside of digging canals and laying track for the new railroads that stretched hundreds of miles into the countryside, there was little for the unskilled to do, and in the cities themselves they fought fiercely over the few available jobs as porters, servants, and longshore-men. The traditional American labor shortage, the most fundamental reason for historically low rates of homicide, among other crimes, had been cited as late as 1837 by the aldermanic committee that helped create the Boston police. But within a decade it was gone, flooded out, in cities all over the North and Midwest.

And just at this time a revolution in small arms, begun with Samuel Colt's invention of the revolver, began to reach full stride. The American gun culture reached back to the early seventeenth century. But when the Second Amendment was passed in 1789, and for decades afterward, there were none as yet that could accurately be called handguns. There were great heavy military weapons, dragoon pistols, and finely crafted single-shot dueling pistols, but both were expensive and bulky. Colt's 1832 invention was not an immediate breakthrough, but after some sputtering it inspired a number of improvements and imitations, and by the 1840s revolvers were being manufactured in quantity. And they contributed in two different ways to raising the number of urban killings.

Small and deadly, easily loaded, capable of firing several shots, these were the first firearms that could be carried and actually hidden on the person; Henry Deringer's models could be fitted into a woman's muff. Equally important, it is far easier, as much psychological research has shown, to overcome the natural inhibition about killing when the only act required is the mechanical one of squeezing a trigger, at a little distance, rather than wrestling at closer range with a living and hard-breathing body.

In any case the new weapons were immediately used to upgrade the arsenals of street gangs. Some states and cities had begun to outlaw possession of slingshots, brass knuckles, and billies, but the constitutional guarantee of the "right to bear arms" stopped them there. For the first time in our history law-abiding citizens in the cities felt they had reason to fear murderous violence; two of the great diarists of the period, New York's George Templeton Strong and Philadelphia's Sidney George Fisher, both independently noted that the men of their aristocratic circles were beginning routinely to go armed, with revolvers, to protect themselves against thugs. So did some cops, but informally, and a little uneasily; city governments, still distrustful of the novel (and not wholly trustworthy) police, did not officially issue any weapons but wooden batons.

And during the same period, finally, the political tensions surrounding the central issue of slavery began visibly to shake the national union, threatening civil war. One effect of the resulting fears was to intensify already high levels of violence against blacks. African-American communities in northern cities grew continually through this period, swelled mostly by freed people pushed out of the South and fugitive slaves fleeing from it. The influx had always been resented by unskilled workers, and now the competition for jobs was more vicious than ever. The growing move to abolish slavery added to hostilities; blacks and white reformers, men and women, gathered to talk together in public meetings, often for the first time, raising sexual fears of "amalgamation," or miscegenation, driving mobs to move in and burn down the halls in which mixed meetings were held. Up and down the social scale, too, African Americans were seen as the root cause of the nation's political divisions: it might somehow help to keep North and South together if they could be kept down, pushed back, driven out. And the same national divisions promoted political instability at the local level, preventing city governments from moving toward truly centralized, impartial, and well-trained police.

In Philadelphia, the first real effort to create a police force began only when Catholic-Protestant conflict reached new heights in 1844. Tension between Irish and Orangemen had often erupted before, much of it centered about jobs in the city's recently mechanized textile industry. Then in 1843 a "Native American" or anti-immigrant party was organized around the key symbolic issue of Protestant Bibles in the schools. After much bluster, invective, parading and counterparading, a young Protestant, George Shiffler, was shot to death the following May 6, and became an instant martyr in this crusade. A counterattack on a Sisters of Charity school the next day sparked a melee that killed two passersby and "many" combatants on both sides. The Irish were badly outnumbered: two more Catholic churches and a female seminary were burned down on the eighth, as rioters defied state troops. And as the city simmered, loudly, into the summer, a mob attacked St. Philip de Neri's Church on Sunday, July 7. As they deployed first battering rams, then rifle fire, some five thousand state troops were called in to protect the city's reputation. The mob, uncowed, finally brought up a cannon, with soldiers volleying back, until at two o'clock the next morning the toll was counted at two soldiers and thirteen civilians dead.

Here as elsewhere, while there were dozens of reasons to riot, race and religion remained the big two. And local government had few resources short of the militia to deal with trouble once it moved past the size of a street fight. Just outside Philadelphia, in 1849, the authorities had to call in an organized street gang to help put down a mob. In October 1856 a local Baltimore election was entirely dominated by such youth gangs: the police either stood by or actively cooperated as Blood Tubs, Stingers, Plug Uglies, and Tigers took over the polls to drive out German and Irish immigrant voters. Pistols, rifles, then cannon were again brought in by the private gangs, and a contemporary historian claims that "more men were killed than were lost on the American side in the battle of Palo Alto, in the war with Mexico," just ten years earlier. In the November presidential election, while the governor of Maryland appealed vainly to the mayor for police help, the toll was 8 dead, 250 wounded. In New York the next year, when the legislature ordered the disbanding of the (Democratic) city police in favor of a new, state-controlled (Republican) "metropolitan" force, the two sets of cops took the battle to the streets. Two days after this was legally—but not physically—settled in favor of the Republicans, the Dead Rabbits and Bowery B'hoys turned out to celebrate the Fourth of July with a fight; when the new Metropolitans tried to move in they were mobbed by both sides, and the militia, again, had to come to their rescue.

Gentlemen, and others, continued to go armed.

4

During these same years, while riot drew the most attention, the murder rate was also climbing, further shattering the dreams of romantic reformers. And in this era, for the first time in American history, a combination of official and unofficial records makes it possible over a period of time to draw at least some statistical generalizations about the nature of ordinary urban homicide cases, most of which fell far outside the realm of romance.

The records in question are not those of the new police departments. Murder, unlike riot, was not high on their list of priorities. Their main contribution in both cases was simply (sometimes) to break up fights. Early police reports typically said little or nothing about homicide. The officers might make arrests in such cases, but so did coroners and ordinary citizens, or constables if someone notified a magistrate and swore out a warrant. In a few cases the intercity telegraph proved useful in tracing known fugitives across the country, as in the case of Albert Tirrell, wanted in Massachusetts and captured off the coast of Louisiana. But if a killer was not known, it was not yet police business to find out "whodunit."

There were "detectives" in every big city, but they were private entrepreneurs, or at best moonlighting cops or constables. Their specialty was recovering stolen goods, for a split or reward, and their expertise, often earned on the other side of the law, consisted almost wholly of knowing who had the stuff and where to find it, with no other questions asked. It took many years to accept this kind of "detection" as even partly a public responsibility. To establish an official "detective bureau," as Boston did in 1846, was to invite an endless round of deals and scandals involving crooks and ex-crooks on and off the city payroll. Bankers and grocers, visiting farmers who had lost watches and wallets, all had business with the cops. But there was no money in "solving" murders, and no one assigned to do it.

Neither the police nor anyone else had any special skills or tools that would help in homicide cases, and no one but the coroner was officially charged with trying to identify a killer. In the relatively few cases that posed mysteries, then, no one had any interest in pursuing matters past the inquest stage, except suspicious neighbors, sometimes angry family, and of course the penny press.

It is in fact the birth of the penny press, with its absorbing interest in murder of all kinds, that when used with court records makes it possible to trace the story of those homicides that came to official attention, from the preparation of indictments to the execution of sentence. And for Philadelphia, second-largest city in the country, midway between the North and the South, it is possible not only to say with some certainty how the justice system dealt with these cases but to add something, with the help of accounts in the papers, about who was involved, when, how, with what, and finally (with many reservations), why.

The official procedure began, as for centuries, with an inquest. In the years under review, 1839–59, most of the city's coroners, like those across the country, were not usually doctors but low-caliber elected officials; it was a literally stinking job to probe into the bloated bodies of drowning victims, or battle maggots over the remains of corpses found in vacant lots. Investigation was rarely intense; a doctor might be called for an autopsy, but taxpayers resented the additional expense, and Coroner Samuel Heintzleman's 1840 reelection campaign turned on the issue of excessive postmortems. The inquest was generally held near the spot where the body was found, on the same day or the next; it generally lasted no more than a couple of hours, although later in the period, in sensational cases, a publicity-hungry coroner could string it out over some days. Many of the jurors, paid a dollar a day, seem to have been regulars, perhaps political cronies, rather than gathered at the spot according to law. In 1845 the city limited their number to six.

In addition to finding a physical cause of death—"John Smith died of a violent blow to the head"—inquest jurors, if they found it a homicide, were supposed to name a specific suspect if possible, either by the traditional formula that this had occurred "at the hand of a person or persons to this jury unknown" or (far more often) "at the hand of James Jones." But sometimes they exercised their broadly political function by going beyond the how and the tentative who to push their way into the trial jury's turf by suggesting why. Infanticides often inspired such verdicts from sympathetic jurors, who might find that a newborn had been drowned by its mother "while in a state of temporary insanity." That effectively blocked later attempts at prosecution; so did an opinionated verdict such as the one that declared, in October 1855, that a dead gang member had died "from a wound in the heart from a pistol in the hand of Robert Doran in defense of his own life, while being pursued and attacked by the deceased and others to this jury unknown."

The great majority of homicides that came to the coroner's attention were "solved" at this level, immediately after the death. Homicide was and is usually an impulsive crime, and few killers thought about effective escape; Catherine Hollinger, having stabbed her husband to death when he said he was not interested in dinner, was found weeping and hugging his body; big John Rox, after taunting his best friend into a drunken boxing match, was too far gone even to notice that the smaller man was dying on the other end of the deserted bar; John Daly was still cursing Daniel Smith, beating his head against a stone curb, when passersby pulled him off. Not yet used to having regular police on patrol, nineteenth-century bystanders often chased down killers on the spot.

If homicide was found, then, at the inquest level, the apparent killer was in most cases easily arrested and identified. The next step in the proceedings was for the coroner to relay the verdict, and ideally the suspect, to a magistrate for arraignment. The magistrate then had the power to ask some questions, hold or not hold the suspect, grant bail or not. If—as in virtually all homicides—the suspect was held, the magistrate was then required to send the case on to the district attorney, who in most urban jurisdictions had long before succeeded the county sheriff as the officer in charge of preparing indictments.

The district attorney rarely contradicted the inquest findings and did little independent investigating, although sometimes he was able to supply a suspect's name, or change one, on the basis of evidence that turned up later. In Pennsylvania he might indict for any of four degrees of homicide. After murder in the first or second degree, voluntary manslaughter was the appropriate charge when there was no evidence of "cool depravity of heart, or of wanton cruelty." Involuntary manslaughter was purely accidental killing, but aggravated by the fact that the accused had been acting unlawfully, or "without due caution," as in shooting a pistol in the street or driving too fast. Having drawn such an indictment, the prosecutor might at any point decide to "nol-pross," or proceed no further on a case, on the grounds usually that it would not pass a jury or that new information made the case moot. Otherwise he in turn was supposed to forward his indictment to the Philadelphia County Grand Jury, twenty-four citizens randomly chosen by lot and charged with deciding whether or not to "ignore" it or issue a "true bill," holding the suspect for trial.

The grand jurors, in deciding whether to return true bills after hearing the district attorney, used their own discretion. Both they and trial jurors were of course all male, their names taken from tax lists, usually settled small businessmen and skilled workers representative of the active political community. The frequency with which in effect they or the prosecution combined to throw cases out of the justice system entirely illustrates the first striking characteristic of the system in these years: like their medieval predecessors, and unlike the severer magistrates of the colonial era, antebellum Philadelphians were reluctant to convict for murder. Between 1839 and 1859, of those accused killers named in indictments, nearly 30 percent never went to trial at all. Of those who did, 98 percent pleaded not guilty: a good bet, because only 50 percent were convicted. In the end, then, only 35 percent of the indictees were found guilty of anything.

The number of indictments for these years—271—must not be mistaken for the actual number of homicides committed, or compared with modern rates calculated on the firmer basis of body counts certified by a medical examiner. In addition to a large number of infanticides, the mid-nineteenth century total excludes those deaths not identified as homicides at an inquest and killers who escaped before being identified. Newspaper stories suggest that there were a fair number of suspicious cases, or dead bodies unaccounted for. There were a few murder-suicides, often involving husbands and wives, which of course escaped prosecution. The indictment totals also include only a fraction of the significant number of homicides committed in the course of riots. The authorities, for political reasons, were often reluctant to prosecute rioters for murder, and jurors were even more reluctant to convict two or three or seven out of the hundreds, even thousands, who may have been involved, nearly all of whom, outside of the defendants, could be counted on to throw smoke, provide alibis, or point fingers in different directions, leaving acquittal as the shortest way out of the resulting fog of testimony.

Rates of indictment, then, with all of their omissions, are substantially lower than actual "murder rates," and can only be compared with each other: the question, how many? can only be answered with reservations. But the relative height is clear: from 3.7 per 100,000 of Philadelphia's population in 1839–45, they moved up to 4.0 per 100,000 during 1853–59—both of them the highest rates of indictment for any comparable period in the whole of the nineteenth century.

A parallel warning applies to those homicides that are analyzed below; based on newspaper accounts, and restricted to the 70 percent of indictments that actually came to trial, they are not a truly representative sample of all the city's killings, omitting many infanticides, riot cases, and other incidents that were ignored by the grand jury or abandoned by the district attorney, as well as killers who escaped custody or died in jail. But this is all the records allow, and it tells us something about both crime and punishment.

Justice in this era was swift, certainly, if not always sure. Virtually all cases of murder were settled within ten months from the date of the

crime to the sentencing. And while big cases might take a week—Philadelphia's leading defense lawyer, D. Paul Brown, could fill a courtroom
with as much wind as Rufus Choate—most trials took no more than a
morning, with deliberations lasting somewhere between a few minutes
and a few hours. But juries took their jobs seriously. Just as grand jurors
often ignored bills certified by the prosecuting attorney, representing
the state, trial jurors were equally independent. Whatever the actual
nature of the crime, it was the custom in Philadelphia for the prosecution to indict simply for "murder"—all but 13 cases of the 271. But
with some instructions from the judge (and sometimes hints from the
prosecution itself), jurors not only freed half of those in the dock but
usually knocked down the formal charge a degree or two when they
did convict.

White jurors, too, once they took their places in the court of justice,
were surprisingly fair in dealing with the city's black community, the
largest in the free states. For urban blacks, the antebellum decades were
the worst since colonial days and slavery. With the right to vote taken
away in New York and Pennsylvania during the 1830s, and by the end
of the era denied in all but two New England states, they were not
counted as full citizens and so were unable to participate in formal civic
life or government, to serve as lawyers or even jurors. In Philadelphia
nearly half were unable to read, write, or figure at all, and even the
educated were shut out of good jobs. They fought back, bravely, against
persecution and above all slavery, defying federal law by helping fugitives escape. But they were outnumbered in all cities by bitterly hostile
Irish competitors, frequent victims of gang raids into their neighborhoods, burned out and beaten in major riots. And yet despite their
segregated, insecure position in the city, judges and juries treated them
in reasonably evenhanded fashion; several independent studies, of Boston, New York, and Philadelphia, have shown little or no difference in
the ways in which nineteenth-century blacks and whites were convicted
or sentenced for crime, whether intra- or interracial.

Philadelphia's population more than doubled between 1839 and
1859, from about 250,000 to 544,000, most of the increase through
massive white immigration. Its African-American population, many
pushed out by persistent persecution, grew more modestly, from about
18,000 to 22,000. Some 25 of the 190 incidents of homicide that came
to trial involved black defendants, an overrepresentation of between

two and two and a half times what would be statistically expected. This is high. But it is hardly surprising, given poverty and misery, and it is not as high as the overrepresentation of the Irish, in some times and places, or later of Italian immigrants. And it is also misleading, given the nature of black homicide in the period.

Many riot murders—almost all of them involving white mobs—escaped the system entirely. And it is striking that in all but one of the black cases the defendants who came to trial acted alone, while many of the incidents involving whites were affrays, mini-riots, or street fights in which not one but four, nine, in one case fourteen defendants were indicted: if the black overrepresentation is measured not in terms of number of homicide *incidents,* each of which usually accounted for a single indictment, but in terms of accused *killers,* it drops dramatically, to well under two. While young blacks did form gangs and fight, they were far less murderous than their white counterparts.

Although generally armed, African Americans were not well armed. In an age in which they might be assaulted at any time, especially if found outside their own neighborhoods and at night, it was only prudent to carry a razor or a knife—and as a result a majority of black killings, far more than white, involved sharp weapons of some kind. Guns, although far more common than earlier, were still relatively expensive. One of the reasons for the overall rise in the rate of indictment in the whole population was an increasing use of revolvers: about 15 percent of cases between 1839 and 1852 were firearm deaths, 25 percent between 1853 and 1859. But it is striking that just one single black case involved a gun: on an October afternoon in 1857 three teenaged boys defied adult warnings by playing with a loaded revolver; when the gun went off it instantly killed eighteen-year-old Eddie Dempsey. (The friends were held guiltless of any crime.)

Only one African American committed murder as part of a robbery: Samuel Zephron was executed in April 1845 for attacking and robbing another black man, Cuffee Todd. Even more notable, there were only three cases in which blacks killed whites. On August 1, 1841, Mary Walker, raving and waving an umbrella, attacked seventy-three-year-old Catherine Murdoch on the street; she was found not guilty by reason of insanity. In May 1847—in the one case involving multiple defendants—a white man, William Siddles, was attacked by Henry Raymond during a riot and then beaten fatally into the ground with the help of

Henrietta Moore and Sarah Crosby. The three were first found guilty of murder in the second degree, and then, after a successful appeal for another trial—a rare procedure—freed on the grounds that while they had clearly been identified as beating someone, it was not clear that the dead man was the victim. The last of the three cases involved a nurse or baby-sitter, Hannah Jones, accused of hitting little Jane Histon with a shovel and depriving her of food; a doctor cleared Jones by testifying that the child was badly diseased and had died naturally.

This scorecard—zero convictions in the end—may be compared to the three cases in which whites stood trial for killing blacks. During the summer of 1849, Thomas Carr, while helping his wife wash clothes in the Schuylkill, chased a bunch of black kids off the dock with a brick; Lewis Jaspar fell off and drowned. The jury found Carr not guilty. Two years later Allen Barber and George Reynolds pushed Alexander Redding off a balcony into the street, cracking his skull. Both were found guilty of manslaughter and drew two years each.

The third case is one of the rare ones in which a gang killing was brought into the system. The novelist George Lippard, in his enormously successful *Quaker City*, published in 1844, suggested that "hunting the nigs" was a kind of sport, with big gangs of hunters, outnumbering their prey, risking little during violent forays into black neighborhoods. And the newspapers did report not only riots but also smaller affrays in which African Americans were at least beaten, perhaps killed. But in May 1847 four white men were accused of breaking Jacob Anderson's head with a club: two of them were found guilty, one of manslaughter, drawing five years, one of second degree murder, drawing six—heavy sentences for the time.

Of incidents involving black principals, two more, other than the Zephron-Todd robbery murder, were thought heinous enough to earn a hanging. James Morris, a sailor, jealous of his beautiful wife, drunkenly chopped down shipmate Aaron Cross with an ax, although the victim apparently had never met the woman; his unusually botched hanging in January 1841 was widely condemned as butchery. Fifteen years later, Peter Mattocks killed his girlfriend, Elizabeth Gilbert, a prostitute known as "Quite Nice." The fact that he had hidden the body was evidence of forethought, or at least afterthought, and earned him a conviction for first-degree murder; he was executed without fanfare in May 1856.

In other respects the black cases much resembled the white: mostly fatal fights, for reasons hard to figure a century and a half later, others involving husbands and wives, a religiously fanatic uncle angry at a faithless nephew, a handful of infanticides.

But the infanticides illustrate the problems not simply of black women but of women generally, especially poor and single women, and the way that the world had changed since colonial times.

It is impossible to measure the actual extent of infanticide, although it is clear that the proportion of cases not reported to a reluctant justice system is bigger, by some order of magnitude, than that for adult homicides. Through the 1850s no record was kept of "dead infants found" in vacant lots, privies, and gutters, but at times during the following decade the reported annual total for Philadelphia reached about one every other day. In addition to these, thousands were reported each year as stillborn, or having died either of suffocation or of a number of other causes impossible for the medical science of the day to distinguish from strangulation, at a time when only a small minority of births were attended by a doctor, none of them among poor women.

During the colonial era the need for men and women to complement each other in the household economic unit meant that few people stayed unmarried long, and quite young children were welcomed as extra hands. But in the wage economy of the midcentury city children were only hungry mouths until they could earn cash. And while most men could easily support themselves, and had little economic need to marry, it was extremely hard for an unskilled woman to make it on her own, utterly impossible while caring for a baby. And to this stark economic fact was added another: there was no way for a poor woman safely to give up a live infant. Wet nursing was expensive, and before the invention of pasteurization, much later in the century, cow's milk was slow death and the poorhouse the last stop for almost all "foundlings" admitted to it.

Abortion was legally an alternative in Pennsylvania, as in most states. The practice was not outlawed until the 1860s or later. Until then, to end a pregnancy before "quickening," usually the sixth month, was not a crime under common law, and a sharp increase in the practice accompanied the move from country to city. But while contemporaries estimated that perhaps a quarter of all American pregnancies were aborted by the 1850s, only the middle and upper classes could afford safe and reliable procedures. Widowed, single, or abandoned women, like Mary Rogers, the young New Yorker whose fate inspired Edgar Allan Poe, could find themselves in real danger.

One of the most sensational Philadelphia murder cases of the period involved such a woman, Eliza Sowers, a mill worker from Manayunk. In the summer of 1838, Eliza, just twenty years old, was "promoted" to a job as housemaid in the establishment of her supervisor, William Nixon. In September she tearfully broke her engagement to an "honest lover" on the grounds that she was "unworthy" of him. On October 3 she left on a mysterious errand in the city; ten days later Nixon and a Dr. Henry Chauncey appeared to tell her incredulous family that she had died of "impacted bowels." Her brothers demanded an exhumation, and found that her intestines had been punctured by a sharp instrument.

At the resulting trial the famous D. Paul Brown, Esq., defended Chauncey, with Nixon and a second doctor, William Armstrong, as accessories. Although Nixon was known for sexually harassing the girls at Eckstein's Mill, the defense insisted that the "honest lover" was the real seducer. And while it appeared that Chauncey, in effect, was house physician to Mary Kingsley's infamous downtown brothel, he insisted that Sowers had administered herself with such ancient (and poisonous) abortifacients as pennyroyal and oil of tansy; he had come, in all charity, only when her condition grew desperate, and volunteered to clean up the afterbirth.

All this time the classic ingredients of sex, blood, and betrayal had brought huge crowds to the courtroom and the streets outside; when the jurors declared that they had reasonable doubts about the guilt of Armstrong and Nixon, and convicted Dr. Chauncey only of medical malpractice, there was loud talk of lynching. D. Paul Brown, unruffled, went on the stage of the Musical Fund Hall the next week to lecture about Shakespeare; the proceeds, with no apparent irony, were donated to a favorite reform, the Society for Meliorating the Condition of Impecunious Laboring Females.

But the condition of too many impecunious laboring females was pregnancy, and those who could afford neither a baby nor a doctor had reason to fear Eliza's fate, and often kept hoping to the end of term that things somehow would work out. Three other cases of adult deaths from abortion came to trial in the period. But this was surely an under-count of the actual number of such fatalities. And infanticide was in effect abortion ex post facto. In reporting on the story of Ann Dowell, a serving girl from a respectable New Jersey family, the *Public Ledger* gushed in November 1840 that "some of its features resemble [Sir Walter] Scott's tale of *The Heart of Midlothian.*" But there was nothing remotely romantic about those that came to trial; these are the only ones about which there is any information at all, and they range between the sordid and the revolting. The *Public Ledger* resorted to its usual early Victorian formula: having teased its readers, it claimed that it "cannot give details" even in the Dowell case. Almost all of the accused were single mothers; several had not reported their pregnancies to anyone, trying to the last minute to hide their bellies under the billowing clothing of the day. Typically they had given birth alone, and then perhaps stuffed the infant's throat with a rag to keep it from crying out, or—having gone to the privy, the only place in the home or boardinghouse where they might safely be alone—had dropped it down, into the vault below, immediately on cutting the cord.

The men who ran the justice system tried to avoid these cases: everyone knew what the problem was, no one knew the solution. It is hard at this date to see why the coroner selected some and not others: unavoidable evidence, yes, in the broken neck, the cord tied around the throat—but beyond that perhaps pressure (or lack of pressure) from the neighbors? The papers report cases in which neighbor women rallied round, either to point the finger or alternatively to protect someone. Once Coroner Heintzleman, holding a hearing over a tiny body, was told to look at one recently pregnant young woman; when she produced a live baby he asked her, in a variation of Solomon's judgment, to prove the child was hers; she passed the test simply by nursing it.

Cases that went on to the grand jury, too, often stopped right there: a large number of indictments bearing single women's names were either ignored or nol-prossed. Just ten cases reached trial; it is not apparent what the jurors saw in some and not others, but one black woman was sentenced for "concealment," and one white—not the mother but a friend—was found guilty of murder in the second degree; the sentences were 1 to 3 and 3 to 6 years in prison, respectively. All the rest were freed.

These ten cases represent nearly half of the twenty-two for which

women were tried. The others fared, statistically, precisely the same as
the men: six guilty, six not. None of them used guns. Of the women's
victims, four were male, eight female. Two of the three accused of
stabbing their husbands were found guilty (as were two of the three
husbands accused of killing wives, not counting one declared insane).
Sarah Bonner, who threw a fatal brick at her drunken son-in-law, was
freed. Two midwives who botched abortions—one was the owner of
an herb store—were found guilty. So was a nursemaid who fed a child
pins and needles; another, a black child, was declared not guilty of
poisoning her charge—the only poisoning case. Hannah Jones, above,
was freed. The other four incidents involved violent attacks on adult
women; three of the accused were freed.

Just one incident resulted in a conviction for murder in the first degree. On July 10, 1840, Julia Ann Jones was seen and heard screaming
by a window, blood all over; neighbors who rushed in found her landlady, Mrs. Sarah Coleman, almost equally blood covered, calmly standing over the body. Coleman, a.k.a. Davis, claimed that Jones had slit
her own throat, but a jury believed she was jealous of Mr. Davis. Apparently shocked by Coleman's seeming callousness as much as by the
nature of the crime, the jurors sentenced her to death. But only three
women had ever been hanged in the Commonwealth of Pennsylvania
(none in the city), the condemned woman had obviously been drinking,
and the governor intervened to commute the sentence to life in prison.

But homicide, as always, was overwhelmingly a male affair, men accounting for a little over 90 percent of indictments, the same figure as
in the Middle Ages. And in a northern city in this period it was specifically an affair of a special subset of poor or working-class white males,
members of a "bachelor subculture" whose values and attitudes con-
trasted strongly with those of the middle class.

Ever since the eighteenth century Enlightenment reformers had been
stressing the need for rational beings to control their anger, or aggressive impulses. This emphasis, reinforced by the romantic movement,
had become by the nineteenth century perhaps *the* main issue in raising
children. By the early Victorian era, as a result, the ideal had in many
cases become reality, and self-restraint was widely practiced as well as
admired.

The men of the middle classes were by then moving away from the kind of physical force thought necessary to run a business or household in the colonial era. Since early in the century, as the business of earning a living moved out of the household and into the office or factory, the home itself had come to be idealized as a gentle "haven in a heartless world," a place of refuge from the competitive struggle of the market-place. Few households kept apprentices any longer, or, in northern cities, male servants who needed "correcting" with a switch. A good wife, firmly removed from anything that might earn wages or profits, could handle a serving girl or two with no more than the moral force that radiated from an idealized version of womanhood. Both roman-tic and Christian reformers agreed that children should no longer be beaten or cowed until their naturally evil wills were broken but rather nurtured lovingly so that their naturally innocent natures could be pre-served into maturity.

At least some of these nonviolent values penetrated far to the south and west. Southerners certainly idealized family love, and many mem-bers of the plantation elite, such as Jefferson Davis of Mississippi, tried hard to live by rules of moderation and gentility. The veteran dueler Sam Houston of Texas, hero of the republic and later state of Texas, was one of those who came to embrace the abolition of capital punish-ment. Two young men growing up in frontier Illinois, Ulysses S. Grant and Abraham Lincoln, both refused on principle to hunt animals, ei-ther for food or sport a position absolutely inconceivable in any ear-lier generation. In his response to dueling, above all, the southern-born Lincoln, whose life was spent moving north through Kentucky, Indi-ana, and Illinois, offers a perfect example of the gradual triumph of the ideal of dignity over honor.

The future president wrote a satirical newspaper piece in 1841 that offended the honor of James Shields, a pugnacious and humorless little Scots-Irish politician, who issued a formal challenge. Lincoln, the one-time wrasslin' champion of Clary's Grove, had the choice of weapons, and was first tempted to suggest cow dung at five paces. The final offer was nearly as absurd: cavalry broadswords, with the duelers teetering along a ten-foot plank just nine inches wide. Shields, doubtless think-ing of the figure he would cut in such a contest, was happy to settle peacefully; an apology was good enough. Dueling did not afterward take hold as part of the political culture of Illinois, and Lincoln never again allowed himself to be maneuvered into such a position.

But the new nonviolent ideals, however far they radiated south and west, were unquestionably northeastern in origin. And they were equally, although not exclusively, middle class. Many ambitious members of the working class saw the advantages of sobriety and restraint as means of moving ahead in the urban economy. The fact that in 1860 nearly *half* of all the adult males in New York City were counted as officers of one or another Protestant organization is testament to the fact that the religious revival reached into many modest households, while the slow progress of the domestic virtues is reflected even more clearly in the dramatic drop in per capita alcohol consumption. But the most striking fact about the Victorian value of nonviolence was less its slow penetration into the working class than its nearly complete triumph over the urban middle class, as the domestic horsewhip followed the duel into obsolescence.

The case of James Wood is illustrative. Wood in 1839 was the well-known owner of a fashionable confectionery store on Philadelphia's Chestnut Street, and had lived comfortably for years, as a widower, with his only daughter, Eliza. When that fall she shattered this cozy domestic arrangement by eloping with a lover, he brooded for two weeks and then walked over to her new household and shot her dead. The case demonstrates that the very emotional intensity of the sentimental family could implode into homicide. But it was doubly rare; Wood was declared insane not only because he was the only male Philadelphian to murder a daughter in the period but also because homicide of any kind did not normally involve any gentleman of education and social standing.

Stories in the papers do not list the occupations of those involved in homicide with any reliability, but it seems that Wood and William Nixon, Eliza Sower's supervisor and betrayer, ranked as high as any. The other "owners" ran places like taverns and blacksmith shops, not far removed in manners and mores from the working class. And the record shows clearly that neither the domestic conditions nor the dignified ideals of the middle class had seeped down among many of those who still worked with their backs and hands, in a more brutal world than that of the gentlemen who directed or paid for their labor. Nor, as yet, had the disciplined behavior that other reformers had been trying to impose through church, school, penitentiary, and police.

Who were Philadelphia's killers, and who were their victims? In the absence of direct clues in the form of reliable occupational descriptions, there is much circumstantial evidence about the social class of those involved. The Philadelphia city directories of the era provide some of it. These books list the names and addresses of all those people—black as well as white, often working class as well as middle class—who were essentially settled residents and wanted family, friends, and perhaps potential customers or employers to be able to find them. Only 34 percent of defendants in homicide cases can clearly be found in these books; 53 percent were definitely not listed; the rest cannot be determined because of duplicate names or lack of addresses. The victims seem roughly similar. And in New York, where Eric Monkkonen has studied coroners' reports, which (sometimes) list place of birth, the estimate for the proportion of foreign immigrants among named killers during the same era ranges up to 80 percent of the total—nearly twice their percentage in the population. While this may be high, it seems clear that these still unsettled newcomers to the city, mostly Irish and German, accounted for far more than their share of urban violence.

The dates of homicide, too, offer clues to the kinds of people involved. The summer months led as usual, but not by as much as in other times. January was tied with June for second place, behind August. The cold weather, in this age when the new railroads were still being built, meant a slowdown in river and road traffic, little construction work, fewer orders in shops or the still-new urban factories. Less employment among the city's workers in turn meant more free time to wander, drink, fight, and get in trouble.

The days of the week offer even better evidence of the importance of underemployment. Nineteenth-century men worked six days a week, in busy or good seasons. The workday usually ran 10 to 12 hours, sometimes fourteen, leaving relatively little free time on weekdays. Saturday was payday—and Saturday nights and Sundays the only times free of the pressures of work or exhaustion. But while between 1839 and 1859 Saturday was the most lethal day of the week, followed by Sunday, the margin was slight; the two days combined, or 29 percent of the week, accounted for only 34 percent of all homicides, a far lower proportion than in times of full and regular employment, such as the 1950s. Among the special subset of young male working-class Philadelphians who did most killings, not much burdened by either family or job, any day, or any night, was time for drinking and fighting.

If, then, most homicides involved unemployed or underemployed young men, disproportionately immigrants or other newcomers, all of the evidence above also suggests the circumstances of the killings. And after time, the best clue is place. Only about 25 percent of them (not counting the infanticides) occurred in the homes of either accused or victim. The dominant site was the street (scene of 39 percent), followed by the saloon (10 percent), with the rest at work or "other"—rivers, privies, rooftops. Newspaper accounts typically tell us only that there was a "fight," or an "attack": few suggest what it was about.

Only a tiny number of urban killers had anything resembling a calculated motive. No known cases involved issues such as inheritance or insurance money, the kind beloved by mystery writers in later years. There were only five robbery murders. Even domestic killings were relatively rare in this period, with a total of seven, and only eight more, aside from the infanticides, involved other relatives or in-laws.

Domestic violence was certainly not uncommon; the earliest known records for the Boston Watch and Police, for example, during the 1840s, show that breaking up fights, probably most of them in private homes, was their biggest single job. But it appears that few of these battles were fought to the death. Of the few, husbands killing wives, as shown in most (but not all) studies of different times and places, had an edge, in this case slight, over wives killing husbands. The numbers, however, are too small to support much generalization about this fact, or about the high conviction rate. The one thing absolutely clear about the Philadelphia figures is that homicide was almost wholly the business of pugnacious young unmarried males.

But there seems a striking difference between the deadly urban fights of this era and those that had led to murder and manslaughter in the Middle Ages. Six hundred years earlier, the typical homicidal quarrel occurred among men who had known each other for years, lived nearby, and—whatever the immediate spark—had probably argued then or earlier over matters of some substance in their lives: property lines, rights to graze on common land, fair share of communal work. But in mid-nineteenth-century Philadelphia only a minority of fatal fights seemed to involve both of those dimensions: long-standing enmity or grudges and substantial issues that might conceivably be settled by confrontation.

The homicides that occurred in homes—often boardinghouses—sometimes combined both elements, as when a married couple attacked a boarder down the hall who persistently woke them up by coming home late and drunk, or a landlord and tenant quarreled over the rent or the noise level. Others involved just one of them. Rival firemen, or their supporters, took shots or threw bricks at one another now and then—long-standing quarrels, little substance. A few men fought over the attentions of a woman at a dance, or in a whorehouse—not long-standing rivalries, but for young folks, at the moment, of some apparent substance.

But in poring over dozens of case studies, a historian is continually struck by the fact that the answer to *why* a given fight erupted has two levels. The circumstances, the people, the background, the spark, are different each time, but the more basic issue involved seems always the same. And at that level *why* remains a mystery, if any rational answer is expected. The answer to What was at stake? is too often, Nothing—except perhaps an alcoholic conception of male honor, a matter as important to underemployed young Philadelphians as to South Carolina grandees or backwoods Scots-Irish.

If this makes little sense on the surface, it did to the members of the bachelor subculture of the antebellum decades. No longer under the quasi-paternal eyes of master craftsmen, with the decline of formal apprenticeship no longer able to achieve the status of "master" themselves, more and more young men simply worked for wages, with little to look forward to. In some big cities as many as 40 percent of the adult men under thirty-five were still unmarried (the Irish were especially used to late marriage and bachelorhood). They lived with no supervision and no responsibilities, usually in boardinghouses filled with others like themselves. And if there was little future, there was always the present: they were still young, they had little to lose, and they could do with their free time what they liked.

What they did, in an atmosphere thick with alcohol fumes and cigar smoke, was watch terriers scramble bloodily around in rat pits, or battling birds tear each other apart in cockfights, pit bulls in dogfights. They gambled in billiard halls, hung out and drank in saloons and whorehouses. They joined ethnic fire companies to fight, and political clubs to fight. There was little else to do: the one truly organized form of recreation was prizefighting, with bare knuckles, by far the most popular of working-class sports in the period. Professionals and semiprofessionals trained hard for these bloody bouts, ended only when one man could no longer stand up: they gave up whiskey, women, and late nights at least for a time. But the spectators, the amateurs, members of a culture that honored strength and violence, could have it both ways, and the very business of enjoying their vices often led to assault. And inevitably, sometimes, assault led to murder.

And so a party of young men, roistering down the street after a dance, encounters a railroad agent who objects to their singing; a fight, a stabbing, a death: two guilty of manslaughter. Two men decide to fight outside a tavern; another declares one of the principals is too drunk to stand up and offers to stand in; a passerby intervenes, takes sides, and is fatally stabbed: ten years for murder in the second degree. One man accuses another of throwing a watermelon rind at him; fatal fistfight: not guilty by reason of self-defense. A ship's mate—maybe— knocks a sailor overboard to drown; witnesses disagree about who did what: mate found not guilty. A man teases another's dog with a knife; the owner's brother objects, the man persists, the brother is stabbed: guilty of manslaughter.

None of this was of much concern to the more settled members of the community who staffed and ran the justice system.

Violent death was a part of life—the early railroads were especially lethal, with boiler explosions and train wrecks—but true accidents were rarely prosecuted as manslaughter, voluntary or involuntary. Given the number of lethal incidents, it is impossible to know why, over the twenty-one years, some thirteen cases of traffic accidents and pistol range misfirings wound up in court—drunkenness? callousness?—but just five of the killers were found guilty, and all were lightly punished.

The rare robbery murders involved, with one partial exception, victims nearly as modest as the killers. Samuel Zephron, as described above, killed a fellow African American. In 1852 Blaise and Mathias Skupinski, Polish exiles, killed and dismembered a sixteen-year-old Jewish peddler whose head, to the delight of the penny press, was later discovered under the ice of the Delaware River. In March 1853 Mrs. Ellen Lynch and her sister, Honora Shaw, respectable but hardly wealthy women—Lynch's husband was a marine—were killed by Arthur Spring, a boarder in the household, ex-convict, and former suitor of Mrs. Shaw, while in search of a hidden cache of $80.

Robbery murder, as in the Middle Ages, was thought an especially heinous crime, and these men were all hanged. So was Peter Mattocks, who killed a woman, his girlfriend, as described above. But these five were the only ones to go to the gallows in the Philadelphia County Jail during the twenty years covered. Three other killers were convicted of murder in the first degree but were reprieved to prison terms. Sarah Coleman, described above, was a woman, and she had been drinking. John Capie and Carson Emos, who stabbed Christopher Soohan to death in 1853, had clearly been talking beforehand about killing someone, anyone—Soohan was a stranger—but they too were drunk, extremely so. To judge from newspaper accounts, a few other cases seem to have involved premeditation and the specific intent to kill. But jurors ignored the legal definitions, used their own common or moral sense, and pushed verdicts down a degree or two; manslaughter was by far the most commonly arrived at.

Juries, then, usually exercised their power to deliver mercy rather than vengeance. Most killings involved furious action, but they were essentially, as in the Middle Ages, the result of sudden flares of anger. The weapons were whatever came to hand. But while fists, feet, sticks, and bricks still outnumbered guns and knives combined, in the heat of the moment it seems that whatever was used, there was an attempt to maim if not kill. From the jury box, however, it was often hard to say who started it, and the outcome was a kind of lottery, in which only a lucky (or unlucky) blow, jab, or shot separated the defendant from the deceased, or indeed made a homicide out of what would otherwise have been no more than a staggering punching match.

American jurists in this period made an important amendment to the inherited English common law. In line with the actual decisions made by jurors since the Middle Ages, judges in many states greatly modified the idea that a man attacked by another had a "duty to retreat." In fact, the leading text for many decades, John Prentiss Bishop's *Commentaries on the Criminal Law,* published in 1856, insisted, not quite seriously, that "if a man murderously attacked by another flies instead of resisting, he commits substantially [the] offense of misprision of felony"—meaning that he himself has, by not standing his ground, criminally encouraged the assault.

In Philadelphia, certainly, the loose plea of self-defense was hard to deny and worked in nearly half of all cases. Drunkenness explained, if not quite excused, most of the others, and jurors were inclined to be tolerant. So were judges: three to six years, the modal sentence, seemed punishment enough.

Unlike riot, after all, ordinary interpersonal homicide in the midcentury city was no real threat to the social order. Stray shots occasionally hit bystanders, or sitters, as when a husband missed his wife and struck a neighboring woman on the backyard privy. But this happened only in poor neighborhoods. A man of dignity might carry a gun, and then often did. But if he chose his friends carefully, and refused to argue with drunken strangers, he had little to fear.

5

But if urban homicide was a minor threat compared to riot, both issues—indeed all issues, as the antebellum years progressed—were overshadowed by the looming threat of civil war. The continued expansion of the United States reached its climax in these decades with the annexation of Texas, the conquest of California and the Southwest from Mexico, and the establishment of northern and northwestern boundaries through treaties with Great Britain. And while there were many occasions for murderous conflict along the frontier, the great westward movement was increasingly dominated, and in part inspired, by the political contest between the free and the slave states.

As always, the advance was marked by conflict with the Indians, much of it murderous. But the Native Americans in this period did little to slow the relentless movement west. From Illinois through Minnesota the woodland tribes, in no position to resist, were continually pushed back; the Black Hawk War of 1832, better described as a "rebellion" by the already subdued Sac and Fox of Illinois, resulted in something close to extermination. The tribes of the old Southwest had already been conquered, with the Cherokee banished across the Mississippi. Elsewhere, in the Middle and Far West, the policy was to get the survivors to sign treaties agreeing to settle onto "reservations," like those of the Five Nations in Oklahoma, where they might be baptized as Christians, taught to farm, and prepared eventually for citizenship. The policy was unevenly followed, with the Indians having little real understanding of what it meant. And it was wholly impossible to apply to the essentially nomadic and formidable horsemen of the plains. Beginning in the 1840s, as Mormons, pioneers, and gold-rushers crossed into Utah, Oregon, and California, they were occasionally attacked by these still unconquered warriors. But well-armed caravans, sometimes with army escorts, were not often bothered; the whites, as yet, were just passing through.

Most violence along the western frontier was then intraracial, much of it the familiar result of neighborhood quarrels and tavern brawls. What was new and most striking in this period was the increasingly murderous character of vigilantism, which like much else fell, not quite neatly, along geographic lines.

Along the northern band of the Midwest, the Lake Plains, farmers and others came in large part from New England and upper New York, settling often in communities, even migrating as whole religious congregations, bringing with them their concept of dignity and their traditionally low rates of homicidal violence. In Marion County, Indiana, typically, mostly rural but including the new capital of Indianapolis, the justice system was largely occupied with the kind of moral issues that concerned eastern reformers: gambling, prostitution, above all drunkenness. From the time the county was organized through midcentury, only eight men were indicted for homicide, four of them in a single incident. Across the Ohio in Kentucky, meanwhile, as in other southern jurisdictions, courts and sheriffs were kept busier with interpersonal crimes, assault and murder, in addition to the traditional concern with keeping slaves in line.

But in both North and South, the first task on the frontier was to establish an effective justice system, and it did not always go smoothly. When rapid settlement outran government, or when raw conditions, corruption, or simple fear allowed criminals to flourish, local citizens increasingly took matters into their own hands. The kind of organized attack on outlawry pioneered by the South Carolina Regulators had for some decades been confined to relatively small movements in Indiana and Kentucky, Illinois and Tennessee. Meanwhile the original name, Regulators, was often transformed into Vigilantes, used in the sense of Thomas Jefferson's dictum "Eternal Vigilance Is the Price of Liberty." And the mushrooming of Committees of Vigilance, beginning in the 1830s, was encouraged by the way in which their self-justifying ideology fit the democratic Age of Jackson.

From the beginning the American Republic had been moving toward democracy, allowing virtually all white males to vote, making more offices subject to direct election. By the 1830s the key officials in county justice systems, sheriffs, prosecutors, and magistrates, were all usually elected rather than appointed. An obvious next step in the devolution of power was direct or democratic justice, imposed by the citizens themselves. Vigilance committees in frontier areas were typically organized by ambitious young men, sometimes land speculators, meeting often in Masonic lodges, anxious to bring order to their communities. Horse thieves and counterfeiters, among others, threatened their property values. And if local law enforcement could not deal with criminals—who often crossed state lines—then vigilantes, bypassing legal authority, could and did appeal not only to the elementary right of self-preservation but to the spirit of democracy, the right of self-rule, justice delivered directly by "the people."

This was much the same argument that was, at the same time, voiced by or on behalf of the less articulate urban mobs, who also believed themselves to be championing the values of their own communities, or subcommunities. It was an obviously dangerous rationale: Abraham Lincoln, as early as the 1830s, warned of "the spirit of lawlessness abroad." But it was also powerfully appealing. Dozens, even hundreds, of vigilante groups sprang up in the antebellum decades, each claiming dozens or even hundreds of members. One of the biggest operated across Alabama and Mississippi during the early 1830s, when fears of "the Murrell Conspiracy," an alleged outlaw plot to foment a slave insurrection, inspired "Captain Slick" to make war on horse thieves and gamblers. Another wave, a decade later, hit Iowa, East Texas, Illinois, and the Missouri Ozarks. Successful movements typically scared off or hunted down outlaws, or those they defined as outlaws, and when the hunt was successful often conducted mock trials, with "guilty" verdicts never in doubt. But while in the early Republic a severe flogging was usually thought warning enough to possible confederates, by the antebellum era those found guilty were more often executed, hanged from a tree.

All of these were homicides: premeditated, first-degree murders in law, "justifiable" homicides in the eyes of the vigilantes themselves. The toll is obviously hard to keep—there are no official records—but the number of "known victims" counted by Richard Maxwell Brown shows at least the direction: 5 victims in the 1830s, 64 in the 1840s, 119 in the 1850s.

In the 1850s, too, just as the verb "to lynch" changed its meaning from "whip" to "kill," vigilantism reached its most famous peak in the new state of California. Following the discovery of gold in 1848, the territory, then state, filled more rapidly than any in history; its immigrants, from many countries, had little in common but the desire to get rich quick. With prices of the most basic necessities relentlessly high, and only a few winners in the gold fields, the state was full of desperate young men wholly without community or family ties. Violent crime inevitably soared. And when in 1851 it was reported that the number of murders in the raw new port of San Francisco had reached over one hundred, many committed by robber bands such as the Sydney Ducks, Australian ex-convicts originally from Ireland, a committee of vigilance was established. The members published an ad hoc constitution, hanged several alleged killers, banished others, and effectively ran the city for two years.

The San Francisco movement of 1851 is a textbook example of what Brown calls "positive" vigilantism. First, as in many other places, the absence of law created a crisis. Vigilantes then established a formal structure, with officers and organizational rules of their own, in effect a kind of parallel government that targeted known criminals with the full support of the law-abiding community. Finally, when the crisis was over, they disbanded and returned the business of justice to constitutionally elected authority.

But not all vigilantes organized formally, enjoyed clear majority support, or disbanded once legal government was in place. As a result armed "Moderators" sometimes formed to challenge them, charging not only that they were defying the law but also that their real purpose was to win the kind of political power that they could not earn through the vote, a response that set off small civil wars, in effect, in Iowa, East Texas, and the Ozarks. Above all the community outrage that sparked vigilante action was often directed not against thieves and killers but at unpopular minorities. In fact the most fateful single lynching in U.S. history involved, in 1844, the charismatic founder of one of the leading American religious movements.

Ever since Joseph Smith published the Book of Mormon, in 1829, his growing band of followers had been persecuted wherever they moved, from New York to Ohio to Missouri. Their experiments in communal living, appeal to the poor, and clannish obedience to "the Prophet" branded them as "peculiar" in all of these locations. In Missouri, during the 1830s, when their growing numbers gave them political control of Caldwell County and threatened dominance over its neighbors, they engaged in several skirmishes with the state militia and local irregulars. Eighteen of them were massacred in one outlying village before the remaining Saints moved east, across the Mississippi. Smith, jailed for treason, was able finally to escape and resume his leadership, and in 1839 he began to supervise construction of a New Zion along the river bluffs of Hancock County, Illinois.

Within two years the Saints' new city of Nauvoo had become the biggest in the state, attracting thousands of converts from Canada and England as well as the East. But neighboring "gentiles," in Illinois as in Missouri, were alarmed by the establishment of a virtual theocracy in their midst—as well as by the threat to local property values. The Prophet's final revelation, that some Mormons, under certain conditions, might be allowed to marry several wives, was the final straw. After several confrontations between armed Saints and local vigilantes, on June 24, 1844, Joseph Smith and his brother Hyrum surrendered to Governor Thomas Ford on a charge of inciting to riot and were lodged in the Carthage County Jail under promise of protection. Three days later a mob burst into the jail as the county militia stood by and shot both men to death. Leadership then passed to Brigham Young, a less inspired theologian than Smith but a brilliant organizer. It was Young who decided to abandon Nauvoo to the weeds and organize the key movement in Mormon history, the great hegira to the desert spaces of Utah.

Through all this turmoil in Illinois, battle lines between Saints and gentiles had been drawn in part along political lines: the big and highly disciplined Mormon vote had been Democratic; the anti-Mormon Vigilance Committee of Safety that was accused of leading the assault on the jail was fiercely Whig. Ten years later it was politics, again, and again ethnic-religious politics, that led San Francisco a second time into vigilantism.

The city in the fall of 1855 was under the control of an Irish Catholic Democratic machine, accused by more middle- and upper-class Whigs of corruptly protecting gambling and prostitution. When a notorious gambler, Charles Cora, shot a U.S. marshal to death that November he was tried by an obviously fixed jury that reached no decision, and so remained in jail while awaiting a retrial. The conduct of the case was denounced by James P. King, a bitterly anti-Catholic newspaper editor of Scots-Irish descent. When King in turn was assassinated on May 14 by City Supervisor James Casey, a former inmate of Sing-Sing Prison, a new committee of vigilance was formed almost immediately, claiming membership in the thousands. On the sixteenth, commanding a cannon, they took the jail housing Cora and Casey, tried them with the usual trappings of formality, and hanged both. Two more hanged, twenty banished, a hundred more scared out of the city, and the job was done.

But by that time the struggles between Whigs and Democrats involved not merely differences in religion and morality but the very survival of the Union. From the founding of the Republic the addition of new territories and states to the Union had been bound up with the issue of political balance, South versus North, slave states versus free. And with the acquisitions won in 1848 through war with Mexico, the contest for the loyalties of the West, from Kansas to California, had helped create a crisis.

6

What heightened this midcentury crisis was the fact that the South was increasingly on the defensive. By 1834, shortly after Nat Turner's rebellion, slavery had been abolished in all of Europe and the Americas except for Cuba, Brazil, and the southern United States. Educated southerners, exposed to the same currents of humane thought that inspired romantic reformers, were painfully aware that their "peculiar" institution was increasingly viewed as barbaric throughout the Western world, and they looked desperately for ways to justify it. One tactic was to insist that slavery was positively good for the slaves themselves, an institution not only sanctioned in the Bible but also ratified by nature and history, which had rescued pagan Africans from sin and misery. A good slave owner then fed, clothed, and protected his charges, as rightful head of a kind of grateful "family." This vision required, for one thing, even greater efforts to promote Christianity in the quarters. Equally fundamental was better protection under law, above all in the law and practice governing interracial homicide.

In general the southern states had lagged in the redefinition of homicide and the change in its treatment; most held on to anachronisms like benefit of clergy, and kept a wide range of capital offenses on the books. But they did move to reform their slave codes. South Carolina, in 1821, was the last state to make the killing of a black slave by a white man explicitly a murder: prior to that it had been a minor crime, misdemeanor rather than felony. And although the great majority of such killings never reached court, the number of formal indictments rose continually, throughout the South, and so did convictions: ten years in prison, heavy by Philadelphia standards, was not an uncommon sentence, and the death penalty was at least occasionally invoked when whites killed blacks.

Blacks themselves continued occasionally to kill whites. But the rate of execution for this as for all slave crimes continued in general to fall. So did the rate of conviction, and in a number of cases the sentence given was that for second-degree murder or even manslaughter, in recognition, direct or indirect, that this form of human property had emotions like other people and that the same kinds of mitigating circumstances and provocations might apply. The highest courts were especially vigilant to ensure that slaves were fairly treated: in Mississippi, between 1834 and 1861, 5 of 13 black-white murder convictions were overturned or remanded for retrial; in Louisiana, between 1844 and 1859, 2 of 5; in Alabama, between 1825 and 1864, an astonishing 9 of 14.

These figures suggest not only the concerns of southern jurists but the relative rarity of fatal attacks on whites as well. Reform had little effect, however, either on northern opinion or on southern jitters. And if one southern reaction to growing isolation was to defend slavery as a civilizing and humane institution, an even stronger one was fear, even paranoia, about outsiders who might foment slave insurrection, and thus the ancient nightmares about murder. After Nat Turner's rebellion in 1831, repressive legislation supplemented by mob activity effectively blocked any public criticism of the "peculiar institution" from the inside. But while no documented "conspiracy" was uncovered between that date and the Civil War, slaves were still tried and occasionally hanged for "insurrection"—which covered a range of defiant behaviors—and panicky rumors of plots coexisted with professions of the loyalty of black "family." Governor Hammond of South Carolina could combine both contemporary southern reactions in the same essay: after praising the "heartfelt" and "benignant" ties that bound master and slave in mutual benefit and even love, he turned to address outside critics: "Allow our slaves to read your writings, stimulating them to cut our throats! Can you believe us to be such unspeakable fools!" But neither argument worked to stop rising criticism, and worse.

Northern mob attacks against blacks and their abolitionist allies continued throughout the antebellum decades. But especially after passage of the Fugitive Slave Law in 1850, which stripped accused runaways of the most minimal of procedural protections, the opposition also took to the streets. Opponents of slavery could use the same ideology as proslavery vigilantes to justify opposition to existing law and practice. Just as committees of vigilance sprang up south of the Mason-Dixon line to harass and sometimes lynch alleged abolitionists, abolitionists in turn organized under the same name in eastern cities to aid escaped fugitives, appealing to a "higher law" than the Constitution. And while initially most abolitionists had been pacifists opposed to physical force, violent rhetoric in time helped inspire violent action. The mob that stormed Boston's federal courthouse in May 1854, killing a guard in a vain attempt to free the fugitive Anthony Burns, was egged on by two of the leading Christian reformers in Massachusetts, the Reverends Theodore Parker and Thomas Wentworth Higginson; eventually it took two thousand armed state militia, federal troops, and local police to escort Burns down to the harbor and a ship back to Charleston.

And in that same year, 1854, the passage of the Kansas-Nebraska Act, designed to allow the settlers of Kansas Territory to decide for themselves whether or not to allow slavery, pushed the sectional contest to bloody new heights. The great majority of these settlers were small farmers who wanted mostly to raise cattle, wheat, and corn—and to keep all blacks out of the territory, whether slave or free. But some were footloose "border ruffians" from slave country, just across the Missouri line, and a few others carried guns sent by antislavery northerners organized as "emigrant aid" societies. Among the abolitionists were the five sons of a fierce old man from Ohio, the religious fanatic John Brown. In the spring of 1855, as southerners massed along the borders to keep the others out—enough of them, Missouri Senator David Atchison trumpeted, "to kill every God-damned abolitionist in the Territory"—Brown himself slipped in with a wagon full of guns and sabers and proceeded to help organize the free-state forces.

No real "vote" was possible as the southerners, although greatly out-numbered, had support from the federal government. But two different governments were elected, quasi-legitimate posses and militias clashed, and in May 1856 the proslavery sheriff of the territory led an attack that destroyed and burned the antislavery capital of Lawrence. When John Brown heard the news he swore to "regulate" matters, and to "strike terror in the hearts of the proslavery people." On the night of the twenty-fourth, Brown led his sons and a few others into a small south-ern settlement along Potawatomi Creek, where the company pulled five men out of their cabins, in front of pleading wives and mothers; Allen Wilkinson's throat was slit; James Doyle, his two sons, and James Harris were hacked to death with broadswords. As Brown saw it, six on his side had been murdered, and five on the other would nearly even the score: "Without the shedding of blood there can be no remission of sins," he believed.

This was a new element in American homicide: ideological murder as an act of terrorism. If there had been any hope for peace in Kansas the Potawatomi Massacre killed it. As both northerners and southerners poured rifles and ammunition into the territory, some two hundred men died in the summer and fall of 1856, with Brown playing a leading role as guerrilla chief, before a determined new governor disarmed and disbanded both sides.

And John Brown was not through. After leaving Kansas and going on a northern lecture tour to help raise money and arms for the anti-slavery forces, he returned to an old dream: to raise an insurrection among southern slaves. While crisscrossing the free states, Canada, and Kansas, he elaborated a plan to invade Virginia, establish a provisional government, and, calling on slaves to rise up and join him, bring revo-lution to the South.

That the old man's biblical eloquence could raise a small party of raiders is hardly a surprise. But it is a measure of the growing despera-tion of the times, of deep northern frustration, that he could draw sev-eral prominent New Englanders into his scheme. The old romantic ideals were gone, victims not only of discouragement but of the fact that antislavery swallowed up all other reforms. Brown's co-conspira-tors, fellow members of "the Secret Six," included the Reverends Hig-ginson and Parker, the old warrior Samuel Gridley Howe, the young idealist Franklin Sanborn, the philanthropic merchant George Luther Stearns, and the country gentleman Gerrit Smith. Fifteen years earlier such men would have been crusading against capital punishment in the name of nonviolence; now, although not aware of all the plans, they were endorsing the use of terror tactics to raise a bloody rebellion.

Whether or not Brown himself was insane, his plan clearly was. On October 16, 1859, the Lord's Day, twenty-one men, five of them African Americans, followed the old man into the arsenal at Harper's Ferry, Virginia. They cut telegraph wires, captured hostages, gathered up a few slaves, and as their first victim shot to death a free black man, the local baggage master, who challenged the raiders along the railroad tracks. The liberated slaves refused to bear arms; no others appeared. Instead, as word of the "insurrection" spread, it attracted a swarm of terrified white men in arms who surrounded the embattled old guerrilla and his little party. One of Brown's black raiders was shot and butchered, his ears cut off; two others were killed under a flag of truce. By the time Colonel Robert E. Lee appeared to take charge, seventeen men had died, including two of Brown's own sons. The leader himself, badly wounded, was captured with a surviving remnant, as Lee, characteristically, ensured that they got immediate medical attention.

Governor Henry A. Wise insisted on trying the six survivors as traitors to the Commonwealth of Virginia, faster than a federal procedure—a grand jury was already in session—in part to forestall a lynching. All were condemned to death. Brown's trial, running between October 27 and 31, was an opportunity for martyrdom that he seized with a skill that undermined the "insanity" defense suggested by a court-appointed lawyer. Several of his fellow captives, still hoping, vainly, to live, denied that they even knew him. But he himself welcomed death, and under sentence was able in words to win at least some of what he had hoped to win at arms. Even the southerners who saw and heard him admired his courage, and most his eloquence. But the South was frenzied with fear, while northern newspapers proclaimed him a hero. Upon his execution, on December 2, Ralph Waldo Emerson, the hitherto aloof philosopher of reform, declared, "He has made the gallows as glorious as the cross." Twelve tumultuous months later, South Carolina seceded from the Union, beginning the final chain of events that led to the Civil War.

7

Just as the years leading to the Civil War were far more murderous than those leading to the Revolution, the war itself was the bloodiest Americans have ever fought. But like the Revolution it was fought with remarkable civility, at least among white men in the eastern theater. And while its domestic effects on the northern homicide rate were paradoxical, to the south from start to finish it was marked by the most momentous nonmurders in our history.

The reasons for the war's high kill rate resulted from a deadly confluence of old lessons and new technology. Virtually all of the successful generals on both sides had gone to West Point, and there studied, as generals do, what had worked best in the last round of wars: in this case the offensive audacity of Napoleon Bonaparte, best symbolized by the bayonet charge. Napoleonic tactics had worked to near perfection during the one-sided Mexican War of the late 1840s. Fifteen years later, improved artillery, Gatling guns, and repeating rifles with several times the range of earlier muskets combined to make such charges nearly suicidal. They remained popular, however, among commanding officers. Modern scholars have estimated that only about 15 to 20 percent of the troops in any given engagement were able to overcome their deep inhibitions against killing fellow humans and actually fire their weapons directly at them. But even with only a fraction of the available firepower in use, bodies piled up quickly at Antietam, Chickamauga, Gettysburg, and Cold Harbor. The end result was that of the 2,500,000 who ever wore either blue or gray uniforms, many of them on short three-month enlistments, some 620,000 men died, or one out of four.

Despite this unprecedented level of carnage, with all the hatreds it generated, the war was largely confined to uniformed combatants, with formal and informal rules about flags of truce, hospitals, and burial details all honored, few civilian casualties, and rare atrocities. As in the American Revolution, one exception was in the west, notably along the Missouri-Kansas border, where the smoldering feud of the John Brown era had never died. William Clarke Quantrill, who had earlier fought on both sides, emerged as a guerrilla captain whose pose as champion of the Confederacy was a thin cover for his real occupation as armed robber, horse thief, and slave stealer. For outlaws like this, the war was an opportunity; with the army busy elsewhere, a band ranging from a few dozen to several hundred seemed invulnerable. In his most notorious single act, Quantrill and several hundred horsemen, seeking revenge as well as booty, raided a rebuilt Lawrence, Kansas, on August 21, 1863, and finding no resistance rounded up about one hundred fifty men and boys, tied them with rope, and over a course of two hours massacred them all in front of their wives, mothers, and sisters.

Among regular soldiers the most infamous exception to the general observance of the rules of combat involved black victims. "Colored" troopers were recruited into northern armies once President Lincoln's Emancipation Proclamation of January 1863 made the abolition of slavery an official war aim, and the Confederate government was deeply disturbed. Many southerners, proud of their military traditions, were simply outraged; President Jefferson Davis, more ruefully, admitted that if black men proved good soldiers the whole argument justifying slavery on the ground of racial inferiority would collapse. General Nathan Bedford Forrest was one of those who could not accept this conclusion, and when in April 1864 his Confederates overran Fort Pillow, Mississippi, they refused to accept the surrender of half of the garrison; blacks, with their hands up, were methodically bayoneted to death, and Forrest later claimed the river ran red for nearly two hundred yards downstream.

On the home front, too, race hatred was a major issue in the most murderous civilian outburst of the war, the New York City Draft Riots of July 1863.

Until that time the Union forces had relied wholly on volunteers, including over fifty thousand Irishmen from New York. But with the early enthusiasm gone with the mounting death tolls, that barrel had run dry. And for the first time in history the government required all men to register for conscription—all except those who could pay $300 to hire a substitute. The move sparked riots in several cities but especially New York, with its heavy concentration of immigrants. Class resentment was an obvious issue, and so was politics; the federal government was Republican, the immigrants were Democrats, and the Democratic governor of New York State declared the draft unconstitutional. As the final provocation to the Irish, the simple sense that this American war was not their fight had been further embittered by the Emancipation Proclamation that winter, which seemed to turn it into a crusade on behalf of their traditional African-American rivals. And so, on Monday morning, July 13, when federal marshals began to spin out names, a largely Irish mob stormed the building, burned the office, and took to the streets.

The streets were theirs by midmorning. With the militia away with the Union army, only a few hundred policemen (many Irish themselves), plus a like number of miscellaneous federal guards, sailors, and marines, were available to take on a mob that panicked authorities estimated at some fifty thousand. The rioters fought everyone, attacked every symbol of authority, beat surrounded cops and soldiers to jelly, and nearly killed the Irish police chief. But above all they targeted the city's fifteen thousand African Americans. Despite pleas from the Roman Catholic hierarchy and heroic action by several individual priests, a mob stripped and burned the Colored Orphan Asylum at Fifth Avenue and Forty-third Street, where only a courageous intervention by one Paddy McCaffrey and several firemen saved the children themselves from massacre. Others were not as lucky. Over the course of several days black men were stripped and lynched all over lower Manhattan, until on Thursday morning, the sixteenth, the tramp of veteran troopers returning from the Battle of Gettysburg heartened the authorities. With a last failed assault on the 7th Regiment Armory on lower Second Avenue, the rioters dispersed on Friday. President Lincoln then announced that the draft would resume.

The riot was the most dangerous in American history, according to Adrian Cook "an insurrection of anarchy, an outburst against any kind of government control by the people near the bottom of society." But careful reading of contemporary records confirms modern findings about mobs: as in most riots—and indeed warfare—the bloody work was carried on by a minority. The authorities were awed by the tens of thousands who filled the streets, mostly to cheer. And the numbers were important: the sheer moral pressure of crowd size, as always, both encouraged rioters and inhibited all but the most determined of bystanders, like McCaffrey, from intervening to help the victims. Actual fighting, however, was confined at any given spot to small bands of young men who already knew each other, as members of street gangs or fire companies. And despite figures greatly exaggerated by contemporaries and many later historians, a careful modern estimate puts the death toll not in the hundreds sometimes claimed but at about one hundred ten. While terrifying to the middle and upper classes—Brooks Brothers was one of the stores broken into and looted—those five days in New York were, for better and worse, not unique but simply the last and biggest of the long series of urban riots that had begun in the Jacksonian era.

Otherwise, on at least parts of the home front, the Civil War had a more calming than inflammatory effect. In some unsettled areas, as along the southern border, violence of all kinds increased. But in New York the murder rate, as measured by coroners' reports, dropped in all years but 1863, the date of the Draft Riots; in Philadelphia the proportionate number of homicide indictments fell by a third. The explanation seems simply that the poor, young, and underemployed males responsible for most urban homicides were drawn off into the army, where killings won medals and applause.

But in the larger history of murder in America, the most important Civil War chapter was written in the rural South.

Historians have argued for years about the causes of the Civil War. The clash between North and South was about two different economic systems, yes, and perhaps two different cultures. Violent northern attacks on the sinfulness of the "peculiar institution" maddened southerners who saw themselves doing no wrong. The North was insensitive, and the South—where in some places a fatal duel or brawl was almost a qualification for office—was aggressive. Recent scholars have stressed the importance of the southern "culture of honor," which branded compromise a cowardly way out of confrontation. But aggravating all of these reasons for conflict, south of the Mason-Dixon line, was the simple fact, as important to the nonslaveholding majority as to the planter class, that slavery was a form of racial domination. And to imagine it gone was to conjure nightmares of murderous revenge.

John Brown's raid pushed this ancient fear to new heights during 1860–61, as events pushed the sides toward war and rumors sparked committees of vigilance to flog out confessions and lynch blacks—and a few whites—all over the South. Talk of "war between the races," the possibility of "utter annihilation of the one or the other," filled the U.S. Congress. One recent historian believes that there may actually have been some black plotting in Adams County, Mississippi, early in the Civil War, to take over several plantations. This single incident seems the closest to the real thing—but even for this there is no firm evidence, no dates, no details, nothing except that 1 alleged plot? or perhaps 2? resulted in 5? or 6? or maybe 40? extralegal hangings by panicked local leaders, about to go off to war and leave their wives and children unprotected.

These Confederates were not afraid of northerners, as they showed on battlefields throughout the war, but they were clearly fearful of what might happen among the slaves back home. The war was fought almost entirely in slave country, and as it went on thousands, then millions, found that as the South crumbled they were free to escape in fact, and more gradually learned that the Emancipation Proclamation had freed them in law. The famous wartime diaries of Mary Chesnut, one of the thousands of women left alone on the plantation, are especially eloquent on her inability to penetrate the impassive "veil" worn by her black charges, indeed the inability of neighboring slave owners generally to predict how house servants or field hands would react to their new condition. As it turned out, hundreds of thousands moved out to meet the Union armies, some timidly, some boldly, many to enlist. A handful even joined the Confederates. A number stayed home and kept at work; a few, encouraged briefly by the federal government, hoped to take over the land for themselves. Still others enjoyed the new freedom to travel, to look for lost or sold relatives, to see the wider world.

The range of reactions was, in short, enormous. But it was not infinite. The freed men and women were confused, ecstatic, sullen, heedless, faithful, ambitious; despite the obvious opportunities they were not, in any number, vengeful. There was no orgy of rape and murder; the white South woke up from its two-centuries-old nightmare long before it had to face the cold dawn of military defeat.

The war ended on a tragic note for both sides. On Friday night, April 14, 1865, John Wilkes Booth shot and fatally wounded President Lincoln at Ford's Theater, as he and the North still celebrated General Robert E. Lee's final surrender, just five days before. And this most famous murder in American history was followed by one of its most notorious miscarriages of justice.

Booth himself, after twelve days of flight, was shot to death in a burning Virginia barn. But the dashing actor had involved several impressionable and dim-witted young men in the plot to kill the president and other major administration figures, and these were quickly arrested, together with Mary Surratt, who ran the boardinghouse where Booth had held court. President Andrew Johnson ordered that they be tried by a military commission—a move of very doubtful legality, as the criminal courts of the District of Columbia were fully available. And so on May 10, less than a month after the crime, the alleged conspirators were brought before nine general officers, with Judge Advocate Joseph Holt presiding.

The prisoners were indicted for conspiring with Confederate President Jefferson Davis, among others, although not a shred of evidence pointed to him. With Holt favoring the prosecution at every turn, Dr. Samuel Mudd was condemned to life in prison for the sole crime of splinting the leg of the fleeing Booth, an utter stranger to him (a sentence later commuted by President Ulysses S. Grant). And while there was little doubt that Lewis Paine, George Atzerodt, and David Herold had in fact plotted to kill Lincoln, much of the public was outraged at the treatment given Mary Surratt. Mrs. Surratt's young son John may perhaps have gone for the plot, but teenagers have always been good at hiding things from distracted mothers, and the pious Catholic widow made an unlikely conspirator. But while no credible testimony involved her directly, and her distinguished volunteer attorney quit the case in angry protest at its proceedings, in the frenzied atmosphere of that summer she was nonetheless found guilty and on July 7 joined the other three on the gallows.

The first presidential assassination in American history and its bungled aftermath brought an appropriate end to a violent era. The three preceding decades, capped by the war itself, had been the bloodiest in the American experience. It is impossible to measure just how bloody. But careful study of the urban murder rate, even through records that omit much actual homicide, suggests that it was the highest in the nineteenth century, while riot, dueling, vigilantism, small civil wars along the frontiers, and the always uncountable brutalities of slavery accounted for much more. And the future, North, West, and South, was still unsettled.

5

The Civil War to World War I, 1865–1917

The years from the later nineteenth century into the early twentieth are in many ways the classic period in American history, as all sections in their own fashion recovered from the Civil War. In the North, East, and Midwest, these were the years of the most rapid industrialization, when almost every index of size and power pointed jaggedly up and the modern physical city began to take shape. In the West, the whole continent between Kansas and California was filled up with new states. In the South, most wracked by the devastation of war, black slavery was replaced by violent intimidation and segregation as forms of racial domination.

Much homicide in every locale was composed of the same familiar elements as always and everywhere: domestic argument, drink, flaring anger, the challenge to honor. But everywhere, too, murder as always both reflected and contributed to social, political, and economic change. Regionally distinctive rates and patterns resulted from racial tension in the South, labor problems in the North, Indian warfare and unsettled conditions in the West. But toward the end of the era these distinctions began to lose some of their earlier force, as a result of the growing power of the urban industrial revolution all over the country, together with the many values and institutions allied with it, from sober behavior to better police work.

I

In the former Confederate states, the first task of the dominant white majority was to restore as fully and as quickly as possible the power enjoyed before secession. And between 1865 and 1877 they won back much of what they had lost in the formal Civil War by turning, in effect, to an intermittent but ultimately successful guerrilla "war of national liberation" based on systematic homicide.

With the Union army on the ground in 1865 and the federal government in charge, reforming northerners wished ideally to remake or "reconstruct" the conquered states in their own image. Many black leaders hoped to break up plantations into smaller units, turning former slaves into small farmers. At minimum, the triumphant Republican party expected to establish itself through friendly governments elected with the support of the new freedmen, white southern allies, and northerners come down either to help reform the region or seize personal advantage in the midst of postwar confusion.

But none of these wishes came true. While the Congress was able to establish Republican rule for varying periods and new state governments struggled to bring the nineteenth century to the benighted Carolinas, the region was simply too poor to support such innovations as penitentiaries, insane asylums, and public schools in addition to the state-supported railroads and other improvements favored by northern capitalists. Belief in the sanctity of private property was too powerful to permit the confiscation of ex-rebel plantations. And while for brief periods it seemed that the white South might accept a black share in political power, the federal government was too divided, inconsistent, and unwilling to commit the money and the manpower needed to ensure real social change.

The two major goals of the resisting southern majority were to get the blacks back to work under conditions as close to slavery as possible and to win back native white rule. The two were related: control of the political and justice systems was essential to uphold "black codes" and "vagrancy laws" designed to keep blacks out of a truly free labor market. And the winning tactic was the same in both cases: armed resistance to Republican state and county governments supported from outside, intimidation of the freedmen through assault and murder.

In the chaos that immediately followed the war, much violence resulted simply from the lack of local law enforcement. But one new trigger for bitter and defeated young men returning home was to find African Americans trying out new roles, defying old rules, and above all voting. During the year following the Confederate surrender in April 1865, federal commanders reported 33 white-black homicides in Tennessee, 29 in Arkansas, at least 70 in Louisiana, all of these figures surely undercounted, at a time when it seemed to some that a black man's life was worth no more "than a stray dog." Murderous race riots, earlier confined to the North, swept into Charleston, Norfolk, and Memphis, where former slaves had taken refuge in unprecedented numbers. On July 30, 1866, as African Americans were holding a political convention in New Orleans' Mechanics Hall, a black man's casual pistol shot at a white newsboy sparked a general assault on the building, and, with the local cops aiding the rioters, some thirty-nine were killed in nearby street fighting before occupying federals arrived.

By that time resistance was taking more organized form. "Patrolers," during slavery a specialized form of night watch, had roamed the countryside in tense times, looking for runaways or simply blacks without passes. After the war this official institution, together with the unofficial "vigilance" tradition, was easily turned to only slightly new, if now illegal, uses. The Knights of the Ku Klux Klan, led by General Nathan Bedford Forrest, the officer responsible for the Fort Pillow Massacre, was only the most famous of the several secret societies that terrorized black and white political opponents across the countryside during the late 1860s.

Intransigent native whites, mostly Democrats, simply refused to recognize the legitimacy of mostly Republican governments elected with black support, and were especially infuriated by armed black state militia. In some states, as in prewar Kansas, two governments claimed the right to rule at the same time, with the outcome in Mississippi, Louisiana, and South Carolina decided by mini–civil wars. And in 1877 the federal government formally surrendered, withdrawing the last blue troops used to support embattled Republican rule, leaving race relations in local white hands. The toll in violent death by then was past counting, with ordinary killings, lynchings, deaths in riots, Klan murders,

and casualties inflicted by or on Republican or Democratic militias almost impossible to disentangle.

And under native white rule after 1877, the South remained the most
murderous section of the country; in fact, Horace Redfield, writing in
1880, commented that "the number of homicides in the Southern
States is proportionately greater than in any country on earth the population of which is numbered as civilized." While there were no reliable
statistics across the whole of the South, Redfield counted the number
of killings listed in the only states with statewide newspapers, Texas,
Kentucky, and South Carolina, a method that almost surely undercounted the number of black deaths, at the hands of members of either
race. But even by this flawed measure, during 1878, just after Reconstruction, these three states had a "murder rate" roughly eighteen times
that for New England.

The reasons, to a more modern observer, are several. Poverty and
desperation are close to the top of the list. Poverty, too, reinforced a
tradition of weak government and law enforcement; it had been hard
since the seventeenth century for sheriffs and justices to catch and convict local bullies in rural counties, and it was still hard in upcountry
Georgia, the hills of Kentucky and Tennessee, and many other jurisdictions where vengeful feuds bypassed the formal system. "Every
man should be sheriff on his own hearth," was an old saying in North
Carolina.

Blacks, too, now often armed, were no longer valuable property, protected by their masters either from racist whites or from each other.
The historian Lawrence Levine has noted that Stagolee, the most celebrated legendary black badman of this period, was a figure "wholly
without social purpose or redeeming qualities," who preyed alike on
strong and weak, men and women. His place in folklore was an appropriate reflection of a former slave's world in which the justice system in
many counties was not protector but predator.

It had always been the hope even of romantic reformers to make
convicted prisoners pay for themselves. In the postwar South, states too
poor to feed and clothe mostly healthy young men in idleness, the hope
seemed more like a necessity. The solution hit upon was the "convict
lease system," through which prisoners were in effect sold for a term to

the highest bidders. The highest bidders in this era were typically the owners of mines, railroads, or swampy timberland, places where free men would not work. Gangs of prisoners could be held in chains. They didn't drink or show up late, and the price of their labor could be pushed down close to zero if maintenance costs, food and clothes, were kept at a minimum. Death rates ran up to 40 percent a year. And the men were easily replaceable: the opportunities for corruption were obvious, as some counties could turn a profit by sentencing numbers of young black men for small or imagined crimes and then selling them off to the mines.

And if some places invented black crimes, others ignored them entirely, even offenses as serious as homicide, so long as they affected African Americans alone. With every reason to distrust the justice systems in most counties, black men and women then resorted to often murderous ways of settling arguments of every kind, in cabins, barrooms, and work gangs.

And for both races, the old code of honor still held in the minds both of men with grievances and of those called to judge them.

A Louisiana lawyer, Thomas J. Kernan, outlined the "Jurisprudence of Lawlessness" for the American Bar Association in 1906, describing the ways in which southerners could get away with murder. A man was expected to fight, even kill, if a woman's honor was involved; the state of Texas officially adopted the otherwise "unwritten law" that justified, in jurors' eyes, the murder of a wife's lover (but not a husband's) caught in adultery. And if many states had abandoned the old common law "duty to retreat" in order for a killing to qualify as self-defense, in Kernan's South it had long been replaced by something like a duty to advance. Almost any insult, or to an outsider the most trivial challenge to personal respect or reputation, could justify a homicide. In practice dueling had long been above the law, and as the old formal code decayed, with its elaborate rules, it was enough to shoot a man on sight so long as he—or the community—knew or should have known that it was coming. Any street brawl that a defense lawyer could stretch into anything remotely like a "fair fight" could qualify as a duel of sorts, and win acquittal. In the South, as everywhere, it was the killer, the survivor, whose story was heard, the victim silent as the grave. And unlike the situation in the North, not only the society's bottom rails but also its social and political leaders were often involved in homicide.

General Goffe repulsing the Indians at Hadley, Massachusetts, 1676, during King Philips War. Credit: Corbis-Bettmann.

Eastern State Penitentiary, in Philadelphia, founded in 1829 as part of a new approach to reforming murderers and other criminals. Credit: Corbis-Bettmann.

California vigilantes executing the orders of "Judge Lynch" during the gold rush, 1850. Credit: Corbis-Bettmann.

Execution of 38 Sioux at Mankato, Minnesota, on December 26, 1862—the largest mass execution in U.S. history. Credit: Corbis-Bettmann.

Murder of Colonel Henry F. O'Brien on July 14, 1863, during the New York City draft riots, the most lethal mob uprising in U.S. history. Credit: Corbis-Bettmann.

Jesse James as a teenaged Confederate guerilla in Missouri, 1864. Credit: Corbis-Bettmann.

Mrs. Mary Surratt, the pious Catholic
widow who ran the boardinghouse
where John Wilkes Booth and others
plotted to assassinate Lincoln. Credit:
Corbis-Bettmann.

Photograph taken by Matthew Brady of the hanging of four Lincoln conspirators,
including Mary Surratt, on July 7, 1865. Credit: Corbis-Bettmann.

Six members of the Mollie Maguires attending their last devotions in the prison chapel, Pottsville, Pennsylvania, June 21, 1877. Credit: Corbis-Bettmann.

A Baltimore crowd being fired upon by the Sixth Maryland Regiment, during the Railroad Strike of July 1877. Credit: Corbis-Bettmann.

A group of white Southerners preparing to lynch a black man, 1882. Credit: Corbis-Bettmann.

Lizzie Borden at about the time of the murders, 1892. Reprinted with the permission of the Fall River Historical Society.

Andrew Borden's body as it was discovered on the couch, August 4, 1892. Reprinted with the permission of the Fall River Historical Society.

Herman W. Mudgett, also known as H. H.
Holmes—America's first famous serial sex killer,
1895. Credit: UPI/Corbis-Bettmann.

When all of these elements came together the result was rural Edge-field County, South Carolina, around the turn of the century. Former Governor "Pitchfork Ben" Tillman, an Edgefield native, was then serving as senator from the Palmetto State, an unashamedly violent man whose father and an older brother had killed men over card games, and whose nephew, also a politician, shot down a hostile newsman in front of the state capitol early in 1903—successfully pleading self-defense. During the same years the murder rate in Tillman's home county was something over 30 per 100,000, bigger even than the carnage recorded in medieval England.

But while the southern white-on-white murder rate was the highest in the country, it was white-on-black killings that in this era reached their most notorious peak. Lynchings occurred in every state of the Union outside of New England—New Jersey had several—with more than 3,700 incidents recorded between 1889 and 1930, and victims of every color. But the South accounted for well over 80 percent of these, and it was only in the South that murder was used in effect as social policy.

The lynching phenomenon fascinated contemporaries at the time, and has occupied scholars ever since. But while southern lynching took many forms, much of its morbid appeal results from the sheer barbarity of many incidents. As often in the past, racial hatred allowed otherwise ordinary men and some women to gather in mobs—the attendance of women and children at these occasions was often noted—and to treat their victims as less than human. The results included the most barbaric episodes in the history of American homicide: special excursion trains took passengers to Paris, Texas, in 1893, to watch a retarded black man die, over the course of an hour, of red-hot irons thrust into his body and down his throat; in 1911 an accused rapist was tied to a stake on the opera house stage in Livermore, Kentucky, and tickets bought the privilege of shooting at him from the seats.

Mass lynchings of this kind often followed certain communal rituals: a prominent site was selected close to the alleged crime, the victim was given time to pray, hanged, and then shot up or burned after death—more rarely before—with the first match, or shot, ceremonially awarded to the injured person or family. In about one-fourth of the cases the victim was castrated or otherwise mutilated, with body parts or bits of rope then sold off as souvenirs and whatever remained left to swing as a warning to the black community. These sadistic orgies were explained then and later in terms of communal horror at "THE Crime," black rape of a white woman; the participants seem often to have ranged across the whole of the local white social spectrum. Senator Tillman boasted that he would gladly lead a mob to avenge such an outrage. In fact all southern defenses of lynching centered on THE Crime, with much success across the country.

In the late nineteenth and early twentieth century, an era of intense racism fostered by the pseudoscience of Social Darwinism even among the most educated, the brutish inferiority of blacks was an article of faith. The sensational yellow press of the era fed on lynching; although most editorials condemned the bypassing of the court system, and certainly torture, there was much clucking about a natural impatience with the law's delays, and the actual news stories were written by sympathetic southern stringers. Feature writers and illustrators reveled in the opportunity to produce socially acceptable pornography, a one-two punch best involving a first-person account of the alleged crime—"The negro seized me. Then I fainted. God was merciful"—followed by a lurid depiction of its aftermath. Meanwhile even the northern-born Episcopal bishop of Arkansas, in 1903, joined a host of other respectable apologists in declaring, "While I do not justify lynching, I can find no other remedies adequate to repress the crime for which it has been made a punishment by the people of the South."

Later psychologists, too, have concentrated on the rape issue, in arguing that, for example, in an era of repressed sexuality white men projected their own sexual fantasies onto blacks and then punished them savagely out of guilt. But these explanations, like those of contemporary apologists, are at best partial explanations for a complex phenomenon. The offenses for which black men, and some women, earned lynching ran a great gamut, from urging fellow blacks to return to Africa through arson, assault, burglary, and horse theft on to "wild talking." Rape, despite all the furor, accounted for only about one-sixth of the alleged crimes; by far the most usual was murder of a white male.

And only a minority of lynchings involved great mass mobs. A careful study of Georgia, where lynching was common, and Virginia, where it was not, estimates that big crowds accounted for perhaps 30 to 40 percent of all episodes. Many of the others were simply illegal on-the-spot executions carried out by gangs of armed men; given the traditional weakness of law enforcement in rural areas, something like the old medieval institution of hue and cry lived on in the South, and the line between a legal posse, an extralegal search party, and an illegal lynching bee was a thin one, crossed only when a fugitive was either caught or shot down. Often, too, when a black allegedly wronged a white a small number of family or friends of the victim would raid a jail to abduct and execute a man whose crime had otherwise failed to outrage many others. A last form, finally, was "terrorist" lynching, usually carried on at night by organized groups such as the Ku Klux Klan and intended specifically as warning to those who might follow a "troublemaker."

Simple racial prejudice, too, fails as a full explanation for lynching. Prejudice was of course involved—some 85 percent of southern victims were black, including virtually all of those subject to barbaric indignities—but while racial prejudice was nearly universal, lynching was quite unevenly distributed across the South, with some areas virtually immune. (Contemporary white South Africans, too, were among those shocked by the American resort to lynching.) Other simple psychological explanations—such as lynching as an aggressive response to inner frustration—fail for parallel reasons. While this may be accurate, it explains too much: frustration is part of the human experience, and all share the biological capacity for aggression, but only in some places, at some times, did southerners or others react to frustration in this specific way.

While general explanations may have some value, then, the most useful explanations for the *why* of southern lynching look closely at the *where* and *when* for clues to the kinds of historic forces and changes responsible for the phenomenon. Interracial southern lynchings, while never absent earlier, began to rise sharply in the late 1880s, peaked in the 1890s, when they averaged about one hundred a year, and then fell sharply through the early twentieth century. As the great antilynching crusader Ida Wells Barnett pointed out at the time, no explanation that hinges on either black male lust or white male sensitivity to it can explain the timing; white women had often been routinely and calmly left alone on plantations full of black men, notably during the Civil War— why the sudden upsurge in concern more than twenty years after? And no general psychological reason can account, either, for the rapid falloff early in the twentieth century. What does best explain the curve are specific and often turbulent internal changes in southern politics and society.

When the federal government left the South to itself in 1877, the place of African-American men and women had not been fully settled. White domination had been assured, but with slavery gone its forms were not yet clear. Millions of black men still voted; others competed for a variety of jobs; and in cities and countryside men and women jostled with whites, testing the limits of subordination. For both blacks and poor whites, the several economic substitutes for slavery, above all sharecropping and a one-sided tenantry, were being fixed in law, accompanied by much resistance to their specific terms. And the political backing for these legal instruments was still not firmly in place; during the later 1880s and 1890s, the message of the Populist party and other appeals to rebellion against the traditional Democratic elite were directed at black as well as poor white voters. The result was continual tension and violence at the polls, as poor whites feared that plantation owners would order black tenants to vote against them and rich whites feared an interracial alliance of the dispossessed.

The geography of lynching supports this analysis. Two kinds of areas stood out. One was the counties where staple crops were grown, notably cotton, the one most valued in the international market and above all in the "black belt" where the population of former slaves was thickest. The other was the fastest-growing counties, as in Texas or South Georgia, newly opened by the railroads and filling with both African-American and white in-migrants ready to exploit new lands through raising livestock or lumbering. In both cases the need to draw sharp racial lines, to validate white "honor" and power by demonstrating black impotence or "dishonor," was unusually strong. The fears of whites in the black belt were exaggerated by their minority status, and in the new areas freedmen and women might prove "uppity" in the absence of local traditions, in contrast to Tidewater Virginia, for example, which had long shown them their place.

The solution eventually found was two-sided, political and social. Elite white fears of black voting were put to rest by a variety of nonviolent exclusionary tactics widely adopted by the late 1890s. Successfully claiming, before the U.S. Supreme Court, that a political party was a kind of private club, Democratic leaders won the right to restrict primary voting, in many areas all that mattered, to chosen white "members." Poll taxes and literacy requirements, with tests administered by white officials, eliminated hundreds of thousands more freedmen. These last requirements eliminated many poor whites as well—but in some states a "grandfather clause" exempted those who could prove that their ancestors were legally registered—at a time when African Americans were of course still slaves.

The other or social side of this bargain, demanded less by the elite than by poor whites, was legal segregation as a means of showing their own superiority. Racial segregation had long been common in the North as well as the South, but nothing approaching the near-total apartheid dictated by legislation passed around the turn of the century. The goal of absolute separation and physical distance made little sense to the elite, long accustomed to African-American mistresses as well as mammies, and was never in fact achieved in practice. But few objected to it in principle, and it made a nicely symmetrical package when coupled with voting exclusion.

The sharp downturn in lynching that followed the turn of the century had many causes beyond this all-white "bargain." Many southerners of education and standing had long opposed the practice, and their objections strengthened as the region developed a more diversified commercial economy and social structure and the old culture of honor and violence slowly crumbled at the top. Formal dueling died out within a generation of the Civil War, and the homicide rate began to fall not long after that. Individual sheriffs and governors had always fought illegal punishment as an affront to the honor of their own competence, a blot on the reputations of the justice systems of their states, and a discouragement to investors. While prosecutions were rarely attempted and never successful, state militias were called on dozens of occasions to ring local jails or escort black prisoners to trial. Courageous white southerners, men and women, worked for the same ends—but never together with—African-American antilynching crusaders like Ida Barnett and the founders of the National Association for the Advancement of Colored People (NAACP), beginning in 1909.

But the most basic reason for the falling curve was simply that lynching was no longer needed. By the early twentieth century the use of murder as social policy had achieved its ends: southern blacks were tightly fixed in place, economically dependent and politically powerless, and nothing more was needed to hold them down.

2

By that time national anxieties had long since stopped focusing on the South and race. The year 1877, traditional end to Reconstruction, was in fact a neatly marked crossroads. That spring the last blue troopers were withdrawn from the old Confederacy, effectively ending federal occupation and closing the official aftermath of the Civil War. But the end of one fearful era was at the same time the beginning of another; a few months later the biggest and bloodiest labor strike in American history spread along the railroads of the upper South, North, and Midwest. And for many members of the middle class, as the clash between labor and industry introduced the nation to wholly new and sometimes terrifying forms of murderous violence, the specter of sectional civil war was simply replaced by the specter of vertical class war.

The great Railroad Strike of 1877 began in a depressed July, when railroad workers in West Virginia walked off the job to protest a 10 percent wage cut, the second in four years. The governor sent the militia to help move the trains, but when these citizen-soldiers fraternized with strikers in Martinsburg, their numbers swollen by working-class supporters, he applied for help from the U.S. Army. President Rutherford B. Hayes, having just ordered U.S. troops out of the South, approved this novel reassignment. But the strike spread next to Baltimore, where fires were set, rocks thrown, and ten men killed in clashes with the jumpy Maryland militia. In Pittsburgh, as in Martinsburg, the local militia refused to act against a local crowd. Elite troopers from Philadelphia, rushed in by the Pennsylvania Railroad, were unable to stop widespread looting and the burning of railroad property; twenty-five men died by the time the federal army took control. Farther west, in Chicago, street fighting between local police and workingmen killed up to fifty more. And all over the country, political demonstrations, marches, and speeches—in St. Louis a weeklong general strike—drove home the point that railway workers were not alone.

America's middle-class newspaper readers were shocked by this apparently sudden outburst. Six years earlier, in March 1871, the city of

Paris, under military siege from outside, had briefly declared a "commune," a kind of worker's state. The brief reign of the Commune was marked both by ambitious reforms and the vicious murders of the archbishop of Paris and more than thirty parish priests before it went down, literally in flames, in house-to-house fighting with French troops. But while it died in France, the Commune lived in the imaginations of middle-class Americans, supplying a vocabulary and set of images as frightening as those of the Haitian Revolt had been to the southern planter aristocracy. It was then easy to imagine that the inspiration for working-class discontent was foreign, that the aim was "communard" or "communist."

In fact, the American labor movement of the late nineteenth and early twentieth century was at best divided and weak, its aims generally modest, even conservative. In a long post–Civil War period of monetary deflation, most strikes, like the one in 1877, aimed at nothing more radical than the restoration of wage cuts. And while the accelerating demands of the industrial era did fuel new tensions between those who earned wages and those who paid them, what was labeled "labor violence" was often simply overlaid on traditional kinds of ethnic, political, and cultural differences that had long inspired murderous conflict in America, and sometimes perverted its system of criminal justice.

One of the best examples of this tangle of motives is the murky history of the Mollie Maguires in the coalfields of eastern Pennsylvania. At one level this was simply a labor dispute, magnified by its position at the very base of the triad of coal, steel, and railroads that powered the new American economy. Trouble in the coalfields was chronic; few jobs in the world are as hard or dangerous as deep-tunnel mining, and after the Civil War the miners sporadically tried to organize as the Workingmen's Benevolent Association. At the same time the region was continually plagued by violence, not only the usual tavern brawls but also ambushes, robberies, or assassinations involving groups of men with blackened faces, apparent strangers to their victims. Several of the targets were the owners, paymasters, or supervisors of small mines; in one case a party of armed men in disguise invaded the home of George K. Smith, on November 5, 1863, and shot him in front of his family; several suspects, arrested by the sheriff, were freed by a mob. Both the national press and the local establishment, long used to branding

Catholics as undercover subversives, blamed these outrages on Irish miners organized as the Mollie Maguires, a secret society that had declared a kind of war on their oppressors.

And the gauntlet was picked up by the other side. Economic leadership in the coal region, by the early 1870s, was exercised by the Reading Railroad, as principal landlord, buyer, and shipper. Reading President Frank Gowen was able easily to crush the Miners' Union with the aid of the economic depression that set in beginning in 1873. But the Mollies were different. The local politicians who ran the county justice system, Gowen believed, were cowed, corrupted, or sympathetic to the miners. His own private Coal and Iron Police—in that country a parallel law enforcement system, legally deputized by the Commonwealth of Pennsylvania—were able to break strikes, and strikers, with the help of a cooperative state militia. But it could not deal with an apparently secret organization that sent unpopular foremen, coal weighers, and owners threatening notes illustrated with nooses and pistols. Gowen's solution was to call on Allan Pinkerton's private detective agency. Pinkerton in turn called in James McParlan, one of his operatives, himself an Irish Catholic. And it was McParlan, as "James McKenna," who showed up at Pat Dormer's Pottsville tavern, on a cold night in December 1873, and by his own heavily stereotyped account in that single evening sang, danced, drank, and fought his way into the hearts of the patrons, as a first step toward penetrating the Mollie Maguires.

"By his own account" (key words, in the absence of reliable outside corroboration), "McKenna" was able to pass himself off as a killer, and the next April won induction into the Ancient Order of Hibernians (AOH), a traditional Irish patriotic organization that allegedly served as cover for the Mollies. Between then and February 1876 he served usefully as an AOH "secretary"—many members were illiterate—and won the confidence of the leadership. And when based on his tips almost two dozen alleged killers were rounded up and put on trial, it was James McParlan who served as the star witness, the one whose colorful testimony about initiation rites and conspiracy to murder revealed secrets, won convictions, and according to most papers brought peace to the families of foremen, owners, and loyal miners all across coal country.

Were there any Mollies in the anthracite fields? Surely yes; the Irish had centuries of experience, back home, with forming secret societies (as well as with treacherous informers paid by their oppressors). Were at least some of them killers? Yes again; Jimmy Kerrigan and Muff Lawlor confessed and saved their lives by testifying against a few others. Were they guilty of all the outrages and murders in the anthracite region? As surely no; this was hard country without them. Allan Pinkerton, while paying McParlan, was also encouraging committees of vigilance to take direct action. So were some local newspapers. And on Friday night, December 10, 1875, a gang of men entered the home of two alleged Mollies in Wiggan's Patch, tied up several of the occupants, shot another, killed Elizabeth McAllister with one panicked bullet, and surrounded Charles O'Donnell in a deadly ring, pumping at least twenty-five shots into his head and torso at such close range that his skin was roasted.

In addition to righteous vigilantes, testimony about the Mollies and their opponents points to many other familiar elements of midcentury American homicide: local political rivalry; rioting fire companies in Mahoney City; strong drink and brawling among Modocs, Buckshots, and Sleepers. The coal country was entangled in a web of often personal vendettas, and the ethnic thread stood out as usual. The Irish had been imported to do the worst jobs, under the supervision of more skilled Welsh or Orange miners. These traditional Protestant enemies ranked high among victims of violence whether or not they had any direct connection with the mines. In August 1875, the wild young Welshman Gomer James, acquitted of killing a Mollie two years earlier, was himself assassinated, by an unknown gunman, while running a beer stand at an outing of the Shenandoah Rescue Hook and Ladder Company. Politics, too, played a role, national as well as local; George Smith, assassinated back in 1863, was apparently unpopular mostly for his support of the Civil War draft, the issue that had cost so many other lives in New York and elsewhere. And Black Jack Kehoe, alleged "King of the Mollies," was convicted in 1877 of a crime committed fifteen years earlier, when Frank Langdon, a mining foreman who had accused Kehoe of insulting the Union cause and flag, was stoned to death by a small mob following a Fourth of July picnic.

But whatever their other crimes or motives, it was as threats to the mines and the Reading that Frank Gowen pursued the Mollies. And the trials were classic examples of what economic domination could do to a local justice system. In the interests of efficiency, twenty accused killers were tried in just nine proceedings for the murders of ten men in three different jurisdictions; all of the victims except for one policemen were mine owners, supervisors, bookkeepers, watchmen, or foremen. Gowen himself, a former prosecutor, played an active role in court as the head of several legal teams invited by the district attorneys of Carbon, Schuylkill, and Columbia counties to assist in the proceedings. Irish Catholics were systematically excluded from all juries. Alibi witnesses in the early trials were immediately convicted of perjury, as a warning to others, if their testimony clashed with McParlan's; one man drew three years. While Jack Kehoe had clearly been angry at Frank Langdon, who had docked his own pay and fired some members of his family, he was never placed at the scene of the 1862 killing; he was nonetheless found guilty of premeditated murder for having said, "You son of a bitch, I'll kill you," sometime before the stoning. And while lawyers hired by the Ancient Order of Hibernians conducted an able defense, every man indicted was convicted, all of murder in the first degree, and all appeals were refused.

It was an awesome show of power, with groups of prisoners repeatedly brought up from jail to court in chains, for the benefit of press and public. And the lessons were brutally underlined by the executions that followed. The convicts were not young gang members but in many cases family men, community leaders of a sort, all of whom took the last rites of the Catholic church on the gallows, most of them still proclaiming innocence. Ten were hanged on a single "Black Thursday," June 21, 1877, four at Mauch Chunk and six at Pottsville; although the Commonwealth of Pennsylvania had banned public executions since 1834, the audience at the Pottsville jail included some fifty newspaper reporters as surrogates for millions of readers across the country. Three more men followed on March 25, another three days later on the 28th, followed by single hangings on June 11 and December 28, a pair the next January 14, another on the 16th, the last October 9, 1879. Twenty executions in less than two years—nearly half the total for the Commonwealth of Pennsylvania during the entire decade of the 1870s—made it quite clear who was in charge of the state and the system.

But while the Mollies and other sensational cases drew international attention, most of the killings resulting from labor troubles did not. Between the Civil War and World War I, while the United States had the weakest labor movement of any major industrializing nation, it also had the most murderous record of labor violence and the most time lost in strikes. Both ends of the paradox are rooted in the same simple fact: the ethnic diversity long unique to America was increasing even faster than the population itself, as beginning in the 1880s a "New Immigration" from southern and eastern Europe began to outnumber older streams from the north and the British Isles.

Before the Civil War the few existing labor unions had been organized much like medieval guilds, as mutual benefit societies, small social clubs, or fraternities. But this simple model was harder to follow as the workforce in individual factories, mines, and railroads got bigger. And as specialized skills were lost to mechanization, with working people reduced in many industries to interchangeable parts, it was easier for employers to take advantage of their differences. Many owners deliberately mixed hostile groups in the workplace, confident that Greeks and Turks, Jews and Italians, would not join a common union. And when Irish miners went on strike, or Italian laborers, there were always hungry Chinese or Poles ready to take their place.

Labor violence rarely pitted workers directly against their employers but more typically against each other. Strikes in this period were acts of last-ditch defiance, in many places not clearly legal, everywhere vulnerable to the labels "radical" or "un-American." For those who walked out, the key to success was to make sure, physically, that no other workers went back in. Strikers saw themselves fighting for their families, while strikebreakers, or "scabs," were typically even more desperate, many of them blacks or others excluded from whole job categories or even industries, as the result more of union or other workers' hostility than by employers. For them a strike was an opportunity. But they knew that they were expendable, that the new jobs would usually be lost even when the strike failed, as most did in this era. With the extra dimension of racial or ethnic tension added to the basic economic conflict, they knew, too, that even if protected by Pinkertons or other hired guns they had to be ready to fight their way to work, and could never fully rest secure at night.

For decades, all across the country, sticks and stones and pistol shots took their toll, one, two, or three lives at a time, in innumerable skirmishes between strikers and strikebreakers. But these routine events did not capture the public imagination as powerfully as those that seemed to threaten the social order more profoundly. The difference between the kinds of killings that did and did not scare Americans is clearly shown in the reaction to two political assassinations in the year 1881.

That July 1, President James A. Garfield, in the virtual absence of security in Washington's Baltimore and Potomac train station, was shot in the back by an unsuccessful Washington lawyer. The assassin, Charles Guiteau, believed (among many other things) that Garfield should have appointed him ambassador to Paris. When the president died of his wounds after two months of pain, Guiteau was charged with his murder. The trial, in which he served as his own counsel, stretched through ten long farcical weeks of interruptions, tantrums, and outbursts enough to prove conclusively that the man was insane, believing "God told me to kill." Judge and jurors, however, reflecting the public demand for vengeance, rejected the obvious verdict of insanity and condemned Guiteau to hang, a sentence he met willingly: "I am going to the Lordy," he wrote, shortly before his execution.

But if Americans were angry at this lone madman, a native middle-class American, they were not frightened. In contrast, the bombing assassination of the popular reforming czar, Alexander II, by self-styled "anarchists" or "nihilists" set off an international wave of fear and indignation that refused to recede for decades. And beginning in 1881, a fledgling anarchist movement in the United States produced just enough inflammatory words and newsprint about dynamite and "the propaganda of the deed" to provide cartoonists and editorialists with convenient symbols for "foreign radicals," helping to fuel an intermittent popular unease that occasionally bubbled up into fear and fury, most famously in May 1886.

Workers at Chicago's McCormick Harvester that year had been out since February, sometimes battling with strikebreakers. On May 1, in an unrelated development, several labor organizations launched a drive for adoption of an eight-hour day, a movement that inspired tens of thousands to quit work and march all over the city. On the third, a crowd of demonstrating lumber workers drifted toward the McCormick plant to help harass the scabs and were met by two hundred policemen, clubs, and bullets. Four men were killed that afternoon, and a leading anarchist, the German-born August Spies, called an indignation meeting for the next night at Haymarket Square.

Long hot speeches, the evening of the fourth, together with cold wind and rain, had by ten o'clock reduced the hastily called meeting to about three hundred men, women, and children. Most of the speakers had left, Mayor Carter Harrison had checked the scene and saw no danger in the oratory, when Police Inspector John Bonfield, at the head of nearly two hundred men, took it upon himself to order the crowd to disperse. His blue column was standing quietly in formation when a bomb, apparently thrown from an alley, landed amidst it. All discipline exploded in the smoky confusion that followed, as the terrified police fired wildly into the crowd and at each other. The bomb itself killed Patrolman Michael J. Degan that night, several in the crowd were shot to death, and during the following several weeks six more policemen died either of bullet wounds or shrapnel.

Over the next few days, the city, and nation, had little more notion of what they were facing than the cops that night on the scene, and reacted in the same way. The fact that many local anarchists had in fact talked long and often about bombing made them obvious targets. But to outsiders all apparent radicals looked alike; hundreds were rounded up and beaten as Cook County District Attorney Julius Grinnell advised the already fired-up police force to "make the raids first and look up the law afterwards." On May 27 a grand jury indicted ten anarchists for murder and conspiracy to murder, all of them foreign-born except for the dashing former Confederate Albert Parsons, who escaped the city before sensationally showing up to surrender in open court. It would have been hard in any case to find an impartial trial jury in Chicago, but Judge Elbert Gary left nothing to chance. Potential panelists were not chosen by lottery, as usual, but by a special bailiff nominated by Grinnell; the eight defendants actually tried quickly used up their twenty peremptory challenges, and the judge allowed none for such causes as prejudice against labor unions or foreigners.

Since no actual bomb thrower could be identified then or later, the prosecution concentrated not on the murder but on the "conspiracy" count in the indictment; it was easy to show that several of the men had advocated the use of bombs in general, if not in this specific case, as a form of social protest. The jury took only a few hours to declare all eight guilty, and under Illinois law to call for the execution of all but one. After all appeals failed, three of the men successfully applied for clemency to Governor Richard Oglesby; the other four refused to beg. Louis Lingg committed suicide on November 10, 1887, by exploding a smuggled dynamite cap in his mouth; Parsons, George Engle, and Adolph Fischer were hanged the next afternoon.

The country was unevenly divided by these proceedings. Most labor leaders, their own movement deeply wounded by the association with violence, had little sympathy for the Haymarket Eight, whose ideas were radically different from their own. Many intellectuals, however, were deeply troubled by the threat to free speech implied in convicting men not for specific actions but for ideas, however naive or even abhorrent. As Chicago calmed down, too, and it became obvious that anarchism was no real threat to the Republic, they were joined by many local business and political leaders. But theirs was still minority sentiment, and it was an act of political courage, even suicide, when in 1893 a new governor, John Peter Altgeld, in granting the three survivors a full pardon, denounced the judge, the trial, and the conduct of the prosecution.

The Haymarket affair, as clearly as the trials of the Lincoln conspirators and the Mollies, reinforced the obvious fact that in times of real or imagined crisis murder trials turned on political opinion. Sometimes that opinion reflected genuine community sentiment, sometimes it could be manipulated, as by Frank Gowen or Judge Gary. In either case, the kind of rough impartiality shown by Philadelphia juries in ordinary homicide cases, and certainly the usual sympathy for defendants, dried up when jurors felt their own place in the social order was threatened.

Usually the label "foreign" or "radical" hung heavily on the necks of workingmen accused of murder in the course of strikes, or conversely helped free policemen or sheriffs' deputies accused of shooting them down. But this was not true always or everywhere. In many places, community sentiment and local politics were in fact pro-labor, and imported strikebreakers, especially blacks or other strangers, were passionately hated. The trigger-happy Pinkertons, too, were highly unpopular in many areas. All of these forces converged in the town of Homestead, Pennsylvania, in the summer of 1892, when the management of the Carnegie Steel Mill locked out union workers and prepared to bring in scabs.

On July 6, six hundred Pinkertons were spotted floating up the Monongahela in covered barges; Homesteaders lined the bank, someone fired a shot, and soon the strikers alongshore and the men on the river were exchanging rifle and pistol fire. Seven of the invaders and nine strikers were dead by the time a truce was arranged, and the surviving Pinkertons were made to run a brutal gauntlet through the town. Company lawyers, in the aftermath, threw a blizzard of indictments for murder and riot at scores of union men. But while the select grand jury of Allegheny County passed these true bills, ordinary jurors would not cooperate; most charges were dropped, and the few men who came to trial were all acquitted.

But the tide still ran against union men in this era. Although the murder charges did not stick, the Amalgamated Association of Iron, Steel, and Tin Workers was effectively broken by the expenses of defending its members in court. And much public sympathy, at first favorable to men defending their homes from invasion, was lost when three weeks after the battle on the river Alexander Berkman, an anarchist with no union connection, attempted to murder Carnegie's leading executive, Henry Clay Frick.

The rest of the century, then, was punctuated by major strikes, most of them failures, several murderous. Given the precedent set by President Hayes, many of them, especially those involving interstate transport on the railroads, the nation's biggest employers, were broken with the aid of state or federal troops. And the new century began with the third presidential assassination in one long generation, as the widely beloved William McKinley was shot down at a reception in Buffalo, New York, on September 6, 1901, by Leon Czolgosz, a lone Polish-born anarchist. McKinley died eight days later. No one, including himself, offered any defense of young Czolgosz, who was indicted, tried, and sentenced in a matter of weeks, hanged on October 29.

3

While both Reconstruction in the South and labor troubles in the North have faded, or been blotted, from popular historical memory, events in the West have not. But the reality of the post–Civil War era of "cowboys and Indians" has been badly distorted by time and the romantic imagination. The fact that small boys and Hollywood producers have changed sides over the years is not enough to set it straight.

The final extermination of the original natives as major players in the drama of American expansion was accomplished within a single generation, a process that began during the war itself. The end, if not romantic, was often dramatic as played out on the deserts, plains, and mountains of the West; but while costumes, scenery, and players all changed, the essential outlines of the plot did not.

The policy of herding Indians onto reservations, adopted before the Civil War, was full of trouble and corruption from the start, and it was impossible to enforce on the warrior horsemen of the West. Many individual chieftains surrendered to it when bribed and harassed by the army. But those who agreed to the reservation treaties, adopted Christianity, and tried to learn farming were often scorned by others, and many young warriors thought of the reservations simply as winter oases, places to wait out the hard weather and pick up rations before returning, refreshed, to a life of hunting and raiding. Many tribes were involved, from the northern Sioux and Cheyenne down to the Kiowa and Comanche of the Texas plains, on across west and south to the fearsome Apache. All these peoples differed greatly in culture, and each had a distinctive history. But with variations the story of the Sioux, the biggest and most famous tribe, is the story of them all.

Originally from the woodlands of the Lake Country, the Sioux had been moving out onto the plains for decades, driving back or killing off other tribes. By the 1850s they had established an empire, becoming the leading trappers and traders of the prairies, continually moving west, north, and south as they decimated the buffalo. Sometimes loosely allied with Blackfoot, Cheyenne, and Arapahoe, bitterly hated by the Pawnee, they dominated the northern plains by the time the white men began first to cross and then to settle them. Several groups signed treaties during the 1850s, but few really understood what a "reservation" was supposed to be, and no chieftains had the authority needed to hold individuals to their terms.

Serious trouble broke first at the Lower Sioux Agency near the ancestral homelands in Minnesota, where Chief Little Crow had tried hard to settle down and learn the white man's way. But traders cheated his people over the price of furs, the promised cash was siphoned off, the flour was wormy and the beef rotten. When they complained, one local trader, Andrew Myrick, sneered, "Let them eat grass, for all I care." The young men heard him. On August 17, 1862, Little Crow himself, dressed in broadcloth and tie, went to Episcopal services as usual at the agency; that same day four young men burst in and shot down a German farm family and their guests at Sunday dinner, to start the biggest Indian massacre in American history.

Over the next few days, under a bitterly disillusioned Little Crow, the Sioux first systematically slaughtered the local traders—Andrew Myrick was later found with his dead mouth stuffed with grass—then fanned out among the local farmers, many of them unarmed Germans and Scandinavians wholly innocent of the long and vicious tradition of frontier warfare. The amount of rape, mutilation, and butchery of children seems to have been exceptional even by the fearsome standards of that tradition. And when the army, after several pitched battles, was finally able to win the release of over two hundred women and children held as hostages and to round up many defeated Sioux, the official records of the new state of Minnesota counted 644 civilian deaths, the army 113 of its own.

The 1,500 Sioux then in army custody were not, however, ordinary prisoners of war; in the view of outraged Minnesotans, and many in the army, they were simply killers. And it was for murder and attendant atrocities that nearly 400 of them, virtually all of the male adults, were tried by a military commission. Some 307 were sentenced to death before President Lincoln personally reviewed the transcripts and, with another and bigger war already on his hands, commuted the sentences of most. But at Fort Snelling that December, 39 warriors were finally hanged on a single snowy day, by far the biggest mass execution in our history.

Little Crow and many of his warriors, though, had escaped. The chief himself was shot—murdered?—by a local farmer the next summer while picking berries in the north woods, but most followed the traditional routes west, moving in among other Sioux tribes and helping spread war across the plains. The Cheyenne were eager to smoke the war pipe with their allies after an entire peaceful village of nearly three hundred, mostly women and children, was murdered at Sand Creek, Colorado, by the local militia under Colonel J. M. Chivington. And for the rest of the 1860s through 1877 the plains were full of hostiles.

By the late nineteenth century, as their numbers and prowess receded, the natives had won many white champions; a few westerners

and many military men admired their courage and way of life, and
eastern reformers were eager to make good citizens of them. The federal
government then always had proponents of a "peace policy." But General William Tecumseh Sherman, in overall charge of operations, was
implacable, and most white westerners agreed with General Philip
Sheridan that "if a white man commits murder . . . we hang him, . . . if
an Indian does the same we have been in the habit of sending him more
blankets." The issues were in any case decided on the plains themselves.

The government repeatedly set aside reservation lands "forever," and
then broke its word, as when for example gold was discovered in the
Black Hills, sacred territory to many natives. On their side many young
Indians saw no need to honor promises made by others, and as the
buffalo were exterminated lived increasingly off plunder taken in raids.
They encountered few cowboys but many wagon freighters and army
convoys; isolated farmers were especially easy targets, the men killed,
the women raped and sometimes captured, in what to the warriors was
traditional warfare and to the whites simply murder and kidnapping,
reason to call out the army and excuse to shrink the reservations further
in revenge.

Indian warfare was like no other. One-on-one most plains or desert
warriors on their own turf were far better fighters than black or white
U.S. cavalrymen, and without native scouts the army was virtually
helpless. But there were plenty of these scouts—Pawnee and Crow,
even Apache, Kiowa, or Sioux who had their own reasons to take arms
against their fellows. Mass cavalry charges were nonexistent, pitched
battles few and mostly won by the army: Colonel George Armstrong
Custer's famous 1876 debacle at the Little Bighorn was a rare exception. Given better tactics, artillery, and no women and children to slow
them, the army could not lose. But what really defeated the Indians was
attrition and loss of habitat. By the early 1880s white hunters with
repeating rifles had helped cut down what had once been millions of
buffalo to a few hundred. Hemmed in by farmers and miners, exhausted by cold and hunger, the last Sioux holdouts were finally pushed
onto their shrunken reservations for good within two years of slaughtering Custer's regiment.

The timing was different with different tribes—a handful of Apaches
under Geronimo held out until 1886—but by then virtually all Indian
people had been effectively disarmed and penned up. And their new

status meant a change in the treatment of Indian homicide that had existed since the seventeenth century.

Throughout this final era, as always, homicide was the most frequent single precipitant of war, or military action, while military action was sometimes, but not always, treated in white law as a legal excuse for it. White civilians who killed Indians were either killed in return by the victim's tribe or, given the refusal of juries to convict, effectively went free. The unrepentant J. M. Chivington, the Methodist minister/militia colonel who had slaughtered a whole village then under the sworn protection of the U.S. Army, went on a dramatic lecture tour with over one hundred scalps as stage props; no one indicted the Tucson vigilantes who killed, raped, and enslaved scores of peaceful Apaches in April 1871. Meanwhile individual Indians who killed whites were either for diplomatic reasons granted some kind of amnesty—as Lincoln's intervention at Fort Snelling—or tried and usually hanged as murderers. Finally, Indians who killed Indians in Indian country were in law ignored.

Early in the Republic, the native tribes had legally been declared "dependent nations." But on the reservation their status was not so clear; charismatic individual chiefs retained much of their influence, while formal power rested with white reservation agents and missionaries. The avowed end was to turn them into American citizens, farmers and Christians, but the end was not clearly in sight. As part of the conversion process, and in the tradition established by the Cherokee generations before, formal "Indian police" and "courts of Indian offenses" were organized on the agencies. But unlike the Cherokee, the plains Indians staffed but did not direct these institutions; the "courts" dealt only with violations of agency rules, and the police were appointed and controlled by the white agent in charge.

The ultimate legal question, as so much in Indian history, was precipitated by a murder, in this case on a Sioux reservation. On the Rosebud Reservation a long political quarrel between Chief Spotted Tail and Captain Crow Dog of the Indian police was settled by gunfire, as the captain, shortly after resigning from the force, simply shot down the chief in cold blood. The killer was immediately arrested by his exmates, and the white courts of Dakota Territory assumed jurisdiction and condemned him to die. But in 1883 the U.S. Supreme Court

ruled, in *ex parte Crow Dog,* that under existing law formal justice did
not cover intraracial killings on the reservation, arguing that it would
be unfair to try a people still moving out of a "savage" state according
to the alien rules of an "external and unknown code." Congress moved
in 1885 to close this loophole: the Indians might settle minor crimes in
their own fashion, but murder, manslaughter, felonious assault, rape,
arson, burglary, and larceny would be tried under the rules of the state
or territory surrounding the reservation. After nearly three centuries, in
short, any homicide in the United States, anywhere, and by anyone of
any race was to be treated under white rules.

Throughout the West, meanwhile, the spaces left by the natives were
increasingly filled with new people and economic activity, ranchers and
farmers, railroads and miners, towns and then cities. The process of
settlement was relatively quiet in some places, notoriously violent in
others. Given continual change and the enormous distances and social
variations between Abilene and San Francisco, it is hard to find any
single theme. But, with some regional exceptions, it may be said that
with respect to murder as with other matters, newcomers brought their
histories with them, and that after a period of sometimes brutal shaking
out new communities tended, with some especially sharp edges, to re-
create familiar patterns.

The farmers who settled places like Iowa and the Dakotas generally
came from either relatively peaceful places back east, the band stretching from Minnesota back through Maine, or from the Scandinavian
countries or Germany. Family men, or men who established families as
soon as they could, they brought settled traditions with them, and even
the hazards of the brutal climate and unsettled world of the Great Plains
could not easily push them over the edge into violent behavior.

It was different among the "cowboys," whose heyday began immediately after the Civil War, when wild cattle were rounded up in South
Texas and then herded hundreds of miles across unfenced plains to the
railheads of Kansas. But while the era of the "long drive" has lived for
generations in memory, it lasted less than ten years in reality before
farm settlement and barbed wire clogged the route. Gamblers and other
hustlers in the "cow towns" along the way were of course delighted in
general by the annual invasion from the Southwest, but not always as
pleased with the behavior of individual cowboys, or with each other.

Still, places like Abilene and Dodge City averaged no more than about 1.5 homicides per cattle trading season, and their marshals mostly concerned themselves, like their eastern counterparts, with arresting drunks and other misdemeanants. And it is a historian's unpleasant duty to inform readers steeped in Hollywood legend that nowhere in the Wild West, not ever, did any two cowboys or anyone else stand in the middle of a street, revolvers strapped to their sides, and challenge each other to a fatal "quick draw" contest.

Far more murderous than the cattle plains were the mountains of mining country, dotted with towns like Bodie, California, that flourished for a few brief years in the late 1870s and early 1880s. Bodie in its heyday suffered little from larceny or burglary and experienced few robberies and no recorded rapes. At the same time, as a town of about five thousand it witnessed at least twenty-nine murders and nonnegligent manslaughters between 1878 and 1882, which translates to the extraordinary rate of 116 per 100,000 annually.

The reason for both the low rate of most thefts and the high rate of killings seems identical; and in terms of murder, classic. Bodie's few women were mostly prostitutes, and in a get-rich-quick atmosphere its dominant male population, in Roger McGrath's classic formulation, was "young, single, intemperate and armed." A few rich drunks were eagerly rolled, but no one was foolish enough to try to rob a bank, barroom, or boardinghouse in a town bristling with shotguns round the clock. Overwhelmingly the killings resulted from fights between more or less willing contestants, the issues rarely money or even women but—as in the saloons of early republican Norfolk, or antebellum Philadelphia—simply honor itself, the stubborn refusal, especially when in liquor, to back down when challenged for the most trivial of reasons. And the tolerance for this behavior, the willingness to honor a plea of self-defense, was even more powerful than in the contemporary South: 40 men were arrested for homicide in the five years studied, 1 lynched, just 7 put on trial, and 1 (one!) found guilty.

The last classic ingredient in Bodie's lethal mixture was racial and ethnic difference: roughly half its 1880 population was foreign born, including 850 Irish, 300 Chinese, and 100 Mexicans. Like antebellum Philadelphians, Bodie's juries could generally treat these foreigners justly when they were brought to trial. But, as in the South and East, much western violence was racial, with the Apache Indians especially

ferocious in dealing with Mexicans, the Mexicans with Chinese, and
the dominant whites with all of them.

The Chinese brought to work on the railroads and later in the mines
were especially vulnerable. Bitterly resented by rival laborers, once the
major roads were built they settled in towns and cities, running small
businesses and doing odd jobs. Wholly unable to count on the white
court system, and often involved in illegal gambling, an honored occupation in their culture, they relied for a rough measure of justice and
protection on fraternal associations, sometimes gangs, or "tongs." Tong
rivalries themselves accounted for much murder within local Chinese
communities, but unlike Mexicans, Indians, or blacks, the Chinese
seem almost never to have retaliated against whites. Interracial homicide, then, ran almost wholly in one direction, with few prosecutions
and several mass killings.

In 1882 the U.S. Congress, responding to racist pressures and a series of violent incidents, mostly on the West Coast, passed the first of a
series of Chinese Exclusion Laws that effectively shut off immigration.
But the violence reached its height three years later in the coal mining
town run by the Union Pacific Railroad at Rock Springs, Wyoming.
Several hundred Chinese were brought into the area following a failed
strike, then a lockout, of angry white miners. After a brief turf battle on
September 2, 1885, a mob gathered outside the local "Chinatown" and
then moved in through its shacks and dugouts, driving out some inhabitants, murdering others, robbing all, and finally burning everything
to the ground. The bodies that remained, dead or alive, were mostly
incinerated; no count was possible, but the estimated number of victims
reached fifty by nightfall.

No one was ever indicted by the local authorities. The railroad was
above all eager to avoid further trouble and quickly put the Chinese
back to work. And with the cooperation of the U.S. Army, called in at
first to help the refugees, the Union Pacific arranged a unique penalty
for murder; known participants in the massacre were simply given back
pay and tickets out of Wyoming Territory.

The national press, in contrast, was almost wholly united in outrage,
but most papers seized on a rationale: "no one single person concerned
in the massacre was a native born American." Rock Springs was instead
the work of "the worst of our European immigrants: degraded Poles,
ignorant and besotted Hungarians, and lazy Italian convicts." This

handy, ironic—and utterly false—explanation helped, in later years, to erase the memory; the kind of violence represented at Rock Springs, which did no credit either to labor or to industry, was not really part of the American historical tradition.

The popular taste in western violence, then and later, ran neither to the drunken brawling of places like Bodie nor to the one-sided killings visited on the Chinese but instead to shootouts involving outlaws and lawmen. Men in both categories—there was much crossover—were almost instantly made figures of Myth, their stories told and exaggerated in the press, dime novels, and worshipful biographies. But there was a core of reality to it all. However encrusted by fantasy, the contemporary West was in fact often filled with murderous gunfire, the result first of the Civil War and always of weak law enforcement in a time of rapid economic development.

The greatest school for banditry after the war was banditry during the war, especially the mini–Civil War along the Kansas-Missouri border that had begun in the John Brown era. Wild Bill Hickok was among several gunmen who had fought on the antislavery side with Brown, but ex-Confederates hold the numerical record. Frank James was among Bill Quantrill's Raiders who burned the town of Lawrence in 1863 and murdered all its male inhabitants; his brother Jesse joined next year, at seventeen, in time to help slaughter seventy-five unarmed Union soldiers at Centralia, Missouri. This one guerrilla band also included the Daltons, the Youngers, and a host of other outlaws later made famous: one historian has found that roughly half of the 296 Raider alumni who can be identified by name went on to violent criminal careers.

Local law enforcement was severely disrupted when these men began raiding, and it remained weak and divided throughout their lives. Some of the West, still not organized into states, was administered by the federal government, which appointed county sheriffs and town marshals; with statehood these officers were elected or chosen by mayors or town councils. Either way the process was political, the lawmen often inept or defied by one local faction or another. And both horses and railroads carried outlaws quickly out of one town, county, or territory into another, where they were either unknown or had sheltering connections.

It was these connections that allowed the James brothers, America's favorite killers, to escape justice for so long. Riding typically with a dozen or so well-armed men, including the Youngers and other local guerrillas turned outlaw, they operated almost entirely in the South or border states during the Reconstruction era, trading openly on their Confederate histories. And Jesse, a strikingly handsome young man who eventually married a childhood sweetheart, had a kind of genius for public relations, granting occasional interviews that helped add a touch of sympathy to the fear they inspired in potential witnesses. The gang was the first to rob banks in broad daylight, the second to hold up trains, and it counted on the postwar unpopularity of rich corporations not only among the Missouri dirt farmers they came from but all over the country. The men murdered several people in the course of their robberies, many of them purely innocent bystanders: the very first was the ride-by shooting of a student at William Jewell College, and one casualty of a raid on the Kansas City Fairground was a ten-year-old girl. But they still managed to project a kind of Robin Hood image that endeared them to credulous readers and, more important, helped them to evade indictment.

In the absence of effective national police, the niche later filled by the Federal Bureau of Investigation, banks and railroads in the West even more than in the East often bypassed the usual machinery of local law enforcement by hiring their own private agents to cross county or state lines, above all the Pinkertons, who were then deputized or commissioned by compliant governors. In the case of the James brothers, however, the detective agency only burnished the legend of the poor outlaw as victim. The Pinkertons did kill John Younger in a shootout in March 1874, but lost three of their own. And the following year they shot themselves spectacularly in the feet. On the night of January 28, 1875, acting on a tip that Jesse was visiting home, several detectives threw a bomb into his boyhood cabin, killing his eight-year-old half-brother and tearing off his mother's arm. (The incident was exploited the next year in one of the Mollie Maguire trials, when the defense tried to discount a witness from the agency by placing him at the murder scene.)

The gang was only broken in the summer of 1876 when in its one move out of the South it attempted to rob the First National Bank of Northfield, Minnesota, got badly shot up by the local citizens, and lost three men killed. Cole Younger, arrested, copped a classic plea by explaining to a sympathetic reporter, "We were victims of circumstances. We were drove to it, sir." While the James boys themselves escaped, it was never the same. Following two unusually brutal railroad murders, the governor of Missouri in 1881 officially offered a huge $10,000 reward for either of them, dead or alive. Jesse, although never indicted for any crime, let alone convicted, was thus declared an "out-law" in the medieval sense of the phrase, a target and a temptation. And it was while living with his wife and children in a small cottage near St. Joseph, Missouri, under the alias "Howard," that he was shot in the back by Bob Ford, one of his own gang, while performing the quintessentially domestic act of adjusting a picture on the wall. Tragic ballads were already written and legends still growing when Frank surrendered five months later; with public sympathy and outrage on his side, he was acquitted of any crime and returned home to live as a quiet farmer.

But many elements of the James story were by then being repeated farther west. Giant railroads crossed the continent as early as the 1860s, and just as the extermination of the buffalo opened the plains to cattle, the impounding of the natives opened the whole country to white entrepreneurs, with ranchers and sheepmen, bankers and miners, gamblers, homesteaders, and speculators contending for dominance. As Civil War veterans with weaker local roots than the James brothers drifted west to find outlets for their talents, some of them murderous, many found robbery a tempting shortcut to all this new wealth, or cattle rustling a profitable supplement to small ranching. While the Missourians had helped make the Colt .45 a famous weapon, most of the serious shooting was done with sawed-off shotguns, as bankers and Pinkertons from Kansas to California alternated between chasing gunmen and hiring them.

The most notorious of these gunmen was William Bonney, a transplanted New York Irishman who moved out of Kansas to New Mexico Territory as "Billy the Kid." Later legend has him killing twenty-one (white) men, perhaps because he was himself just shy of his twenty-second birthday when shot down by a onetime friend, Sheriff Pat Garrett, for a $500 reward. An ugly little man, with none of the romantic qualities of Jesse James, contemporaries knew him simply as a "low-down, vulgar, cutthroat" and hired killer; but for a historian he is important above all as a symptom of the troubles afflicting the post-war West.

New Mexico was the most turbulent of territories, thinly settled, full of conflict between its long-established Mexican farmers and sheepherders and incoming cattlemen from Texas, who often staked out territory that had belonged to the older inhabitants for generations, while the Apache preyed on them all. It is symptomatic that the Kid's death total was usually given with a cynical caveat—"not counting Indians or Mexicans"—and that one of his employers, the cattle baron Colonel John Chisum, routinely ordered that any Indian or Mexican trespasser on his immense acreage be shot on sight. Chisum was the biggest single rancher in the territory, but his dominance in Lincoln County was challenged by several other banking, merchant, and grazing factions willing, like their counterparts all over the West, to hire their own gunmen whenever local sheriffs were either weak or hostile. Bonney was one of those brought in to fight the resulting Lincoln County War of 1875–81, before turning to simple banditry toward the end. But his own exploits pale before the estimated total of two hundred lives lost in that contest and the legacy it represented.

Racial hostility continued throughout the history of the territory. While the Apache were eventually confined to reservations, during the 1870s and 1880s, the Mexicans did not go away. Local champions like Elfego Baca contested Anglo dominance in the justice system directly, running successfully for sheriff, while Juan José Herrera organized the Gorras Blancas, or White Caps, an all-Mexican vigilante group that was accused of using murder as well as sabotage to fight against railroads and others who were strangling their way of life. Herrera's later move into elective office only underlined the deadly serious nature of politics in New Mexico, a place where sheriffs and local officials were routinely killed by the losing side. Uniquely in this country, in fact, political assassination seems to have established itself as a part of territorial culture, sometimes reaching to the highest levels. Albert B. Fall, New Mexico's leading politician and later its first senator, was suspected by many of arranging the 1896 murder of crusading Judge Albert Jennings Fountain and his little boy along a lonely road outside of Las Cruces, just as Jennings was leading a grand jury investigation of criminal activity in Lincoln County.

New Mexico is clearly an extreme case, and most western towns and counties were usually quiet places, their sheriffs little concerned with homicide and marshals more worried about stray dogs than killers. But the exceptions were real and numerous, and many boom areas hired enforcers with violent reputations to bring "order" with little concern for "law." Between 1886 and 1895 Sheriff John Slaughter, one of the richest ranchers of Cochise County, Arizona, simply shot twelve men to death while they were in his official custody; there were no official repercussions. And as Virgil and Wyatt Earp, their friend "Doc" Holliday, and scores of others moved easily from work as private guards to public lawmen, and occasionally to gambling, rustling, or robbery, it is impossible to keep score. Given the encrustations of legend, the fact that there were at least two sides to many of these men and every town they worked in, there is no one reliable version of what happened even during an encounter as famous as the 1881 Gunfight (or ambush?) at the O.K. Corral in Tombstone, Arizona; the killing of Frank and Tom McClaury and Billy Clanton by Holliday and the Earps may in fact have been murder, manslaughter, or justifiable homicide. In any case, the day of the gunfighter passed fairly quickly.

One barometer both of the extent of banditry and the weakness of regular law enforcement is the toll of deaths taken in formal vigilante movements: of over seven hundred known victims across all of American history, Richard Maxwell Brown has counted more than five hundred between 1860 and 1900, mostly in the plains and Far West, with Montana Territory leading all others. But as the various contenders for riches in the Wild West either won or lost, and as justice systems settled down, the count by decade shows a clear pattern: even as western populations shot up, the trend was down, with 179 during the 1860s, 125 in the 1870s, 107 in the 1880s, 25 in the 1890s, and just one lone "outlaw" hanged between 1900 and 1909. By that last date Billy the Kid was just beginning to be resurrected as a kind of hero, while the last of the famous bandits, Butch Cassidy and the Sundance Kid, had been driven out of the country by pursuing Pinkertons. And as of April 1915, when Frank James deprived Kearney, Missouri, of its only tourist attraction by dying peacefully in the cabin he had been born in, the business of train robbery, shootouts, and cattle rustling had pushed all the way west to the little town of Hollywood, California.

But violence in the West did not die out with the traditional badmen, nor did the Pinkertons and other private gunmen die out when they were no longer needed to fight them. Instead the focus simply shifted, as it had earlier across most of the nation, to issues involving capital and labor, with a murderous intensity seen nowhere else.

The more quickly and richly the West developed, the more it resembled the rest of America in the Age of the Robber Barons, but on a bigger western scale. As access to water and railheads became critical on the plains, small ranchers in general gave way to big ones. On the Pacific coast, operations once as simple as commercial fishing and lumbering increasingly demanded capital and large-scale operations. Nowhere was the change more dramatic than in the Rocky Mountains, where the quirky lone prospectors of legend soon gave way to giant mining corporations. As the more easily gathered precious metals on the surface quickly played out, mining for gold and silver became the kind of capital-intensive, technologically sophisticated business that mining for copper, lead, and coal had always been. At the same time mining, like other western industries, required unskilled laborers of a kind, and under conditions, that virtually guaranteed violence: single men mostly, concentrated in large numbers, employed by big impersonal corporations traditionally denounced for lacking "a body to kick or a soul to damn." And it was around the mines that labor trouble reached its most spectacular peaks.

The men who organized the Western Federation of Miners (WFM) were westerners and miners, wholly familiar with rifles and shotguns, professional experts in the use of dynamite. And when in 1892 the owners of the lead and silver mines around Coeur d'Alene, Idaho, locked them out after losing a strike, a small war broke out. Pinkerton guards killed a union man in July, the miners killed a Pinkerton, and at the cost of five more deaths blew up a refining mill, took two captives, and at gunpoint drove strikebreakers and guards out of the town. The state militia could not cope, court injunctions were ignored, and the governor called in the U.S. Army.

Ever since its 1877 withdrawal from the South, the army had been involved in labor disputes, usually helping to break strikes; with the end of the Indian Wars that became its main domestic duty. And in Idaho the Coeur d'Alene area was simply turned in effect into a military district, rebellious miners herded into outdoor bullpens and deported without trial.

From that date well into the twentieth century, elements of the same scenario were replayed continually throughout the mountains: armed confrontations and shootings, sometimes involving several hundred men on both sides, the militia, occasionally the army, martial law, bull-pens, and deportations. The justice systems in mining country, where the sole employers also owned everything from the boardinghouses to the grocery stores, were wholly distrusted—usually by the unions, sometimes by the owners. And in between the bigger strikes, murder and intimidation were part of the contest, dynamite blasts and shotgun ambushes sometimes monthly occurrences.

The Western Federation of Miners was the biggest single union to endorse the founding of the American Socialist party, in 1901, but peaceful reform within the political system was not enough for militants like Big Bill Haywood, the charismatic leader of the union. A year after failure in the Colorado Labor War of 1903–04, Haywood led his men into a wholly new kind of labor organization, the Industrial Workers of the World, or IWW, nicknamed the Wobblies. A full generation after the great Railroad Strike of 1877, nearly twenty years after Haymarket, the worst fears of much of middle-class America were realized. In powerful contrast to all older unions, and to the Socialist party, the new union in June 1905 declared its belief in revolution, renouncing politics in favor of direct action, including sabotage. Six months later there was apparent confirmation of what that might mean. On December 30, 1905, former governor Frank Steunenberg of Idaho, an old enemy of the Wobblies, opened the gate to his home in Caldwell and was blown to pieces by a bomb tied to a fish line.

The state of Idaho next day put up $15,000 in reward money, a sum that drew the immediate attention of the head of the Denver office of the Pinkerton Agency—the aging James McParlan, once the scourge of the Mollie Maguires. A shady sometime bodyguard of a high WFM official, a man then operating under the name "Harry Orchard," was quickly arrested; McParlan arranged to have him put in solitary confinement, with himself as sole visitor and confidant. The old detective proved a psychological master, flattering, threatening, and filling his subject's dim but suggestible brain with stories of his own glory days back East, and with visions of going free at once if he turned state's evidence. Orchard soon broke down and dictated a wild confession in which he not only admitted to scores of murders but painted a picture of the Wobblies that remarkably resembled the Mollies, with an inner circle covertly gathering to plot some twenty-six assassinations. Idaho officials then attempted to extradite Big Bill Haywood and two other WFM officers out of Colorado; failing that, they simply kidnapped them illegally and put them on trial for conspiracy to murder Frank Steunenberg.

No other issue had ever aroused American radicals like this one. Still comparatively weak but growing in numbers, socialists and Wobblies mounted huge demonstrations across the United States, singing the Marseillaise, talking national strike, even revolution, if the three should be convicted. The trial opened on May 9, 1907, as a powerful symbolic contest. Haywood was a colorful proletarian defendant, an ex-cowboy and homesteader who had lost one eye in a mining accident. The prosecution was led by young Idaho Senator William Borah, the opposition by a law partner of Colorado Senator Tom Patterson, together with Clarence Darrow, the most famous defense lawyer in the country. Borah established that Haywood knew that Harry Orchard had done the deed, but he had no other evidence besides the bomber's own baroque confession. Darrow ripped that document, and James McParlan, to pieces, and in final summations he had no oratorical peer. The judge, swayed neither by President Teddy Roosevelt's pretrial denunciation of Haywood nor by New York parades in his favor, instructed a jury mostly of Idaho farmers that Haywood was simply not guilty as charged. The other two defendants were later freed as well, while Harry Orchard, shortly sentenced to hang, had his sentence commuted to life.

But Haywood and the IWW would not stop scaring middle-class Americans. Besides miners, his Wobblies appealed on the ground mostly to western itinerants, often immigrants, lumberjacks, fishermen, and migrant agricultural workers, and on paper to radicals of every kind. His union organizers were hard to tell from railroad tramps; romantic figures, experts at propaganda, song singers and orators, they went where the trouble was and tried to make something out of it, organizing men whom no other union would or could help in any way. Given their numbers, a few union men, inevitably, were criminals; a few more, violent fanatics. On October 1, 1910, after months of street fighting in Los Angeles, John and James McNamara of the Iron Workers blew up the rabidly antiunion Los Angeles *Times* building; the explosion, which went off at 1:07 A.M., killed twenty people, all of them cleaning women and others working late, none of them bosses or edi-

torialists. Even Clarence Darrow could not free the brothers, who confessed in midtrial. But the most famous Wobblie martyr was Joe Hill, a
genuinely gifted songwriter, who was convicted of the robbery murder
of a Salt Lake City grocer in 1914. The jury did not buy his classic
alibi—that he'd spent the night with a married woman he gallantly
refused to name—and under Utah law he was shot by a five-man firing squad on November 19, 1915; his last shouted words were "Don't
mourn for me, boys—Organize!"

But however murderous a few of their number, members of the
IWW were far more often victims than perpetrators of violence—shot
by company guards, hounded by sheriffs, sometimes lynched by ill-
organized and panicky "vigilantes." More than the occasional picket
line fatalities back East, involving blacks or Hungarians against Irish
workers, killings involving the Wobblies represented direct confrontation between labor and capital, reminding Americans everywhere that
murder was one of the weapons in both arsenals and keeping alive the
illusory specter of Red Radical Revolution in the United States.

4

But the great irony of the period following the Civil War was that while
the conflict between labor and capital was often murderous, and created
fears even wider than those of slave insurrection before the war, the
dominant tendency of the contemporary urban industrial revolution in
most of the country was to push homicide rates down, well down from
their antebellum peak.

What happened after the war was in some ways what reformers had
worked toward before it. The abolition of slavery was obviously important; wage labor, whatever conflicts it generated, did not rest on the
continual use of physical force. But some of the other antebellum reforms also took hold, even in areas where slavery had not reached directly. The ones that worked best were those directed at creating a more
orderly society—among other things, a less murderous society—rather
than those romantic reforms that attempted to change hearts and souls
more profoundly.

Attempts to abolish capital punishment, to make penitentiaries truly
reform their inmates, to abolish prostitution—none of these died, but

none was fully relevant to the demands of the new industrial order, and none flourished as they had earlier. In contrast, the police, the temperance movement, the public schools—the items on the reform agenda designed to discipline the population—were successful as never before. And underlying all of them were the direct demands of the new kind of work itself, which helped create a whole new social psychology. And as the urban industrial revolution finally took off in the United States, the most dramatic single index of this change in mass social psychology was a substantial drop in the homicide rate—a phenomenon noted all over the developed world—together with a rise in suicide.

One striking difference between the antebellum and postbellum years was that big urban police departments decisively won the battle for the streets. Some elements of the move toward a more effective force were already in place before the Civil War ended. New York had uniformed its reluctant cops as early as 1853, Philadelphia in 1860, Chicago in 1863. Telegraphic communication between big city stations was generally established by the 1850s. The effect of the Draft Riots was to kill any reluctance to provide the men with revolvers, and the outcome of the war helped establish a stable two-party system, from the local level on up, and provide the authorities with the continuity and confidence to use the force decisively.

The volatile combination of street gangs, volunteer fire companies, and racial/ethnic tensions did not disappear immediately, and riot did not recede without a fight. At the same time, as noted, the conflict between labor and capital often heated up dramatically. But as city departments put a heavy emphasis on battle-readiness and drill, only the great Railroad Strike of 1877 proved, in general, too much for them to handle on their own. Sometimes the reluctance of local cops to step in against strikers made it necessary to call in the militia, and during a few race riots, mostly in the South, they stood by without seriously intervening. But otherwise the most famous urban "riots" of the late nineteenth and early twentieth century were simply occasions when, as at Haymarket Square, the cops or the military attacked badly outgunned and often peaceful demonstrators.

With every passing decade the police advantage grew. As late as 1870, in Philadelphia, a raid on a downtown gambling house had been successfully thrown back by small arms fire; just ten years later that would be unthinkable. Call boxes, signal systems, then telephones and paddy wagons that could deliver ten or fifteen beefy men to the site of a disturbance, and, by the second decade of the twentieth century, automobiles—all made it easier, whenever the will was there, to put down most riotous occasions before they got out of hand and truly murderous.

The job was eased still further by a host of changes in the nature of big city life. The level of violence among arriving immigrants was determined both by their earlier history—that is, the culture they brought with them, especially their attitudes toward drinking, fighting, and social authority—and by the state of the cities they settled into. No ethnic group in the later nineteenth or early twentieth century, neither the Jews fleeing pogroms nor the Italians devastated by cholera, was as desperate as the midcentury Irish, or as collectively pugnacious. The growing urban industrial economy and a variety of support systems made it easier to absorb newcomers. The outcome of the Civil War, too, helped cool racial violence. African Americans, no longer in the eye of the storm, now had the vote, some political protection, a few jobs on the police force. Equally important, the once easy sport of "hunting the nigs" got more dangerous as black communities got bigger and better able to fight back.

Young men still joined street gangs, and the bachelor subculture did not wholly die out. The line between horsing around with the guys and deadly combat was still thin. Owen Wister, in another context, caught it right: "When you call me that, smile." But there were now alternatives to fighting as a form of entertainment; ethnic ball clubs and prize fights among African-American, Irish, and Jewish gladiators helped sublimate aggression short of homicide. By the 1890s, in an important move, boxing matches were fought with gloves on. Bicycle expeditions to amusement parks, later cheap movies, provided truly harmless things to do, and organized rackets and political street work were less mindlessly violent than random riot.

But the drop in homicide rates that began during the late nineteenth century is far too widespread to be explained in terms of cutting down on riot deaths in American cities. Everywhere it has been studied in the developed world, from Stockholm, Sweden, south to Sydney, Australia, from London across the Atlantic to New York and Philadelphia, then on west to Oakland, the rates of all violent crime, however measured, were declining at the same time. A phenomenon that broad is best explained in terms of the most fundamental economic and social change in the period: the urban industrial revolution itself.

Before the Civil War, the efforts of reformers and businessmen to create a more orderly workforce, as described in chapter 4, had been swamped by the invasion of disorderly Irish immigrants. But the Irish were, or remained, disorderly mostly because of chronic underemployment: during the 1840s and 1850s there was simply too little unskilled or semiskilled work to do in cities. It was in the decades after the war, the most economically expansive in our history, that the urban industrial revolution really took off. This was the era that created the physical city that still exists: high-rise buildings, libraries, ball parks, and museums, all of them enabled by the great manufactories, then new, now all but gone. And at the same time as this upsurge in blue-collar opportunities, the invention of the typewriter, the telephone, and the department store, together with expanding local government, created an explosion in white-collar office jobs as well. The common denominator in all this work was regular, predictable, cooperative behavior, the same kind that made the trains and trolleys run, and kept great crowds of tens or even hundreds of thousands of people moving peacefully to and from work, every day, at the same hours.

Increasing sobriety was essential to the change. Despite much hypocrisy and corruption, liquor control was the biggest single item on the police agenda. Cops arrested drunks in staggering numbers, and were charged by lawmakers with limiting the days, hours, and number of places where liquor might be sold, sometimes to hold off the more extreme reformers, led most famously by the Women's Christian Temperance Union, who legally dried up whole towns, counties, and states. Saloon keepers cooperated with cops by throwing out unruly customers, cooling off potential trouble. By the time of World War I, across the nation, the average yearly alcohol intake had dropped substantially, and the federal government was on the eve of prohibiting the sale of liquor altogether.

Education, with its stress on schoolroom discipline, was almost equally important. While public schools had been established in much of the country during the 1850s, attendance had not usually been required by law. But between 1870 and 1900 the average yearly number of school days per pupil jumped from seventy-eight to ninety-nine, the average number of eligible children attending from 57 to 72 percent. In the context of controlling violence, as important as the three Rs was the continued stress on learning how to do repetitive tasks, cope with boredom and frustration, and curb impulsive behavior and aggression.

Factory and office, finally, reinforced and rewarded this learned behavior and (relative) sobriety. And a measure of the successful change in mass social psychology is provided by the statistics of homicide in Philadelphia, then the city with the broadest industrial base in the United States. Between 1839 and 1859, measured by indictments for homicide as described in chapter 4, the city's murder rate stood at 3.6 per 100,000 annually. That number dropped between 1860 and 1880 to 3.2, and between 1881 and 1901 to just 2.5, the same downward trend observed in much of the developed world.

But while these homicide figures help describe what was happening, and when, they do not explain why. Two additional sets of clues help provide a psychological explanation for what was happening in the industrial city: the statistics for the other kinds of violent death, suicide and accident.

On the one hand, while the urban industrial revolution created wholly new ways of dying—through electric shock, or falling down elevator shafts—in Philadelphia the rate of old-fashioned or "simple" accidents such as drowning fell dramatically. During 1869–71 the age-standardized rate of drowning was 18.5 per 100,000 a year; by 1899–1901 it had fallen to 8.0. And while the statistics of suicide are notoriously unreliable, as friends and family sometimes cover up what is thought a shameful death, the opposite movement here is even less mistakable. The suicide figures, standardized to account for a slightly aging population, more than doubled between the 5.8 per 100,000 officially recorded in 1868–72 and the 12.2 in 1899–1901.

How to account for these three strong trends in violent death? Social scientists have long noticed that homicide rates are often high in groups whose suicide rates are low, that moving from the bottom toward the top of the scale of income and education the homicide rate falls as suicide rises. An even sharper focus is offered by the suicide-murder ratio, or SMR, the result of dividing the suicide rate by the sum of both rates.

The SMR, invented by the psychologist Martin Gold, is based on the concept that both kinds of death are expressions of extreme frustration, manifested as aggression. Homicide is the result of aggression directed outward, at others; suicide results from aggression directed inward, at the self. Another way of putting it is that homicide is characteristic of people of "honor," suicide of people of "dignity." A low ratio, as among low-income groups, indicates a tendency toward outward aggression; a higher number, as among the educated middle class, indicates a tendency toward inward aggression, and the equation as a whole shows that both rates tend to be higher among groups, such as males, with a stronger tendency toward aggression in either form. The figures for accident, in this model, tend simply to reinforce those for homicide, the accident prone being remarkably similar to the homicidal in their tendency to alcoholic, reckless behavior, to the quick acceptance of physical challenges along the riverbank or on the street.

Put in motion, over time, the SMR explains exactly what was happening to the whole of the urban industrial population, indeed the whole of the United States after the Civil War. Even more important than income, among men, was the nature of occupation and education. American suicide rates, in the late nineteenth century, were lowest among people who did the older kinds of work: merchants and traders as well as farmers and teamsters. The rates were higher among those whose work demanded formal education, close supervision, or both: modest mill workers and clerks as well as higher-status doctors and lawyers. And in Philadelphia as a whole, over time, as the population grew less free-swinging and more sober, regimented, and introspective, suicide rose as murder fell.

The connection between this change and the nature of work is best illustrated by the different histories of three different ethnic groups.

The city's Irish, once infamous for their violence, over the late nineteenth century went to parochial school, got their knuckles rapped when they got rambunctious, and graduated into jobs in factories, offices, and most famously the civil service, where they again learned to stand in line, keep out of trouble, do the job, and wait for promotion. And as they stopped spitting into each other's drinks and settling disputes with fists, feet, and bricks—earlier in the century bricks had been known in some quarters as "Irish confetti," sprinkled freely about on festive occasions—their murder rates dropped. Once the highest of any major group in Philadelphia, toward century's end the rate among those of Irish surnames fell to 1.8 per 100,000, or well below the citywide average.

The direction among African Americans was tragically different. No group in the city, or indeed the nation, made greater strides in education, as the postwar promise of freedom and legal citizenship made schooling the apparent key to opportunity. In Philadelphia, between the 1850s and the 1890s, the black literacy rate soared from about 20 percent to over 80 percent; even in the South, by century's end, the majority at least of young adults could write their names and figure. No period in African-American history witnessed more cultural achievement, as colleges, newspapers, and churches multiplied and knit communities together in mutual support.

Across the whole of the country the number of the highly educated, doctors first, many of them women, and then lawyers, grew at an astonishing pace. But in terms of economic gain, all of that learning, for most, went heartbreakingly for nothing. Few African Americans could afford to hire the professionals who had sacrificed so hard for their degrees, and fewer whites wanted to. And as a result, after reaching a peak in 1910, the proportion of doctors and lawyers in the black population plummeted and did not recover for three generations. There was simply no basis of economic support below the professional level. In an age of truly implacable "scientific" racism, the most qualified of school graduates were unable to ring their dark faces with white collars, to join the new urban army of clerks, typists, and salespeople. Unions and employers combined to keep blacks out of the new factory work, too, for which they were fully qualified, and many were driven out of the older kinds of blue-collar skilled work as carpenters, masons, and plumbers, jobs that they had long held in many cities. They were not only denied a chance to grab at the fabled American "ladder of opportunity" but in many cases actually kicked off.

The effect of denial and despair, of being confined to medieval jobs in a modern world, was ominous. Many of the most ambitious were driven into dangerous careers in bootlegging, gambling, and prostitution, where business disputes had to be settled physically, without taking them to the courts. African Americans living in high crime areas, still fearful of whites, carried guns, once rare in their communities, more often than whites. And in Philadelphia, inevitably, their rate of indictment for murder, in the antebellum years only moderately high and lower than the Irish, rose raggedly just as the Irish sank, and it had reached 11.4 per 100,000 by the 1890s.

By that time, however, these rates were exceeded by those of a third group, those born in Italy, whose story further underlines the point. Philadelphia's "murder rates" for the early twentieth century are for technical reasons measured not by indictments, as above and in chapter 4, but by the comparatively lower rate of actual convictions, sentences to death or the penitentiary. Between 1901 and 1907, this rate among non-Italian whites was just 1.3 per 100,000 annually; and among blacks, 12.9. But the Italians, arriving often as single men, came from the nation with the highest homicide rate in Europe; their dispositions not improved by the ocean voyage, their arsenals upgraded by the American gun culture, as newcomers they killed each other and occasional bystanders often enough to reach the truly astonishing homicide conviction rate of 26.5 per 100,000.

But unlike the blacks, the Italians were admitted into factory work, won some security, settled down into lives with legitimate economic futures for themselves and their families. And while the African-American conviction rate stayed high, the Italian rate went down, and by 1908–15 had fallen to about the black level, at 11.4 per 100,000 and dropping fast.

For the whole of the first two decades of the twentieth century, meanwhile, as evidence of the power of the urban industrial revolution to change murderous behavior, the rates among non-Italian whites continued to fall, as they had for decades, reaching 0.7 in 1915–21.

Throughout most of the period after the Civil War, the nature of homicide in Philadelphia remained much the same as before it, with some changes in names and ethnicity. The stories behind all indictments through 1901 and a sampling of indictments plus arrest reports in the years 1902, 1908, and 1914 tell us that men and women were still being killed over cards, words, and dirty looks. The great majority of the killers, as before, were not clearly found in the city directories: young men mostly, with few skills, often transients or new arrivals to the urban industrial city, with only an occasional member of the middle or upper middle classes.

One form of homicide, however, did typically involve people of respectable status—that is, murder-suicide, as would be suggested by the concept of the SMR. These killers, not as young as most, were usually married, often white-collar workers, skilled craftsmen, even professionals. And while not available for either arrest or indictment through the justice system, beginning in 1914 they were listed and described in incident reports filed by the Philadelphia police. There were seven cases that year, a significant fraction of the sixty-seven of all kinds; all but one of them involved passionate love, jealousy, or domestic despair, as when, just before killing themselves, forty-two-year-old Wesley Wharton shot thirty-eight-year-old Agnes Welch for refusing to live with him, or thirty-five-year-old Alexander Glaser, going blind, shot his sleeping wife.

Otherwise, the proportion of incidents occurring in the home after the Civil War stayed nearly the same as before it, at about 25 percent, and so did those occurring in the street or saloon, which moved from a little under to a little over 50 percent. Rational motivation of any sort remained rare; in the three twentieth-century years sampled, although the accounts are murky in many cases, just 2 among 174 incidents of murder and manslaughter clearly involved robbery or intent to rob. In fact robbery at gunpoint was so rare in the urban East that when there was a holdup in a Bronx saloon, in November 1895, the story was headline news in Philadelphia and ran for a week; the New York cops could figure only that it must have been done by troupers from Buffalo Bill's Wild West Show, then playing the town.

Statistically the most significant increase over the years was in the use of firearms; after holding flat for most of the nineteenth century at about 25 percent, the proportion of gun deaths in the early twentieth century leaped up over 40 percent. The jump is the clear result of a population shift, the upsurge of immigration, and especially of murder indictments among African Americans and Italians, two groups more likely than others to carry lethal weapons.

By then a third race was established in the city; a small "Chinatown" had evolved in the 1890s, composed mostly of fugitives from violence and intolerance out West. The newcomers brought their institutions with them, on a small scale, and the peace of Race Street, as in San Francisco, was occasionally disturbed by tong rivalries and pistol fire. The rare crime brought to the justice system posed serious fair trial problems, with the official interpreter in at least one case a member of a tong hostile to the accused. And it was a "tong war" that led to the proceedings against Jung Jow and Mock Kung, two young men who were hanged in March 1908 for shooting a rival leader, on orders, they insisted, of the dominant Hip Sing.

Infanticide remained the same dreary problem throughout the nineteenth century, but during the early twentieth century indictments all but dried up, the apparent result of two changes that greatly eased the situation of single mothers. The more important was the invention of pasteurized cow's milk, which made it far easier for desperate young women to leave infants at the poorhouse or foundling home with some real hope that they might survive. The other was the growing practice—although still not routine, especially for poorer women—of giving birth in hospitals, with care available and witnesses about.

The fact that murder and other crimes were clearly more common among the poor had, in the era of antebellum reform, suggested that the causes might be environmental, that crime was the result of deprivation, the lack of decent family life, bad education, desperation. But since then there had been a dramatic change in the prevailing intellectual climate, the result in part of the growing prestige of the sciences, above all biology, as the result of the widespread intellectual acceptance of the Darwinian theory of evolution. And by the late nineteenth century the dominant idea was no longer that criminals were basically souls like the rest of humanity, who might ideally be reformed, but that they were truly different, mentally and even physically inferior to other people, and looked it.

The change was the work specifically of Cesare Lombroso, an Italian psychiatrist, who published a book in 1876 that claimed, on the basis of skull measurements taken in prisons and insane asylums, that murderers were brutish types, with low foreheads, beetling brows, and small brains. These and other criminal types were "atavisms," he argued, throwbacks to an earlier stage of human evolution. This was an idea taken from the pseudoscience of Social Darwinism, which had flourished even before Charles Darwin's 1871 publication of the *Descent of Man*, and (with no support from Darwin himself) attempted to range people, indeed whole races, along an imagined scale from "low" to "high." In the United States, the sociologist Robert Dugdale in 1877 published *The Jukes*, a highly influential study of a clan of upstate New

Yorkers full of crazies and evildoers of many kinds. Despite his often inaccurate genealogies and vague definitions, Dugdale, like Lombroso, helped to underline the idea that crime, perhaps especially homicide, is primitive, inherited behavior and, at the extreme, that killers and other lawbreakers are a kind of distinctive subspecies.

But however popular in intellectual circles, the idea that murderers are obviously "primitive" did not fit the vicarious experience most Americans got through their newspapers. Much of the appeal of Jesse James was his romantic good looks, and while homicide was statistically most common among the poor and desperate, it was not the routine street fights but murder among the respectable, ideally the rich and famous, that got the ink and the attention. The most notorious cases of the day involved schoolteachers, ministers, or congressmen, colorful incidents like the shooting of Wall Street speculator Jim Fisk by another one, Ned Stokes, in 1872, or in 1906 the death of the leading architect Stanford White at the hands of Harry K. Thaw, a jealous husband and young heir to millions. And while few in Philadelphia got national attention, among its many hundreds of killings there were a sprinkling involving professionals and other members of the middle class such as Dr. Albert Goerson, hanged in 1885 for poisoning his wife and daughter. And then, beginning in 1895, the case of thirty-four-year-old Herman Webster Mudgett more than compensated for any earlier lack of local notoriety.

From the perspective of our own day, one of the most striking things about analyzing the long string of homicide indictments in the City of Brotherly Love is the near-absence of rape or sex killings among them: just one child murderer in the 1870s, another, homosexual, in the 1890s. Throughout the nineteenth century murders of this type were rarely prosecuted, in part because sex killers, however crazy, were more likely than most others to act secretively and escape the undeveloped system of criminal detection of the day, and in part, it seems, because there were simply not as many of them as there are now. And during the century's final decade, neither Philadelphia nor the nation was ready for cases like that of Mudgett, or Dr. H. H. Holmes, who long held a unique place in the annals of American crime.

Mudgett's bizarre and almost incredibly complex story began to come to light when he was arrested in Boston on November 16, 1895, and transported to Philadelphia for arraignment in an elaborate murder-for-insurance scheme. It was in Chicago, the previous year, as Dr. H. H. Holmes, that he had persuaded one Benjamin Pitezel and his very reluctant wife, Carrie, to go along with a plan to insure Pitezel's life for $10,000 and then fake his death, substituting a stolen corpse. It was with this in mind that Mudgett set up Pitezel in business in Philadelphia as "B. F. Perry," and then—skipping the part about another body—caught him in a drunken stupor, chloroformed him, and set up a small fake explosion that obliterated some of his features.

Over the next several months, simultaneously trying to conceal her husband's death from Carrie and diddle her out of her share of the scheme, Mudgett in effect kidnapped three of the Pitezel children, took them traveling over much of the Northeast, strangled and buried little Howard outside Cincinnati, then gassed Alice and Nellie in Toronto. But the scheme was revealed by one Marion Hedgepath, a train robber with whom Mudgett (at the time posing as "H. M. Howard") had been jailed for an unrelated swindle in St. Louis. Mudgett had promised the bandit a share of the Pitezel insurance money if he would help find a cooperative lawyer. Hedgepath did supply a name, heard about the $10,000, and when he got no cut wrote directly to the Fidelity Mutual Company.

Once Mudgett was in custody and Pinkertons and others hired by Fidelity began to trace his path across several states, it was found that he was married to three women, was wanted in Texas for horse theft, and had lived for several years in Chicago. It was there, as Dr. Holmes, that he ran a drugstore and with various legal and illegal funds built a huge and curious many-chambered "castle" full of trapdoors and chutes, leading to a giant incinerator. Up through his trial, in late October, he continued to assert innocence of murder but admitted to fraud, to having planted an already dead body in Pitezel's place, freely volunteering that as a former medical student, with much knowledge and curiosity about human anatomy, he had often trafficked in corpses for purposes both of dissection and deception. Toward the end he changed the story to read that Pitezel had committed suicide. And once convicted, in the months before his hanging in May 1896, he opened up another line entirely, giving out several "confessions" to a fascinated reading public, in the last of which he boasted of some twenty-seven murders all told, mostly by asphyxiation, strangulation, and chloroform.

A handsome man of thirty-four, his brown beard barbered as neatly as his fashionable clothes were tailored, Mudgett was as full of lies as of charm: some of his alleged victims turned out to be still alive. But the old "castle" back in Chicago, examined shortly before it was destroyed in flames, did in fact yield burned traces of human remains, and several people closely associated with him, many of them young women, boarders and mistresses, had in fact disappeared mysteriously. He admitted at one point to raping young Alice Pitezel, then fifteen, before her death, and there were at least hints of necrophilia in the accounts of some killings.

Mudgett's criminal career coincided closely with that of London's "Jack the Ripper"; the papers, having exhausted "fiend" and "monster," invented the word "multi-murderer" to describe him. The term "serial killer" would not be coined until late in the twentieth century; by whatever name, he appears to be America's first.

5

Philadelphia's justice system evolved slowly over the years. The clearest trend was the declining role of the trial jury, a change noted all over the United States. Criminal and especially homicide trials in the colonial era had been dominated by magistrates, often part-time amateurs; the early Republic had for ideological reasons stressed the role of citizen-jurors. But in an age when the legal profession above all valued order and efficiency, jurors were the unpredictable wild cards in the system. As always before, the twelve men in the box often undermined careful precedents and black letter law by in effect finding excuses to punish folks they thought had earned it and to free those who had not on the basis not of the evidence but of their own moral judgment. A favorite out, whatever the law might say about the M'Naghten rule, for example, was "temporary insanity" as a means of exonerating attractive women who had killed faithless lovers, or abandoned servant girls who had strangled newborns. And elite reformers were notably worried about the intelligence and impartiality of immigrant juries, especially in cities.

But to counter these unruly amateurs, the nineteenth century witnessed the rise of the professional public prosecutor. In many states and jurisdictions it was still the coroner who played the key role in homicide investigation, such as it was. That role often pushed out of the realm of simple fact, or cause of death, into the realm of law, or legal responsibility for death. Drawing on common law distinctions, a coroner's jury might find not only that a given case was an "excusable" homicide—that is, an accident, with no legal liability involved—but "justifiable" as well. This last category stretched from the clearest case—legal execution—to others not always so clear, in the absence of surviving witnesses, as when a policeman shot down a criminal while defending his own life (the only case in which such a homicide was generally "justified") or a home owner in mortal fear killed an armed invader. This kind of decision short-circuited the whole indictment/trial process entirely and was one of the reasons why district attorneys, as in New York, now took charge of cases from the beginning.

But prosecutors had their own ways of getting past juries. This was the period when for the first time many cases were disposed of through plea bargaining among defendants, their lawyers, and the district attorney. The issue was not overcrowded dockets, the pressures of too many cases, but simply uncertainty on both sides about what a jury might do. Guilty pleas, once rare, were now routinely exchanged for shorter sentences. Accused killers in the late nineteenth and early twentieth century were often indicted for more than one count of homicide, both murder and manslaughter, allowing not only juries to decide at the end of trial but defendants to choose before or even during it. In first-degree cases in the city of Philadelphia only 7 such pleas, still, were recorded in the twenty years between 1860 and 1880, but the number then shot up to 149 between 1881 and 1901. During the 1890s more cases were pleaded than went to trial; and although the proportion dropped early in the next century, it still remained high, at nearly 40 percent.

One clue to an increasing professional efficiency in the prosecutor's office, and his ability to dominate grand juries, was that fewer and fewer indictments were for any reasons dropped before trial. Back in the period 1839–45, fully 28 of 96 men and women indicted for homicide were never brought to the dock; by 1895–1901, only 9 of 215. And at the same time, from the 1870s on, district attorneys exercised their authority in another way, bringing in charges of voluntary manslaughter for incidents involving clearly accidental deaths.

What this change reflects is an increasing if left-handed stress on the importance of life, an insistence that homicide of any kind is intolerable, that any killing must be weighed and judged through the full official mechanisms. In the late nineteenth and early twentieth century, incidents that would never in earlier times have gotten past a coroner's inquest were brought further into the justice system, deaths from exploding boilers or firecrackers, "no-fault" traffic accidents—a trend that underscores the fact that more serious voluntary homicides were actually in decline.

The urban industrial city's insistence on peaceful behavior, its lower threshold of tolerance for violence, is reflected also in the tendency of jurors to favor the prosecution. However gradual, the shift was striking: while only a little over one-third of murder indictments had resulted in convictions of any kind before the Civil War, the proportion reached nearly two-thirds during the late nineteenth and early twentieth century. Consistent, too, with the growing condemnation of killing of any kind, Philadelphia's justice system was ever more reluctant, in most cases, to invoke the death penalty.

The city's prosecutors still headed the list of indictments in most cases with murder in the first degree, and jurors agreed in a few— twelve in the three sampled twentieth-century years. But eight of those convicted were spared in the end, less through the judicial process of appeal than through the essentially political process of commutation by the governor.

Just one of the twelve first-degree convicts, Harry Shappello, won an appeal. On retrial his 1914 sentence for shooting his wife was reduced to second-degree murder. But Philadelphia's homicide trials, conducted in the regular quarterly county courts, were not often appealed successfully to the supreme court of Pennsylvania, and never beyond that to the U.S. Supreme Court. Across the country in general the grounds for appeal, although loosening somewhat, were still extremely stiff by the standards of the late twentieth century. The Bill of Rights was not then generally held to apply to the states, which interpreted their own criminal codes as they chose and often allowed, for example, evidence found in searches without warrants.

The most careful study of the criminal appeals process for the period is of Oakland, California, between 1870 and 1910, and there, too, criminal appeals were rare and successful ones rarer still. While any death sentence called for an automatic appeal in California, as in a few progressive states (Pennsylvania was not one of them), only two of seven sentenced to hang escaped the noose. And in noncapital cases appeals were expensive, the grounds thin and stiff, most convicts poor and without influence; only 4 percent of all murder convictions were appealed on any ground, with the same general lack of success. From coast to coast the county criminal courts were for all purposes laws unto themselves, with higher courts far away and the federal system virtually nonexistent.

Philadelphia's Judge Robert Ralston in 1911 published an indignant book entitled *The Delay in the Execution of Murderers,* outlining what he believed was a process entirely too cumbersome and lengthy. In the city, since only one judge served on a first-degree case, an immediate appeal might be made after the verdict to a panel of three other county judges, on the grounds that the decision was against the weight of the evidence. Appeal to the state supreme court could be made only after sentence had been passed. After the high court affirmed a conviction the matter then went to the governor, whose decision as to whether or not to commute or pardon was reviewed with the help of a board of pardons, consisting of the lieutenant governor, attorney general, secretary of the commonwealth, and secretary of labor, or any three of them. The next to last step was the governor's signing of the death warrant. Then, given a decent interval for the condemned to reflect and perhaps repent, the hangman took over for the last one.

Despite Ralston's impatience, the process was reasonably brisk, given the several steps involved. Of the 66 first-degree verdicts declared in Pennsylvania between 1896 and 1902, the modal time between calling a jury and execution was between 10 and 11 months, with only 18 stretching a year or more, the longest just 2 years. The modal first-degree jury trial, including the selection of the panel, took just 2 days, with the longest lasting only 17, and a handful 10 or 12. Appeals to the three-judge review panel were in fact "almost invariable," at least in Philadelphia, and 41, or nearly two-thirds, were appealed to the state supreme court. But there were only two second trials granted, one by a Philadelphia three-judge panel, one by the supreme court on the grounds that inadmissable evidence of a prior conviction had been allowed. And there were only two other reversals (involving a single case, with two defendants), on the grounds that detectives had not shown that a confession was properly obtained. In one other case the highest court ruled that a condemned man, on the record, had not been asked to say anything before sentence of death was pronounced upon him: Jonas Preston Jr., of Chester County, was then allowed a two-month respite, given his say, and lawfully hanged on May 20, 1899.

The political process, as represented by the board of pardons, was a better bet to save men from execution than the process of legal appeal. After reviewing supporting letters and petitions, the governor and his allies commuted thirteen death sentences to life in prison, about a fifth of all cases. But even more political, and far more merciful, were the trial juries who, reflecting the sense of the community, convicted so rarely of first-degree murder in the first place.

Pennsylvania's general reluctance to take life was fully in tune with national trends, as the antebellum movement to make death discretionary, even in first-degree murder cases, reached more than half the states. While real prison reform was mostly stalled, around the turn of the century the optimism of the Progressive Era helped revive the long dormant movement to abolish capital punishment, and Arizona, Oregon, Washington, Kansas, and the Dakotas all joined in during the first two decades of the new century. Meanwhile actual judicial executions had in fact been declining raggedly across all of the United States since its founding, the most spectacular drop occurring just as the nation emerged from the colonial period—when in some years it had occasionally reached 35 per 100,000 (counting slaves)—down to between 3 and 4 per 100,000. By 1900 it had fallen well below 2, the figures swollen by hangings in the South and West, far lower in the industrial North and East. In the Commonwealth of Pennsylvania itself the great urban industrial cities of Pittsburgh and Philadelphia accounted for proportionally far fewer executions than the more rural counties. And in Philadelphia at least, by the early twentieth century there would have been very few indeed, except for an ominous racial trend.

Throughout the later as in the earlier nineteenth century, the justice system—like those in Boston, New York, and even bloody Bodie, California—had treated all races with remarkable evenhandedness. In Philadelphia, barring the murky problems posed by riots, blacks who killed whites got the same kinds of verdicts and sentences as whites who killed blacks. White victims in these cases, when not obvious aggressors on the street, were typically co-workers, lovers, or drinking companions

of the accused African Americans, men or women of some social distance from judges and most jurors. While Philadelphia's black community was until the first decade of the twentieth century the biggest
in the North, the city did not share white southern fears or paranoia
about blacks. Among other things the rare cases involving alleged interracial rape were handled like all others, and the prevailing racist stereotype, at least among the elite, was voiced by Judge Peter Gordon in
1893: "There is nothing in history that indicates that the colored race
has a propensity to acts of violent crime; on the contrary, their tenden-
cies are most gentle, and they submit with grace to subordination"—a
fact the judge ascribed to centuries of servitude.

Both stereotype and treatment, however, changed with dramatic
suddenness in the late 1890s. In 1897 Marion Stuyvesant was for a time
accused of murdering his middle-class white employer, and then in
1898 Face Epps and Sam Dodson pushed an elderly grocer to her death
during a clumsy robbery. But the real turning point arrived symbolically in the century-turning year 1900, when three black transients
robbed a socially prominent lawyer, Roy Wilson White, and beat him
to death with an iron bolt just outside the Broad Street Station. The
three accused men, in order to avoid any charge of legal lynching, were
fiercely defended in an unusually long trial by a group of volunteers
from the Philadelphia bar. But they were sentenced to die nonetheless.
And two years later William Lane found no champions at all.

Lane, a butler in the household of Mrs. Ella Forbush, a moderately
rich widow, stabbed his employer to death during a quarrel on April
Fool's Day, 1902. He then summoned her two little girls, aged seven
and ten, into the kitchen and slit their throats. He was arrested immediately, at a time when the grand jury was in session, indicted that afternoon, pleaded guilty the next morning, and despite obvious signs of
insanity—he had made no attempt at concealment, and claimed not to
remember anything after the first murder—was sentenced to death the
day after that and hanged just fifty-one days later, a local record that
still stands.

In the early twentieth-century years sampled, following these dramatic incidents, blacks accused of homicide were found guilty some 80
percent of the time, far more than whites. Although most of these killings involved other African Americans, and the system in one sense was

showing sensitivity to the deaths of black victims, the result of a new stereotype that added fear to the earlier contempt is most clearly shown in the disparity in legal executions.

All told in a city averaging about a million and a half people, roughly 6 percent black, some twenty-four persons were hanged between 1900 and 1916. Of the twenty-four, eleven were black. Five of them had murdered whites: Lane, the three who killed Roy White, and Samuel Archer, a newcomer from the South who panicked and shot a policeman when stopped for acting suspiciously outside a downtown store. All of the rest, like most of the white convicts, had killed wives or sweethearts; not really dangers to the wider community, they had simply violated the general sense that men should not kill women, and as African Americans they found little sympathy among the jurors or board of pardons who decided their fates. Here, too, the Philadelphia story mirrored national trends: it was always easier to condemn black men to death than white, and it may be noted that none of the states that abolished capital punishment in this era had substantial black populations.

The last man hanged in Philadelphia, indeed Pennsylvania, was James Reilly, in March 1916, following the age-old rituals from last meal to final blessing and last words, with the press ready to pronounce whether he had "died like a man" or a coward, repentant or defiant, quickly or at length. At that point the commonwealth introduced a new means of capital punishment, an electric chair at the state prison in Rockview.

New York State had begun the movement toward electrocution, billed as more humane than hanging. The proposition was hard to prove; the subjects themselves were in no condition to testify, and the first witnesses were not convinced, on August 6, 1890, after watching the pioneering wife-killer, William Kemmler, strain and thrash about in the midst of noisy sparks, smoke, and the odor of burning flesh. Other states were slow to follow. Most clung to hanging, except for Utah and Nevada, dominated by Mormons who believed literally in the idea of blood atonement and shot murderers by firing squad in order to fulfill the verse from the Book of Noah. About a quarter of them, all over the nation, had converted to electricity by the time Pennsylvania made the move, most, for reasons of economy, moving the procedure out of county jail yards into a single state prison where the one chair was conveniently housed. On July 17, 1916, Jacob Miller, a twenty-one-year-old white man who had shot a policeman during an attempted robbery, became the first Philadelphian to die at Rockview.

6

The move toward professional efficiency and "science" evidenced both by the growing authority of prosecutors and by adoption of the electric chair was also reflected in two other closely related trends: an increased reliance on police detective work and on forensic expertise. Both movements were slow to start, and erratic, but the difference between the Civil War and World War I eras was in the end immense.

Virtually all rational or scientific aids to detective work were pioneered in Europe or its colonies, then spread reluctantly to a conservative England and even more slowly to the United States. The idea of rogues' gallery photographs of known criminals was born in Belgium during the 1840s, adopted by the Paris Sureté and Scotland Yard, and finally crossed the Atlantic twenty years late. Another and more precise means of identification, the "Bertillon system," was invented in France by Alphonse Bertillon during the 1880s. Elaborate measurements of ear, nose, and finger lengths, cranial circumference, and the like, were found to be nearly unique to every individual and were kept in central offices and prisons. This in turn was supplanted, beginning in the 1890s, by the even surer method of fingerprinting, used first in India and Argentina, then England, although neither the Bertillon system nor fingerprints were widely accepted in the United States before the turn of the century.

One result of Bertillon's method, over time, was finally to kill Lombroso's idea that criminals as a class are physically set apart from their law-abiding fellows. While Lombroso fascinated academics for a generation, by the early twentieth century careful measurements had clearly established that there were no consistent physical differences between criminals and professors of sociology and that Europeans had no bigger craniums than Africans.

Neither Bertillon nor rogues' gallery pictures were of much use in homicide detection anyway; killers, unlike many burglars, counterfeiters, and shoplifters, were rarely repeat offenders with records conveniently on file. Much more helpful were advances in medicine, especially pathology and toxicology. In many cases of murder, the victim's body is the best single source of evidence; as the nineteenth century progressed, doctors were better able to analyze it for clues.

Medical testimony in murder trials had been commonly used since the eighteenth century. The very first step in proving any case a homicide was to establish the cause of death. But in the United States that job was in the hands of an inquest jury; most of the coroners in charge were political hacks, some of them undertakers eager to expand their clientele, few of them doctors. Massachusetts in 1877 threw out the whole system in favor of investigation by trained medical examiners alone, but no other state followed during the nineteenth century. Elsewhere doctors might be called into the inquest, but taxpayers' reluctance to pay their professional expenses was added to a traditional aversion to disturbing the dead, and only about 8 percent of late nineteenth-century inquests involved autopsies of any kind.

In law any causal connection between a killer's action and a death made the case a homicide, and when an alleged victim had hung on for some days, weeks, even months after being beaten or shot, under common law anything less than a year and a day, doctors for prosecution or defense might wrangle about whether it was the resulting injury or some wholly unrelated illness or heart condition that had finished him off. These contests in court left much to a jury's discretion, for several reasons. "Expert" testimony in court was legally distinguished from ordinary or eyewitness testimony. Experts, once their qualifications were ratified by the trial judge, were allowed to draw inferences, or conclusions, not simply to describe the nature of a wound, for example, but to offer the opinion that it had been delivered by a knife, club, or bullet. But American jurors were traditionally resistant both to circumstantial evidence and to experts of any kind, their resistance sharpened in this case because judges allowed any physician to testify as "expert" and because the few Americans trained in pathology were mostly specialists in infectious disease rather than violence, and nobody in the room really knew what they were talking about.

France was the leader here, in determining cause of death from the nature of wounds or condition of heart and lungs and time of death from lividity or rigor mortis. Late in the century Professor Alexandre Lacassagne, who held the chair of Pathology and Forensic Medicine at

Lyons—there were no such experts in the United States—was especially famous for identifying bodies from bits of hair, bones, and teeth and finding the differences among various red or brown stains under a microscope, distinguishing human blood cells from animal. Lacassagne, too, in 1888 was the first to venture that a specific bullet had been fired from a specific revolver, having carefully counted and measured the individually unique rifling marks made by each gun. And he and other continental colleagues and rivals continued, as before, to find new and better methods of detecting poisons, not only isolating the inorganic metals but the more complex organic compounds.

Poison was in fact a special case. While this was—apparently—an extremely rare method of committing murder, accounting in the Philadelphia series for less than 1 percent of all those treated by the justice system, it had a special place in folklore and the popular imagination. The stealthiness of the method, its violation of the cozy sanctuary of home and kitchen, had scared slaveholding Virginians in the eighteenth century, and continued to scare thereafter. Virtually by definition this was a first-degree crime, deliberately premeditated: the horror it invoked is reflected in the fact that Sarah Jane Whiteling, convicted of poisoning her husband and two little children, was in June 1889 the first and only female hanged in Philadelphia since the American revolution (perhaps because she had neither youth nor good looks in her favor). Unlike barroom brawling, poisonings often involved people of high status, disproportionately women, motivated by jealousy, greed, and lust. This was the stuff both of high drama and of the increasingly popular genre of detective fiction that reached its peak, late in the nineteenth century, with Arthur Conan Doyle's celebrated *Adventures of Sherlock Holmes,* which badly misled readers about the nature of most ordinary cases.

Arsenic was the potion of choice, in both real and fictional incidents, trailed at some distance by cyanide of mercury, and American readers followed several celebrated British cases in the course of the nineteenth century while contributing a few of their own. Cordelia Botkin set a long-distance record in September 1898 by mailing a box of loaded bonbons from her home in San Francisco to Mrs. Elizabeth Dunning, her lover's wife, then living in Dover, Delaware. Dunning and her sister ate them and died four days later. Three months after that, in Manhattan, socialite Raymond Molineux anonymously sent a bottle of Bromo

Seltzer laced with cyanide to Harry Cornish, athletic director of the Knickerbocker Athletic Club, who had, he believed, dishonored him by winning a public weightlifting contest. It was Cornish's landlady, Katherine Adams, who ultimately drank it and died in convulsions. And over the next decade Belle Gunness, a widow from LaPorte, Indiana, may have set a numerical record by poisoning and then robbing as many as fourteen suitors and then, with the help of a confederate, burying them about the place.

Gunness escaped prosecution; in April 1908 a body that did not much resemble hers was found in the burned ruins of her farmhouse, and she was never seen again. Botkin nearly got away with her crime, Mrs. Dunning's family doctor having mistaken arsenic poisoning for an excess of corn fritters. And it was only after the Cornish-Adams incident that the club doctor got suspicious, and Molineux was found to have earlier poisoned Harry Barnett, a fellow Knickerbocker and his rival for the hand of one Blanche Cheeseborough. But while medical ignorance accounted for a number of undetected nineteenth-century murders of all kinds, the bigger problem by far was the indifference of the justice system at the level of intake and investigation.

In dealing with possible homicides the two related issues were money and class, or more precisely, taxpayer dollars and community standing. In the great majority of cases, the facts that homicide was obvious and that there was an immediate suspect made detection easy and cheap. When the dead person was a known member of the community, coroners and police, with the press looking over their shoulders, were increasingly willing at least to begin the often expensive and time-consuming business of finding out what had happened and who was responsible. But it was a different matter when anonymous "floaters" were pulled from the river, or under suspicious circumstances the bodies of poor people were found in the street, and no one of any influence or standing had reported them missing. The business of "detective work" as we now know it had been made a public responsibility only a few decades earlier; even public prosecution was a relatively recent American invention. And in the late nineteenth century homicide detection was still a relatively low priority.

City police departments, in their published annual reports, typically boasted above all of their ability to "keep order," to cut down disturbances on holidays or during parades, to put down strikes or riots.

Some of them, like Philadelphia's, also proudly published lists of property reported stolen and then recovered. In an age in which the majority of citizens lived far closer to real poverty than we now do, most missing items were pathetically small, shoes and shirts and sealing wax, pillowcases and socks. Detectives were most happy to deal with the bigger cases, bank burglaries and jewel thefts, which might result in legal rewards or illegal deals. They could then use their extensive knowledge of and connections with the criminal underworld, maybe even the rogues' gallery. But there was still no money or prestige in homicide, and little mention in the annual reports.

A semiofficial history, *The Philadelphia Police: Past and Present,* published in 1887, listed all the city's detectives by name. There were thirteen of them, including two clerks who never left the office, for a city of close to a million. Just one was a specialist, in horse theft. In thirty-two dense pages, describing the men's histories, exploits, and notable captures, overwhelmingly of thieves ranging from larcenous servant girls to bank robbers, there are only five mentions of homicide, commanding just forty-one lines of type. Henry Clay Mintzhouser had however earned the nickname "the Murder Detective" by contributing to at least two cases; the second, in which he had been called out of town to Chester County, involved a killer who had fled to Italy, and "the county commissioners would not incur the expense of having the murderer extradited and brought back."

Under these conditions coroners were under pressure not to make waves. To declare a dubious and unidentified corpse a homicide rather than a suicide or an accident victim would rarely lead to a solution, and won no points with the police who would have to handle it. Inquests found homicide "at the hands of a person or persons unknown" when there was an obvious gunshot wound to the head, but a broken skull was more likely to be labeled the "result of a fall while in a state of intoxication," and in May 1900 a dead transient found in the Delaware, his hands tied behind his back, with bag, wallet, and money missing, was labeled a "suicide." It is impossible to say just how many of these cases were neglected or mislabeled, but in the five years 1839–41, 1870, and 1900 combined, the Philadelphia *Public Ledger*—a relatively conservative paper, although not averse to street sales—reported 174 possibly suspicious deaths, just 82 of which resulted in murder indictments.

It was not that police detectives were either wholly corrupt or utterly helpless, but simply that they had no tools, standing, or expertise that set them aside from other citizens. Nineteenth-century policemen in general inspired no awe and not much respect. They were often attacked on the beat, sometimes killed, and when they themselves attacked or killed were subject to the same criminal processes as others, tried and not infrequently convicted for assault or manslaughter. They did make homicide arrests, but so did coroners, magistrates, and, often, private citizens. Urban crowds routinely acted as unofficial posses, blacks and whites cooperating in chasing down killers on the street, even braving bullets without waiting for official help. The only thing that distinguished the police was their habit of making dozens of dragnet arrests in especially frustrating and well-publicized cases (one of the problems that makes homicide arrests, in that era, an untrustworthy index to the actual "murder rate"). But in terms of homicide their major contribution was simply prevention, through breaking up small fights and bigger riots, rather than detection.

As of the early 1890s, the state both of police detective work at its average and of scientific expertise at its best is well illustrated by the single most famous murder case of the century. It was ten minutes past eleven in Fall River, Massachusetts, on the stifling Thursday morning of August 2, 1892, when Lizzie Borden summoned the family maid, Bridget Sullivan, from the second floor of the modest house on Second Street: "Come down quick. Father's dead. Somebody came in and killed him." Bridget was then directed to get the family doctor and to fetch a friend, for comfort. A neighbor woman also hurried in, and sent her yardman for another doctor. It was a passerby, overhearing all the excitement, who first thought to call the cops.

Dr. Bowen arrived well before the police and found Andrew Borden on the couch in the downstairs parlor, virtually unrecognizable, his face shattered from numerous head wounds, dead perhaps twenty minutes or so. Patrolman George Allen followed shortly, informally deputizing a gawker to guard the door and bar all but police, physicians, and family, a post the poor man held faithfully, quite forgotten, all day long. A small crowd inside was then tending to Lizzie, who seemed calm enough, and Dr. Bowen went out to telegraph her elder sister, Emma, who was visiting on Cape Cod, when someone noticed the absence of

Andrew's second wife, Abby. It was two frightened women, not police-men, who then ventured upstairs and found a second body, as battered as the first. The blood in the second-floor bedroom had started to co-agulate, and Bowen calculated that Mrs. Borden, stepmother to the sis-ters, had been killed some time before her husband.

Andrew Borden was the old city's leading banker; Fall River simply ground to a stop, as every mill and shop in town emptied out on word that he and his wife had been butchered in broad daylight, in their own home, on a busy street full of houses just a few feet apart. And the case has inspired much of the same fascination ever since. There was no sex involved, with elderly victims and Lizzie a plain spinster of thirty-two. But there was certainly violence, and above all there was mystery.

The house at number 92 was much like the "locked box" puzzle beloved of later writers. Front and back doors had been fastened through most of the day, except when Lizzie or Bridget briefly ventured out. Emma had spent the night many miles away, and the one other surviving member of the household, a visiting uncle, had left early in the morning and could account for nearly every move. Imagination first conjured a "wild-eyed" or "bushy-haired" stranger—maybe one of those new immigrants—or perhaps an enemy of Andrew Borden, a no-toriously cold, tight, and unpopular man. But while the key figures in the case were observed coming and going, their own accounts mostly backed by neighbors and others, no one saw anyone else, or heard a sound.

Suspicion fell on Lizzie partly because of her manner, her restrained New England response to the deaths, and partly because of a number of mildly inconsistent or improbable stories she told at the time and then at the inquest, suggesting for example that someone might have tried to poison the family earlier that week. It was said that she or some-one like her had tried to buy poison earlier that summer. Gossip also had it that she and Emma, whose mother had died years before, did not get along with Abby, their stepmother; until the double murders Andrew's remarriage may in fact have deprived them of at least some part of a $500,000 inheritance. And then, despite three close searches for evidence by Fall River police and detectives, on three separate days, looking among other things for a weapon or bloodstained clothing, the very next morning Lizzie was observed burning a blue dress with dark stains. It was old paint, she said.

Lizzie was arrested after the inquest, which, since Massachusetts had dispensed with the coroner and his jury, was a private affair with no counsel or cross-examination allowed. But she was a rich as well as a sympathetic figure, able to hire the Pinkerton Agency—the Fall River police actually resorted to a private detective of their own—and her three-member defense team was headed by George D. Robinson, former governor of the Commonwealth of Massachusetts. The trial opened on June 5, 1893, before three judges of the state supreme court, with two regional district attorneys conducting the prosecution. Some 108 panelists were carefully interviewed to yield the twelve jurors, mostly nearby farmers, none from the town itself.

With tens of millions of international readers hanging on every reported detail, Robinson, the very image of the shrewd old Yankee, was the star of the trial. He successfully moved to have Lizzie's inquest testimony disallowed as evidence, on the grounds that at the time she was "virtually" under arrest, had not been allowed counsel, and had not been told of her right, under the constitution of Massachusetts, to remain silent for fear of self-incrimination, advice that was then "customary" although not strictly required. A druggist's rather vague testimony about her possible attempt to buy poison was also disallowed as irrelevant. In cross-examination, the friend who had seen her burn a dress made it clear that it was not the dress she had seen Lizzie wear on the fateful morning. And Robinson had a field day with inconsistencies in testimony by the police.

But it was the expert witnesses brought by the prosecution itself to establish the time and manner of death who proved the most important to the defense. The district medical examiner and another one from Boston were joined by two Harvard professors, a doctor and a toxicologist. Mrs. Borden had suffered nineteen head wounds, probably from an ax; she had not cried out and the first blow had hit her straight on, implying that it was wielded by someone she knew. Andrew had almost certainly been napping on the couch when he got the first of ten, probably from the same weapon. Neither had any trace of poison in their systems, disallowing Lizzie's public suspicions. But Robinson helped bring out that the amount of spattered blood must have been enormous; many witnesses had agreed that his client was spotless, only minutes after Andrew's death, although the house had no bathrooms and running water only in one downstairs sink. The toxicologist, judging from the state of Abby's stomach contents, testified that she had died at least an hour and a half before her husband; neither Bridget nor anyone else suggested that Lizzie, in the long interval between physically strenuous crimes, had looked or acted abnormal. She had also never left the house, barn, or yard. And while there were three axes or hatchets in or about the place, none in good order, toxicological tests established that the hairs on one of them had come from a cow, and the stains were rust; Dr. Edward S. Wood testified that if human blood had been on any of them it was physically impossible in a short time to have washed or rubbed off enough to escape his microscope.

The defense witnesses were then an anticlimax. With no blood and no weapon, twelve good men and true were not going to convict a pious female Sunday school teacher, beyond all reasonable doubt, of two violently gory acts of murder. It took them just over an hour to confirm that, on June 20. It was not their job in law to solve the puzzle, to determine "whodunit," only to do justice by the book and according to the evidence. But both contemporaries and posterity have naturally wanted more.

It still seems almost inconceivable that anyone from outside the house could have killed the Bordens. Andrew may have had enemies, but why would an intruder so viciously attack Abby, how could he slip in, and where would he hide for an hour and a half, dripping no blood, in a narrow ten-room house in which Lizzie and Bridget were continually coming and going, until Andrew's return for his morning nap? At the same time no single trace of physical evidence ever pointed to Lizzie, a woman of spotless prior reputation and behavior. The same lack of clues applies to Bridget, whom no one suspected at the time, and who, despite possibly greater opportunities to smuggle an incriminating package out of the household, had no apparent motive for such a passionate outburst.

Most later historians have gone along with the verdict expressed by contemporaries:

> Lizzie Borden took an axe
> And gave her father forty whacks;
> When she saw what she had done
> She gave her mother forty-one.

But the little ditty is quite wrong about the number of blows and the sequence of events. At least.

7

In the last two decades before World War I, the gap between "police" and "expert" detective work shown in the Borden case closed markedly, as advances were made on both fronts.

American police work still trailed behind other advanced countries, simply because the criminal justice system had no single "capital" such as Paris, London, or Berlin. The federal role in ordinary law enforcement had been confined mostly to the appointment of local marshals in the territories, a job that shrank close to the vanishing point when territorial New Mexico, in 1912, was admitted as the last of the adjoining forty-eight states. Postal inspectors had been created in 1836, and the Treasury Department founded the Secret Service in 1864, mainly to guard against counterfeit money and excise stamps, although in time the officers proved flexible servants of several government agencies. The establishment of a small Bureau of Investigation inside the Justice Department, beginning in 1908, helped the federal government again to expand its modest role in law enforcement, when as part of the moral spirit of the Progressive Era the Congress passed the Mann Act in 1910 and the Harrison Act in 1914, concerned, respectively, with interstate prostitution and the sale of certain drugs. But none of these agencies had much prestige, certainly neither the authority nor the resources to deal with homicide in the states, as Scotland Yard or the Paris Sureté had in their countries.

The looseness built into the federal system made it far easier than in more tightly governed European nations for men like Herman Mudgett–Howard Holmes to marry three women and perhaps to kill an unknown number of victims. England in 1837 had required that all death certificates be registered in London as a reaction to the discovery that one woman had poisoned a number of people in several jurisdictions, each of them ignorant of what was happening in the others. But the registration systems adopted in this country—Philadelphia, typically, required records of all births, marriages, and deaths beginning in 1860—applied only to individual counties, hundreds of them, at best to some of the forty-eight states, with no central file keeping.

Individual police departments and detectives, however, had very early begun informally to swap rogues' gallery photographs and "wanted" notices. And as part of the late nineteenth-century push toward the prestige and efficiency of "professionalism," a number of occupations actually or potentially involved in law enforcement founded associations designed to help them, among other things, to trade experience and information across state or even national lines. This was the era when both the American Bar Association and the American Medical Association were organized; the American Prison Congress was founded in 1870, the International Association of Chiefs of Police in 1901. And by the twentieth century there was an accelerating amount of information to share in this way.

Gunsmiths, for many years, had occasionally been called to testify whether a given bullet had come from a large- or small-caliber gun, for example, or to judge whether a suspected murder weapon had recently been fired. (Spider webs in the barrel were a good clue, and rust.) But in 1902, aware of early European experiments, Judge Oliver Wendell Holmes of the Massachusetts Supreme Court set up a demonstration in which bullets were fired from a defendant's gun into a wastebasket full of cotton, then microscopically compared to those found in the victim's body. The resulting conviction, widely noted, helped establish a whole new era in the study of guns and bullets. And although methods were crude, and still subject to the errors made by self-trained "experts" with more flair for dazzling juries than using microscopes, the science of forensic ballistics was unquestionably launched.

Forensic medicine made even longer strides. One key year was 1904, when Dr. Charles Norris, trained abroad, took a post as professor of pathology and head of the chemical and bacteriological laboratory at New York's Bellevue Hospital. Norris quickly expanded his role; a champion of the medical examiner system all over the country, he won his first major victory in 1915 when, nearly forty years after the Commonwealth of Massachusetts, New York City threw out its elected coroners. Norris himself was soon appointed chief medical examiner, and proved a man with a powerful flair for publicity and organization. As a phone line made his expanding laboratory available to the police twenty-fours a day, his office was soon screening thousands of reports of suspicious deaths every year, while he and his assistants, some on call, others installed as pathologists in each of the city's five morgues, performed autopsies in up to a third of them.

The crisp new methods that Norris introduced in New York were typical of the Progressive Era, a time that stretched from the end of the nineteenth century well into the second decade of the twentieth. One key to the successes of the period is that the spirit of reform was buoyed by an economic expansion of unprecedented length, which enabled local taxpayers to pay for sometimes expensive innovations. While farm products had been the major American contribution to the international economy since the seventeenth century, now, especially after victory in the Spanish-American War of 1898, American manufactures increasingly joined cotton, wheat, and beef in the export market. When World War I broke out in 1914, tragedy in Europe proved an economic stimulus to the still-neutral United States, which supplied food, arms, and capital to the warring powers.

Progressive reforms had begun, and were always strongest at the local level, with attacks on municipal waste and corruption. And the stress on moral, orderly behavior, the same impulse that led to federal laws against drugs and prostitution, found its first targets in patronage-ridden city police departments, with their traditionally profitable relations with protected brothels, speakeasies, and thieves. As the successes of the urban industrial revolution helped enrich local treasuries, the introduction of civil service was followed by higher pay and expansion in number. In Philadelphia the fifteen detectives of 1898 were more than doubled to thirty-three in 1903, and the force as a whole was increased by nearly a third between 1900 and 1910. And most important was a shift, all over the country, in the priorities and mission of local police.

American police had from very early been used as the eyes, ears, and right arms of local governments and given a wide range of duties while roaming their beats, lighting gas lamps, cleaning streets, running health inspections in plague years and soup kitchens in hard times. But other departments took most of these jobs as local governments expanded. And as the Progressive Era opened, there was a special objection to the old practice of putting up homeless people in the station houses at night, condemned as inefficient or "unscientific" charity, which made life too easy for the lazily unemployed. In New York City Police

Commissioner Theodore Roosevelt, in a key symbolic shift, ordered the lodging ended in 1896. By the early twentieth century, in New York and in most other places, cutting down on the functions of police was promoted as a way of freeing them for the two jobs they had left: controlling traffic and fighting crime. And fighting crime came to mean among other things an increased stress on homicide detection.

One turning point in Philadelphia was the Mudgett case. Fidelity Mutual Insurance had a financial stake that led to hiring the Pinkertons and others to help convict Mudgett of Benjamin Pitezel's murder. But it was a Philadelphia special officer, Frank Geyer, who traveled at city expense over much of the Midwest and into Canada during 1895–96 to find the bodies of the three Pitezel children, a business that involved a good deal of time and ingenuity. Although at the trial his evidence about the deaths of Howard, Alice, and Nessie was ruled irrelevant, it is significant that the city accepted Geyer's mission as a public responsibility, undertaken at public expense, and perhaps even more important that in dramatizing the business of homicide detection he became a kind of public hero.

It is even more significant that in this country the use of fingerprints for purposes of murder detection was championed not by a doctor or scientist but by a policeman, Detective Sergeant Joseph A. Faurot of New York. Faurot, for years in charge of a small registry of criminal identification, had a passion for learning new methods, and finally wangled a trip to Scotland Yard to learn the state of the art firsthand. On his return he was able to demonstrate the newfangled technique in sensational fashion, when in the spring of 1908 the body of Nellie Quinn, a pretty young nurse, was found in an Upper West Side rooming house, with an empty whiskey bottle under her bed. Faurot dusted the bottle for prints and found that they were not Quinn's; after taking inked impressions from several boyfriends he found a set that matched; a young plumber, George Cramer, confronted with this novel evidence, then confessed to having murdered the woman in a drunken rage. As this and later cases made headlines across the country, other departments bought first the idea and then the equipment.

In the years after 1910, detectives in Philadelphia began routinely making careful incident reports of each reported homicide, taking photographs and in some cases looking for prints. Perhaps of most symbolic import was the adoption of a new feature in the department's annual reports. Beginning in 1913 there was each year an official column de-voted to all "murders" reported, together with a case-by-case listing of the results: arrest if any, indictment, trial, and verdict. This "box score" treatment had earlier been reserved for important property crimes and, when the heat was on, during the Progressive Era, for violations of the gambling and liquor laws. It was a clear sign that in the City of Broth-erly Love, as elsewhere, the solution of homicide cases had become, at last, a major departmental priority.

Between 1865 and 1917, the last shots fired in the Civil War and the first after American entry into World War I, differences across the United States had been narrowing. The conquest of the Indians, thick-ening settlement, and economic advance brought eastern problems to the trans-Mississippi West. The South, struggling to modernize, was solving its own economic and racial problems to the satisfaction at least of the dominant whites. And in a time of apparent peace, progress, and prosperity, as the era of the badmen, vigilantism, and lynching slowly faded, murder rates fell all over the country, following the lead of east-ern cities, indeed of the Western world in general, where the urban industrial revolution was transforming mass behavior. But in 1917 that Western world had been learning for three years what Americans would shortly discover, that peace, progress, and prosperity cannot be taken for granted, and that nothing in history moves along straight lines with-out interruption.

6

World War I to World War II, 1917–1941

The First World War opened a new chapter in American history, a period of awesome international power and prestige. The several American colonies had first been settled as distant outposts on the fringes of the emerging world marketplace, and even through the expansive nineteenth century the new nation remained in some ways an economic colony to the Continent. In 1914 the United States was still a net debtor, absorbing capital and technology from more advanced European nations, when the Western world was rocked by the outbreak of war. By the time the United States entered the conflict just three years later, it was a net creditor; with victory in 1918 it emerged as incomparably the strongest economic, military, and political power on the planet.

American dominance continued through both the prosperous 1920s and the depressed 1930s. But unlike Britain in the previous century, or France in the eighteenth, the United States was never able to enjoy an unchallenged cultural superiority to match its economic and military power. And it was only partly from jealousy that many Europeans thought of this country as still barbaric, crude, and immature. One key index to the "uncivilized" nature of this giant upstart was the persistently high U.S. murder rate, as compared with other Western nations, a charge that was hard to deny,

World War I itself was followed by a round of pent-up violence. And during the 1920s, the "Lawless Decade" that followed the passage of the Eighteenth Amendment to the Constitution, prohibiting the sale of drinking alcohol, many thoughtful Americans were both fearful of and embarrassed about murderous violence and what it seemed to imply about "the national character," judicial institutions, race relations, and other sensitive issues.

These concerns led among other things to the reform and strengthening of police, above all to the growing power, at the national level, of the Federal Bureau of Investigation. But in fact, as older regional differences continued to flatten, the urban industrial revolution strengthened its hold—even during the Great Depression of the 1930s—and old forms of violence faded out, the murder rate by the end of the period was clearly in decline.

I

World War I was for the Europeans a war of carnage much like our own Civil War, and for many of the same reasons. But for the Americans the engagement was short and satisfying; war was declared in the spring of 1917, but fresh troops reached the battlefields in number only in 1918 and pushed the Allied cause over the top that summer and fall. As measured by the figures of the Bureau of Vital Statistics, the national homicide rate took a dip during that year. Sigmund Freud, in *Civilization and Its Discontents,* wrote in 1931 that during wartime a nation might bind itself together in love, directing internal aggression outward toward a common enemy. A simpler explanation for 1918, as for 1861 – 65, was that a number of aggressive young men were away, killing with the army instead of on the streets. With its many diversities and tensions, the United States has only rarely been a nation united, certainly not bound in love, and the immediate effect of world war was to promote several kinds of ugliness.

Given traditional isolation, and the reluctance of many ethnic groups to fight Germany on behalf, it seemed, of the British Empire, the United States government felt the need to justify our involvement by taking both the high road and the low. That is, while President Woodrow Wilson called on the nation to "Make the World Safe for Democracy" he also defended the need to segregate African Americans from the rest, in the name of reducing racial frictions, and the new Committee on Public Information poured out propaganda to teach people to hate Germans. Once hailed as half of the dominant "Anglo-Saxon race," they were now denounced as "Huns." But the war lasted too short a time to slake this officially cultivated thirst for violence, and with only a relative handful privileged to go and fight abroad—a million troops—the mass of fired-up Americans had to do their hating at home. And they tended to focus on the usual suspects: foreigners, radicals, and blacks.

Anti-German hysteria reached a tragically ironic peak on April 4, 1918, when a crowd in Collinswood, Missouri, far from the action, lynched Robert Paul Prager, a young man with a German name and accent who was suspected of "disloyalty"; it was discovered only afterward that he had earlier tried to enlist in the U.S. Navy, to fight on behalf of his adopted country, but was rejected because of a glass eye.

Fear of radicals had never died down, especially in the West, and was inflamed further when the Russian revolution, begun in the spring of 1917, was taken over by the communists that November. The most obvious American target was then the Industrial Workers of the World, since the early twentieth century the leading target of local antiunion violence. Once the war broke out Big Bill Haywood and other leaders of the "Wobblies," like the American Socialists, declared their opposition as pacifists on principle, although many individual members had signed up to fight. The federal government jailed dozens for obstructing the war effort at the same time as local raids and lynchings were stepped up. Official harassment continued after victory in 1918 into the "Red Scare" of 1919, led by Attorney General A. Mitchell Palmer and J. Edgar Hoover, the young head of the Federal Bureau of Investigation. As hatred of Germany segued into fear of revolutionary Russia, the IWW organized an unsuccessful but scary general strike in Seattle, with all of the city's working people called to quit work at once. And that fall witnessed the culmination of several years of beatings and killings in the Pacific Northwest. During a celebration of Armistice Day, November 11, parading American Legionnaires in the lumbering town of Centralia, Washington, exchanged shots with Wobblies inside their Union Hall. Three Legionnaires were killed; the others rushed in and seized Wesley Everett, himself a veteran, who shot down one more before he was castrated and hanged from a railway trestle over the Chehalis River.

The Wobblies had in any case always won more publicity than members, and in the long run it was impossible to hold out against murderous intimidation, combined with government pressure. Americans had mostly gotten over their communist-anarchist Red Scare jitters by the fall of 1920, and refused to panic that September when a bomb blast outside the House of Morgan killed thirty-four passersby on Wall Street. And by the time a broken Bill Haywood skipped bail and sailed for Russia in 1921, the IWW, indeed American radicalism more generally, was effectively dead.

It was harder to stop the African-American push for jobs and recognition, stimulated both by wartime rhetoric and war production. Blacks had been leaving the South for years before 1914, pushed out by poverty, the invasion of the boll weevil in the cotton fields, and the success of the lynching campaign to deny them civil rights and the vote. But as the United States was called to make arms for British, French, and finally American troops, the need for labor created new job opportunities in northern cities and factory towns. And unlike Bill Haywood and many radicals, W. E. B. DuBois of the NAACP, by then the dominant leader of the American black community, was persuaded by President Wilson's democratic oratory to support the war effort. Thousands of African Americans joined the army, a few of them, unlike in the Civil War, as officers; the government had to warn the unsuspecting French not to treat these black soldiers like the rest of the liberators, but it was hard to deny their pride and high expectations.

Black pride and entry into new places combined with white resentments to make murderous trouble all through the war. In East St. Louis, bursting with war workers, blacks in July 1917 answered months of harassment by firing at white invaders, accidentally killing two policemen; the riots that followed cost thirty-nine black lives, officially, and nine white. That August outside of Houston a crowd of African-American soldiers marched toward the city, after a clash between white cops and black military police, and shot down two of the local officers; it took units of the Texas and Illinois national guards plus six hundred federal troops to put down the invasion: thirteen men were hanged for murder. Washington, D.C., Charleston, South Carolina, and Longview, Texas, all witnessed major race riots between then and the war's official end. The biggest hit Chicago, in the summer of 1919, following two years of gang fights, house bombings, and jockeying over boundary lines in parks, bars, streets, and factories. After an incident sparked

when on July 27 an African-American kid drifted over the unofficial
line separating black and white bathers at a beach on Lake Michigan
and was either drowned or stoned to death, three days of fighting took
twenty-three black lives and fifteen white.

But while the excitement over foreigners and radicals retreated, the
blacks did not. Factory jobs ebbed away as the war ended, but African
Americans continued to flow north into the cities, expanding their turf,
insisting on their rights. Between 1917 and 1920 the very term "race
riot" was redefined; no longer helpless victims of mob invasion, blacks
were fighting and firing back. And these newly urban people not only
voted and built communities but also earned a new place in city and
nation. Their contributions to popular culture, long hard to deny,
earned special recognition in the unofficial Jazz Age nickname given the
1920s, just as the authors and artists of the Harlem Renaissance im-
pressed their white peers with their inventive talents. A corner was
clearly being turned, however slowly; one by-product of the Chicago
riot was the appointment of a commission that produced a pioneering
sociological study of conditions in the city's ghetto, the result of discrimination in jobs, schools, and housing. And as Social Darwinism
waned and the racial climate changed, Americans all over the country
joined the NAACP in protesting violent outrages; one woman, on a
cruise to a Europe devastated by the loss of millions of war dead, wrote
to the attorney general of the United States that she was offended by
having constantly to explain such barbarities to foreigners.

2

But even without the indignities provoked by racism, Americans had
much explaining to do over the Roaring Twenties that followed the
war, a time when the national murder rate, problems in law enforcement, and apparent flaws in the justice system got more national and
in many cases international attention than ever before.

For most observers, the key issues centered around the Eighteenth
Amendment to the Constitution, the culminating moral reform of the
Progressive Era, which in 1919 forbade the sale of drinking alcohol.
One result was to involve tens of millions of ordinary Americans in
routine lawbreaking, as every working-class beer or middle-class cock-

tail party involved an offense against the United States. The other was to inspire, on a giant scale, a largely new form of crime.

Since the nineteenth century organized gangs had been involved in extortion and labor racketeering, bullying at the polls, gambling, and sometimes liquor sales. For ambitious young urban entrepreneurs, once Irish, more recently Italian or Jewish, this was a traditional if crooked way up the American ladder. But now the need for both bullets and brains was greater than ever. The old games were still played, from running brothels to cracking safes, but the new one was different. It required planning and cooperation as never before, first to make or import illegal alcohol, then to distribute it across a given state or city, all without interference from either rival gangsters or local, state, or federal authorities. These human obstacles could be cut in or bribed, or they could be intimidated or killed. The stakes were huge, and if killing was needed, many of the players had come home from the war with an expertise in automatic weapons. Even more important, during the 1920s, were mass-produced automobiles, which as mobile striking units or "getaway cars" were the most important technological aid to murder since the invention of the revolver, especially when bristling with tommy guns.

Gangs in different states or cities sometimes cooperated. But unless or until a monopoly was established over a given territory, rivals fought for control of the turf, hijacked each other's beer trucks, executed troublemakers, and killed civilians while careening around corners and spraying gunfire across city streets. The death toll in some places was appalling: the Chicago Crime Commission estimated that in that city alone, during the Lawless Decade, there were some four hundred gang-land murders, virtually all officially unsolved, the killers speeding away in Buicks or dumping bodies in the river or in abandoned lots, leaving no witnesses willing to talk. During the same period one estimate is that across the nation the enforcement of Prohibition directly cost a thousand lives, as sheriff's deputies, patrolmen, and treasury agents shot up and were shot down by gangsters.

The nation and the wider world were appalled, and also perversely delighted. The gangster world was so quintessentially *American*: fast, high-tech, violent, and full of colorful rags-to-riches stories. However immune to successful prosecution, the leading figures were generally well known; boasting was more their style than hiding, as an air of power and ruthlessness was part of the mystique of success, and publicity was not only heady stuff but a useful weapon as well. These men did not pretend to the gallant or Robin Hood fantasies that had earlier clung to Jesse James, but Americans were still ready to romanticize Dutch Schultz, Owney Madden, and Jack "Legs" Diamond in New York, the Purple Gang in Detroit, and above all Scarface Al Capone in Chicago.

Alphonse Capone had been imported from Brooklyn in 1919 as a battle-tested thug, then still in his teens, to work for Johnny Torrio. Chicago's notoriety over the next several years resulted from an unusually vicious series of turf wars, with Capone commanding a small army of enforcers. He himself, it was said, personally murdered with tommy guns and revolvers, and in one case a baseball bat, used to obliterate the heads of two allegedly traitorous underlings helplessly tied to their chairs. Torrio, his nerves shot, got out of the business in 1925, but Scarface loved it, grandly granting interviews to newspapermen and reformers, holding forth in a silk dressing gown, waving a cigar. By 1929 he was able to arrange his most famous killings with a phone call from his Palm Island estate on Biscayne Bay.

George "Bugs" Moran was the last threat to the Capone monopoly of the Chicago liquor trade. And early on the morning of February 14, five men in a squad car parked outside Moran's headquarters in a North Clark Street garage, three of them dressed as cops. The men inside clearly thought this was another routine or sham official "raid" and obediently lined up, hands against the wall: six gangsters and an optometrist, Dr. Reinhardt E. Schwimmer, one of the wide-eyed hangers-on that badmen then attracted. The five visitors then machine-gunned all seven to death and left within minutes of their arrival. No one was ever tried for this St. Valentine's Day Massacre, but everyone knew who was responsible: Moran himself, badly shaken, commented, "Only Capone kills like that."

3

And the fascination with murder did not stop with the new breed of gangsters. Sensationalized violence had been a staple of the popular press since the 1830s, but it reached new heights throughout the Lawless Decade as one notorious case chased another across the headlines in a nearly continuous stream. A careful count revealed that between November 8 and December 8 of 1926 the New York *World* was devoting about 15 percent of its total space—including advertising—to crime news; and the tabloid *Daily News*, 33 percent.

During most of that month the national focus was on "the Case of the Minister and the Choir Singer," which included all of the traditional ingredients, sex, blood, and mystery, the difference being the 200 reporters and 50 photographers who covered it, and the estimated 12 million words it generated by wire. The case had its origins when in the summer of 1922 the Reverend Edward Wheeler Hall of New Brunswick, New Jersey, was found dead in a local lover's lane, together with his mistress, Eleanor Mills. Both had been shot, but their throats were also slit and their bodies arranged in a kind of embrace in the midst of a scene strewn with their love letters. No action was taken by a grand jury at the time, but four years later the governor, smelling publicity, demanded that the case be reopened on the basis of alleged new evidence involving the widow, Frances Hall, and her brothers, Henry and Willie Stevens. The evidence proved flimsy, and the bespectacled defendants, high in the middle class and well into middle age, made unlikely villains; after an excruciating month in court the jurors set them free in a matter of hours. Later speculation about the killings pointed to the Ku Klux Klan, then active in New Jersey and elsewhere as self-described guardians of Protestant values and sexual virtue. The conclusion was suggested by the obvious staging of the scene, a kind of warning of the wages of sin, and by the fact that Mrs. Mills, profane singer of holy songs, had had her tongue and vocal cords cut out. But no investigation followed, and the case again faded.

A very different puzzle was offered the next year when Judd Gray and Ruth Snyder were tried for the murder of her husband, Albert. The mystery here is the lack of mystery. Although the lovers had faked a burglary, and she at first blamed Albert's bludgeoning on "a foreigner. I guess. Some kind of Eyetalian," they were utterly inept murderers, and soon confessed and turned on each other. Perhaps it was their very Long Island suburban ordinariness that appealed to millions of readers, or the detailed accounting of their affair together, but they held center stage for eighteen days in the spring of 1927. Snyder in fact managed to seize one more front page in January of the next year, when as a

climax to the pornography generated by the case a reporter smuggled a
camera into Sing-Sing to catch her likeness in the very act of becoming
the first woman ever to die in the electric chair.

But the unease about executing Ruth Snyder was minimal next to
the debate about the judicial process and the death penalty generated
by the other two most publicized cases of the decade, the very different
murders of a little boy in Chicago and two shoe company employees in
New England.

In the spring of 1924 Bobby Franks, just fourteen, was picked almost at random as the victim of a "perfect crime" plotted by his distant
relative, eighteen-year-old Richard Loeb, and Loeb's friend and sexual
partner, Nathan Leopold, then nineteen. The two youths, pampered,
rich, and brilliant, respectively the youngest graduates ever of the Uni-
versities of Michigan and Chicago, had tired of committing vandalism,
setting fires, stealing small items, and cheating at cards. A bigger thrill
would be murder, best done after a kidnapping, best yet after collecting
a ransom. The plan was made and rehearsed, the ransom note already
composed on a stolen typewriter, when after cruising the North Side and
losing a couple of prospects they spotted Bobby and talked him into their
rented car. With Leopold driving, Loeb butchered the boy with a chisel,
and after he had bled to death the two stuffed him into a culvert.

But for all their intelligence—Leopold was supposed to have an IQ
of 200—the teenagers failed to destroy all the evidence, and an intensive manhunt (the officers joined by a too-talkative Loeb) turned up the
body, the chisel, the typewriter, and Nathan Leopold's eyeglasses. The
two soon confessed, each blaming the other. As Leopold's father begged
Clarence Darrow to take their case, the Chicago *Tribune* offered to
broadcast the trial over the radio.

There was no hope with a jury, the "sense of the community." "Fun-
Killers" to the popular press, the two were Jewish, homosexual, rotten-
spoiled, "moral imbeciles." Darrow chose a bench trial, before a single
judge. He then pleaded his clients guilty for an astonishing thirty-three
days, mostly devoted to disagreement among "alienists," or psychiatrists, brought by both sides. The strategy was announced before it all
began: "While the state is trying Leopold and Loeb, I will try capital
punishment."

Capital punishment was then in fact healthier than either of the defendants. The actual number of hangings or electrocutions continued

to slide, but legal abolition had lost its political appeal. While in most states reserved as a practical matter for murder, execution for rape was not uncommon in the South, almost always for blacks, and Kentucky, having adopted the electric chair in 1911, reinstituted hanging in 1920 as a more painful alternative for this crime alone, following an especially vicious child rape and murder. Much more rarely robbery or kidnapping might earn death for those convicted. The sporadic legislative abolitions of the Progressive Era had dried up, and Washington, Oregon, and Arizona all reversed themselves as a result of the violent emotions stirred during and just after World War I. The only states that did not practice capital punishment in the 1920s were then Michigan, Wisconsin, and Rhode Island, the three that had signed off during the antebellum period of romantic reform, together with Kansas and the Dakotas, which had joined them during the Progressive Era and weathered the war. Illinois was emphatically not on the list.

But Clarence Darrow, playing to a national audience as well as to Chief Justice John R. Caverly of the Cook County Court, summed up in an eloquent twelve-hour plea that some papers printed in full. Aside from the traditional argument that state-sponsored hanging was barbarous both in itself and in its effect on society, he made two substantive points. First was that his clients were "mere boys," not that much older than their victim; Illinois had never executed anyone that young, and almost never anyone, of any age, who had voluntarily pleaded guilty to murder. The second was more controversial: he did not know, or care, Darrow insisted, whether they were "insane," medically or legally. (In fact, given the planning and the attempt to hide evidence, it was clear that they did not qualify under the M'Naghten rule.) But there was clearly something wrong with them: "somewhere in the infinite processes that go to the making up of the boy or the man something slipped." Perhaps it was heredity, perhaps Leopold's reading of Friedrich Nietzsche on "the superman" or Loeb's obsession with crime stories. The alienists had been divided, or uncertain, except for one Dr. William Krohn, who, Darrow pointed out, had abandoned the practice of medicine sixteen years earlier to make his living solely as an expert witness for prosecutors willing to hire him. But no expertise was needed to see that his clients were sick, "emotionally defective": the very lack of comprehensible motive that made the crime so horrible was itself a proof that his clients were in some sense not responsible actors.

In the end Judge Caverly sentenced Leopold and Loeb to life in prison without parole, largely, he said, because of their youth. Reformers were moved by the rest of Darrow's argument, but much of the public, partly influenced by rumors of his million-dollar fee, was outraged by his success. As the New York *Morning Telegraph* put it, "Law, the bastard daughter of justice, handed her mother a frightful beating in Chicago yesterday." (Both sides on the capital punishment issue felt vindicated by the eventual aftermath: after years of highly pampered life in Northern Illinois Penitentiary, Richard Loeb was stabbed to death after a failed homosexual rape in 1936, while Nathan Leopold, paroled in 1958, went to work as a lab technician in an impoverished Puerto Rican church.)

The outcomes were different for Nicola Sacco and Bartolomeo Vanzetti, accused of robbery murder in the spring of 1920. The crime involved five men who on the afternoon of April 15 drove up to the Slater and Morrill Factory in South Braintree, Massachusetts, just as the shoe company's payroll arrived, shot down Paymaster Frederick Parmenter and his guard, Alessandro Berardelli, and then escaped with $16,000 in a touring car of unidentified make. Sacco and Vanzetti, one a skilled shoemaker, the other a fish peddler, were arrested on May 5, after they had stopped by a garage to ask for what may have been the bandits' car. Both were found to be carrying guns and radical pamphlets, and—unsure of the charge—gave evasive answers when asked for alibis.

This behavior was not unusual among the little group of Italian anarchists to which both men belonged, and whose members, during the last stages of the postwar Red Scare, were being continually questioned, illegally rounded up, asked to betray their friends, and sometimes beaten and deported by agents of the Federal Bureau of Investigation. And over the next seven years, while the case grew enormously complex both legally and technically, the issue of political belief remained at its core. Supporters argued that principled pacifist champions of the working class could not possibly have committed such a brutal crime, an obviously professional job, in which the robbers had not only executed two ordinary workingmen but afterward, during the escape, had sprayed gunshots at witnesses peeking out from factory windows along the route. At the same time, although not unanimously convinced of their guilt, Pinkertons, federal agents, and state and local police be-

lieved in general that "Godless atheists" and radicals made especially
satisfying suspects, and what were they doing with loaded revolvers?

But at the time of the arrests, the issue for the prosecution was how
to turn suspicion into guilt, especially since the nearly fifty eyewitnesses
to the murders, although on the whole agreed that Italians were involved, were otherwise hopelessly divided about nearly everything they
had seen. The biggest problem was that while Nicola Sacco's unremark-
able face might be made to fit some descriptions, it was hard to fix the
unforgettable Bart Vanzetti, with his piercing eyes, hawk nose, and
dramatic swooping mustache. The ingenious solution arranged by District Attorney Frederick Katzmann was to try Vanzetti that June for an
aborted holdup in nearby East Bridgewater, the previous Christmas
Eve, also by a gang in a car. Sacco had punched his factory time card
that day, but a handful of the many witnesses, changing their inquest
testimony, identified Vanzetti as one of the bandits—one of them knew
he was an immigrant "by the way he ran." A lackadaisical defense relied
wholly on the apparently solid alibi that Vanzetti had spent the day
delivering eels, a traditional treat, to his usual Italian Catholic customers in North Plymouth. The all-Yankee jury (Vanzetti's attorneys had
challenged no one) did not buy the stories of a dozen foreigners, and
the defendant had next to face a murder trial with a record for attempted murder and robbery of a shoe company payroll.

That trial opened on May 31, 1921, Katzmann for the prosecution,
before Judge Webster Thayer, who had already presided over Vanzetti's
conviction. The defense, supported by modest contributions from
friends, neighbors, and anarchists, was led by Fred Moore, a flamboyant
Californian with a reputation as a radicals' lawyer, who soon alienated
local opinion with his long hair, casual courtroom clothing, and above
all interviews denouncing American capitalist justice. Confused and
contradictory eyewitnesses for the prosecution were matched by alibi
witnesses for the defense who had some trouble remembering just what
they were doing on a particular day more than a year earlier. Jurors,
resentful at being sequestered, had a hard time with the ballistics testimony, "a wilderness of lands and grooves." Two for the prosecution
claimed that the bullet that killed Berardelli was "consistent with" one
fired from Sacco's Colt .32, while two for the defense denied it. The
defendants testified on their own behalf, and with the judge's permission were questioned extensively about their politics, their dodging of

the draft during the recent war, and their atheist religious views. Judge Thayer, who freely gave out interviews criticizing the defense, had told reporters, "You wait 'til I give my charge to the jury—I'll show 'em." He delivered on July 14, summing up the case for the prosecution, in a speech heavily flavored with references to God and Country, and in a matter of hours Sacco and Vanzetti were convicted of murder in the first degree.

To that moment this one case had commanded little national attention, given the crowded American criminal calendar. But Fred Moore's tactics were more successful at making martyrs of his clients than freeing them, and within months there were bombs and demonstrations outside U.S. embassies from Rome to Montevideo. And as Moore was replaced with William Thompson, American supporters began to rally also, civil libertarians and radicals joined by a few conservatives like Thompson himself, who simply believed that two innocent men had not gotten a fair trial. Thompson filed a motion for retrial on the grounds that the verdict was against the weight of the evidence; five supplementary motions were added over the next two years, mostly based on the impeachment of prosecution witnesses. Another one was based on an affidavit from former state police captain William Proctor, who had testified about Sacco's gun for the prosecution and had since changed his mind. All of these motions, under Massachusetts law, had to go though Judge Thayer. He denied them en masse on October 1, 1924.

One month later Celestino Madeiros was arrested for killing an elderly cashier in a bank holdup and locked up next to Nick Sacco in the Dedham jail. Young Madeiros was a member of the well-known Morelli Gang, which many law enforcement officers thought had done the job in South Braintree as well. The next year, after his own murder trial, he confessed to it, in a statement marked both by apparently inside knowledge and elementary mistakes about the case. Defense investigators meanwhile crisscrossed the country, interviewing witnesses and prisoners, filing dozens of affidavits involving changes of testimony, alibis, and confessions, all of them countered by the state. After the Supreme Judicial Court of Massachusetts in 1926 turned down appeals from Thayer's denials, Thompson filed another motion based on the Madeiros confession. Thayer quashed that as well; the Supreme Judicial Court of Massachusetts upheld him, on the grounds that it had no power to review the facts of the case if there were no technical errors.

Four days later, on April 5, 1927, Judge Thayer condemned Sacco and Vanzetti to death.

But the case was still not over. The antiforeign bias shown in the Dedham courtroom helped fan anti-American bias abroad, where the appeal of radicalism was far stronger than in the United States, and the electric chair, so very American, inspired a special horror. The Italian government had sent representatives from the first, and the death penalty sparked not only huge demonstrations in Moscow and elsewhere but also formal protests from the Vatican, the French Chamber of Deputies, and the German Reichstag. Both men had won passionate partisans in this country as well, Sacco as a hardworking family man, Vanzetti for his powerful combination of humility and a peculiar eloquence in broken English. On the other side, all of this unprecedented support from abroad and from the left created a resentful backlash among more conservative citizens of Massachusetts, who felt their whole judicial system was being put on trial. Caught in the political crossfire, Governor Alvan T. Fuller was persuaded to appoint a special three-man commission, headed by Harvard University president Lawrence Lowell, to advise him about clemency.

In addition to reviewing existing evidence, the Lowell Commission brought in a new expert, Calvin Goddard, to do the ballistics all over again. As it happened, roughly between the time of the murders in 1920 and the death sentence in 1927, three Americans, Charles A. Waite, Philippe Gravelle, and Goddard himself had in effect revolutionized the still-controversial study of ballistics. The United States for the first time was moving into the forefront of a key forensic science, and one of special importance in this country. The majority of American murder cases by then involved guns, and although the guns themselves were often ditched, investigators almost always had bullets to work with, and usually shells. While the self-taught "experts" at the trial and afterward had peered through glasses and microscopes, taking notes and making pictures, Goddard now had a new invention, the comparison microscope, which allowed him—and others—to see two bullets and their unique markings simultaneously. Armed with this, he concluded—and persuaded two previous defense experts—that the bullet that killed Alessandro Berardelli had been fired from the Colt .32 that Nicola Sacco, with fatal foolishness, was still allegedly carrying three weeks later.

The Lowell Commission was convinced, and Governor Fuller refused clemency on August 3. But expert testimony is not always convincing, especially in cases involving ideology or high emotion, and given the possibility of switching guns or bullets over the years—the prosecution, and indeed the defense, had not always played fair—the partisans were not persuaded. The month of August was filled with a hot blizzard of appeals and exceptions: to Thayer again, who turned down a motion charging himself with judicial bias; to the Supreme Judicial Court of Massachusetts; to members of the federal circuit court and Supreme Court of the United States. All were denied, Justice Oliver Wendell Holmes of the Supreme Court ruling that the federal judiciary had no right to intervene in a state criminal case unless the proceedings there were "absolutely void," that is, in blatant violation of the Constitution.

As the final gasp of organized anarchism in the United States, that month was also punctuated with bombings of the homes of jurors, legal officials, and churches. As the fatal day approached the city of Boston was filled with local, state, metropolitan, prison, and Cambridge policemen, more uniformed force than at any time since the American Revolution. And on August 23, 1927, more than seven years after the murders, millions mourned as Sacco and Vanzetti were finally electrocuted, together with the nearly forgotten Celestino Madeiros, the only three condemned men in the history of Charlestown State Prison to refuse the final ministrations of a clergyman.

But their deaths, even their funerals, the most spectacular in the history of the state, did not truly close the most technically and legally tangled case in American history. Francis Russell, its leading historian, after rerunning the Goddard tests again in 1961, came eventually to agree with Carlo Tresca, the dean of American anarchists, that Sacco was guilty but Vanzetti was not. But this emotionally unsatisfying (if quite possibly correct) conclusion only dramatizes the fact that the case left scars, doubts, and divisions that would not easily heal.

4

Whether struck by the very differing stories of Al Capone, Bart Vanzetti, or Richard Loeb, thoughtful Americans at the close of the 1920s had reason to worry about murderous violence and problems in the

justice system. President Herbert Hoover commissioned an unprecedented study of law enforcement in the United States, and the resulting
Wickersham Commission report, issued in twelve volumes beginning
in 1931, summed up the prevailing wisdom about crime and criminality, police, prosecution, prison, and parole. And the next year, reflecting
many of the same concerns, Professor H. C. Brearly published the first
scholarly study of the subject, *Homicide in the United States.*

Brearly was interested less in the famous cases than in the ordinary
ones that made up the "homicide rate." And he was concerned above
all with four questions: Was this in fact "the most lawless of civilized
nations"? Was the rate going up or down? What were the patterns of
homicide? And how, finally, to explain both patterns and rates?

He recognized that the available national statistics, based since 1906
on the registration of death certificates, were seriously flawed. But the
comparisons used to answer his first question were bigger than any possible errors: the figures showed that during the 1920s the American
homicide rate was 8.4 per 100,000, more than 10 times Japan's 0.8,
5 times the 1.6 for Ontario, nearly 17 times the 0.5 for England and
Wales, and 47 times the Swiss 0.18. Only the provinces of southern
Italy had higher rates than the overall U.S. average, but even there the
22.0 for Sicily was topped by the 30.0 for the state of Florida.

The statistical problem made it harder to judge direction, but while
suspect, the same figures showed a ragged upward trend from 1906 to
1929: from 5.0 to 8.5. The differing geographic patterns, however, like
the gaps between rates in the United States and other nations, were big
past all denying. Vermont had the lowest rate at 1.4, Florida the highest
at 30.0; in general the South led all regions, followed by the Far West,
the Midwest, and finally New England and the northern plains.

The most obvious change in the patterns of homicide was the increased use of guns. During the mid-1920s, Brearly's figures showed,
guns were responsible for 71 percent of all deaths, a few points higher
in rural areas, lower in urban. An independent and more recent sampling of 513 homicide indictments in Philadelphia for the years 1920,
1926, and 1932 underlines the point: 64 percent of the nonaccidental
victims died of gunshot wounds, a sharp rise from the 42 percent for
sampled years earlier in the twentieth century and far greater than the
25 percent for the whole of the nineteenth century. Shotguns and rifles
in rural areas were economic tools for most and recreation for many;

the guns involved in city shootings were almost always revolvers, economic tools only for robbers, but widely owned and sometimes carried by fearful people of all kinds. The surging urban prosperity of the period made cheap pistols more affordable than ever, and the publicity given crime news added to the fear, as the issue of handgun control took on a new intensity, with several national organizations and state legislatures taking up the cause.

African-American men and women were especially vulnerable to gun deaths, and across the country, as earlier in Philadelphia, accounted for proportionally more of them than any other group. This was still an era in which blacks were more likely to be murdered by whites than vice versa, and had more reason to be afraid downtown at night. For more than a century their own neighborhoods had been zoned, by the dominant powers, as "red-light districts," and the nasty underside of the Jazz Age was that places like Harlem, Beale Street, and Storyville were full not only of music but also of prostitutes, gambling halls, illegal speakeasies, and wired-up strangers looking for action. And for many residents, in the North as well as the South, the justice system was no ally, and instead of a beacon of help in time of danger a blue uniform was seen as a red flag. Police brutality was one of the major targets of the Wickersham Commission. And in an era when the Philadelphia department averaged about 7 killings a year, New York 22, and Chicago nearly 45, too many of the victims were black men.

One result of the vicious circle of gun carrying was that every encounter in the black ghetto was potentially lethal; the weapons carried for protection against gangs and strangers turned too often against family and friends. The result was another vicious circle: while the African-American population in most cities was still a small minority, it was increasingly identified with the crime of murder. The black death rate from homicide, according to Brearly's figures, was between seven and eight times the white death rate during the middle of the 1920s, and while the largely rural South had the highest rates overall, both black and white rates were highest in small cities and heavily publicized in big ones like Chicago and New York. Still largely denied the regimenting experience of office and factory, which raised the suicide-murder ratio among white immigrants, African-American newcomers encountered the city only as a place of marginal employment, full of unfamiliar tensions and troubles. Even among the relatively well-off policyholders of the Metropolitan Insurance Company, Brearly pointed out, homicide among young adult black males ranked third as cause of death, behind only tuberculosis and pneumonia, two diseases then essentially incurable.

Among whites, the most notorious major change during the 1920s was the number of gangland murders: the Illinois Crime Survey counted 130 of these in Chicago during the two years 1926–27, roughly 18 percent of all nonaccidental killings. And while this was an unusual sample, taken at the peak of Al Capone's campaign to establish a racketeering monopoly, other places from Los Angeles to Philadelphia reported the same kinds of deaths in lesser number. The common denominators were the evident efficiency of the execution, the fact that if they did not simply speed away immediately the killers dumped the victim's body in a river, park, or empty lot, the lack of cooperative witnesses, and as a result of these a dismal record for successful prosecutions. Not one of the 130 Chicago cases cited above resulted in a conviction of any kind. In Philadelphia the number is hard to count; a number of killings that in court were said to involve self-defense or no apparent motive at all were rumored to be related to the activities of Mickey Duffy, the Lanzetti brothers, and other local mobsters. The one thing clear is that in a city where the police claimed to "solve" nearly 95 percent of all killings, either through arresting or at least naming a fugitive suspect, about half of the twenty-five "unsolved" cases in the three sample years were identified as gangland killings.

The other half of the unsolved killings were mostly the result of armed robberies, another category that shot up during the 1920s. These had earlier been rare crimes in the urban East. But by the 1920s headlines continually advertised the fact that automobiles had opened up exciting possibilities to up-to-date versions of the Jesse James gang, like those who held up the South Braintree payroll, while more modest lone gunmen stuck up grocery stores, gas stations, and late-night celebrants on city streets. Death was always a danger in armed robberies, unlike the muggings or drunk-rollings that had been routine earlier, but the exact figure for robbery murders is hard to count, and the indirect toll was even more important.

It is relatively easy for a historian working from official or newspaper accounts to find reliable numbers for things like "race" or "weapon"; but "robbery" is one of the harder categories to define, and in dealing with motives the historical record is full of flaws and holes. The Chicago Crime Commission found that seventy-one people, exactly 10 percent of the victims of nonaccidental killings during 1926–27, were victims of holdups. This is almost exactly the percentage for Philadelphia for the sample years, when both indictments and "unsolved" killings are added together. But a significant fraction of the fatal shootings by policemen also involved robbery suspects. On the other side, armed robbery was one of the things that helped to make this a dangerous time to be an officer of the law. Brearly noted that fully one in seven murder victims in the southern cities of Atlanta, Birmingham, Memphis, and New Orleans during 1921–22 were policemen, and while the attempt to enforce Prohibition was said to have cost many deaths, armed robbers accounted for all of the four Philadelphia cops killed in the sample years and probably most of the twenty in Chicago during 1926–27.

The presence of guns, too, quick reactions and quick deaths, helps make it hard to pin down what really happened in the many cases involving card games and crapshoots—was the victim cheating, or being robbed? Meanwhile the very threat of robbery meant that growing numbers of small businessmen kept revolvers within reach, especially those involved in illegal sidelines like the numbers racket or liquor sales. In Philadelphia during the sample years, save for a single chiropractor who strangled his mistress and a University of Pennsylvania student accused of shooting a visitor from Dartmouth, all members of the middle class indicted for nonaccidental homicide were grocers, saloon keepers, or the owner-managers of gas stations. Whether directly or indirectly, the victims in these cases died as the result of growing nervousness about guns and cars, the vicious circle that was making the city seem a place in which people had reason to fear strangers at night.

And at the same time there was reason to fear family as well; the last major category of homicide to show an increase during the 1920s was domestic. This is an easier figure to calculate than those for robbery. In Chicago during 1926–27, 42 husbands and 13 wives were killed by their spouses, or 8 percent of the total. But the Chicago figures evidently do not include common-law marriages; in Philadelphia the total number of domestic killings during the sample years was 55, the proportion twice as great, at 16 percent. Both figures are bigger than those for earlier periods.

In terms of the history of marriage in general, the rise suggests both good news and bad. The good news is that the relations between urban husbands and wives were in some ways growing closer over time and that more members of the working class—as always the great majority of killers and victims—were entering long-term relationships. The bad news is that in the city marriage for many working people had always been an economically unstable relationship and that the underside of love and affection is possessiveness, jealousy, and tension.

Both points are most strikingly illustrated by the situation of black Philadelphians. During the 1920s as earlier, most of the city's African-American adults were married, and the great majority of children were born into legitimate two-parent families. But the strains on these families were enormous. As always, the move from country to city meant a movement from a family unit in which shared work was essential to a family unit in which husbands and wives worked separately; among the poor one paycheck was not enough, and children were almost wholly consumers, with no earning power until they were twelve or so. For black men the problem was aggravated by the fact that while they were still excluded from industrial and office jobs, their wives were far more employable. For black women the problem was that the jobs, while available, were mostly in badly paid domestic service, the best of them as live-in maids—situations that left little room for successful marriage or children.

This uneven situation led to a high rate of separation, divorce, and jealousy, and so to an even higher rate of domestic killings among Philadelphia's blacks than others; in the sample years fully 30 percent of African-American murders involved husbands and wives. And beyond this high rate was as always a distinctive pattern of gender roles as well. Black women, historically, had rarely been held in by the narrow roles allowed to middle-class whites. And the fact that they went where the men went, did what the men did, and often held the high cards in the marital and sexual games played by men and women of all races meant that they were more likely than white women to play the kind of aggressive roles that might lead to murderous assault.

Across the country, of 161 women committed to prison for homicide in 1926, some 124 were African American, just 35 white, and 2 of "other races." This suggests, however crudely, a huge imbalance in actual rates of nearly 30:1. In Philadelphia during the sample years it was even bigger. Just 3 white women were indicted for nonaccidental kill-ings, and another, Irene Etter, committed suicide in the spring of 1932 after shooting her steelworker husband and Gwendolyn Shinn, a twenty-two-year-old boarder in their household. But 17 black women were indicted; with the black population about one-tenth the white, that is a ratio well over 40:1.

These black women were involved in a range of incidents. Constance Thomas, who had put up most of the money for their West Philadel-phia restaurant, shot and killed her abusive husband in 1926, and while there was clearly malice aforethought, a jury decided that she was pro-voked, and she was sentenced to 9 to 18 years for second-degree mur-der. Eva Coleman, in the same year, had an argument with her landlady over her child's noisy behavior, slashed the woman to death, and fled. As a dramatic example of the growing importance of ordinary homicide detection in police work, she was arrested twenty-two years later, in Chicago, under a new name, and returned to receive a suspended sen-tence for manslaughter in 1948. Six women killed other women, 11 killed men, mostly husbands, at home, during parties, in back yards and streets. Six used guns, 8 knives or other sharp weapons, 1 a lighted oil lamp, and 1 an iron bar. Very strikingly, 5 of the 11 who killed men did not use guns, or physical "equalizers," but knives, at close quarters, showing a kind of strength and confidence almost unknown among white women at any time.

Almost as striking is the utter absence of indictments for infanticide in Philadelphia, among either black women or white, or among black women in Chicago during 1926–27. While infanticide accounted in England for nearly a third of all homicides and was important on the Continent, Brearly's figures show that by the 1920s it had dropped un-der 2 percent of U.S. homicide deaths. This reflects, not just the quea-siness about prosecuting such cases that had been growing since the Puritan era in New England, but a real drop in their number. Living standards, women's wages, and hospital birthings continued to rise, and the 1920s marked an especially important turn in the nature of adop-tion. While black communities, always sympathetic to the plight of single mothers, had a long tradition of informal adoption, white cou-ples well into the twentieth century preferred to "foster" healthy boys already old enough to work. Only in the 1920s and 1930s did "sentimental" adoption overtake this hard-headed economic approach. And as celebrities such as Babe Ruth, Al Jolson, and George Burns and Gracie Allen helped to publicize the adoption of infants, especially girls, some of the worst pressures on pregnant unwed mothers were eased.

5

But whatever the specific patterns of homicide in the United States, Professor Brearly was interested above all in why there was so much of it. And his survey is a marvelous guide both to the questions and prejudices of contemporary laymen and to the answers provided sometimes by common sense and sometimes by sociological expertise.

Were American murder rates so high, first, as the underside of our go-getting spirit, a by-product of the nation's wealth and power? Clearly not, Brearly pointed out; the impoverished South had the worst record of all sections, the rich Northeast the best. Was it the aftermath of war, the glorification of killing? Again not; compare the lower rates of European nations far more affected than we. Was it the American media, the movies and the papers? This made more sense, and various experts were worried that the gunplay in Wild West silents created violent fantasies in delinquent kids. But children themselves, when surveyed, did not identify with movie villains, remembering mostly that they all died or went to prison. The sensational papers made better targets, together with books and dime novels that glorified criminals like Jesse James. And although again there was little hard evidence to go on, at least one well-publicized killing had an apparent "copycat" effect.

One of the few individual cases described in Brearly's study was that of Edward Hickman, a young man who in 1927 kidnapped, ransomed, murdered, and mutilated a little girl named Marion Parker in Los Angeles. Sex murders were still not routine events in that day—there were only three reported in the sample years for Philadelphia, two in Chicago during 1926–27—and the heavy coverage of Hickman's crime seems to have inspired at least four imitators; the New York City superintendent of schools felt the need to warn teachers about letting pupils go home in the company of adults not their parents.

Continuing with his list of possibilities, Brearly dismissed the popular idea that foreign immigrants pushed up homicide rates; with the possible exception of the Italians, no group was as violent as natives of the South and West. (It may be added that despite the publicity surrounding Al Capone, Prohibition era gangsters were often ethnically Jewish, Irish, Polish, or white Anglo-Saxon Protestant.) Nor was the mixing, the continual contact and sometimes friction among ethnic groups and cultures, responsible; no place was more polyglot than New York City, and New York in his day had lower homicide rates than the nation at large.

The equally popular idea that the American school system encouraged criminal behavior by neglecting the teaching of values in favor of an emphasis on secular success and competition was harder to test. But Brearly did note that murderers in general had little schooling of any kind and that the best schools were in the West, the worst in the South, while the East had the lowest homicide rates of all.

Prohibition was no answer either: American homicide rates were high before the Eighteenth Amendment was passed. Neither was the simple fact—compare Canada and Australia—that we were a new nation, with a long frontier tradition.

But above all, Brearly was at pains to disprove the theories of the late nineteenth century, the age of Social Darwinism, Robert Dugdale, and Cesare Lombroso. The idea that criminals were born and not made, that an inherited "stigma of degeneracy" distinguished them physically, mentally, and morally from other citizens, was no longer tenable. It would be hard, on this basis, to explain why the citizens of Wyoming were three times as murderous as those of neighboring Idaho. Careful tests of the "IQs" of convicts compared favorably with those of draftees during World War I. And although murderers seemed to score lower than others, wardens reported that they also tended to be model prisoners, by no means "moral degenerates."

Himself a white South Carolinian, Brearly followed his attack on hereditarian dogma by abandoning racist explanations as well. As the result of recent studies, he and others were coming to believe that the undeniably high incidence of murder and manslaughter among African Americans was simply the result of poverty, discrimination, poor education, and a history of abuses by the police and justice systems. And although more information was needed, it was at least possible that if researchers could control for all these environmental factors "approximately equal homicide rates might be found for the two races."

What underlay all of Brearly's conclusions was that as sociology and criminology moved toward the middle of the twentieth century they were returning to the explanations discovered during the era of romantic reform, a century earlier. While neither he nor the experts surveyed for the Wickersham Commission's 1931 *Report on the Causes of Crime* were as optimistic as these distant ancestors about the ease of setting things straight, they agreed that crime in general and homicide in particular were best explained not by heredity but by environment, by history and culture. Murder was clearly related, as among blacks, to poverty and lack of education. Beyond that, the two most important contributors to high rates of homicide were rooted respectively in the family and personality and in the legal or justice system.

Entering the 1920s, Brearly was appalled by the fact there was 1 divorce in this country for about 8 marriages, compared to 1 in 96 in Great Britain and 1 in 161 in Canada. Experts found that family instability was clearly related to juvenile delinquency. And with respect specifically to murder, they believed that such instability contributed to the most common type of homicidal personality.

There were a number of personality types, described in now outmoded psychological jargon, that according to current theory seemed especially prone to homicidal behavior, beginning with such obviously twisted sadists as Leopold and Loeb. But in looking over the range of homicidal incidents, Brearly was struck above all by the senselessness of most of them, the brawls that seemed to erupt over little or nothing. These he thought were the result of a low "sociological age," a failure to mature, to move out of the infantile stage of ego into altruism. Sometimes, not wholly ruling out the influence of heredity, he believed that the failure might result from feeblemindedness or epilepsy. But more often it resulted from failures in upbringing, from being spoiled as a child or, without firm parental guidance, from learning antisocial behavior from a delinquent "gang." In either case individuals under stress expressed their personal weakness and lack of self-control through a kind of fatally infantile temper tantrum.

Brearly offered no solution to the problems of family and child raising. But when he turned to the law and the justice system his policy prescriptions, although sometimes implicit, were entirely clear. The most obvious single explanation for high American murder rates was the legal availability of guns, above all concealed revolvers, and the fact that carrying guns was associated with manliness especially in the South and West. This alone was nearly enough to account for our differences with other nations, he pointed out. But there were other issues as well.

On the question of deterrence, Brearly, like most contemporary experts, was opposed to legal execution, if only on the less than passionate grounds that it was so rare (there were then about one hundred a year) that it was irrelevant to most cases. Far more important than severity was that punishment be both swift and certain. And here again the United States compared badly with continental Europe, where the judicial system, relying on trained experts, was briskly run by unelected and presumably dispassionate judges.

There was no question that the American justice system was both lax and inefficient. While rates differed in every region, state, and county, the bottom line was that in a 1923 sample that included most of the country, the rate of imprisonment for homicide was 3.6 per 100,000, while the homicide rate itself (measured by the death certificates) was 8.1, meaning that only about 44 percent of killings resulted in any serious punishment at all. Some of this resulted from the weakness of police detection; the number of wholly unsolved crimes was smaller in European nations, where forces were centralized and enjoyed far more prestige than in the United States. (And where, it might be added, automobiles were still relatively rare, and guns rarer yet.) And if the police were a problem, the courts were a disgrace.

The disgrace, Brearly believed, was rooted both in popular and in legal culture. Americans, historically, were tolerant of violence, and in all well-publicized cases an often irrational "sympathy for the slayer" attached even to such obviously guilty parties as William Gray and Ruth Snyder. But other citizens were always irrationally eager to avenge death, whatever the evidence against the accused, and very often murder cases were decided before they began, through the contest between defense and prosecution over composition of the jury. Again there were two sides; American juries were "miniature mobs," their group passions easily aroused, while, on the other hand, the professor suggested, many reformers would reduce the number needed to convict from twelve to ten. The whole emphasis on contest subverted the search for real truth, or justice. Public confidence was badly shaken by the obvious fact that rich defendants with skillful lawyers fared far better than poor folks and that the legal profession, "like primitive savages," worshiped ritualism and outdated precedents that allowed the guilty to escape or win new trials on the barest of technicalities.

And if capital punishment was no deterrent—Brearly again turned to statistics, with noncapital Rhode Island having far lower homicide rates than capital South Carolina—the evasion of tough punishment sent the wrong message about the sanctity of life. As of the mid-1920s, the average murder or manslaughter sentence handed down in the United States was about twenty years for males, fifteen for females (far higher, it may be noted, than in any earlier time). But as the result of casual pardons and paroles (rarely granted by the kind of experts the professor favored), the men typically served only about five years, the women three, a kind of "lenient treatment" that helped to explain, he believed, why murder rates stayed high.

But while Brearly's statistics were a useful rough guide to many aspects of American homicide, he was quite aware that the national registration figures he cited were deeply flawed. One of the problems with death certificates as a source of "murder rates" is simply that "homicide" is a not a medical but a legal term and that doctors tended to write "skull fracture" or "renal failure" without indicating how or why these had occurred. And with respect to the important issue of comparison across time, the apparent ragged rise from 5.0 per 100,000 in 1906 to 8.5 per 100,000 in 1929 is an utter illusion. In fact, while there are no truly definitive figures, the actual "murder rate" across the United States during the early twentieth century almost certainly continued the long downward slide of the late nineteenth century, or at worst remained flat with a modest upward zig during the "Roaring Twenties."

The death certificate "registration area," first, did not yet include all of the states. The system was pioneered among those with more advanced medical-bureaucratic procedures, above all in the less murderous North and East, and gradually added others from the South and West. The apparent 1906–29 "rise" then mostly resulted from starting with states with low homicide rates and adding new ones with high rates. If the same places are compared across time, the rise disappears; of the 23 states included in the "registration area" in 1912, 1 showed no change by 1922, while with a neat symmetry, 11 rose and 11 dropped.

Many places in the very earliest years also classified automobile accidents as "homicides," as police departments did, and the time in question neatly spans the internal combustion revolution. Motorcars, a rich
man's luxury in 1906, had become items of mass consumption by 1929.
Traffic control was still primitive, and elderly pedestrians were more
used to calculating the oncoming speed of horse-drawn milk wagons
than of Studebakers, so that deaths from automobile accident were proportionally far more common than now: in Philadelphia there were
roughly three hundred a year, on average, by the 1920s. These were technically "homicides," of course, but not in the sense used either earlier
or later, and the inclusion in any number of the arrests, indictments, or
death certificates based on them pushed up the "murder rate" artificially.

Some historical studies, then, uncritically using these misleading "official" figures, have published graphs and charts showing wholly erro-
neous rises for the early decades of the century. But if the object is to
find the "real" murder rate, it is quite clear it was dropping markedly
outside, perhaps, of the big cities of the Northeast and Midwest.

The western gunfighter, on either side of the law, was after all a figure
of the past, with movies stars like Tom Mix taking the place of romanticized real figures like Wyatt Earp. Labor violence continued into the
1920s and 1930s, with brutal jockeying along picket lines and occasional serious outbreaks, as around the Kentucky mines of "Bloody"
Harlan County, or in the Memorial Day Massacre of 1937, in which
pro-union men and women marching on a Republic Steel Plant in
South Chicago were charged by police; none of the ten men killed in
that one were armed, and six were shot in the back. But after the brief
antiradical flare-up around World War I, there were no truly sustained
episodes comparable to the Rocky Mountain "labor wars," or those that
had everywhere dogged the International Workers of the World.

Racism, too, while still intolerably high, accounted for fewer direct
casualties than in earlier decades. Across the South, its leadership eager
to be accepted into the modern world of the twentieth century, the day
of literally murderous politicians like Pitchfork Ben Tillman was done.
After the flare-up around World War I, race rioting, while it never really
ended, subsided markedly. So did lynching; another partial victory in
the long and never-ended battle against racial violence occurred following an episode in 1931, in which nine young black men were accused
of the capital crime of raping two white women in a boxcar passing

through Alabama. The "Scottsboro Boys" were tried in a court of law, not lynched; in a case that drew in the NAACP and national attention, the result of a series of appeals was that over the course of a decade four were freed, one fled to Michigan—which refused to extradite him—and the remaining four got prison instead of the chair.

The Native Americans, finally, had been disarmed entirely, and those unable or unwilling to join the dominant culture were shut up on reservations. During the New Deal of the 1930s an end was made to the long and misguided attempt to destroy their tribal structure entirely. The reservation still remained a dismal place for most, and for those who ventured off to clash with white neighbors in nearby grazing areas or barrooms the dominant system of justice remained one-sided or incomprehensible. But at least the ancient cycle of interracial murder, massacre, and revenge was long dead.

Why, then, all the publicity about the "lawless decade" of the 1920s? Simply that these faraway declines in murderous violence were of little concern to most middle-class readers and opinion makers. The census of 1920 had marked an enormous demographic milestone: over half the population of the United States now lived in "urban" areas—a category that covered "suburban" developments as well. And there is no doubt that the kinds of homicide that filled the news directly concerned these people. Armed robberies and gangland slayings happened close to home. Al Capone, Nicola Sacco, and Bart Vanzetti were scary representatives of the new immigration filling the cities. The marked increase in urban black crime was helping push whites out into the suburbs. The most famous cases, as always, involved people from backgrounds much like their own: Hall and Mills, Gray and Snyder, Leopold and Loeb.

Did the increase in gun crimes and robberies actually push up urban rates? Maybe. But the ongoing urban industrial revolution was still demanding the kind of rational regimented behavior that had been pushing them down since the 1870s. For all of its failures in other ways, national prohibition did work in cutting down much casual drinking among the working class, and with it casual fighting. The public schools were reaching more kids for longer periods of time, teaching them, as always, to sit still, take turns, and mind their betters, helping to raise the suicide-murder ratio. And the ongoing power of this kind of socialization, together with its absence, may be shown through the still contrasting experiences of Philadelphia's Italians and blacks.

Among Italian immigrants and their descendants, as they were slowly absorbed into the urban industrial revolution, the rate of imprisonment for murder and manslaughter (eliminating auto and other accidental homicides) fell by close to a factor of two and a half between 1901 and 1926, from about 17 to 7. Among excluded African Americans the same rate, starting at lower than the Italian at 10, climbed by more than a factor of one and a half, to 16. During the same period, the rest of the population, including the long-resident native WASPs, Germans, and Irish, even the newer Jews, Greeks, and Poles, bumped along at a rate that varied from a little over 1 per 100,000 at the beginning to a little less than that at the end.

Starting in 1931, in response to complaints voiced by scholars like Brearly and the Wickersham Commission's *Report on Criminal Statistics,* the Federal Bureau of Investigation, now headed by J. Edgar Hoover, began to collect and publish an annual series, *Uniform Crime Reports for the United States,* based on the number of incidents reported to police departments across the country. And while these, too, especially in the early years, were flawed and incomplete, they provided a relatively trustworthy check on the differently gathered mortality statistics, which finally covered the whole nation in 1933. And with various yearly zigs and zags, the direction of both indices from the early 1930s and for decades afterward was sharply and unmistakably down.

6

Publication of the *Uniform Crime Reports* was only one symbol of the many ways in which the federal government was becoming more involved in crimes like homicide, which had earlier been left almost entirely to the states. Congress had begun the process by stretching federal law to involve prostitution, drugs, and most famously the sale of alcohol. But even as the Eighteenth Amendment was repealed, the federal judiciary and even more the executive branch began to expand their roles, a trend much dramatized during the 1930s.

The federal government in fact had a number of weapons to use against crime. One of them was exercised following public outcry over the brazen St. Valentine's Day Massacre, when state and local authorities seemed powerless to deal with Al Capone. It was finally agents of the U.S. Treasury who convicted Capone in 1931, not for these and other murders, his real offense, but—just a year before Prohibition was ended—for evading federal income taxes on his illegal gains.

At the same time, too, the U.S. Supreme Court began for the first time to move against local injustice in criminal cases. The legal key to the defense of the Scottsboro Boys, mentioned just above, was that the Court took on a role that it had earlier refused, notably in the case of Sacco and Vanzetti just five years before, in reviewing the record of a capital case tried in a state court and deciding on grounds of substance and not mere constitutional technicality that the trial had not been fair. In an extremely important ruling, the Court in 1932 held in *Powell v. Alabama* that the Fourteenth Amendment to the Constitution, which guaranteed that no state could "deprive any person of life, liberty, or property without due process of law," meant that the Bill of Rights applied to the states as well as to the federal government. While the nine accused had been assigned attorneys just before the trial opened, the Court ruled that their defense had been so minimal that the defendants, contrary to Article 6, had in effect been denied "the assistance of counsel" and so reversed their death sentences and ordered another trial. Three years later, in the same case, the right to intervene was broadened when the Court ruled that systematic exclusion of African Americans from the jury made the retrial unfair by definition.

But while in practice the Supreme Court over the next two decades moved only hesitantly to expand its role, the Federal Bureau of Investigation, under the direction of J. Edgar Hoover, positively charged into new territory as new crimes caught the public imagination.

The most notorious of these was the kidnap-murder of little Charles A. Lindbergh Jr., son of the first man to fly the Atlantic solo and the most internationally famous American of the era. The toddler, just twenty months old, was stolen out of his second-story bedroom in the little community of Hopewell, New Jersey, on the night of March 1, 1932. Next day hordes of state and local police clumsily destroyed any clues to the kidnapper, notably the sole footprint found at the scene. Several ransom notes were, however, delivered to the family, and a frantic Lindbergh was determined to pay. But he was long unable to make contact, despite desperately running through a series of odd and sometimes criminal would-be intermediaries. On April 2, finally, Dr. John F. Condon, a retired school principal, passed $50,000 in marked bills to a mysterious stranger in a Bronx cemetery. The child was never delivered; six weeks later his body was found in a shallow grave four miles from home.

It was over two years later when, largely by accident, a German immigrant named Bruno Hauptmann was caught with some of the ransom money. There is little doubt that Hauptmann was the mysterious stranger in the cemetery, cashing in on the crime. But the great emotional need at the time was to put full closure to the case, to the family's grief and the public's outrage, and he was tried for the actual murder. At the trial in Trenton, given the utter lack of eyewitness testimony of any kind, the sole link between the defendant and the actual killing was the rickety makeshift ladder used to reach the bedroom—Hauptmann was a professional carpenter by trade—which a wood expert testified had been made of materials taken from his attic. Discovery in later years of an FBI memo that called this testimony "fabricated" (with more apparent skill than the ladder itself) has cast some doubt on this; but at the time, in an apparent victory for "scientific" evidence, it was good enough for twelve men to send Hauptmann to the chair.

More important in the long run was that given the state and local bungling in New Jersey, the case inspired Congress to pass the "Lindbergh Law" in 1933, making kidnapping across state lines a federal offense. And the list of such offenses, with the FBI responsible for enforcement, was quickly expanded into other areas, notably bank robbery.

Historical changes are always mirrored in cases of homicide. In Philadelphia, as the prosperous 1920s turned into the Great Depression of the next decade, in the single year 1932 Wallace Mitchell, father of five, was fatally shot by a grocer as he stole a bottle of milk from a back door; a railroad guard killed Nathaniel Austin, a black teenager, as he tried to steal a bag of coal from a freight train; Joe Garnet, another black man, tired of being teased by his wife and others for being unemployed and living in a public shelter, turned on his tormenters and stabbed one of them to death. Jurors, sympathetic to all parties involved in these little tragedies, ruled all of them cases of involuntary manslaughter, with light or suspended penalties. But while incidents like these illustrated the strains of daily life among the poor, the attentions of press and public centered around more dramatic cases, and decreed in effect that murderous bank robbery was the characteristic Crime of the Era.

During the early 1930s, with money hard to get, these robberies multiplied especially across the South and Midwest, seriously dividing communities, as those who had had their mortgages foreclosed quietly cheered and those with life savings on deposit—in a day before federal insurance—were wiped out. As before, local lawmen were easily frustrated (sometimes bribed, or scared) by men with machine guns and getaway cars speeding quickly out of their jurisdictions. Taking stolen cars across state lines had been a federal offense since 1919, and in 1934, eager to use Hoover's government "G-men" against gangsters of all kinds, Congress made it a federal crime to kill a federal officer, to transport stolen money or flee prosecution for major crimes across state lines, or to rob a national bank.

Romance had attached to bank robbers since the days of Jesse James, and during the depression, with banks and bankers more unpopular than ever, the ancient free-floating David and Goliath and Robin Hood legends were easily attached to the latest crop. The most notorious was then John Dillinger, a sometime farmboy from the Indiana heartland whose athleticism and trickery made fools of pursuers all over the Midwest. By 1933 not only Dillinger himself but Baby Face Nelson, Pretty Boy Floyd, and Homer Van Meter, all loose associates, had become famous names as they killed lawmen and citizens, broke jails, and robbed banks from Ohio across to South Dakota. Eager to join the hunt, Melvin Purvis of the FBI's Chicago office got word in the spring of 1934 that members of the mob were relaxing at Little Bohemia Lodge, in Rhinelander, Wisconsin. Dozens of agents surrounded the place on the night of April 22, and while Dillinger and friends slipped off spent the dark hours destroying the fishing resort with gunfire and killing an innocent guest, while to compound the embarrassment one of the G-men was shot dead in the pursuit that followed.

This fiasco proved a death warrant for Dillinger and the gang, as a furious Hoover offered a huge reward and issued an order to shoot to kill. A deal was finally made with an East Chicago prostitute who knew the leader's whereabouts. Betrayed by this Lady in Red, his date for a movie, John Herbert Dillinger (or was it really him?) was shot down outside the Biograph Theater on the night of July 27. The bureau called a triumphant press conference the next morning. And while romantics mourned the gangster's death—one old girlfriend joined a carnival to tell his story—Hoover's masterful publicity machine won the day.

The other mobile tommy-gunners of the era were soon crushed in the same way. Bonnie Parker and Clyde Barrow had been blasted by a posse, in rural Louisiana, a month before Dillinger, but "the feds" made the most spectacular hits. Homer Van Meter was gunned down in a Minneapolis alley that August. Bureau agents in October shot down Pretty Boy Floyd outside of East Liverpool, Ohio, far from the Oklahoma hill country where he was a local legend, and in November—at the cost of two more dead G-men—killed Baby Face Nelson in a machine-gun duel in rural Illinois. The bureau's deadly reputation was further enhanced the next year when they won another bloody shootout, outside of a Florida lake resort, with Ma Barker and Fred, the last of her bandit sons still alive and free.

Over the rest of the decade, the director continued to label various gangsters "Public Enemy Number One" just before his G-men killed or captured them; Hollywood loved it, as gangster movies came to rival westerns. Hoover himself was flown in personally to arrest the kidnapper and murderer Alvin "Creepy" Karpis in 1936, and three years later handcuffed Louis "Lepke" Buchalter, head of Murder, Inc. Both men were delighted with that one. Buchalter's loosely organized killers did work on contract for various New York labor racketeers and gangsters; conviction on a federal drug charge gave him several years to try, vainly, to pull the old familiar strings and avoid trial and execution for murder in New York. And the surrender to Hoover, of course, arranged by the radio personality Walter Winchell to take place publicly, in busy downtown Manhattan, was another public relations coup for the bureau.

By then the FBI was working, despite some opposition, to remedy an old constitutional problem by creating a kind of voluntary pyramid of state and local law enforcement agencies, with itself at the top. Many local lawmen were resentful of the FBI's publicity machine, and Augustus Vollmer, a notably innovative head of the International Association of Chiefs of Police, was in turn an obvious target of the director's jealousy. Vollmer, improving on early experiments by Cesare Lombroso, had by the 1920s helped devise a polygraph machine that might serve as a "lie detector" by measuring a subject's blood pressure, pulse, sweat, and respiration rate under questioning. But its results were not accepted as "expert" evidence in federal courts, or for many years in states outside of Vollmer's own California, in large part because of Hoover's opposition. The director, too, since the early Red Scare days, had been the target of criticism from the political left for his growing paranoia about domestic radicalism and subversion, while civil libertarians complained continually about the FBI's trigger-happiness and evasions of constitutional rights. But there was no denying that once Hoover took charge in 1924 the bureau had earned a reputation as tough, efficient, and incorruptible. And the expansion of federal law gave its agents the right (when they were asked, and willing to accept the challenge) to enter a number of otherwise local cases, as of homicide, when kidnapping or the crossing of state lines was even suspected.

The long move toward better crime detection, begun late in the nineteenth century, had been continuing at several levels. But at the bottom, the move toward eliminating the coroner system in favor of medical examiners was largely stalled, as politicians preferred to keep the coroners and simply hire forensic pathologists as needed. The need for Washington's leadership was clear. The International Association of Chiefs of Police had been urging a centralized system of fingerprint registration for decades when, in 1930, Congress authorized establishment of the Division of Identification within the FBI to keep a file, always expanding, of all prints taken in the United States. Two years later the bureau opened a laboratory, in part inspired by the Chicago Police Department's embarrassing inability, after the St. Valentine's Day Massacre, to evaluate ballistic evidence. Beginning in 1932 the bureau's expertise was then offered free of charge to any local department that asked for it. This was an often slow process, and rarely used, but one that came to involve not only ballistics but also, in cooperation with university experts across the country, a truly impressive range of physical evidence from blood and hair to soil, dust, and metallic traces.

The evolving pyramid was capped when in 1935 the Justice Department opened the National Police Academy, in which local officers took a series of courses staffed by bureau agents. From the beginning its graduates, returning to head divisions and departments back home, formed an elite of loyal law enforcement officers, connected to each other through the bureau. By the 1940s, then, through initiatives formal and informal, taken by the Congress, the Supreme Court, and the FBI, the United States had moved almost as far as the federal system would allow toward the kind of centralized national system of criminal justice that had long reigned across the Atlantic.

In terms of crime in general and murder in particular, the decades following World War I were full of rapid changes. After a period of unsettled violence at the very beginning, followed by the spectacular Roaring Twenties, the nation settled into the Great Depression with clearly falling rates of homicide and greatly improved ways of dealing with it. But as the 1930s turned into the 1940s, the European continent, once the symbol of superior civilization, loomed as a place of menace and fear. Beginning in 1939 Adolf Hitler's Nazi Germany conquered most of its neighbors and made an alliance with imperial Japan, which was mounting the same kind of aggression on the other side of the world. On December 7, 1941, Japanese planes unexpectedly bombed and strafed the U.S. naval base at Pearl Harbor, Hawaii. This first foreign attack on American soil since the War of 1812 pulled us into the Second World War, blotting out most other issues, and it was not at all clear what might follow.

7

World War II to the Vietnam War, 1941–1963

As it turned out, the outbreak of World War II marked a period of unrivaled prosperity that began during the fighting and continued for decades, a period marked by much progress and confidence on nearly every front except for fear of Russia abroad and subversion at home.

The United States had moved out of the depression and into World War II with a government far more centralized than ever and its citizens far more united. War production, already begun on behalf of European allies, was a tonic for the economy and the blue-collar workforce. The need for labor created new factory and office opportunities for blacks and for women. After December 7, 1941, there was no need to whip the nation into hating distant enemies, given the universal anger stirred by the attack on Pearl Harbor. Nearly 11 million American men and women went into uniform; and while the 330,000 who died were only a fraction of the 50 million killed worldwide, it was clearly the United States that dominated the war, and then the world, as confirmed with the dropping of the atomic bomb and the final victory in August 1945. And this time the triumph was not wasted, as the mistakes of the World War I era were avoided and the economic and social gains of wartime held through the later 1940s and 1950s.

The result was that in several areas, notably race relations North and South, urban living, and murder rates, this was a period of extraordinary promise.

I

As often before, and for the same reasons, the murder rate, as carefully measured by the Bureau of Vital Statistics, dropped during wartime. And this time, despite a brief upward blip in 1946–47 as the servicemen came home, it kept dropping afterward, and none of the violent developments of the 1920s and 1930s were echoed in the 1940s and 1950s.

Although relations with wartime Russian allies soon turned bitter, the resultant fear of communist subversion, or the Red Scare, involved neither bombs nor murderous vigilantes. Labor and capital, with booming prosperity to divide between them, kept their competition largely free of bloodshed, supervised by federal rules and agencies created during the New Deal. Returning black men in uniform, some of them with new ideas about civil rights, were not greeted with a wave of race riots or lynchings. Those who had won places in factories were enlisted by national unions, which sometimes helped ease friction with white co-workers and neighbors while protecting their new jobs.

The FBI was stronger than ever, basking in its role as protector against Russian spies and communist subversives, and the day of bank robbers wielding tommy guns seemed as dead as that of outlaws with six-shooters. Urban gangsters did not go away, and in some ways the business of vice, especially drugs and gambling, was run more efficiently than ever. But while there were some shootouts and casualties, the very purpose of "organized" crime—involving loose cooperative and territorial arrangements among otherwise separate groups—was to cut down on the kind of murderous competition associated earlier with Al Capone's Chicago. The city of Las Vegas, which began to rise out of the Nevada desert during the early 1940s and soared through the 1950s, was one sign among many that a new generation was working toward quasi-respectable and "front" operations, relying less on triggermen and more on lawyers.

Newspaper readers, as always, had murder to read about, and just after the war the widely publicized case of William Heirens sounded dim echoes of Leopold and Loeb for them to talk about. Heirens, from a rich suburban family, was a brilliant student who skipped the freshman year when admitted to the University of Chicago. That June 1945 he slashed a middle-aged woman to death when she discovered him burglarizing her North Side apartment, and in December he shot and

stabbed a young nurse under the same circumstances, writing, in lip-
stick, a note on her bedroom wall: "For Heaven's sake catch me before
I kill more. I cannot control myself." Six months after he had killed and
dismembered six-year-old Suzanne Degnan, in January 1946, he was
finally captured while attempting another burglary.

In an age fascinated by Sigmund Freud, and by the promise of scientific advance, the Heirens case was red meat. During the war, although American intelligence had failed to come up with a drug to use
in breaking enemy agents, psychiatrists did discover that sodium pen-
tathol might unlock buried memories in shell shock victims, easing
them into talking about matters that they had been suppressing. Billed
as "truth serum," it offered the exciting possibility that criminal suspects, too, might be made to talk, unable to lie to police. And in the
summer of 1946, for the first time in a criminal case, it was used on
William Heirens.

The effect of injecting young Heirens with the drug was that he at
first described the crimes, in detail, but as the work of someone else,
evidently an alter ego he called "George Murman," whose surname
amateur psychiatrists were able to translate as "Murderman." Later he
offered a more coherent confession. As a boy, incapable of normal
sexual relations, he had spent much time pasting Nazi pictures into a
scrapbook, playing with guns, setting fires, and burglarizing houses. His
gruesome obsession with the bodies of his three victims had given the
papers much to hint at; and the issue of his sanity together with his age
were mitigating factors that helped a judge and prosecutor to agree to
sparing him death, after a guilty plea, in favor of three life sentences
without parole.

But while many clung to hope in the potential of truth serum, as the
ultimate "scientific" aid to police work (and perhaps psychiatry), its
apparent magic quickly faded under assault from two professions. Psychiatrists found its effect on the mind to be wholly unreliable, as in
the Heirens case, and the Illinois Supreme Court condemned its use
without permission as a clear violation of the Fifth Amendment right
against self-incrimination. The business of "lie detecting" was left,
then, to the more familiar polygraph machine. This was still viewed
with some skepticism, but beginning in 1947 its results were allowed as
expert evidence in most states, provided both prosecution and defense
stipulated in advance that they would use them.

But the big news in the postwar era was in any case not crime but communism, and the biggest capital case involved not homicide but espionage, the result of the shock administered by the Soviet Union's explosion of an atomic bomb in September 1949. In the context of the developing Cold War, the blast shattered not only the previous American monopoly on atomic weapons but American nerves and complacency as well. The FBI then found that the wartime bomb project in Los Alamos, New Mexico, had been penetrated by foreign agents, explaining how and why the Russians had so quickly mastered the technology. The key scientific information had been passed, it turned out, by Klaus Fuchs, a British citizen and communist refugee from Nazi Germany who had joined the project in 1944. Fuchs was arrested in England in February 1950, and shortly offered a confession that led back to the United States.

With much work and some luck the FBI was able within months to identify the go-between between the scientist and the Russians as a Philadelphia chemist named Harry Gold. Gold, like Fuchs, confessed to having worked to advance the ideals of Soviet communism, which had since the war disillusioned both of them. And he provided another name, David Greenglass, a former technician at Los Alamos who had supplied some of the nuts-and-bolts to make real bombs of Fuchs's theory. After first protesting ignorance Greenglass and his wife also confessed to passing secrets, and they named as the head of the spy ring David's brother-in-law, sometime machine-shop partner and longtime mentor Julius Rosenberg.

Harry Gold pleaded guilty. Julius Rosenberg, his wife, Ethel, his longtime friend, Morton Sobell, and David Greenglass were all indicted for espionage, together with a long-departed minor Russian "diplomat." The trial opened in March 1951, at the very height of the war begun a year earlier when the United States had come to the aid of South Korea, invaded by the communist North. Greenglass pleaded guilty at the outset, so that the proceedings involved the Rosenbergs and Sobell only. No testimony implicated Sobell, who refused to take the stand, in the specific trade in atomic secrets. Most of the government's case was built on Gold and Greenglass, plus other witnesses who testified to the defendants' communist views, their plans to flee to Mexico after Fuchs's arrest, and other acts deemed incriminating. With Sobell mute, virtually the only defense was the testimony of the Rosenbergs themselves, who simply and stubbornly denied all involvement in spying and insisted that Greenglass, who had fallen out with his brother-in-law, was maliciously lying. The verdict of guilty, on March 29, was no surprise. But the sentences were. Klaus Fuchs, in England, had already drawn the British maximum of 14 years; Harry Gold, 30. In this case Judge Irving R. Kaufman handed 30 years to Sobell, 15 to Greenglass, and on April 6, as courtroom observers gasped and even screamed, condemned not only Julius but also Ethel Rosenberg to death in the electric chair.

Since the founding of the American Republic the number of crimes that earned capital punishment had been shrinking steadily, although an occasional scare or case suggested new ones, in some states, such as assault by a life-term prisoner, bombing, or kidnapping. As of 1951 there were still a number for which no one had been executed in decades—15 states had "carnal knowledge" on the books, 7 bombing, 4 arson, 2 train wrecking. "Treason" against an individual state had resulted in no deaths since John Brown, in 1859, was hanged by the Commonwealth of Virginia. Only 6 of the many states that provided death for kidnapping had actually carried it out since 1930; for assault by a lifer, the figure was 1 execution in the 5 states that made it a capital offense; for armed burglary, 2 of 4; robbery, 7 of 10; rape, 18 of 19. Only murder was in practice as well as in law a capital crime in the majority of states, all 44 of those that legalized the death penalty. But a federal capital case was largely new country, and while the Rosenberg trial itself had created little public outcry at the time—the Russians, firmly in control of Communist parties the world over, had no wish to publicize it—the sentences did.

The protests in some ways echoed those inspired earlier by Sacco and Vanzetti, and only partly because all parties were highly conscious of that earlier case. Again the fact that much of the campaign that denounced either the trial or the sentence was inspired by Soviet Russia did not account for protests from the Vatican, or among many non- or anticommunist citizens across the Western world. While neither Rosenberg had the charismatic eloquence of Bart Vanzetti, the very ordinariness of their middle-class life and looks counted for them; while a strong case was made for their involvement in specific acts of espionage, it was hard to believe David Greenglass's unsupported allegations that they were spymasters on a grand scale. Ethel in particular had played at most a helping role, as in typing notes, and the traditional aversion to executing women was compounded by the fact that the couple were evidently devoted parents to two small boys.

Less of the uproar than with Sacco-Vanzetti centered on the Rosenbergs' possible innocence, more on the harshness of the sentence. Tried during the height of the McCarthy era, when accusations of communist sympathies often pointed to "New York Jewish intellectuals," the fact that the jury that convicted them included no Jews was a sore point, despite the ethnic backgrounds of both Judge Kaufman and the prosecutor, Irving Saypol (both surely chosen with this in mind), and the notable lack of sympathy from B'nai B'rith, the leading watchdog against anti-Semitism.

Legal scholars had a stronger point. The two had been tried for conspiracy to commit espionage in wartime, but the war in question had been with Nazi Germany; despite mutual hostilities, the United States had not then or ever been at war with Soviet Russia, the nation to which the secrets were passed. And Judge Kaufman, in a sentencing speech rich in references to the evils of International Communism, gave his opinion that the Korean War was in part the result of the defendants' "treason." No American had in fact ever been executed for treason against the United States (John Brown had betrayed Virginia), a crime to which a special horror attaches, and that was not the offense with which the two were charged or convicted. But all judicial appeals on these legal grounds failed, and with the Cold War raging President Dwight Eisenhower refused to grant clemency on grounds of compassion. Julius and then Ethel Rosenberg, still protesting innocence, were accordingly electrocuted at New York's Sing-Sing Prison on Friday, June 19, 1953, just before a late sundown announced arrival of the Jewish Sabbath.

2

That the Rosenbergs pushed murder out of the headlines for a while was no surprise, partly because of the excitement surrounding the Cold War and partly because of the lack of excitement then surrounding homicide.

Marvin Wolfgang's classic study, *Patterns of Criminal Homicide,* published in 1957, was based on an analysis of all 625 cases reported to the

Philadelphia police between 1948 and 1952. Wolfgang, a criminologist, was able to follow the homicide unit as it did its daily work, and so to offer far more detail and accuracy than any historian working out of dusty and reluctant paper records. In retrospect the five years of his study covered the very height of the ongoing urban industrial revolution, and clearly showed its long-term effects, as the collective portrait Wolfgang drew from life (and death) was of a less threatening series of big city homicides than would have been possible at almost any time before or certainly since.

Philadelphia, as in earlier eras, was as nearly representative as any other city. Based on the 588 cases that were labeled neither "excusable" nor "justifiable," its "criminal homicide" rate over those five years averaged 5.7 per 100,000 annually, putting it almost exactly in the middle of some eighteen of the biggest reporting American cities. Those ahead of it were Miami, at 15.1, followed by Dallas, Washington, D.C., Kansas City (Mo.), Baltimore, Chicago, Cincinnati, and Seattle. Trailing Philadelphia were, in order, Boston, Columbus, Los Angeles, New York, Pittsburgh, Akron, Buffalo, St. Paul, and finally Milwaukee, at 2.3.

In most other respects, too, Wolfgang's findings fit those for other places. The national average of 5.4 over the same several years was just a shade lower than Philadelphia's, as improved education, population shifts, stronger local institutions, and cultural changes continued to pacify the countryside, pushing rural rates in many areas below those for the bigger cities. The largely agricultural South was, however, still in the lead, with the West no longer so wild as when Brearly had surveyed it in the 1920s.

Philadelphia was typical, too, in that after decades of advances the homicide squad was by then at the top of the police department's ladder of prestige, commanding the services not only of experienced detectives but also of specialists in handwriting, fingerprinting, photography, and ballistics, among others. An expert forensic pathologist worked for the coroner, who in turn worked closely with the cops; the growing respect given police may be measured by the fact that in addition to the twenty-three mostly trolley and auto homicides that an inquest ruled "excusable," all but one of the fifteen killings by police were deemed "justifiable," the only ones that earned that label. Just one policeman, as a result, went through the whole court process: after indictment for involuntary manslaughter, a white motorcycle officer, pleading self-defense, was acquitted of shooting down a black motorist for resisting arrest.

In some broad ways the patterns of urban homicide followed familiar lines, some of them stretching back to the Middle Ages. Murder and manslaughter were committed mostly by men, 82 percent of cases, and especially young men. Wolfgang was able to specify closely that those between ages 20 and 24 had the highest rates, at 22.7 per 100,000, followed by ages 25 to 29 and 30 to 34; teenagers between 15 and 19 were in fourth place, and those under 15 had nearly infinitesimal rates at 0.3. Roughly 90 to 95 percent of all offenders—he could not be more precise—were "in the low end of the occupational scale," working with hands or backs. And in this and other ways offenders and victims tended to resemble each other; 94 percent of all killings occurred within racial lines, although in this era—for the first time—the twenty black-on-white homicides outnumbered the fourteen white-on-black. The nearest exception to the rule of resemblance was sexual, if a little complicated: there were significantly more female victims—24 percent of the total—than offenders—18 percent—meaning that men killed women more than women killed men, but that both sexes killed mostly men, the women usually husbands and lovers.

As always, the courts were more lenient with these and other women than with men, convicting them at a lower rate but above all of lesser degrees of homicide, carrying much lighter sentences. In domestic cases especially, juries tended to believe wives about provocation and the need for self-defense. There were an even 100 of these domestic cases, with a slight edge, as usual, to male murderers: 53 husbands were accused of killing wives, 47 wives of killing husbands. Some 10 men in effect convicted themselves by committing suicide, 1 ran away, 6 did not come to trial for various other reasons; of the 36 who did, all but 2 were found guilty, or 94 percent. There were no suicidal wives in the group, no fugitives, and only 5 had not been tried when Wolfgang wrote; of the 42 who had, just 26 were convicted, or 62 percent.

In a pattern continued from the late nineteenth century, the great majority of all suspects arrested were in fact convicted of some degree of homicide: the Philadelphia figure was 66 percent, compared to 63 percent for big cities generally. And the rank order of conviction rates, when classified by motive, followed even more ancient patterns. At the high end (leaving aside just 3 rape-murders, 1 of them unsolved), jurors were most likely to convict offenders accused of robbery, 81 percent, as a reflection of their own fears and moral views. At the other end, none of the eight defendants whom the police (as distinct from the defendant) reported had acted in self-defense was convicted of anything at all. Those who took cold-blooded revenge were condemned at a rate only second to robbers, followed by those who killed in arguments over money. Domestic killers ranked behind these others mostly because the wives were so often freed; the husbands, by themselves, were even more likely than robbers to be convicted. The biggest group by far, and as always, were those involved in fights for trivial reasons, pushes and shoves, angry words, insults to honor—and again, as always, they ranked at the bottom of the conviction scale, next to (and overlapping) those who killed in self-defense.

The rate of reported murder and manslaughter among African Americans, as earlier in the century, was far higher than that for whites. By this time the black minority in the city, 18 percent of the whole population, accounted for a substantial majority of all of Philadelphia's homicide deaths, fully 73 percent. The racial difference in the city was bigger than that across the country not because its black population had notably high rates but because its white population had notably low ones, since urban whites in the North and West, especially in manufacturing cities, were far less violent than those in southern and often rural areas. But most important, the black-white gap in the city was no longer growing, as it had been between the Civil War and the 1920s. Although, as too often, the available measures are not strictly comparable, black Philadelphians in the 1920s had been *convicted* of murder and manslaughter sixteen times as often as whites, while their homicide *arrest* rates in Wolfgang's study, at 24.6 per 100,000 annually, were just fourteen times the white 1.8.

Much of this difference, as earlier, was related to gender roles, as the difference between black and white women soared well above those for the men. With infanticide by this time of negligible importance (the word does not even appear in Wolfgang's index), white women were very rarely involved in homicide of any kind, just sixteen of them in the five years studied. In this, too, the city's racial and sexual patterns mirrored those across the United States.

Another continuing trend, also in line with developments across the country, was toward treating homicides less tolerantly, not only in terms of conviction rates but also in terms of the seriousness of the offense for which killers were found guilty. Whatever the race of defendants, verdicts were more likely than in earlier years to be murder in the first degree, at 20 percent; second-degree verdicts were returned in 29 percent of cases, voluntary manslaughter in 36 percent, involuntary manslaughter in 15 percent. But at the same time, apparently and paradoxically registering the same insistence on the value of life, but in a different key, judges and juries were more reluctant than ever to use the supreme penalty: of the 77 first-degree verdicts, just 7 carried the recommendation of death, and during the period only 5 Philadelphians actually went to the chair at Rockview State Prison.

But in historical perspective, what is most striking about homicide in Philadelphia is the way in which it represents the urban industrial revolution at its height. The one way in which patterns in the city differed both from those earlier and from other places across the United States was the relatively low percentage of gun killings. Some 33 percent of victims in Philadelphia died of gunshot wounds, 55 percent in the nation as a whole. While this was in part an urban-rural difference—countryfolk had always had more access to firearms—it also represents a drop from sampled years in the city itself, earlier in the century, and from the percentages that Brearly reported for the whole of the United States in the 1920s. One reason for fewer gun deaths was simply the decline in the Italian-born population, with the great slowing of European immigration. But even more important was the fact that all Philadelphians at midcentury—notably African Americans, who were no longer much threatened by roaming white gangs—felt safer than before, with less need to stash or carry firearms.

Certainly the overall "murder rate" had dropped markedly, in both city and nation. During the mid-1920s Philadelphia's mortality statistics—roughly comparable to those used by Wolfgang—had stood at 9.3 per 100,000, compared to 5.7 in 1948–52. In the latter period the homicide squad was able to "clear" 91 percent of its cases by arresting a suspect. This was almost identical to the national rate of a little over 90 percent, and it says as much about the nature of the cases as about police efficiency. Mid-twentieth-century patterns, as compared with those for the nineteenth century, or even the 1920s, showed a marked drop in most of the kinds of cases that were hardest to solve: those with multiple defendants (as in riots or mini-riots), those involving strangers, those occurring on the streets. Of the hard-to-solve variety, only robbery murders were (apparently) up, although there were only forty-nine in the five years, many brought into the totals as a result of greatly improved detective work. In the overwhelming majority of cases, the police were able to make an arrest the day of the killing, some 78 percent; and in 88 percent, within a week.

The ease of arrest was in part the result of what may be called the "domestication" of homicide by the 1950s. The term is among other things quite literal: the home had become by far the most frequent site, with over half of all cases, only partly because homes by then were more attractive places to be in at night, with central heating often, radios usually, and even televisions sometimes. Given the move indoors, the time of year made less difference than in earlier periods, with only a slight favoring of the warm months. The victims, again in over half the cases, were close friends or family of the offenders, a pattern especially noted among African Americans, and most of the rest were acquaintances.

"Domestication" does not imply a lack of violence; in general murderous attacks tended in fact to grow wilder as the relationship between victim and killers grew closer, as the fury of betrayal, or years of anger, were reflected in the number of shots, blows, or cuts inflicted, often on an already lifeless body. What "domestication" means rather is that as homicide was more fully restricted to the home, and to a circle of family and friends, fewer strangers were in danger. These few, aside from those hit by robbers, tended to be attacked in streets or barrooms by roving groups of belligerent young white bachelors full of liquor, not as common as they used to be but still active.

Victims as well as offenders, finally, tended to be people with prior police records, usually for violent crimes such as assault, and both had typically been drinking at the time of the fatal encounter. Sober, peaceable folks, again, had little to fear. And even the aggressive fraction of the population that was at risk showed some real signs of settling down, had they been given a little more time to do it. Both killers and victims were typically young but not teenaged people, often married, used to the rhythms of workweek and weekend. In an era of full employment and busy factories, the period between Friday and Sunday accounted for two-thirds of all killings, Saturday alone for nearly one-third. Dropping into a local bar, especially after work on payday, was a widespread habit among working people of all groups, and could sometimes lead to trouble. Those involved in criminal homicides, like tens of thousands of other blacks and whites across the city, had a little time off, money to spend, and liquor in the blood; it was just this once that the anticipated pleasures of sex, a party, or a night on the town turned suddenly into a nightmare, forever changing their lives or ending them.

3

The domesticated pattern of homicide emerging among urban black Americans was a small sign of a bigger social change. While the Cold War was the most important international development of the era, the most important at home was the narrowing of the great black-white divide that had plagued America since the seventeenth century. No period since the Civil War showed greater promise. And for an understanding of that promise and what was happening to it, the story told by murder and murder rates, South and North, is less well known and in some ways more illuminating than the familiar narratives of growing acceptance, legal change, and civil rights.

The assault on racial discrimination began during and even before the war, reaching full intensity just after it on a number of fronts. Well before 1954 and the famous *Brown v. Board of Education* decision, the U.S. Supreme Court, with the support of leading members of both major parties, had been picking away at the foundations of legal segregation, and the Democrats had formally endorsed equal opportunity in housing and jobs. Building on the breakthroughs of the 1920s, serious writers as different as Ralph Ellison, Richard Wright, and, later, James Baldwin won the appreciation of their peers, while in the bigger arena of mass popular music the last unwritten taboo was broken when male crooners like Billy Eckstein and Nat "King" Cole joined Ella Fitzgerald and other black women in singing love songs to white teenagers over the radio. Hollywood, gingerly, began to deal with themes of racial injustice in movies like *Pinky* and *Intruder in the Dust*. And with much greater force Jackie Robinson with the Brooklyn Dodgers, Marion Motley with the Cleveland Browns, and Nat "Sweetwater" Clifton with the New York Knicks swept away the absurdities of diehards who had claimed that African Americans lacked the cool physical courage to play team sports. City by city, as the 1950s advanced, college by college, team by team, white fans across the North and West found themselves rooting for black athletes.

But the white Deep South was still unmoved, and what finally cracked it were not the rich and famous, not decrees from above, and not outsiders of any color, but rather the extraordinary courage of ordinary black southerners. The story of Rosa Parks and her refusal to move to the back of a Montgomery bus in the fall of 1955 is justly famous, and so are the stories of Martin Luther King Jr. and others who built a nonviolent movement out of thousands like her. But there is another story, too, best told through the bloody history of Mississippi, hardest of the hard-core states, which had historically lynched more blacks than any other.

Throughout the twentieth century, African Americans who found Mississippi intolerable had simply moved north, above all taking the Illinois Central "freedom train" straight up to Chicago. In the 1940s this was the poorest state in the Union, and as cotton production mechanized unskilled jobs were harder to get than ever. With blacks segregated from whites in almost all matters public or social, condemned to inferior schooling, often hungry and sick, blocked off from politics, there was little apparent hope for either collective or individual advancement. But following World War II, more and more men and women who loved the state decided not to leave but to change it. Many of them had seen a different world, and a number of returning veterans like Charles and Medgar Evers of Decatur boldly registered to vote (although they did not actually vote), and with G.I. benefits went on to college.

For ten years after the war the state stayed calm, with African Americans quietly organizing in many places under the banner of the NAACP. Lynchings were slowly fading away, and in 1952, for the first time ever, there were none recorded anywhere in the South. But when in May 1954 the Supreme Court kicked down the last legal prop to segregated schooling, many white Mississippians rallied desperately to save the old order. The weapons were familiar, and together with economic pressure one of them was the policy of murderous intimidation that had worked so well three generations earlier.

A "death list" with the names of African-American organizers was published in several Delta newspapers in the spring of 1955. The Reverend George Lee was on it; that May he was shot dead from a passing car while driving his Buick in Belzoni; a coroner's inquest ruled the death an accident, possibly from a heart attack, and labeled the metal fragments from a faceful of buckshot as, perhaps, "dental fillings." In August Lamar Smith, who had been registering voters, was shot dead on the courthouse lawn in Brookhaven. Later that same month, fourteen-year-old Emmett Till, back visiting from Chicago, was teased by some friends into acting up with Carolyn Bryant, a white woman in a Delta grocery store; that night her husband and his half-brother came for the boy at his great-uncle's cabin. Three days later Till's body was found in the Tallahatchie River. Roy Melton was shot dead at his gas station in September. In November Gus Courts, who had succeeded Reverend Lee as head of the Belzoni NAACP, was severely wounded by shotgun blasts from a car driving by his grocery store.

Threats, bombings, killings, the foreclosure of mortgages, and the stoppage of credit had an immediate effect in driving many African Americans off the voting rolls and some of their leaders out of the South. Charles Evers, his several businesses wiped out, had to leave for Chicago to recoup. The name of Medgar Evers, now state director of the NAACP, was on the death list. But he stayed. So did Amzie Moore, Richard West, Bernice Robinson, Louie Redd, and Joyce Ladner, men and women from all over the state. Reverend Lee's widow, Rosebud, refused to take her name off the voting lists.

It was growing clear during that summer of 1955 that things were changing in Mississippi, as the lynching of Emmett Till drew more national protest and attention than any in history. Given Mississippi's dependence on federal money and outside investment, Roy Bryant and J. H. Milam were actually arrested and tried for it within weeks, with Medgar Evers and other leaders active in seeking out witnesses. And while a white jury acquitted them in a little over an hour (the two later boasted of the killing in a story sold to *Look* magazine), observers noted that the courthouse was surrounded by angry black men, some of them carrying weapons. The teenager's death and its aftermath had not intimidated but energized local African Americans, especially the younger men and women of what Ladner has called "the Till Generation."

The threats and house bombings and drive-by shootings continued for several years, Medgar Evers was beaten, and some were killed, but there was far more noise than there were actual deaths. White men were no longer assassinating "uppity" blacks in broad daylight; they were speeding by anonymously, in cars without license plates, too fast and too far away to be sure to hit their targets, fearful of getting close. When James Meredith entered the University of Mississippi in September 1962, an armed mob of two thousand surrounded, harassed, and sometimes shot at the handful of federal marshals assigned to protect him, but only under cover of night. In an atmosphere full of smoke, whiskey, and defiance, two bystanders were killed in the darkness. But Meredith stayed. Over the next few days firebombs were thrown at an activist doctor's medical clinic, and the homes of two NAACP branch presidents. They stayed too.

That same year Medgar Evers led the state NAACP into an alliance with the young people from SNCC, the Student Non-Violent Coordinating Committee, and with members of CORE, the Congress of Racial Equality. SNCC and CORE, much like Martin Luther King Jr.'s SCLC, or Southern Christian Leadership Conference, had been involved in nonviolent protests across the South. The several groups had many differences, but they were united in their ability to risk pain and even death. As segregationist whites reacted to this new alliance, with its threat to register blacks across the state, the Evers home was firebombed in May 1963. And finally, as his children woke to the sound of his car, returning from a brutally hot day's work at 12:30 in the morning of June 12, Medgar was shot dead, in the back, in his own driveway, by an assassin hidden in the weeds.

The sniper left his Enfield in place, and the local police, no longer indifferent, sent a fingerprint and .30-caliber bullets to the FBI crime lab in Washington. This was the first step in collecting a train of evidence that took three trials—the first two deadlocked—and thirty years, but eventually led to the murder conviction of segregationist Byron de la Beckwith in February 1993. But the most dramatic event of the day after the killing was the return of Charles Evers, who left several thriving legal and illegal businesses in Chicago to fly back home and join widow Myrlie in tending to his brother's body. When the national NAACP wondered "Who's going to take Medgar's place?" Charles cut off the question: "Don't look no further. I'm here." If there had been any doubt before, there was no longer: what had worked in the 1890s was not working in the 1950s and 1960s. Murder as social policy was bankrupt; while out-migration continued as always, many African Americans were not only staying in the Deep South but coming down and back to it, and the movement would not be stopped.

4

But in the meantime, up North and in the cities, things were more complicated.

Among nostalgic older Americans, later in the century, the 1940s and 1950s would come to seem a kind of golden age of progress and prosperity. And while nostalgia is a drug that distorts perception as badly as any other, it is hard to deny that for two groups especially, urban Americans and above all African Americans, these were in fact the Good Ol' Days. The two groups in fact overlapped more than ever before. Decades of flight from Mississippi and the rural South, accelerated in the war and postwar decades, had resulted in an epic transformation, as the census of 1960 announced that for the first time in history proportionally more blacks than whites were living in cities, 73 percent to 70 percent.

The cities they lived in were more livable than ever, and the streets were safer; the trolleys ran on time, and the smoke was only the price of industrial progress. Zoos and movies and ball parks, concerts and museums, were increasingly open and affordable for men and women of all races, and just as the Dixieland revival helped move jazz out of the South Side further into the mainstream, the quirkier sound of bebop was a reminder that Harlem had not run out of ideas. People raised in the depression were heady with the money and the apparent security that came with jobs in Chevrolet, Westinghouse, and RCA factories. And for African Americans the world war had marked a truly revolutionary watershed in employment.

Before that time, fully 60 percent of black women in the money economy had found work only as domestics, at the bottom of the ladder of pay and prestige. Within two decades the percentage had fallen dramatically, to 36 percent, as jobs in government and business opened up. Among men, the proportion of white-collar and skilled jobs also climbed steadily, and in 1953, during the Korean War, the black unemployment rate reached a historic all-time low of just 4.5 percent. The most significant change of all was registered in the same 1960 census that showed blacks were proportionally more likely than whites to be living in cities: as a proportion of all those employed, by a margin of 25 to 20 percent they were also more likely to be working in factories.

Almost all of the indicators of social health went up in these decades: personal income and longevity, education and home ownership. The most important of those that went down was the murder rate, as measured by national mortality statistics among both blacks and whites. The white rate of 2.6 per 100,000 annually in 1950 dropped to 2.5 ten years later, and the black rate plunged even faster, from 28.0 to 23.1, so that by 1960 the combined national average, 4.7, was the lowest ever recorded for any census year.

In the early 1930s Brearly had believed it possible that high rates of homicide among African Americans might be the result of nothing more complicated than poverty. But Marvin Wolfgang, by the 1950s, found racial differences persisting even among people of similar jobs and incomes, suggesting that there were important differences in what he called "norms of conduct," or learned cultural responses to potentially aggressive situations. And while he did not speculate about the reasons for this, the falling black rates of the 1950s offer a strong clue, and in the context of the time a hopeful one.

All culture is the product of history, the result of a given group's experience over time. The cultural "norms of conduct" specifically responsible for rises or falls in either suicidal or homicidal behavior are those that help direct aggressive impulses either inward or outward— or best, in utterly harmless directions. This is a quite specific, and small, segment of the range of any group's culture, having little directly to do with theology or music, attitudes toward children, aging, or death, accomplishment in cookery or art. And across the developed world, broad changes in the suicide-murder ratio had resulted from an equally specific although widely shared historical experience. That is, those directly involved in the urban industrial revolution—whether Protestant or Catholic, winners or losers in the world wars, citizens of democratic or authoritarian regimes—all experienced statistically falling rates of interpersonal violence and (although harder to demonstrate) rising rates of suicide.

From this global perspective, what was beginning to happen among black Americans was simply what had long been happening among white Americans, together with Australians and Swedes, Germans and Englishmen, starting sometime in the nineteenth century and continuing into the mid-twentieth century. And the promise was that with economic inclusion, at last, African Americans would follow the paths already taken by Irish and Italian Americans, whose own violent norms of conduct had been settled out in a generation or two by the behavioral and psychological demands of office and factory.

But it would not be that easy; the same kinds of statistics that showed the promise also suggested a threat to it. Racial discrimination was declining but not dead, and its long-term effects were still strong. Philadelphia, typical of older industrial cities, reached its peak size at over two million in the census of 1950; over the next ten years the fact that tens of thousands of blacks moved in helped inspire an even bigger number of whites to move out to the suburbs. In the same years the kinds of industrial jobs that African Americans had just begun to win began also to move out, even to dry up. Across the country, after hitting its historic low in 1953, the black unemployment rate began to rise, reaching double digits by the end of the decade. The highest percentages were those among young men in cities. And after a little lag the homicide rates reported by the FBI, which had pointed unevenly down since the *Uniform Crime Reports* were first published in 1931, began in 1959 to climb ominously upward.

Even less noticed at the time, meanwhile, and halfway across the globe, American "advisers" were beginning to filter in to help the little demi-nation of South Vietnam, abandoned by its onetime French colonial masters, as its leaders tried to avoid absorption by its more vigorous twin in the communist North.

During the years between 1941 and 1963, then, the United States had taken and held as high a position as any nation ever had in world affairs. The mixture of jealousy and admiration that older European democracies had shown following World War I was shifted further toward gratitude following World War II. After having helped a second time to hold off German expansionism, the Americans turned, through a variety of political and economic initiatives, to holding off the Russians, in the process rebuilding the tattered world capitalist market. And at home, too, a new maturity was shown by a clear decline in the violent behavior and racial divisions that had so long provided ammunition to foreign critics and thoughtful citizens both.

In fact as the 1950s moved into the 1960s it seemed to optimists that the whole of the world was moving closer, not just in terms of buying Coca-Cola, radios, and blue jeans but also in terms of values, standards, and behavior. Regional differences were flattening out in this country, and partly for the same reason it was expected, or at least hoped, that global differences would flatten in the same way; as the urban industrial revolution spread over the world, peoples everywhere should grow more prosperous, contented, and rational than ever before. Americans believed of course that the threat of Russian and Chinese communism must be contained, but especially following a 1962 crisis over the installation of missiles in Cuba, the United States and the Soviet Union were communicating better than ever, both apparently committed to peaceful solution of their disputes. But then history took a new turn, in this country marked by unexpected events during 1963–64.

8

The Sixties, 1963–1974

In dramatic contrast to the optimistic progress of the late 1940s and 1950s, the long decade that lasted from the fall of 1963 into the summer of 1974 was one of the most troubling in the whole of the American experience. Increasing involvement followed by retreat and defeat in the civil war in Vietnam, halfway across the globe, dominated American foreign policy. Reaction to that war back home had a heavy impact on domestic politics and attitudes as well. The economy, booming halfway through the period, began in 1968 to slow in ways that suggested that the long postwar period of American dominance was eroding. But there is no single explanation for the nature and pace of change during the 1960s, as prosperous young members of the middle class flocked into an antiestablishment "counterculture" while urban African Americans boiled over in riotous fury in the midst of successful drives for civil rights and political recognition.

Certainly with respect to murder, as much else, the 1960s was an era that witnessed more rapid, worrisome, and sometimes paradoxical new developments than any earlier. As television replaced newsprint as the major source of information, new and heinous kinds of murder, including assassinations and killings for ideological reasons far more complex than those of the Civil War era, were publicized more graphically than any before. The result was to lift questions involving the causes of criminal violence and the effectiveness of legal procedures out of scholarly journals and the several states into national politics and the public arena. And all of this was happening just as, in response to deep-seated

changes in the nature of the economy and work, the long downward
international trend in homicide rates was strikingly reversed.

I

Historians are used to using wars, or revolutions, to divide time into
periods; but this key transitional era in American history was signaled
instead with a single act of murder. At 12:30 Dallas time, on the afternoon of November 22, 1963, while John F. Kennedy's motorcade
passed below, a rifleman perched in the Texas Book Depository building squeezed off two rounds—or three?—and blew off the top of the
president's head. That is a moment that older Americans will always
remember, and it ushered in a decade of bloodshed, turbulence, and
confusion that few of them were ready for and almost none of them
understood.

Just what happened during the five or six seconds it took to assassinate the president of the United States, and why, has been subjected to
more intensive investigation than any comparable act in our history.
But the results only underline the stubborn human ineptitude that
guarantees that much about murder remains mysterious. It took the
presidential limousine just eight minutes to rush Kennedy to the nearest emergency room, at Parkland Memorial Hospital. Dr. Malcolm
Perry found him on his back, heart beating but all other vital signs at
stop, and nervously performed a futile emergency tracheotomy that destroyed the contours of a hole in the front of his throat. Having seen—
and through the operation destroyed—that throat wound, he answered
press queries half an hour later by saying Kennedy had been killed by a
shot from in front.

In the meantime, one Lee Harvey Oswald had been seen fleeing the
Book Depository building, and his description was flashed to Dallas
police. Stopped by Officer J. B. Tippitt at 1:15, Oswald shot Tippitt
dead, ran to hide in a nearby theater, and was arrested within minutes
of Perry's press conference. The world was told that the assassin had
been found; he was then interrogated ineptly by a crammed roomful
of city and county detectives, Texas Rangers, FBI, and Secret Service
agents, none of whom would either surrender jurisdiction or remember
to provide a stenographer. Late that evening he was arraigned for the

murder of Officer Tippitt, while the FBI worked to confirm his ownership of the rifle used to kill Kennedy.

By that time, the president's body had been flown back East, where, beginning at 8:00 P.M. EST, a three-hour autopsy was performed at Bethesda Naval Hospital under the direction of the head pathologist, James Hume. Commander Hume, unfortunately, had no experience with either forensic pathology or gunshot wounds; he and his team only later learned that Dr. Perry's tracheotomy had obliterated an exit (entrance?) wound. But having seen the back of the president's head, unlike Perry, they found that his skull had been pulverized by a shot from behind. They also traced a wound in the back that oddly had neither an apparent exit nor a bullet at its end; they later offered the theory that the bullet had somehow fallen out on its own, back in Dallas. And back in Dallas, three and a half hours after the autopsy, at 1:30 A.M. local time, Lee Harvey Oswald was arraigned in local court for murdering the president of the United States.

All this time the nation and the world were in a collective state of shock, wondering what it was all about. Had the Russians been behind it, or Cuban dictator Fidel Castro? Would it mean war? Was it the notorious right-wing fringe centered in Dallas itself, enraged by Kennedy's liberal politics? Worst of all—could it have been ordered by Lyndon Johnson, the vice president from Texas, now constitutionally president of the United States?

Few knew anything about the clumsiness of the investigation thus far, and it was expected in any case that Oswald himself would provide the answers to these questions. To protect him from possible vigilantes, it was decided to transfer him from the city to the county jail; to accommodate the television cameras, the transfer was scheduled not quietly, for the wee dark hours, but for the camera-friendly light of midday. And amid all the publicity and confusion, Jack Ruby, owner of a nightclub strip joint, somehow slipped by (was guided through?) police security in the basement, and at 12:21 Sunday afternoon, with one .38-caliber bullet to the midsection, assassinated the assassin in front of millions of haggard viewers of NBC. An hour and a half later Oswald died, like Kennedy, at Parkland Memorial, and all hope of definite answers died with him.

Only a few facts about the mystery man were immediately apparent; a former marine, with vaguely Marxist sympathies, he had lived for a

time and married his wife, Marina, in the Soviet Union. Within the
week, in the hope of quieting national unease, President Johnson appointed a distinguished bipartisan commission headed by Chief Justice
Earl Warren to investigate the case. Ten months later the Warren Commission reported the most comforting of conclusions: that Oswald was
indeed the man, that he had acted alone, that there was no conspiracy
of any sort.

The commission told the nation what it wanted to hear. But the
weight of the twenty-six volumes of reports and exhibits it used to back
its conclusions was not enough to squash the original rumors about
Russia, Cuba, the far right, and Lyndon Johnson; while Jack Ruby, with
his sleazy underworld connections, had added "Organized Crime" to
the list of possible suspects. Criticism began almost immediately, and
new books and theories are still appearing, encouraged by the Warren
Commission's often hasty methods, its lack of access to key autopsy and
other information, its reliance on FBI and CIA employees who had
their own reasons to conceal prior agency contacts with Oswald.

And by the time the Warren Report was published, in September
1964, America was sliding into the kind of mutual distrust that naturally encourages conspiracy theories. Lyndon Johnson, the president
created by Kennedy's murder, was then running for reelection against
Barry Goldwater, the most conservative Republican candidate in decades, and the issues raised in that campaign were beginning to split the
nation more sharply than at any time since the Civil War.

2

Lyndon Johnson's bottomless sense of inferiority, following the charismatic Kennedy, helped shape his political course and American history.
Kennedy had sent 16,000 "advisers" to the failing government of South
Vietnam and flushed Russian missiles out of Cuba; Johnson determined to take an even harder line in faraway Indochina, and in the
campaign summer of 1964 the president escalated American involvement in the local civil war by bombing North Vietnam. At the same
time, as a southerner he was highly sensitive to suspicion that he might
weaken his predecessor's perceived commitment to racial progress and
opened the year 1964 by announcing a "War on Poverty," followed by
a strong Civil Rights Act.

Bombing North Vietnam did not immediately become a big political issue; support for African Americans did.

Attacks on voting restrictions and segregation in the South continued that year and afterward with general success. As the murder of Medgar Evers in the summer of 1963 had only strengthened the cause, so did the murders of James Chaney, Mickey Schwerner, and Andrew Goodman, three young SNCC activists, in the summer of 1964. These deaths in Philadelphia, Mississippi, not only outraged voters outside of the state but led to a major legal and institutional breakthrough in dealing with such crimes, further strengthening the role of the federal government in dealing with cases of homicide. J. Edgar Hoover's FBI, long hesitant to get involved in such issues, was galvanized by the three killings, and the Justice Department decided to move on its own. Given the failure of the Neshoba County authorities to prosecute the crime as murder under state law, the department made it a federal case. Its weapon was a Reconstruction era statute that made it illegal for two or more persons to "conspire to injure, oppress, threaten, or intimidate any citizen . . . in the free exercise of any right [granted by] the Constitution or laws of the United States." That December, based on evidence provided by FBI informants to a federal grand jury, nineteen men, Klansmen and law officers, were arrested for effectively depriving young Chaney, Schwerner, and Goodman of their civil rights simply by murdering them.

This legal tactic, upheld by the U.S. Supreme Court in 1966, was used successfully later in the decade to prosecute several racially motivated killings in southern jurisdictions where local prejudices made murder convictions impossible. But in the same 1964 summer that Chaney, Goodman, and Schwerner were assassinated, the term "white backlash" was coined to describe the beginnings of a paradoxical countermovement up North. Segregationist Alabama governor George Wallace, running against President Johnson, won over one-third of the vote in a handful of presidential primaries that spring, and beginning in July Barry Goldwater's campaign brought the issue of "crime in the streets" into national politics. And by 1967, the year when eight men were finally sentenced to terms of three to ten years for "conspiracy" in the Neshoba County murders, violence against southern blacks had decisively given way as a political issue in favor of violence by urban blacks.

The background to this issue was simply that all through the 1940s and 1950s, as the accelerated African-American move into the cities helped inspire an even greater white exodus, the complexion of urban crime had changed. White Americans—even contemporary social scientists—were not then generally aware of the historical statistics that would show that black murder rates were dropping through most of the period and black-white differences were narrowing. But they were vividly aware, and frightened, by the more obvious fact that as big cities turned blacker, so did big city homicides.

Generations of experience with the southern justice system, and an untold number of big city confrontations, had taught many African Americans not to trust the police. At the same time white Americans were learning to count on police as never before. As their efficiency increased and civil service rules took hold, their actions were in practice rarely reviewed by prosecutors or judges, and all over the country, as in Philadelphia, coroners and medical examiners routinely labeled police homicides "justifiable" and so kept them away from grand or petit juries.

As neither local politics nor police tactics changed as rapidly as the complexion of big cities, the longtime tensions between white cops and black civilians simmered ever more angrily, fueled by the televised sight of southern sheriffs beating and siccing dogs on peaceful demonstrators led by Martin Luther King Jr. and by the evident fact that the Neshoba County sheriff and his chief deputy were deeply involved in the Chaney-Goodman-Schwerner murders. And then, just after the Republican National Convention, in July 1964, the fatal shooting of a young teenager by a New York policeman was shortly followed by another, after a protest march over those three murders in Mississippi turned into a violent clash with the cops. Suddenly Harlem erupted in riot.

The widely televised outbreaks that spread that summer from New York to Rochester, St. Louis, Philadelphia, and many smaller cities helped redefine the term "race riot" for the third time. The one-sided nineteenth-century white invasions of black neighborhoods had been much like anti-Semitic European pogroms. By World War I they had become armed clashes between whites and blacks finally numerous enough to fight back. In the summer of 1964 they had evolved still further, as sprawling ghettos erupted in self-destruction, with residents burning and looting their own neighborhood stores, often white owned. The fighting pitted local blacks against police and sometimes national guardsmen, modern successors to the old state militias. As the violence was almost wholly confined to the ghetto itself, with little physical danger to those outside it—most of the nine deaths that first summer were of rioters "justifiably" shot by the authorities—the white majority was reduced to the passive role of sitting on the sidelines, rooting for the cops and cursing at the tube.

During that campaign season outrage at southern brutality still outweighed "white backlash," and admiration for the courage of Martin Luther King Jr. and the young activists to the south helped conquer the Republican appeal for more "law and order." Lyndon Johnson then easily beat Barry Goldwater that November. But the backlash had a real effect, as analysts noted that five Deep South states went Republican for the first time since just after the Civil War. And the issue of crime in the streets did not go away, and never has.

Over the next four years Johnson's presidency went on to splinter the nation. His decision to try to please both ends of the political spectrum by expanding both the war in Vietnam and the War on Poverty satisfied no one. Resentment of American actions in Vietnam and fear of the draft contributed to a collegiate counterculture, greatly expanded drug use, and hostility to authority in all forms. The civil rights coalition blew up as young militants turned on old white allies in the name of "Black Power." Activist blacks themselves were pulled in several directions, followers of Martin Luther King Jr.'s Christian pacifism competing with militant young black nationalists on one side and leftist Black Panthers on the other. And back of all the increasing anger and division were the mounting death tolls, not only in Southeast Asia but in the nation's cities as well.

The Vietnam War, with its typically small actions and media censorship, was not as telegenic as the urban riots, and as each "long hot summer" in the ghettos brought more of them the players all came to know the script, as sketched in the nightly news and special reports brought into their homes. Trouble almost always began as a conflict between police and local residents, maybe a "justifiable homicide" or even a minor arrest that sparked a fight and drew a crowd. The officers were then surrounded, jeered, and stoned; windows were broken next; and if there was no effective resistance, the mood changed from angry to light-headed as the crowds got bigger and the looting began. At that point, if the local police could not quickly restore order, crowds surged through whole districts while buildings were torched, firebombs thrown, sometimes even snipers set up in windows to shoot at cops and firemen. When the national guard was sent in serious killing began.

Nothing but the infamous New York City Draft Riots of 1863, with its 110 victims, approached the number of homicides in these outbursts. Dozens of cities were hit each year. Among the biggest, in August 1965 some 34 died in a six-day riot in the Watts district of Los Angeles; in July 1967, 23 died in Newark, New Jersey. In Detroit the same month, where the national guard was joined by U.S. paratroopers, the total reached 43. The body count in Detroit included 33 blacks and 10 whites (the latter total much bigger than usual). Rioters themselves killed no more than 2 or maybe 3 of these, including 1 white civilian hit by a shotgun blast; storekeepers shot 2, and 4 more were burned or electrocuted to death by fallen power lines. Most of the rest, including some women and children, were killed by police or the ill-prepared guardsmen, in an atmosphere of smoke, fear, anger, confusion, and much indiscriminate gunplay. The well-disciplined paratroopers, many of them black themselves, had, in contrast, an obvious calming effect; they knew what serious combat looked like, refused to panic, and shot down just one man.

White viewers were enraged, and scared, by all of this. It was especially maddening, and to most incomprehensible, that these riots should erupt after two decades of racial progress, just as segregation was crumbling and a host of antipoverty programs were moving out of the Congress and into the cities. Divisions over the role of police were especially deep, as white voters in several cities promoted the political careers of tough cops while paramilitary organizations like the Black Panthers flourished in the ghettos, demanding home rule, denouncing blue-uniformed "armies of occupation," and telling the cameras that they were out to "off the pigs," meaning kill the cops. And immediately after the holocaust in Detroit the president appointed the National Advisory Commission on Civil Disorders, headed by former Governor Otto Kerner of Illinois, to draw on the experience of social scientists, policemen, community leaders, and politicians to find just what was happening and why.

Two years later the Kerner Commission issued a report. Its first conclusion, based on far firmer evidence than that of the Warren Commission three years earlier, was that as in most historical riots there was no conspiracy behind these, no "outside agitators," although once they had broken out on their own, various groups and movements had tried to use or interpret them to their advantage. Other findings were not so reassuring. It was no more possible to blame the outbreaks on rootless drifters than on outside agitators or plotting by the Panthers; most of the participants were quite typical local people, the most active of them long-settled young men from the neighborhood, with jobs, if anything a little better educated than most of their peers. The report concluded that the anger was real and deep-seated, the product of years of denial and discrimination.

Much of the *Kerner Report* fit with what historians were finding about the historic pattern of riots in France, England, and the United States over the previous two centuries. Popular protest does not break out in times of real despair; the truly desperate have neither the hope nor the energy for it. Instead protest riots—even revolutions—tend to follow periods of progress, when expectations outrun the pace of change and frustrations boil over into action, in Western societies usually directed not at persons but at property, or such symbolic targets as police stations. The most disturbing prediction to follow from this was that despite all the improvements in race relations, the split between inner cities and the surrounding suburbs was creating two nations out of one, and if the trend continued more violence was inevitable.

In fact, by the time the *Kerner Report* came out in 1969, the worst of the rioting was over, less the result of official tactics than, quite literally, burnout. Almost no riots occurred twice in the same city, as disillusioned ghetto residents woke the morning after to find their neighborhoods in smoky ruins, with no place to buy bread or milk and little to show for the excitement. The report itself sold two million copies; its moderate explanations for the events of the mid-1960s still make some sense, and many city governments did move to try to heal relations with a growing black electorate. But television was a far more powerful medium than print, and at the national level another legacy of urban violence was millions of white voters seething at the sight of activists shouting "Burn, Baby, Burn!" into the cameras and riflemen in battle fatigues holding press conferences to talk about Black Power. If Kerner's explanation for urban violence made sense, his call for massive new domestic spending on antipoverty and social programs was hopelessly ill-timed, doomed both by the need to finance the war in Vietnam and by political backlash. And then, just as the riots began to subside, in 1968, murderous violence took yet another ugly turn.

3

Martin Luther King Jr. had been awarded the Nobel Peace Prize in 1964, just as his nonviolent tactics were beginning to win the battle against legal segregation in the South. But the very next year he set two much harder targets. One of them, inspired in part by the futile rage of the riots, was the extralegal segregation, discrimination, and above all poverty in big city ghettos. The other was the escalating war in Vietnam. Neither campaign was as widely popular or successful as his earlier assault on the segregated South. Death threats had always followed him almost everywhere. And on April 4, 1968, while visiting Memphis, Tennessee, in support of a garbage strike, chatting with supporters on the balcony of the Lorraine Motel, King was fatally shot, his spinal cord severed by a bullet from a rifle with a telescopic sight.

African Americans again reverted, briefly, to rioting in protest of King's assassination. The apparent killer, who did not trouble to recover his belongings from a motel room just two hundred feet from King's, was shortly identified as one James Earl Ray. It was not at all clear why this longtime petty thief and robber, with no known political views, had chosen to assassinate the most internationally revered American of the day; but his name was put on the FBI's "Ten Most Wanted" list, and a search was mounted.

Political leadership of the antiwar movement had by then passed to New York Senator Robert Kennedy. With the unpopular Lyndon Johnson having bowed out, the murdered John Kennedy's younger brother and closest political confidante was seeking the Democratic nomination for president of the United States. Consciously reaching out to King's admirers, he was also seen as the one white politician who might heal the racial wounds of the era, both by supporting social programs and by opposing a war whose American casualties—given student draft deferments for collegians and a variety of dodges for the well connected—were disproportionately counted among the poor, ill-educated, and black. And then on the night of June 5, as the candidate celebrated victory in the crucial California primary, a young man named Sirhan Bishara Sirhan worked his way through the crowd in the Los Angeles Ambassador Hotel, raised a .22 pistol, and shot him point blank in the head; Kennedy died twenty-five hours later.

Not yet recovered from the assassination of Martin Luther King, the nation was stunned again. Just two days after Kennedy's death James Earl Ray was captured in England, on his way to Brussels—raising questions about how and why a provincial hard luck loner with no apparent source of funds had become an international traveler, eluding a manhunt by escaping to Canada on a false passport, moving on to London, to Portugal, then back again to London. Sirhan Sirhan was meanwhile insisting that he had killed Kennedy, with no outside help, as a blow for the liberation of his native Palestine from Israeli rule.

The possibilities were bewildering. King and the two Kennedys had been assassinated, clearly, for ideological reasons—but what reasons, from what political direction? Sirhan's confession made little sense; the senator from New York was indeed a supporter of Israel, but so were virtually all American politicians, and the matter was scarcely an issue in his primary campaign. Just what (or who) was behind Oswald had died with him, and Ray avoided the kind of explanation that a trial might produce by abruptly pleading guilty, in March 1969, without implicating anyone else. Once in prison, to keep the pot boiling, he repudiated his confession, insisting that he was in fact innocent, hinting at possibilities he had never revealed, and continuing vainly to ask for a new trial.

And these three were only the most famous assassinations of the era, as over the next several years the number of broadly "political" or terrorist murders multiplied in frightening fashion. Middle-class white Americans by this time were long familiar with southern killings of civil rights activists, and occasionally they read about events from what seemed faraway arenas, such as the bitter rivalries within the dimly understood Black Muslim sect that led, in February 1965, to the assassination of the charismatic leader Malcolm X, shot down as he addressed a crowd in a Harlem theater. But during the late 1960s and early 1970s lives were taken by and among policemen, privileged young people, movie stars, and often random victims of a kaleidoscopic variety of ideological rages that burned far closer to home.

The civil rights coalition had all but collapsed before King's murder, and in the resulting confusion about ends and means young black activists founded a number of organizations, some promoting movement back to Africa, some self-government within the boundaries of the United States, still others a leftist world revolution in cooperation with white radicals. What all of them shared was a taste for paramilitary uniforms, violent rhetoric, and guns. During the mid- to late sixties, nothing beat the kind of publicity that came from confrontations with policemen, and when members of a Cleveland group called the Black Nationalists of New Libya killed three of them in a shootout on July 23, 1968, the incident inspired three days of rioting. But the most famous and, to policemen, notorious organization was the Black Panthers.

The Panthers were born in several different cities during 1966. Their ideas and activities varied with time and place; some groups set up ghetto soup kitchens and educational programs, others pulled off armed robberies and burglaries, while their official ideologies moved irregularly back and forth between nationalist and leftist. But the most visible Panthers were headquartered in Oakland, California, where in effect they patrolled the city's patrol cars, heavily armed, following the cops everywhere through the ghetto and monitoring arrests for signs of racist abuse. State laws allowed the public display of loaded weapons— and when the police tried to tighten California's gun control legislation, the Panthers provided great photo-opportunities by prowling the halls of Sacramento in protest, draped with bandoliers and automatic rifles. It was the Oakland Panthers who identified the cops with "pigs," a nickname that spread as fast as television, and in October 1967 the local leader, Huey Newton, was severely wounded and arrested following a stop and shootout that resulted in the death of Officer James Frey. But as the cry "Off the Pigs" reverberated through the ghetto riots of that summer, it also served as the death knell for the Panthers themselves, who officially organized as a revolutionary political party in 1968.

Governments had far more resources and firepower than the thinly manned Panther organization. Hoover's FBI was inclined during the

1960s to see "domestic subversion," communist influence, and possible
revolution in a number of small and otherwise isolated groups. More
important in targeting the Panthers was the bureau's less official role as
capstone of the nation's law enforcement establishment and ally of local
police; and if the "off" talk was mostly wind, it was an ill-wind, a threat
with enough substance so that the cops would not tolerate it. Nothing
was easier than for the FBI to infiltrate the organization, and others
like it, using the threat of criminal charges to recruit African-American
informers.

  Black radical groups, all of them new and continually changing their
policies and people, full of big egos and clashing ambitions, were easily subverted through rumors of betrayal true and false. In January
1969 Bunchy Carter and Jon Huggins, two University of California-
Los Angeles student members of the Black Panther party, were gunned
to death inside of Campbell Hall, on the Los Angeles campus, by members of the African nationalist US organization, perhaps on the basis
of misinformation supplied by the FBI. On December 4 of that year
the Chicago police dealt more directly with Panther Fred Hampton,
deputy director of the national organization, by illegally raiding his
apartment at 4:30 in the morning, guided by a planted agent, and
shooting its several inhabitants, killing Hampton and Mark Clark in
their beds. And as in a spirit of rampant suspicion Panthers across the
country turned on, sometimes tortured, and executed each other, two
groups of them, in New Haven and New York, were arrested and beginning in 1970 tried for "conspiracy to murder" suspected informers. As
further evidence of the growing national split, the New Yorkers were
freed, given a jury's suspicion of FBI tactics and informants, while several in New Haven were convicted.

4

Meanwhile "pig" had also become part of the white radical vocabulary.
As the war in Vietnam spread, collegiate antiwar protests increasingly
spilled over into riots and occasional firebombings, with rocks and
bottles thrown at squads of "pigs" called in to quell them. Many young
people, repelled first by the government's involvement in Vietnam,
then by all of the manners and mores of their parents' generation,
dreamed vaguely of social revolution and spread the epithet beyond the

police and other "fascist" agents of government to the whole class of "bourgeois" from which virtually all of them had come. And it was the word "pig" that provided some of the especial horror, and key links, to the most notorious murders of the decade.

On Sunday morning, August 10, 1969, Winifred Chapman reported for her job as housekeeper at an isolated Beverly Hills estate rented to the movie director Roman Polanski, looked briefly about, and ran screaming to a neighbor. The police, quickly summoned, found five bodies in and around the house, beginning in the driveway with Steven Parent, a local teenager, shot dead in his car. The coffee heiress Abby Folger and her lover, Wojichiech Frykowski, were found in bloody heaps on the lawn. She had been stabbed so often that the police thought her white gown was actually red; he had been shot, beaten, and slashed repeatedly. Jay Sebring, an internationally famous hairdresser, was found in the living room, a rope around his neck thrown over a rafter; at the other end was the actress Sharon Tate, Polanski's wife, eight months pregnant. Sebring had been shot, and both, like all but Parent, savagely and repeatedly stabbed after as well as before death. The single word "Pig" was written in Tate's blood on the living room door.

The next day two more bodies were found in another mansion in the Los Feliz district of Los Angeles; Rosemary La Bianca had been stabbed forty-one times, her husband, Leno, a supermarket executive, twelve, not counting fourteen puncture wounds from a serving fork. The killers had then calmly eaten a meal and apparently played with the family's dogs. The word "War" was scored on La Bianca's abdomen, "Death to Pigs," "Rise," and "Healter Skelter" [sic] daubed in blood on the walls. At the time one young detective remembered that the bloody words "Political Piggy" had been found ten days earlier, in another jurisdiction, at the scene of the murder of a young music teacher, Gary Hinman. But no one in charge thought to make the connection; it was the rich and famous who were terrified, as Frank Sinatra went into hiding, Mia Farrow was afraid to go to her friend Sharon Tate's funeral, and one sporting goods store in Beverly Hills sold two hundred shotguns in two days.

But it was the Hinman murder that broke the case that fall, despite investigative delays and slipups resulting from the several different agencies handling the killings. A young man named Bobby Beausoleil was found driving the dead musician's car on August 6; his prints matched a set found at the crime scene, and he was arrested on suspicion of murder. Two months later, in mid-October, Inyo County sheriff's officers raided a remote ranch in Death Valley, where they rounded up twenty-four members of a "hippie" cult known as the Manson Family on a variety of charges from arson to grand theft. Two teenage girls living on the ranch then approached the officers asking for protection, and one of them said that a fellow "family" member, Susan Atkins, had helped Beausoleil kill Hinman. Atkins was duly arrested; while in detention the next month she gleefully told two prostitute jailmates that she was one of the party that had killed Sharon Tate and her guests.

The story that emerged over the next few weeks was especially chilling to those ordinary middle-aged Americans who followed it through the media. Beginning in the late 1960s tens and maybe hundreds of thousands of middle-class youngsters had been dropping out of school, experimenting with drugs, and leaving home in rebellion against their parents while talking socially radical talk. California was a favorite destination, a place where many floated at least briefly into communes, as substitute for their abandoned families, and a number inevitably drifted into prostitution, theft, and other minor crimes just to keep alive. Charles Manson was clearly different, a thirty-five-year-old son of a prostitute and lifelong petty crook who had discovered, in the middle sixties, a remarkable gift for enticing young people, especially teenage girls, into his own extended "family." But the young people themselves were as ordinary as Manson was not, stray dropouts who seemed achingly familiar to parents across the country, unusual only in the way they had become entrapped in the "family" and in murder.

No one was ever fully able to explain the Charles Manson phenomenon, but for the two years between his arrest and trial his picture was everywhere, as people tried to understand the secret of his charisma from his physical appearance. Short and slight, he would be easy to overlook in a crowd. Hair and beard consciously modeled after those of conventional pictures of Jesus Christ were not unusual in that day, but there was clearly something truly extraordinary, and scary, about his eyes. It was a combination of those eyes, drugs, and sex that apparently allowed Manson to mesmerize his LSD-addled "family"—Susan Atkins thought he was both God and Satan—with a philosophy of revolution built partly on the Book of Revelation and partly on the notion of a coming race war, with Manson picking up coded messages in songs from the pop group the Beatles. Whatever he ordered (and his commands were often bizarre), there were followers to do it without question.

Bobby Beausoleil, it turned out, had been ordered to kill his friend Gary Hinman—who was tortured over two days, Manson cutting off an ear—for some $20,000 he was mistakenly supposed to keep in his house. Manson then ordered the murders of whoever lived in Polanski's isolated Beverly Hills estate—Sharon Tate and her friends were wholly unknown to the "family"—simply to make a kind of statement, or perhaps get Beausoleil, then in jail, off the hook. It was "Helter Skelter" time, he told his followers, a lyric phrase from the Beatles current White Album hit. Four of them took the assignment. Young Parent, a casual visitor, was killed when he surprised them inside the gates; then while Linda Kasabian stood guard, the others, in a drugged frenzy, tied up and slaughtered Tate and her guests, Atkins and Patricia Krenwinkle acting as sadistically as big Tex Watson. The next night these four, plus Manson himself and two others, did much the same to the La Biancas; people equally unknown to them, and for equally vague reasons.

These were a series of killings then unique in the annals of American homicide, with an accordingly unique fascination. And while the "family" were scarcely revolutionaries in any real sense—no one else could read the two harmless "Revolution" songs in the White Album the way that Manson did—they had an odd appeal to another group of young people at least marginally less insane than they were. The surface or "lifestyle" radicalism of the hippies was different from the deeper criticisms of racism, imperialism, and class oppression preached by more thoroughgoing radicals. While there was some overlap between the two kinds of protest and protesters, their aims and means were quite different—Manson himself was virulently racist—and they normally had little use for each other. For many of those seriously interested in political change, hard drugs and defiantly flamboyant clothing were seen as frivolous as, to hippies, all-night meetings were square. But for a small group on the radical extreme—known as the Weathermen, a title taken from a Bob Dylan lyric—the sheer mindlessness of the Manson murders made a shivery sense of its own.

In late December 1969, just as the Manson Family was being arraigned for the murders, the Weathermen, by then a tiny splinter off the student

New Left, convened in Flint, Michigan. It was a deeply discouraging
time for the left. President Richard Nixon had taken office earlier that
year, defeating Democrat Hubert Humphrey in part by winning the
"law and order" vote from segregationist Alabama governor George
Wallace and in part by promising to win rather than end the war in
Vietnam. Many Weathermen, their earlier hopes of radical reform
nearly buried in defeat, greeted each other with three upraised fingers,
signs of the serving fork stuck in Leno La Bianca's belly. "Dig it," one
young woman exulted. "First they killed those pigs, then they ate dinner in the same room with them, then they even shoved a fork into a
victim's stomach. Wild!" At the convention Sharon Tate became, in
death, an unlikely villain, a symbol of privilege, her shredded fetus dismissed as one less white American imperialist-to-be. And with Fred
Hampton assassinated that very month, the Panthers in disarray, the
urban riots sputtering out in failure and bombings in North Vietnam
intensified, several in attendance decided that Flint would be their last
public appearance. They vowed instead to go underground and to revive an old anarchist tradition, virtually dead since the era of Sacco and
Vanzetti, by carrying on a terrorist bombing war against "the System."

Five of them were heard from, loudly, later that winter. Early in
March 1970, Cathy Wilkerson, a recent honors graduate of elite
Swarthmore College, moved with Kathy Boudin, Bryn Mawr '66, and
several others into her father's elegant and temporarily empty Greenwich Village townhouse. On the morning of the 6th the block was
shaken as the building exploded. Wilkerson, wearing only blue jeans,
was seen running off down West 11th Street, together with a wholly
naked Boudin, and disappeared for years. Back at the townhouse they
had left three friends. Ted Gold, a Columbia graduate, was not found
until that night, crushed under the rafters. It took a week to identify
the fragments of Diana Oughton, of Bryn Mawr and the Peace Corps,
from the print on a severed little finger. Ted Robbins, a Kenyon College
dropout, was wholly obliterated; in the absence of physical remains his
presence at the scene was deduced, later, from messages left by companions. Under the rule of felony murder, both Boudin and Wilkerson, as
involved in the illegal bomb-making project, were legally liable for all
three deaths.

A few months later the years of less extreme collegiate unrest reached
its own bloody climax on two widely separated campuses. Early in May,

in protest against President Richard Nixon's bombing of hostile supply lines in the neutral nation of Cambodia, students at Ohio's Kent State University engaged in a series of demonstrations climaxed by the burning of the campus ROTC building. Governor Rhodes called in the national guard, which on Monday morning, the third, lobbed tear gas at rock throwers, moved forward and then back, and ordered a crowd of hundreds to disperse, a group including many peaceable onlookers or passersby. And then at 12:35 P.M. several nervous guardsmen, without warning or orders, fired sixty-one shots into the crowd. They told investigators later that they had felt threatened. Of the thirteen casualties, a presidential commission later found that only two were hit from in front. Of the four students killed, the closest, Jeffrey Miller, who had at one point been harassing the troops, was 85 yards away; Allison Krause, at 110 yards, may have thrown rocks; the other two, 130 yards distant when hit by fatal fire, were William Schroeder, himself an ROTC candidate, and Sandra Scheuer, on her way to music class.

Episodically, over the next ten days, partly in protest against these events up North, partly against the war, partly against racial discrimination, students at Mississippi's all-black Jackson State College engaged in another series of confrontations, with school authorities, passing white motorists, and police. The night of May 13 they threatened the ROTC building. The next night, units of the national guard, the state highway patrol, and city police faced a group of 75 to 200 jeering students behind a chain-link fence in front of Alexander Hall; without warning or orders, as at Kent State, the officers fired more than one hundred fifty rounds into the crowd. Several later claimed they had been shot at. An investigating commission could not confirm this: police radio tapes, full of references to "nigger gals" and other victims, said nothing about sniping. But among the many casualties were Phillip Gibbs, a married junior, and James Earl Green, a high school student, both killed instantly.

Grand juries were called but indicted no one for the homicides at either Kent State or Jackson State, which simply added to the political polarization of the nation. And during the early 1970s Americans kept killing each other for ideological reasons. On September 9, 1971, New York State's Attica Prison was taken over by mostly black inmates, holding hostages and demanding prison reform, the demands to be negotiated by, among others, Minister Louis Farrakhan of the Black Muslims.

Four days later, after two hostages were injured, the place was stormed by state police and prison guards, killing ten hostages and twenty-nine inmates. Later that fall someone blew up the Army Mathematics Research Center at the University of Wisconsin, killing a graduate student inside the building. A handful of Black Panthers reacted to the effective death of the organized party by going underground as the Black Liberation Army, abandoning all other avenues of reform in favor of the stark simplicity of killing cops. In New York, between the spring of 1971 and winter of 1972, the group claimed credit for killing four of them, in black and white pairs, to underline the point that the issue was not the color of the policemen's skins but of their uniforms. This desperate program, combined with a radical rationale for bank robbery, appealed at the same time to the surviving remnants of the Weathermen; Kathy Boudin belonged to the same circle as Joanne Chesimard, or Assata Shakur, who was arrested in a fatal shootout with the New Jersey state police in 1973.

And then the reading public was in effect blindsided from another angle entirely, as the grievances of Native Americans, forgotten for generations, were dramatized in a violent confrontation with federal agents at the historically resonant site of Wounded Knee, South Dakota.

5

As had been true of most conflicts between Native Americans and white governments since the seventeenth century, it was an act of murder that sparked the train that led to the armed takeover of the little hamlet at Wounded Knee. But as equally true, there was more to the conflict than that.

Official U.S. policy toward the Indians had changed over the generations, the original aim of assimilation abandoned during the 1930s, then resumed in the 1950s. By the end of the 1960s some 300,000 of the 800,000 surviving Native Americans had moved off the reservation into the cities, many of them badly prepared for the "mainstream" they were encouraged to join. When the American Indian Movement (AIM) was formally organized in 1968, inspired in part by the current demand for Black Power, its founders played on old issues and new ones. The old ones were the corruption and indifference of the Bureau of Indian Affairs (BIA), its use of cooperative native stooges to run tribal governments, its continued subversion of land rights. The new ones involved the plight of Indian people in the cities. Several native groups made headlines in the late 1960s with demonstrations such as the occupation of Alcatraz Island, in San Francisco Bay, when it was abandoned by the government. But it was hard to crack the indifference of most inhabitants of the reservations, sunk in poverty and desperation, with unemployment over 50 percent in many western states, alcoholism and suicide rampant, and a homicide rate twice the national average.

And then Russell Means, a Sioux from Cleveland and one of the founders of AIM, was told about Raymond Yellow Thunder. Yellow Thunder, a middle-aged Oglala Sioux farmworker, was found dead in a panel truck, outside of Gordon, Nebraska, late in February 1972. The local authorities first claimed he had died of exposure, but his sisters saw evidence of mutilation on the body, and an autopsy found evidence of "foul play." The story later pieced together was that Yellow Thunder had stepped drunkenly out of a local bar and was picked up for sport by a group of whites in a car, locked for a time in a trunk, beaten and burned with cigarettes, and at one time forced to dance, naked from the waist down, for the amusement of a crowd at the American Legion Hall. It was after this ordeal, missing for a week, that the victim turned up dead. And when under insistent family pressure Leslie and Melvin Hare, two influential young heirs to a ranching fortune, were finally arrested for the crime, they were charged with no more than second-degree manslaughter and released without bail. The sisters then turned to AIM.

For Means "it was a turning point," requiring wholly new tactics. Placards and protests were not enough: "We could not allow Indian people to be murdered." And he proceeded to organize a caravan of Sioux from the Pine Ridge and Rosebud reservations, over five hundred men and women in a hundred cars, to descend on little Gordon, waving American flags upside down in the traditional symbol of distress. The demonstrators occupied the town for three full days, terrifying the inhabitants. And when the Hares were jailed, a cop suspended, and the town fathers promised to end all discrimination against Indians, AIM's reputation soared not only locally but across the country.

The occupation of a whole town was a truly novel tactic, and Means, with a genius for publicity, over the next several months organized a number of well-televised demonstrations in Washington and elsewhere.

At the same time the visceral, and traditional, murder issue struck a special nerve among Indians across the country. Among the notable deaths were those of the activist Richard Oaks, ambushed in a California park, Philip Celay, a "justifiable homicide" shot in the back by a deputy sheriff in Arizona, and the "excusable homicide" of the highly honored special forces veteran Leroy Shenandoah, an Onandaga iron-worker beaten and shot by Philadelphia police in a case of tragically mistaken identity.

But for Russell Means the ancestral homelands were in South Dakota, and it was there that just a year after the Yellow Thunder murder he was again called to intervene in a homicide case, this one the killing of Wesley Bad Heart Bull, shot dead in a gas station lot in the town of Buffalo Gap. Again the white killer was charged only with second-degree manslaughter, again released, this time on minimal bail, and again AIM organized a demonstration, on February 6, 1973, this time at the courthouse in Custer, a name with special resonance in Indian history. But backing up state police and national guardsmen by this time was the FBI, as Director J. Edgar Hoover was convinced that AIM was subversive, communist, potentially revolutionary; and the protest was broken up. At that point, frustrated not only by the opposition of local, state, and federal agencies but also by the corruption and brutality of native BIA police, under control of the tribal leader—a man then threatened with impeachment—Means turned not outside but inside the Pine Ridge Reservation. On the evening of February 27, he and two hundred armed supporters took the highly symbolic step of moving into the little hamlet of Wounded Knee, site of the killing of Sitting Bull during the last massacre of Sioux by the U.S. Cavalry in the winter of 1890.

AIM then occupied the Church of the Sacred Heart (with the support of the resident priest) and the local trading post (without support from the traders), together with the local museum and post office. Means and his group demanded a U.S. Senate investigation both of the current management of the BIA and of historic treaty violations going back to 1868. The group was soon blockaded by BIA police, U.S. marshals, and FBI agents, but during the early days allies managed to slip in and help build and supply defensive bunkers as the confrontation escalated. Shots were fired on March 9, and, except for occasional cease-fires for negotiations, the two sides continued to shoot at each other for several weeks. Some federal agents were wounded, one seriously, but AIM was badly outgunned, and on April 27, the killings of two supporters, Frank Clearwater and Buddy Lamont, helped to force a fragile truce on May 4.

The event helped to further polarize national opinion. Conservatives across the country rallied behind the FBI, for so long the symbol of hard-line, incorruptible law enforcement, while liberals and civil libertarians denounced it. Accounts of the siege varied enormously, but one thing was clear: American citizens, acting on the basis of deeply held beliefs, were exchanging deadly fire with a small army of federal agents, in a confrontation that lasted for several weeks. The nation, as yet, had never seen anything like it.

6

Throughout all the murderous turmoil of the 1960s and early 1970s, meanwhile, the U.S. Supreme Court continued its long drive to clarify the rights of criminal defendants, which toward the end of the period resulted in the effective suspension of the death penalty for any offense, with powerful political repercussions.

The *Powell* case, which in 1932 had demanded a new trial for the Scottsboro rape defendants, was one key landmark in the movement, begun in the nineteenth century, that allowed federal courts to oversee the operation of the criminal systems of the several states. The concept that the Bill of Rights applied to state proceedings was a powerful legal lever, and under the regime of Chief Justice Earl Warren, beginning in the late 1940s, the Court did not hesitate to use it. While Warren and his colleagues rarely moved past precedents set either in the federal courts or in the more historically liberal states, such as California or Massachusetts, what it did in effect was to insist on a single, national, and high set of standards for criminal proceedings across the whole of the country.

And so, in *Mapp v. Ohio* (1961), the court ruled on the basis of the Fourth Amendment that evidence found by police without proper search warrants could not be used in a criminal trial. In *Gideon v. Wainwright* (1963), it held that the Seventh Amendment guaranteed that any defendant in a felony trial had the right to a lawyer at state expense. On the basis of the Fifth Amendment's right against self-incrimination,

Griffin v. California (1965) forbade state judges and prosecutors from implying guilt, in addressing jurors, as a result of a defendant's decision not to testify in court. The next year *Miranda v. Arizona* (1966) demanded on the basis of both the Seventh and Fifth Amendments that people arrested in a criminal case had to be informed of their right to a lawyer and to remain silent.

Another set of rulings dealt with the rights of convicted prisoners, based on the Eighth Amendment's prohibition of "cruel and unusual punishment." The early-nineteenth-century hopes that prisons might be places of reform and rehabilitation had depended, in part, on the absolute authority of wardens to impose their own benign intentions on the wicked wills of the inmates. These early hopes were long gone, and by the 1960s many prisons had become places abandoned by the authorities to the better organized inmates, especially racial gangs or groups like Hell's Angels or the Black Muslims. Attorneys for prisoners then sought no more than to make incarceration less brutal, insisting that even murderers condemned for life—for whom "rehabilitation" was irrelevant anyway—retained some basic legal rights. The federal courts agreed, notably in *Talley v. Stephens* (1965) and *Holt v. Sarver* (1970), both cases from Arkansas. The first held that arbitrary whippings must end, the second that the state's whole corrupt, trusty-run, and often brutal penal system was unconstitutional and must be drastically reformed.

All of these general rulings in favor of the rights of criminal defendants and prisoners were spiced by decisions in individual cases, including one that reversed the most notorious murder trial of the 1950s. On July 4, 1954, Dr. Sam Shepard told police he had been knocked out after struggling manfully with a "bushy-haired" intruder into his suburban Cleveland home (bushy hair apparently a standard feature among such strangers), before awakening to find his pregnant wife, Marilyn, dead in their bedroom, bludgeoned some thirty-five times with a blunt instrument. Neither police nor jury believed him, given no apparent physical evidence for the existence of any outsider. But in 1966 the Court granted a new trial on the grounds that sensationally biased press coverage had made it impossible to impanel an impartial jury, and Shepard's celebrated defense lawyer, F. Lee Bailey, found a forensic expert on retrial to testify that some blood samples found in the house belonged to neither occupant. The doctor was set free.

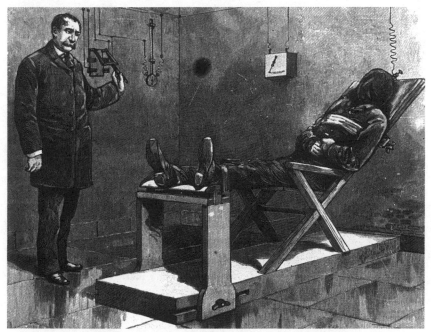

An early version of the electric chair, billed as a humane alternative to hanging, 1890s. Credit: The Bettmann Archive.

Bartolomeo Vanzetti and Nicola Sacco in court, Dedham, Massachusetts, 1923. Credit: UPI/Corbis-Bettmann.

Nathan Leopold and Richard Loeb, flanking Clarence Darrow, at their sentencing, Chicago, June 13, 1924. Credit: UPI/Corbis-Bettmann.

Ruth Snyder, the first woman executed in the electric chair, New York, 1927. Credit: UPI/Corbis-Bettmann.

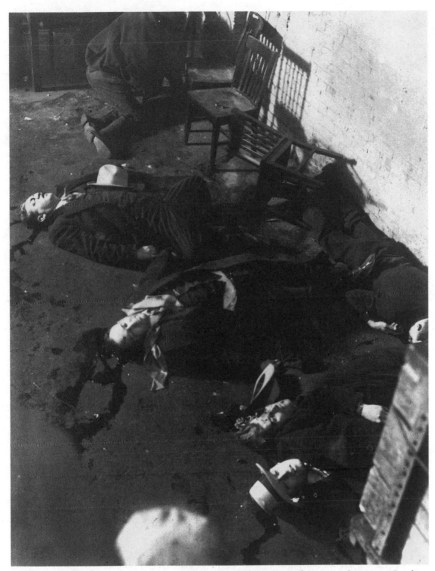

Victims of the St. Valentine's Day Massacre, Chicago, February 14, 1929. Credit:
UPI/Corbis-Bettmann.

Al Capone leaving the court in Chicago, shortly before his conviction on a federal tax charge, 1931. Credit: UPI/Corbis-Bettmann.

William Heirens, a serial killer and
the first suspect in a criminal case to
be questioned under the influence of
"truth serum," Chicago, 1946.
Credit: UPI/Corbis-Bettmann.

One of 10,000 national guardsmen standing ready during the Watts riots of August 1965. Credit: UPI/Corbis-Bettmann.

Richard Speck, convicted of murdering eight student nurses on the night of June 13–14, 1966. Credit: UPI/Corbis-Bettmann.

Charles Manson, leader of the group responsible for the Tate-La Bianca murders, Los Angeles, 1969. Credit: UPI/Corbis-Bettmann.

American Indian Movement sentries on guard at Wounded Knee, South Dakota, March 3, 1973. Credit: UPI/Corbis-Bettmann.

In terms of the legal treatment of most homicide cases, none of the Warren Court's decisions had a truly dramatic effect, although some created real changes and others speeded up processes already under way. Most states, even Arkansas, had over the years been improving conditions in their prisons with little direct federal prodding, simply because rising prosperity and living standards on the outside seeped inside their penitentiaries, as relatives and other voting visitors insisted on such basics as running water, ample food, and some time for rest and recreation. The right to a state-appointed lawyer guaranteed by *Wainright* was already well established everywhere in homicide cases. *Griffin*'s restriction on prosecutors and judges had some impact in those states that did not already follow it, but it had been standard practice in all federal trials since 1893. And the kind of illegal search and seizure addressed in *Mapp* was rarely an issue in murder trials.

Miranda, then, was the only one of these landmark rulings to have a widespread and routine effect in homicide investigations. Some cops grumbled at the time about the need to read an arrested person a short list of warnings about self-incrimination, and to respect any silence, but the legal issue was hardly novel: three generations earlier it was the lack of such a warning that had allowed Lizzie Borden's lawyer to keep her inquest testimony out of her trial. *Miranda* did have some effect in cases of crimes, such as arson, that were typically committed by professional or semiprofessional criminals, who had much experience with the system and knew that police were forbidden to beat or otherwise force confessions out of them. But except for the relatively few who acted as hirelings of organized gangs, killers were and are overwhelmingly first-time amateurs, and so their proceedings were much less affected, as detectives still found it possible to get them to talk without consulting lawyers. The usual game was rigged in favor of the police—smart, educated, and experienced in such cases—against the great majority of homicide defendants—never up on such charges before, ill-educated, jittery, hoping to get on the good side of the law. Interrogation rooms, strange and frightening places to murder suspects, were a detective's home turf, and as one "good cop" played on a suspect's natural and often overwhelming desire to tell his side of the story, to lie, boast, justify, or confess, another "bad cop" played on his equally natural fear of authority. And so despite complaints, the number of confessions in homicide cases did not drop markedly after *Miranda*.

But if most of the Warren Court's decisions were reformist rather than revolutionary in effect, without much political impact, the same could not be said of its decisions concerning the death penalty.

The background to the dramatic suspension of capital punishment in the United States was the long slow decline in the practice. During the 1950s, in another move to make legal execution as humane as possible, many states had substituted death in a gas chamber for the electric chair. But neither was much used in the postwar era. The number of executions actually carried out sank to double digits as early as 1950 and fell to just seven in 1965, one in 1966. And then, with the 1967 gassing of two convicted murderers, a black man in California and a Puerto Rican in Colorado, the death penalty simply stopped operating all across the United States. No new humanitarian arguments were added to the old ones, and there was no big popular movement in favor of abolition. But for decades there had been an unevenly dropping percentage of Americans who favored capital punishment when asked by opinion pollers. And now on top of the long-standing general reluctance to take life there was added a new set of legal and constitutional objections.

One effect of the 1932 *Powell* decision was that the number of capital executions appealed all the way to the Supreme Court soared from a little over 3 percent in the 1930s to nearly 33 percent in the 1960s. The expense to the states involved was considerable, and so was the embarrassment of the trial or appellate courts whose judgments were overridden. By the mid-1960s, the drive to overturn the death penalty altogether was being led by the Legal Defense Fund of the NAACP, whose key argument was that in practice it was disproportionately reserved for racial minorities, especially blacks, who accounted for well over half of all who died at the hands of the state. The evidence was in fact overwhelming. Roughly 90 percent of all those executed for rape, over many decades, had been black. And among those accused of murder, scholars carefully going over the evidence, case by case, holding constant all other factors such as the nature of the crime and the age and sex of victims, clearly confirmed that what had been true in Philadelphia beginning in the twentieth century and in the South throughout its history applied as well to the United States as a whole: African Americans were far more likely than whites to be sentenced to death.

The evidence was certainly strong enough to convince the states of the need, in effect, to suspend all executions until the Supreme Court laid down firm guidelines. During 1968, in *Witherspoon v. Illinois,* the standard prosecution practice of excluding potential jurors from capital trials on the grounds that they opposed the death penalty was held unconstitutional, under the Fourteenth Amendment, because it deprived a defendant of a jury "representative of the community"—just as excluding black jurors did. No state, then, could safely execute anyone convicted in such a trial. For four years capital punishment was suspended while the key test cases worked their way up through the system, with both prosecutors and defense lawyers metaphorically holding their breath. In 1972, finally, the California Supreme Court and then the U.S. Supreme Court issued two more historic rulings.

In California, *People v. Anderson* held that gassing was "cruel and *unusual* punishment," simply because it was so rarely done, carried out in only a tiny percentage of potentially capital cases, and was thus unconstitutional in that state. The federal ruling in *Furman v. Georgia* was less extreme but followed in part the same logic. It was a close 5 to 4 vote, with the majority turning in five different opinions. Some of the winning justices held in effect that while the death penalty was not on its face unconstitutional (past executions were not invalid), it had in effect *become* unconstitutional under the Eighth Amendment, just as California had ruled, because it was so seldom imposed. The others in effect ruled that death at the hands of the state resulted from something like a lottery, as no firm guidelines dictated why *this* crime, or criminal, deserved execution and *that* legally identical one did not. And while leaving the way open, in theory, for a new legislative approach, the Court followed the argument of the NAACP by quite clearly forbidding execution at the discretion of (usually white) jurors, as being liable to arbitrary or prejudiced abuse.

This reasoning was an ironic reversal of the nineteenth-century movement to soften mandatory executions in cases of first-degree murder, rape, and other offenses by allowing judges and jurors some discretionary leeway in which to exercise the quality of mercy. But while scholars might puzzle over that point, the one that hit the fan was that it invalidated the capital sentences of all the 120 men then on death rows across the country, threw state law into confusion, and underlined the nation's already powerful ideological polarization.

The timing was especially critical, and to many painful. All through the rising turbulence of the later 1960s the Supreme Court, as the Founding Fathers had intended, had marched to its own drummer, ignoring the prevailing political climate by pursuing a line of legal reform begun in a quieter era. As the "law and order" issue grew more explosive every year, the justices calmly followed *Talley* with *Miranda, Witherspoon* with *Holt*. But 1968 marked a series of key turning points. That was the year when both Robert Kennedy and Martin Luther King Jr. were assassinated, the year when Richard Nixon won the presidency in part by running against urban riot and "crime in the streets." It was also, with ironic timing, both the last year in which a bare majority of Americans, when polled, still opposed the death penalty and the first year in history when no one officially suffered it.

The issue of capital punishment had always provoked strong emotions, and the late 1960s were especially aggravating to those who believed in it. One of the most frightening killers of the era was known as "the Boston Strangler," a man who in just a year and half, between 1962 and 1964, raped, killed, and sometimes sadistically mutilated thirteen female victims. Women who lived alone anywhere in eastern Massachusetts were terrified by the Strangler, who broke into locked apartments and attacked victims ranging in age from eighty-five-year-old Mary Mullen, who was found with a cord tied in a neat bow under her chin, to nineteen-year-old Mary Sullivan, left with a broom inserted in her vagina and a "Happy New Year!" card between her toes. Early in 1965, F. Lee Bailey, attorney for a man once falsely accused of these crimes, identified an inmate in an institution for the criminally insane, one Albert De Salvo, as the real Strangler. The evidence was strong, but the authorities took no legal action, evidently embarrassed by the fact that they had arrested De Salvo twice during the early 1960s without connecting him to the murders. The Commonwealth of Massachusetts implicitly agreed with Bailey by transferring the alleged Strangler from Bridgewater State Hospital to Walpole State Prison, for what was in effect a life sentence; he had been sent to Bridgewater, hearing voices, after an arrest for nothing more than breaking and entering an apartment. But the public was outraged, and a major political issue was made of the fact that De Salvo was never put on trial for his life.

And then, the year after the Strangler revelations, a drifting petty criminal named Richard Speck shocked the nation by calmly and one by one murdering eight student nurses from South Chicago Community Hospital, raping one of them, during a single hot July night in 1966. Speck was widely considered a kind of monster, a notion encouraged by a brief return to Cesare Lombroso's Darwinian theory that criminals are physically different, biologically born and not made. During the excitement surrounding early exploration of genetic structure it was thought that carrying an extra Y, or male-determining, chromosome explained not only Speck's gaunt physique and deeply pockmarked face but his super-macho murderous behavior. Unlike De Salvo, he did not escape a murder trial or a death sentence, as pronounced by a Cook County jury in June 1967. But the next year the Supreme Court's ruling in *Witherspoon* invalidated that decision, forcing a resentencing to life in prison, which to many voters suggested somehow that he had gotten away with murder.

And by this standard Speck was not alone. Both the King and Kennedy families urged that their respective assassins not be sentenced to death, but much of the public felt cheated by their life sentences—in the case of Sirhan Sirhan, forced by the *Anderson* decision after he had been condemned to die in California. The same thing happened to Charles Manson, the apparent embodiment of sheer evil, and to all of his "family," together with brutal robbery murderers, cop killers, and child rapists across America. And as politicians accused the courts of coddling criminals and "tough cops" all over the country won office as big city mayors (a development inconceivable in the previous century), Richard Nixon worked throughout his first term to restructure the Supreme Court. He had barely squeaked to victory in 1968; the second time around, in 1972, the tested appeal of "law and order" helped him to reelection, just months after the *Furman* decision, by the biggest electoral margin ever won by a Republican candidate for president.

7

The headlines, as always, dealt with the big ones; the assassinations and ideological killings, the hideous, sensational, or mass murders. But far more important numerically than these, again as always, were the "routine" homicides among acquaintances in bars, family members in kitchens, robbery victims in streets and gas stations. These, too, were climbing sharply in the anxious decade 1963–1974. And the explanations offered by contemporary sociological experts were no more helpful than those of contemporary politicians, liberal and conservative.

Political conservatives tended to blame Democratic administrations, the Supreme Court, the decline in capital punishment, the "handcuffing" of police by judicial decisions, the defiance of settled law by protesters like Martin Luther King Jr., and various campus radicals. More privately, or with various code words, they also blamed blacks. Liberals, when not claiming that rising homicide rates were simply a figment of the FBI's imagination, blamed poverty and racism. Sociologists, heirs to an academic discipline that since its nineteenth-century beginnings had idealized small traditional communities, blamed urban growth, using a number of ugly words at the very top of the alphabet—"alienation," "anonymity," and "anomie"—to describe the unhealthy mental state of city folks. But all of these attempts at understanding ignored both the hard statistics and the history of homicide in America.

The "murder rate" had begun its rise in the late 1950s, under the conservative Eisenhower administration, and peaked in 1973 under Richard Nixon. It had never shown any correlation with rates of execution, rarely involved college students of any political persuasion, and was moving up among whites as well as blacks, Iowans as well as New Yorkers. The rise was recorded in death certificates as well as crimes reported to the FBI, and so were as "hard" as any criminal statistics could be. It kept moving up through a generally prosperous decade, when the number of blacks and whites counted under the official "poverty" line was falling dramatically. And while during the 1960s metropolitan rates did generally move up and past those for the countryside, this was a very recent development. To blame the rise in violence on the growth of cities was to ignore the fact that through most of American (and English) history cities were generally more peaceable than the countryside; that while various social ills (including crime) were officially counted better in urban jurisdictions than in rural ones, as late as the 1950s the "murder rate" in New York was lower than the national average, and that during the 1960s, as always, it was far higher in many small cities than in the big ones like Chicago and Los Angeles.

All parties simply wanted to blame "crime in the streets" on their favorite villains. Being American and optimistic, all but the academic sociologists also wanted to blame it on something they could "cure," or at least promise to cure, either through tougher cops and courts or through more antipoverty programs. And being American and parochial, they remained largely ignorant of the fact that the rise in murder rates was at the same time afflicting a variety of nations with widely different political and justice systems, economies, and racial compositions.

The first American colonies had been founded as part of the then-new worldwide international economy, and the United States had always been deeply involved in that economy, more deeply involved, and with wider implications, than most of its citizens recognized or understood. And at the most basic level rising violence in the United States was part of an international shift of great significance, nothing less than the reversal of the long decline in homicide rates and other indices of criminal behavior that had begun in the middle decades of the nineteenth century.

The problems of records and definitions that make it hard to find comparable measurements over any long period within a single jurisdiction are multiplied many times over in any attempt to stretch comparisons not only over time but across space, as between nations. But careful studies by Ted Robert Gurr have shown movements in international homicide rates, by far the most well measured and "trustworthy" of criminal statistics, that are far too long and steep to be denied. Gurr draws in part on my own more detailed work for the (mostly urban) United States over the same period, and despite some differences in timing and degree, the picture for the several Western countries is roughly the same. If drawn as a sketch it would look like a long distended U-curve, or perhaps a reverse J-curve, with high rates from the earliest available nineteenth-century statistics dropping to lows somewhere in the middle twentieth century, as in Marvin Wolfgang's Philadelphia, and then shooting up sharply in the 1960s.

This giant U is of course pretty ragged, responding to a number of short-term phenomena in each locale, but even some of its zigs and bumps are common to many nations. In the middle of the twentieth century, the drop in recorded homicide rates during World War II and its rise immediately afterward echoes the experience not only of World War I but of the American Civil War, and (in England) it seems the

Napoleonic Wars as well. There are national variations, too: English homicides drop more steeply than American, on the left side of the *U,* as do Stockholm's convictions for murder and attempted murder. In Sydney the index for high court convictions for murder and assault plunged at the most dramatic rate, falling by a factor of ten between the 1830s and the end of the nineteenth century. The bottom, too, was hit at somewhat different times in these places, and in various European nations. But the sketch still works, in its rough way, and the jump in the late 1950s and certainly the 1960s is unmistakable everywhere: in Stockholm, with no Vietnam War, virtually no blacks, little poverty, no liberal Democrats (or conservative Republicans), the rate of conviction for murder and attempted murder soared by 600 percent between 1950 and 1970.

There are many possible explanations for this international crime wave, or right-hand upturn in the U-curve, but the most fundamental is that it represents the decay of the conditions that caused the left-hand downturn in the first place. That is, just as the downturn represents the force of the urban industrial revolution in the mid- to later nineteenth century, bottoming out in the mid-twentieth with the full maturing of that revolution, the upturn represents the move into what was already, in the 1960s, being called the "postindustrial era."

Homicide in the modern world has been mostly an irrationally impulsive crime, committed by young men, especially poor and aimless young men energized by frustration and anger. And in the 1960s two sides of the economy, both consumption and employment, combined to heighten frustration, release the curbs on irrationally impulsive behavior, and fill the streets with aimless young men.

Frustration, even desperation, was never absent from the world of the nineteenth century, as people lived close to the edge of genuine hunger, and in hard times property crimes tended to go up as men and women had to beg or steal clothes, shoes, and bread. But the urban industrial revolution worked to curb impulsive behavior, as the hard discipline of mass schooling, backed up by cops and courts and moral lessons, reinforced the basic requirements of the new kinds of work itself. The regimen of routinized work and long hours through all seasons of the year was made tolerable, even desirable, not only by more material abundance, the basic promise of more, here, and now in terms of clothes, shoes, and bread, but also by such future possibilities as home ownership and family advancement. The moral lessons of self-control and the private and governmental institutions of social control reinforced each other and the built-in demands of office and factory. At the very minimum the regularity of work and the demand for sobriety narrowed the opportunities for drinking and fighting to a few hours in the week.

But by the 1960s the very abundance of the postindustrial economy was creating whole new layers of frustration. Modern marketing techniques, such as mass advertising and open shelves, virtually cried "Take!" to all comers, and property crimes soared even during times of prosperity. Television greatly magnified "relative deprivation," encouraging people who by earlier standards were well fed and clothed to compare their own conditions, in great detail, to the lifestyles of the rich and famous, and so created demands for "More!" that were almost impossible to satisfy legitimately. And at the same time it grew harder for many to satisfy more basic needs through ordinary work.

The new postindustrial economy required, and still requires, levels of schooling that the human species has never known before, more years of demanding that young people sit still, take turns, mind the teacher, and listen for the bell. For those who drop out after a few years of this, absorbing some of the discipline but few of the fine points, there had once been jobs in factories. But by the 1960s these manufacturing jobs, traditionally the best paid for those with few educational skills, were shrinking in number. And as competition stiffened for those in low-level white-color work, the prospects for good money and advancement shrank there as well.

Once there was a clearly apparent reward for putting up with the boredom and frustration of mass education, for obeying the cops, staying out of trouble, learning to curb the appetite for mind-altering drugs. But once the decay of the urban industrial revolution diluted these payoffs, the moral lessons came to seem irrelevant and the institutions of social control simply tyrannical. And at a level of prosperity high enough so that anyone could afford alcohol, with an expanding pharmacopoeia of other drugs widely available, without steady employment and with much time on their hands, a growing number of young men in the postindustrial age drifted into impulsively violent criminal behavior.

The story above is international in scope, but during the 1960s and early 1970s its American variation had some features of its own, as the result of the erosion of American economic dominance, the Vietnam War, the problem of race, and the unique character of cities in the United States.

The year 1968, pivotal in many ways, witnessed a major crisis in the international money market. The resolution of that crisis both reflected and contributed to the fact that the U.S. dollar could no longer act as the basis of the world's currencies, as the result of chronic deficits in our international balance of payments. Some of this resulted from economic developments beyond any American government's ability to control, but to try at the same time to fight a Vietnamese war in Indochina and a war on poverty at home greatly added to the strain. In any case the long postwar economic surge that had so lifted the prospects of urban working-class Americans, especially blacks, was coming to an end.

Hidden under the prosperity of the era, the older manufacturing cities like Philadelphia continued, as they had since the late 1950s, to lose population and jobs. The good-paying factory jobs that lives and families could be built on were the ones that black men, in particular, had just begun to win in the postwar era; as "postwar" segued within a few years into "postindustrial," these men discovered that they had in effect been piped aboard a sinking ship, welcomed into the urban industrial age just as that age was fading out. At the same time there was a loss even in the less desirable, wholly unskilled jobs as messengers, elevator operators, and porters that had once been open to them.

While many Americans, black and white, were able to move up and out of poverty during the 1960s, for many of them moving up meant moving out of the inner city. The majority of Americans, unlike Europeans, had long felt uneasy about cities. Florence, Rome, Paris, and London were monuments to a nation's history, outposts of high culture and civilization; Chicago and New York were dirty and sinful, full of strange, distasteful, sometimes scary people—in the nineteenth century foreign immigrants, by the late twentieth African Americans. And as the jobs moved out to the suburbs, so did the people with the jobs, black and white, abandoning the central core of the older cities to the unemployed and desperate.

Vietnam was no help: for the first time in history, there was no drop in the murder rate even at the height of a major war. Instead the fighting simply drained federal dollars and attention away from the domestic economy and social issues. The fact that it was so deeply resented kept terms of duty short and morale low. By its late stages, after 1968, the Pentagon reported that about a third of all the troops in Indochina were abusing drugs, while refusal to obey direct orders, even the murder of unpopular officers—those who insisted on more fighting—had become serious problems. And when finally rotated home, veterans hardened to violence were greeted not with parades but indifference, even vilification, and the same tightening job market many of them had enlisted to escape.

Those who returned to the inner cities after 1969 found that the destruction of the Black Panthers had not brought peace but new troubles. Some of the Panthers, those not suicidally attacking the police, had provided some sense of hope, some positive programs. In their absence purely local youth gangs swelled in importance, power, and arrogance, representing no ideas but their own existence, robbing strangers, killing each other in turf wars. One result was the new record in homicides set in 1973. And not only the number but the patterns of these killings confirmed that the United States was pushing up the right-hand side of the historic U-curve in homicide rates, as shown, once again, by the Philadelphia story.

Not all places moved at the same pace. In Houston, for example, never an industrial city, the coming of the space age in the shape of the National Aeronautics and Space Administration only slowly changed the old southern attitudes toward homicide. For over a century Texas had put down in black and white what other places honored only as an "unwritten law": that a husband (not wife) who caught a spouse in the act of adultery had a right to murder the guilty party or parties. Carrying concealed weapons into ordinary social situations was an old state tradition, and until the code was revised in 1974 the defense of private property, certainly the barest hint of personal self-defense, defined a killing as "justifiable." In that year lawmakers agreed that Texas had too long "provided private citizens with wide discretionary power to kill their fellow citizens legally and with impunity." As a result, one study of all Houston's killings in the year 1969 showed that, even before the stage when defense lawyers got to strut and fret in open court, police, prosecutors, or grand jurors routinely dismissed an absolute majority of

known killers without formal trials. Hearing, of course, from the survivors of these mostly barroom or family disputes rather than the losers,
they based their decisions on the time-honored ground that, as the result of some combination of lowdown lyin', cheatin', braggin', stealin',
or coldhearted double-dealin' in general, the victim had in fact deserved
to die. (It is interesting that in this *macho* jurisdiction, perhaps because
guns, as "equalizers," wiped out the physical difference between men
and women, more wives killed husbands [15] than husbands killed
wives [9]. *None* of them served any time as a result.)

But Philadelphia, like most northern jurisdictions, was not and never
had been as tolerant as Houston: during the late 1960s and early 1970s
the problem in the City of Brotherly Love was not that homicide was
often excused by the justice system but that it was beginning to run
away from it.

In 1972–74 another study of Philadelphia's Police Homicide Division, asking the same questions as Marvin Wolfgang had a generation
earlier, came up with dramatically different answers. The number of
arrests for homicide among whites had climbed from just 1.8 per
100,000 annually in the mid-twentieth century years to 2.8 at the verge
of the century's last quarter, a gain of 56 percent. In part as the result
of the explosion in gang activity, the number of black arrests meanwhile
shot up from 24.6 per 100,000 at midcentury to 64.2 in the early
1970s, a jump of 261 percent. The gap between black and white, then,
which had been closing in the 1940s and 1950s, was again widening.
Most significant, in a city now full of young African Americans with
little work to do, as over a century earlier it had been full of young Irish,
were the specific patterns of homicide. That is, the patterns of the early
1970s, on the right-hand upside of the U-curve, in many ways more
closely resembled those of the left-hand downside, way back in the
nineteenth century, than they did those of just a generation earlier, or
1948–52, at the bottom of the curve, the time that had marked the full
maturity of the urban industrial revolution.

As a result of the fact that one day looks much like the rest to the
unemployed, during both 1972–74 and 1839–1901 the fraction of
killings occurring on weekends was just one-half of the total, in contrast to the nearly two-thirds during the mid-twentieth-century years,
when sobriety (and exhaustion) reigned during the workweek and
the time for drinking and fighting peaked around payday. On both

sides of the *U,* in comparison with the mid-twentieth-century bottom, there were proportionally more killings of strangers, and in the streets, fewer at home; more deadly brawls involving many contestants, fewer one-on-one domestic fatalities; more robbery murders; proportionally fewer women arrested; more interracial murders, fewer involving family, friends, or acquaintances.

All of these changes after midcentury, too, were precisely of the kind that made homicides harder for police to solve. And as the national "murder rate" measured by mortality statistics more than doubled between the 1955 low of 4.5 and the 10.2 per 100,000 annually reached in 1974, the percentage of those that could not be "cleared by arrest" plunged in parallel, roughly doubling from less than 10 percent to about 20 percent.

In January 1973 a ceasefire in Vietnam was followed by an exchange of prisoners; despite some diplomatic fudging it was clear that the United States had lost. By then even defeat was a relief, closing a decade of more rapid change and frightening domestic events than any since the Civil War. But while the events are over, we are still living with many of the changes they created, politically and socially. And in terms of homicide, we are still struggling, among other things, with the problems of the international postindustrial economy, as national murder rates are still nearly as high as those reached by the upside peak of the long-term international U-curve in murder rates.

9

Murder in Contemporary America, 1974 to the Present: A Historical Perspective

In America, history has always moved too fast to be analyzed on the fly, and every generation has believed that its own experience is unique, that in the rush of change it has broken with tradition more decisively than any other. Sometimes even a professional historian is moved to agree: yes, it is at least partly true that this is a genuinely new time, without useful precedents in the past. There is no question that the patterns of homicide have changed over the last quarter of the twentieth century and that we approach the twenty-first in the midst of some unique developments, many of them troubling. But history is rarely transcended outright, and the historian's basic credo is that it is impossible to know just where we are or to predict where we are headed without some knowledge of where we have come from.

Ever since the 1960s the "crime issue" has been part of our national political discourse, and as murder heads the list of crimes most feared and publicized, the level and direction of the "murder rate" is a matter of continuing concern. But there is little agreement about what it means. In late December 1993 the chair of the U.S. Senate Judiciary Committee, charged with oversight of the several federal agencies devoted to fighting crime, announced that "the United States is the most dangerous country in the world. No country in the world has a higher per capita murder rate than the United States." A little more than two years later the cover story of a national news magazine declared, "Finally, We Are Winning the War Against Crime."

Both of these declarations were based on the latest statistical evidence. The senator began his speech with the murder total from the FBI's *Uniform Crime Reports* for 1992; the magazine relied on an interim report from the same source that showed a 15 percent drop for the first six months of 1995 (later cut back to 8 percent). Statistics like these stimulate scholarly commentary at regular intervals; the backyard arguments follow more often on dramatic events, the abduction and murder of little Polly Klaas, the O. J. Simpson trial, the latest drive-by shooting of innocent victims in Chicago or New York. But as experts and laypersons, liberals and conservatives, argue about whether or not there is a "crisis" in violent crime, and why, they share only a common refusal to look much beyond the immediate past.

The simple fact is that in terms of both homicide and its treatment in law, the continuities are even more impressive than the changes. Murder itself stretches back into prehistory, and the death penalty almost as far; the outlines of the modern criminal process go back to the Middle Ages, and so do many enduring patterns of criminal homicide. While other patterns, punishments, and procedures have come and gone over the history of the American Republic, still more have moved along relatively predictable lines.

Some acquaintance with the past is needed, then, if only to tell what is genuinely novel in our contemporary world from what is not. The list of debated issues is a long one, and this book has not even tried to deal with all of them. Its focus, much more modest, is limited to those that the specifically historical evidence may help to clarify. These clues from the past have no respect for political or ideological boundaries; readers will already have found that neither those labeled "liberal" nor those labeled "conservative" in contemporary debate can find consistent comfort in the historical record. But if approached with an open mind, history may provide much useful perspective. At the least it may help to steer current debate away from the more obvious dead ends; at best, help scholars and voters to build their several arguments on stronger foundations.

To now the book has concentrated on placing homicide firmly in the context of the wider history of America. The conclusion will deal briefly with several of the questions it promised to help solve way back in the introduction. That is, what is the current "murder rate" and how does it compare with those in past times, and of other nations? What has changed since the early 1970s in the nature and levels of homicide? Last and hardest: What does history suggest about the usual explanations for murderous behavior, from the family, police, and courts on to the economy, guns, and the cultures of region and nation?

I

The single question most often asked of a historian of criminal violence is, How do murder rates today compare with those in past times? Readers by this time will understand that there is no simple answer; the historical equivalent of Murphy's Law is that people in past times did not record the kind of information we would now most like to have. But there is some firm comparative information about the present and recent past. And after that it is at least possible to provide a series of respectably educated guesses, growing shakier as we move in effect backward through this book, out of the twentieth century into the nineteenth, eighteenth, and seventeenth, returning finally to medieval England in the fourteenth and thirteenth centuries.

If the question is confined to this last quarter of the twentieth century, the answer is simple: not much has changed. In 1974 the murder rate was 10.3 deaths from homicide per 100,000 residents of the United States, as recorded in the official U.S. statistics of mortality. Since then it has zigged and zagged along a line averaging something over 9.0, between a high of 10.7 in 1980 and a low of 8.3 in 1985, turning down some in the mid-1990s. If this represents a crisis—and in ways not measured by mere statistics, this may be argued—it is not because of any sharp rise in the numbers.

These numbers are high by historic standards, but not dramatically so. And the ups and downs among them, while not negligible, are in perspective not great either. According to the same standardized set of national mortality statistics, the murder rate for the late 1920s and early 1930s was close to what it has been in this past generation, reaching 9.7 in 1933, the first year in which the mortality statistics covered the whole of the United States. From that apparent earlier peak the rate then dropped fairly steadily and quite sharply to lows in the late 1940s and 1950s. In some years it dropped under 5.0—the figure for 1955 was 4.5, or less than half those averaged in either the 1990s or the late 1920s. The accompanying chart shows that while the figures for the forty-odd years between the onset of the Great Depression and the end of the Vietnam War make a fairly neat U-curve (with the usual upward blip just after World War II), those from 1974 to the present simply oscillate up and down around an essentially flat line trailing off the right-hand peak of the *U*.

Before the 1930s, the comparative question gets progressively harder to answer as the figures get less reliable. The national mortality statistics, as explained in chapter 6, were first compiled just after 1900; on paper the murder rate rose fairly steeply between then and the late 1920s. But given the problems in the way the statistics were compiled, it is quite certain that if they had been properly, uniformly, and completely collected they would have shown comparatively little change between the beginnings and the 1920s. This means in effect that a graph for essentially the whole of the twentieth century would show a long, wavering but basically flat line trailing to the left of the 1932–74 U-curve which would match that shown in the chart, on the right.

Before 1900 there are no national figures at all. And for the whole period stretching back from then into the 1830s, there is only one provable conclusion and one firm guess.

A variety of records from several places, notably homicide indictments from the city of Philadelphia, as described in chapters 4 and 5, fit with other nonstatistical evidence to show that in the major industrializing cities of the United States, as in the rest of the developing world, the general trend of the murder rate was down for most of the nineteenth century, certainly from the turbulent and riotous decades just before the Civil War.

That is the trend that may be taken as proven; the firm guess is that across the country as a whole, during the same period, the murder rate was considerably higher outside big cities than inside. As late as the 1920s the official mortality figures show that the New York City rate was lower than the national average. If trustworthy figures for the whole nation were available from the 1830s into the early twentieth century,

U.S. Death Rate from Criminal Homicide per 100,000 Population, 1933–1994

Y-axis (left): Average Number of Homicide Deaths per 100,000 Population for Two Years — scale 0 to 12

X-axis categories (two-year periods):
1933-1934, 1935-1936, 1937-1938, 1939-1940, 1941-1942, 1943-1944, 1945-1946, 1947-1948, 1949-1950, 1951-1952, 1953-1954, 1955-1956, 1957-1958, 1959-1960, 1961-1962, 1963-1964, 1965-1966, 1967-1968, 1969-1970, 1971-1972, 1973-1974, 1975-1976, 1977-1978, 1979-1980, 1981-1982, 1983-1984, 1985-1986, 1987-1988, 1989-1990, 1991-1992, 1993-1994

Each bar represents a two-year average

Sources: Vital Statistics, 1933–92, Uniform Crime Reports, 1993–94

the rural-urban difference would in all probability be the same or even bigger, given the levels of murderous violence especially in the rural South and parts of the West.

But the "actual" figures for either the downward urban trend or the rural-urban difference—figures that would correspond to the modern statistics of mortality—simply do not exist. The records that *are* available present enormous problems to historians. A potpourri of arrests, indictments, imprisonments, and executions, with a few runs of coroners' reports, they are not easily comparable to each other, they rarely span many years or decades in any given township, county, city, or state, and the standards used in all of the thousands of such jurisdictions across the United States differ in ways impossible to measure. Above all they undercount, to some unknown degree, the number of killings actually committed.

Modern mortality figures come quite close to the "actual" number of homicides committed in the real world, and so the "dark figure" for those that are never officially counted is nowadays quite low. But that dark figure is by definition higher, often far higher, when the count is based on anything other than number of victims found by the authorities. Many killings do not result in indictments, indictments do not always lead to convictions, and only a fraction of convictions lead to executions. And given the relatively primitive police and detective systems of the nineteenth century and above all the sometimes selective interest of coroners in pursuing cases of homicide, it is impossible to compare the numbers for the late twentieth century with those for earlier times with any certainty.

In big nineteenth-century cities, the authorities often bungled and even covered up when faced with the murdered bodies of poor people or transients, and this is one of the factors that make all the reported statistics suspect. But the biggest wild card in counting urban homicides is infanticide, a crime that from medieval times into the twentieth century was sometimes pursued vigorously but more often ignored. The killing of newborns was always easy, almost always impossible to detect. In mid-nineteenth-century Philadelphia "dead infants" were often found in gutters and privies several times a week. And given these sad routine discoveries, the generally high level of infant mortality, and the many ambiguous "causes of death" reported by desperately poor women and families, the dark figure for infanticide was surely far higher than the official one.

And while the unrecorded murder of newborns is historically a major block to an accurate count, it is greatly overshadowed by the unrecorded murders of nonwhites across much of the country. While the Civil War was legally followed by Emancipation, of a sort, the African-American population of the southern states was only slowly and irregularly brought into the formal systems that counted and seriously prosecuted white-on-black or even black-on-black killings. And it was not until the 1930s, with the Supreme Court's intervention in the Scottsboro case, that the federal government even began to pressure the several states into bringing black citizens into their legal systems on the same basis as whites.

In cases of homicide the legal status of Native Americans was also confused, at least into the 1880s, when the last of them were herded into reservations and subjected to white jurisdiction. Until then the line between interracial murder and warfare was always ambiguous and troublesome. Meanwhile, killings among and between Indians, who were in law supposed to be in some sense subject to the United States, were rarely subject to official action by either tribal or white authority.

So what was the "real" murder rate for the period? In the cities, even at its height in the antebellum decades, the murder rate was probably not as high as it is now, at least among teenagers and adults. If the number of infanticides were actually counted it might well be higher, even much higher. And outside of the cities, these were decades of murderous interracial and intraracial violence not only in the South but in the West, where it involved not only the mutual hostilities of whites and Indians but massacres of Chinese and Mexicans. When these are added not simply to the routine drunken brawls among family, friends, and barroom acquaintances but to the toll taken by urban riots and in mining camps, by vigilantes and gunfighters, by strikers and strikebreakers, it is evident that whatever the numbers they were surely higher than those of recent decades.

For the years between the American Revolution and the 1830s, as always, homicide varied enormously among regions. Very few hard numbers are available, except for executions, which were dropping sharply, but there are other strong clues in the record. The Native Americans, still a real threat, often killed and were killed. But the cities were quieter than they would be in the violent 1840s and 1850s. In settled communities generally, within an increasingly nonviolent middle class, and even along the frontiers, homicide among white citizens was not considered a major problem—except in the South. There the relations among whites were increasingly infected by the often murderous violence essential to wringing work out of unwilling blacks, and homicide was widely tolerated, even celebrated, so long as it could be justified, often with much stretching, as "honorable" self-defense.

For the colonial period, the racial and regional divisions among the inhabitants of the several American colonies were even sharper than they would be later, and the paradoxes greater. Warfare was a way of life for American colonials, much of it sparked by acts of murder between Indians and whites. Middle- and upper-class heads of household raised their children and treated servants and spouses with far more routine brutality than they would in the nineteenth and twentieth centuries. Racial slavery, still new to both Africans and Europeans, was an even harsher institution than it would later become. Much of the white population was made up of indentured servants, even convicts, transported from England. But partly because of their rarity, the number of trials and executions for capital offenses of all kinds may be traced in many colonies with some care, and it is quite clear that in settled communities along the Atlantic Coast the white-on-white murder rate was very low, by the standards either of later times or of the imperial England that ruled them all.

And finally, to complete the sense of paradox, and to underline the point that history does not move in straight or simple lines, there is the evidence from medieval England. The records for some counties during much of the thirteenth and fourteenth centuries are more detailed than for any other sizable British jurisdiction until the eighteenth century, or American until the nineteenth. Coroners' rolls and court proceedings do omit some kinds of homicide, from infanticides to the murderous behavior of the rich and powerful and their outlaw protégés. But even without these, they show that in a nation that lacked most of the usual "causes" experts assign to modern murder, neighbors killed neighbors and robbers killed victims at rates roughly twenty times those of modern Britain and up to double those that trouble us in the contemporary United States.

2

But the numbers across time do not fully answer our concerns about murder, and Americans have also worried, historically, about our image abroad and our record relative to other nations. In declaring in 1993 that "no country in the world is as dangerous as the United States," the chair of the Senate Judiciary Committee was of course defining "danger" narrowly. Not since 1865 has a war been fought on American ground. He was evidently discounting also the undeclared but monstrous ethnic hostilities then wracking Bosnia and Rwanda, the murderous rebellions afflicting much of the Southern Hemisphere, the state-sponsored killings and acts of terrorism authorized in many other places. This has never of course been "the most dangerous country in the world." But by the narrower definition, does it have "the highest per capita murder rate"?

This is not hard to test; for some decades the United Nations has been recording deaths from homicide. And while the counts from some member states are even less trustworthy than those for this country earlier in the century, some real comparison is possible. And the answer to the senator's second proposition is again no.

While the United States has averaged 9 to 10 homicides per 100,000 over the past quarter century, the World Health Organization (WHO) reports that a number of other nations, mostly in South America and Africa, have had rates double and even triple ours; so has Russia, since the early 1990s, during its hard climb out of communism. Some of these foreign rates would probably be higher if counted more strictly, the reporting states having often clumsy recording techniques, great sensitivity about their international reputations, or both. (The WHO figures include police and military killings of civilians, in addition to ordinary murders and manslaughters. Syria, whose sponsorship of terrorism abroad is matched only by its record of repression at home, was reported to have averaged 0.05 homicides per 100,000 people during 1979–81, a figure perhaps credible to believers in the Tooth Fairy.)

But however exaggerated, the senator's concern about relative murder rates in the United States is neither new, unique, nor ill founded.

The meaningful comparison is not with those of unstable and impoverished nations across the globe but with those of other economically advanced societies with trustworthy records. And here the contrast is undeniable. Japanese murder rates have averaged well under 1.0 a year, while German, French, and English have all hovered somewhere close to that figure. Our near neighbor Canada has sometimes broken 2.0, and Italy has pushed past 2.5, but no developed nation in recent years has averaged as high as 3.0, in contrast to our own 9.0 to 10.

In short, while American murder rates have remained essentially flat during this last quarter of the twentieth century, they are still high. Certainly they are far higher than those of the other nations that otherwise most resemble us. But the statistics alone tell only part of the story: whatever the numbers, the nature of homicide in America has been changing since the early 1970s, and some of those changes reflect important social developments.

3

That homicide rates have stayed relatively flat over the last quarter of the twentieth century is not surprising: murder has always reflected its historical context, and by the traditional measures this has seemed a relatively flat period in American history generally. A series of small military engagements, no big wars; economic good news and bad, without surging prosperity or major depression; national elections occasionally pushing government from the moderate right to the center left, checks and balances preventing dramatic movement. But just as underneath the larger surface much has happened, the numbers alone do not tell the full story about murder, and there are legitimate reasons to worry.

The statute of limitations never runs out on homicide, and some old memories never fully fade. On August 23, 1977, the fiftieth anniversary of their executions, Governor Michael Dukakis of Massachusetts declared "Nicola Sacco and Bartolomeo Vanzetti Memorial Day"; the state legislature twice turned down attempts at posthumous vindication during the following decade. Cathy Wilkerson of the Weathermen, last seen fleeing her Manhattan townhouse in 1969, turned herself in during the summer of 1980; her companion Kathy Boudin was arrested the next year as part of a team of armed robbers. In the spring of 1996 alone, Richard Thomas, once a Black Panther, was arrested in Chicago for the execution of rookie Philadelphia patrolman Frank Von Colin back in 1970; Dr. Samuel Shepard's son, Sam Jr., worked to clear his father's name by identifying a new suspect in the 1954 murder of his mother; and the United Methodist church formally apologized to the Cheyenne and Arapahoe for the Reverend J. M. Chivington's leadership of the Sand Creek Massacre of 1863.

Through all these years, too, people have killed each other for all of the old reasons, money and honor, the numbers on bits of bone, paper, and plastic, hot glances and cold dinners, the differences between Jeanne and Joanne. But at the same time a number of unique and frightening kinds of homicide have occurred since 1974. And while some have been truly isolated events, or simply dramatized old issues in new form, others have pointed in genuinely new and scary directions.

The most notorious of isolated murders were the work of the so-called Unabomber, object between 1978 and 1996 of the biggest FBI manhunt in history. The bureau finally accused Theodore Kaczinski, a brilliant mathematician turned hermit in the woods of Montana, of mailing explosive devices over the years to targets from university professors to airline executives, selected nearly at random for their apparent involvement in what he considered the high-tech destruction of the planet. Three victims were killed in this cold-blooded fashion, several badly maimed or injured. In the fall of 1995, the bomber blackmailed the New York *Times* and Washington *Post* into publishing his rationale, "Industrial Society and Its Future," a call for a revolutionary return to a simpler society.* This manifesto, an odd mixture of the sophisticated and the naive, was nearly as unique as a fingerprint; it was his younger

---

*The author, then at work on this history of criminal homicide, discovered that a homicidal criminal was a reader of his work when contacted by reporters and federal agents in connection with this manifesto; in support of his argument that the industrial revolution demands regular, rational, sober behavior—to a degree he considers excessive—the bomber cited some of my earlier work, similar to that described in chapter 5. In the original note to the publishers, this serial killer worried that the quotations used might be so long as to violate copyright law(!), and so suggested an alternative, shorter, footnote, which was gratefully accepted.

brother's recognition of characteristic thoughts and phrases that led him to suspect Kaczinski's identity and turn him in, after a reported $50 million and a million manhours of federal detective work.

There are no real historical precedents for the Unabomber. The same may be said of the very different but equally extraordinary series of events that led the highest authorities of Philadelphia, on May 13, 1985, to order the bombing of some of their own constituents from a borrowed state police helicopter. But these were rooted not in one man's twisted mind but in the long-standing and widespread racial tensions that mark urban America everywhere.

The homicidal confrontation in West Philadelphia had its origins in another, seven years earlier, between the city's police and a radical back-to-nature group called MOVE. Like the Unabomber, the members of MOVE used sophisticated high-tech equipment—in their case loud-speakers, ranting obscenities—to express their yearning for a simpler life. Unlike Theodore Kaczinski, they lived in a city neighborhood, where repeated threats and conflicts with nearby residents, cops, and health officials led in the fall of 1978 to a raid on the heavily armed MOVE house and the killing of a policeman. When the remaining cult members later moved to another place, much the same scenario was played out, but in a different and complicated political context.

In Philadelphia, as in many other cities, it takes both black and white votes to win political office, a simple fact that guides much police work. The members of MOVE were black, as were their outraged neighbors. Frank Rizzo, the law-and-order mayor who had ordered the 1978 raid that killed Officer James Ramp, was white, sensitive to being tagged a racist. As former chief, his popularity with the police force was unshakable, and he was careful to mount an operation that put the safety of policemen second to that of the women and children of MOVE. But Wilson Goode, elected in 1983 as the city's first African-American chief executive, had the opposite problem. The city's black community would forgive him almost anything, but he was afraid, politically, to risk the lives of mostly white cops. And so when after months of delay and mutual warnings an assault on 6221 Osage Avenue was finally ordered it was planned so as to minimize any danger to the attackers. The street was evacuated, the area turned into a war zone, and at long distance firefighters hosed down the house and police fired an American record of ten thousand rounds at it, their usual arsenal fortified by machine guns, tear gas, and an antitank weapon. When no one surrendered it was ordered finally that a homemade packet of explosives be dropped onto a fortified bunker on the roof. The packet detonated a gas tank, the place exploded in flames, and while the authorities and firemen looked on, taking no action, and hundreds of thousands watched on television, the blaze went out of control, incinerating eleven men, women, and children in the house and destroying an entire city block.

No one was indicted for these homicides. Eleven years later, in the spring of 1996, the one surviving adult member of the house joined relatives of the dead in suing the city for personal injuries and civil damages. At the trial ex-mayor Goode denied all responsibility, and, playing on the long-standing tensions between blacks and police, defended his absence from the scene with an improbable but frightening excuse: several rogue cops, he claimed, had been planning to assassinate him in the confusion.

The Unabomber will find no like again; neither will the conflagration on Osage Avenue, although the problems it underscored are still with us. But a third kind of "unique" homicide is not a one-time event but a whole category, one that threatens to expand into the next century. The ideological turmoil of the 1960s and early 1970s has never really gone away, and in more recent decades there has been a steady toll taken in killings by a range of True Believers: vaguely Marxist or African nationalist groups, supporters of Puerto Rican or of Native American independence, pro-life activists, racist hate groups, and religious cultists. Violent clashes between federal agents and armed militants have grown since the original 1973 siege and showdown at Wounded Knee, South Dakota. The 1993 confrontation with David Koresh's armed Christian cultists in their Waco, Texas, compound was a clear turning point, as after some clashes in February resulted in the death of four federal agents a misbegotten assault was ordered on April 19. The resulting firefight, explosions, and mass suicides killed some eighty people inside the compound, seventeen of them children, a disaster that led the FBI to reexamine the tactics, inherited from the G-man days of the 1930s, with which it approached hostage crises and other armed standoffs. But in terms of their implications for ordinary Americans, the most frightening murders in our recent history have been terrorist bombings: those of the World Trade Center in Manhattan in 1993, of the Alfred P. Murrah Federal Building in Oklahoma City just two years later.

Terrorism in America is as old as John Brown. Defined as murder or other violence directed at noncombatants, designed to make an impact on a wider audience and on public policy, it is almost always a self-defeating tactic, often degenerating into senseless acts of protest or revenge. The one major exception in this country was the white-on-black terror of the post–Civil War South, where it had widespread popular support to begin with. Otherwise the historical record here has been thin. Dynamitings popularly associated with "red anarchism" date from the late nineteenth century. Right-wing segregationists took up terrorist bombing in the 1950s and 1960s, and the Weathermen revived an old left tradition, dormant since the era of Sacco and Vanzetti, with their explosive campaign of the late 1960s and early 1970s. But for all the public fear of anarchists, they caused only a few deaths directly in this country: the casualties at Haymarket, in 1888, were mostly shot by panicky policemen. And however cold-blooded the Weathermen, they were usually careful to destroy property rather than people. All of these actors, too, generally attacked specific targets clearly identified with "the enemy." Both the scale of the more recent bombings and their indiscriminate nature is something entirely new, as men, women, and children of all races and beliefs were massacred for purposes of propaganda and protest.

The towering World Trade Center in Lower Manhattan was attacked, on February 6, 1993, through a car bomb in an underground garage; 8 people died and many more might have, as over a thousand were injured, and only heroic work by firemen, helicopter crews, and ordinary citizens saved others from the smoke and flames. On April 19, 1995, the explosion of the Alfred P. Murrah Federal Building in Oklahoma City showed the deadly potential in such incidents, as a truck bomb, parked on the street, set off a blast that killed 168 people, including 19 children, most of them little ones attending a day care center for government employees.

Sorrow is one natural result, as expressed by the flowers, notes, and teddy bears left to decorate the chain-link fence that long surrounded the Oklahoma City site. So are anger and fear. The technological ability to blow up big targets is widespread. The assassinations of the 1960s

had already shown that ideologues may strike from any direction, sometimes in ways not only impossible to predict but even to re-create after
the fact. In the fall of 1995 ten Islamic fundamentalists, led by an Egyp-
tian, Sheikh Omar Adel Rahman, were convicted in federal court for
the World Trade Center bombings. A year later two American anti-
government right-wingers, Timothy James McVeigh and Terry Lynn
Nichols, also awaited trial on federal charges for the mass deaths in
Oklahoma.

And what is most frightening is that neither the foreign hatreds generated by the American government's support for Israel nor the domestic hatreds inspired by its role in the lives of paranoid citizens begin to
exhaust the list of the world's deadly grievances. As terrorism has spread
worldwide since the early 1970s, characteristically insisting that there
are no innocents, the open society of the United States is obviously
vulnerable. The end of the old Cold War has made America the focus
of angers and resentments across the globe just as domestic politics has
taken on new and often irrational intensity. What we have seen so far
may be only a harbinger of things to come; the alleged murderers in the
Manhattan and Oklahoma City bombings have all denied involvement,
pleading not guilty, and we have not yet in this country encountered
the truly deadly suicide killers whose fanatical lack of self-concern
makes them almost impossible to stop.

Ideological killings are still too rare to have much impact on the annual
statistics—something close to 25,000 homicides are reported each
year—but they have a disproportionate power to worry us. The same is
true of two other trends in murder: mass killings clearly and serial killings probably have been on the rise since the early 1970s.

Mass killings are those that claim a number of victims in a single
short span, committed by men—never women—whose motives are
personal rather than political. They always make national headlines and
so draw more attention than their number alone would deserve. But
their unpredictability, and the generally random way in which they
claim their victims, makes them scary in some of the same ways as ideological murders. The record set by Charles Whitman, who shot 16
people from atop a tower at the University of Texas in 1966, has since
been approached or beaten several times, notably by James Huberty,
who killed 21 visitors to a San Diego McDonald's in 1984, and George

Hennard, whose toll was 22 at a coffee shop in Killeen, Texas, seven years later. Typically white and middle class, these killers often have the kind of obviously disturbed personality profiles that point more strongly to suicide than homicide. None of them escape, and many do not even try, as they either commit suicide, are shot down by police, or surrender passively. While psychologists have studied them in some detail, the specific reasons for their brief homicidal outbursts generally die with them, and given their idiosyncratic personal histories it is hard in any case to place them as part of deeper social currents. But it is safe to predict that their numbers will grow, as the increased firepower of modern weapons makes it easier than in earlier times to claim multiple victims in a matter of minutes.

Serial killers, defined as those who kill three or more people over thirty days or more, are also typically white and often middle class, but they are otherwise quite different from mass murderers, and even more frightening. There are more of them: hundreds have been interviewed since the 1970s. They are even harder to classify: usually but not exclusively men, usually but not always loners, they kill for a bewildering variety of motives, including robbery, revenge, and the satisfaction of sadistic impulses. Some act out sexual fantasies of a sort guaranteed to draw media attention, not only rape but necrophilic mutilation of bodies, even cannibalism, as in the case of Milwaukee's Jeffrey Dahmer, alleged killer of seventeen young men before his arrest in 1991. Those who are caught often lie, and with the cooperation of their proud captors greatly exaggerate the number of their victims. Many are not caught at all. Unlike mass murderers, while serial killers may be psychotic they are also secretive, clever, often charmingly seductive; the modern archetype is Ted Bundy, who beginning in 1974 reputedly murdered eighteen young women across several states. And like Bundy, who was not arrested until 1979, they are able to escape detection at least for some time.

The cleverness makes it impossible for a historian to say how many of them operated in the past. H. H. Holmes in the 1890s and the poisoner Belle Gunness in the early 1900s seem in their different ways to fit modern profiles exactly. But there are not many such historical exemplars. There is one purely material reason why serial murder is easier nowadays than it would have been in the past: many such killers (not all) use cars or trucks to abduct victims beforehand and/or transport bodies afterward—Alaska's Robert Hansen used a private plane—which would have been difficult before the 1920s. But this is clearly outweighed by the fact that the state of homicide detection in the nineteenth century made it hard to capture even one-time sex murderers, and with every generation back in time it would be easier for both missing people and killers to go unnoticed, especially if under the federal system they crossed state or even local lines. Social security cards, an aggressive FBI, and national fingerprint files are all essentially creations of the 1930s, and for any earlier time we have few clues.

Still, the extant historical records simply do not smell of serial killings in any number. The leading experts are probably right to note that they have sharply increased since the middle 1970s, for reasons still unclear, and it is likely that the longer historic curve has been climbing as well. And while some of the apparent increase may result simply from better detective work and wider media coverage, our heightened recent fears seem firmly rooted in reality.

The fearsome nature of ideological, mass, and serial killings is easy to understand. But the statistical trends in the other, more common kinds of murder and manslaughter are even more troubling, if less well understood.

Some characteristics of American homicide have stayed as flat as the murder rate itself. From the early 1970s into the middle 1990s the percentage of killings committed with firearms has crept up only slightly, according to the FBI's *Uniform Crime Reports,* wavering between a little under and a little over two-thirds: roughly the same as in the 1920s, lower than the 1950s. Toward the bottom of the "means" list, poison has as always remained out of style everywhere but in the pages of mystery novels, rarely reaching over ten to twelve incidents a year. About three of four victims and nine of ten arrested for homicide have been men, figures again close to historic averages stretching back into the Middle Ages.

The racial figures have held equally steady. With the black population of the United States at roughly 12 percent, the number of black homicide victims has hovered close to half: 50 percent in 1974, 51 percent in 1994. The number of African Americans arrested for homicide has meanwhile remained several percentage points higher: 57 percent in 1974, 56 percent in 1994. While much has rightly been made of this racial disparity, black rates eight to ten times higher than white are again no novelty, dating from the earliest trustworthy national records in the 1920s and 1930s. And if homicide in recent years has been the leading cause of death among black male teenagers, in the 1920s company records showed that it trailed only pneumonia and tuberculosis, two long-forgotten threats, among the relatively elite group of black male adults who carried commercial life insurance.

The FBI lives in a world more black and white than most of us, and its figures for other races have appeared only erratically. The cultural grouping "Hispanic" was listed for the first time in 1980, accounting for 16 percent of arrestees, a significant but not enormous overrepresentation in terms of their percentage in the population; but after a few years the category was dropped. American Indians, occasionally listed, are overrepresented among victims both of homicide and of suicide, an unusual parlay and sad reflection of the continued misery of life on the reservation. All other racial groups are underrepresented. In any case, of over 22,000 murder victims in 1994, after "black" and "white" there were fewer than 500 "others" and less than 200 listed as "unknown."

But if race, sex, and over the last quarter century overall rates have proved historically steady, there have been changes in other categories. Two of them are cause for real concern: type of crime and age of offenders. The kind of "domesticated" urban homicide of the post–World War II era had already receded by 1974, and the trends apparent then have continued strongly.

Back in 1974 the South still strongly led all regions in homicides, with a rate of 13.3 per 100,000, the Northeast trailing with just 7.4. By 1994 two long historic trends, population shifts and the nationalization of culture patterns, had closed this gap by about one-third, 11.0 to 7.0. A related but entirely opposite shift has meanwhile continued a trend, evident since the midcentury years, by raising metropolitan rates, historically low, to a point where they are now over twice those in the countryside. The 1974 rate for metropolitan areas was 11.0; rural areas, 8.0; and smaller cities, 6.0. In 1994 the metropolitan figure was 10.0; and those for both smaller cities and rural areas, 5.0.

In terms of type, in 1974 a little over 12 percent of homicides involved spouse killing spouse (counting common-law marriages). The sexes were fairly evenly divided at that time, wives only slightly more likely to be victims, 52 to 48 percent. With other relatives included, family killings accounted for about 23 percent, or almost a quarter, of the national total. But by 1994 only 5 percent of killings were spousal, husbands committed 70 percent of them, and family killings altogether had fallen dramatically to 12 percent, almost half the earlier levels. The proportion of homicides among friends and acquaintances, too, had fallen: in 1976, the first time that figure was released, it was 54 percent; and by 1994 it had plunged to 35 percent.

All of this continues developments begun earlier, following the low point in homicides in the midcentury years. And they all play on deep-seated cultural values and fears. From the earliest records, in the Middle Ages, it has been clear that family killings and homicides among ac-quaintances have not been thought as threatening as other kinds, al-though men who kill women, including wives, have usually been punished harshly. Whatever the statistics show about domestic danger it is strangers—robbers, rapists, or other criminals—who truly scare us, and murder as mystery. Armed robbery has clearly been on the rise. So has interracial homicide, another frightening category. While the great majority of killings remain within racial bounds, as always, one long trend has reversed an older pattern; in 1994 proportionately twice as many white victims were killed by blacks, 12 percent of the total, than vice versa, at 6 percent. In the late twentieth century it is whites who fear blacks downtown at night, just as historically it was blacks who feared whites.

All of us meanwhile fear the unknown, and during the 1990s one of the biggest categories in the FBI's list of motives and relationships has been just that: "Unknown." This is a category that did not even exist in 1974; it now contains well over a quarter of all homicides: victims of robbery? revenge? thrill seekers? drug dealers? And its size reflects an-other ominous trend: the fact that the percentage of killings "cleared by arrest" has been dropping steadily over the decades. Homicides among family, friends, and acquaintances have always been easy to solve ("slam dunks," in detective jargon), but part of the fear inspired by most other kinds is that they are not. The "clearance rate" in 1974 was 80 percent, a percentage already well down from the midcentury record of about 90 percent in most big city departments. By 1994 it had fallen to 64 percent.

And on top of these longer historical trends there is a genuinely new one. We did not use to fear kids, but we do now. Well into the second half of the twentieth century, killings by teenagers were relatively rare. In 1974 the number of homicide arrests among those under eighteen had climbed to a little less than 5 percent of the total; by 1994 the proportion had more than doubled, to 11 percent, and more and more early teens were involved. The importance of this fact is reinforced by another. Since murder is usually the work of young males, overall homicide rates are at least in some part affected by the percentage of young males in the population. By historic standards the proportion of male teens between the early 1970s and mid-1990s was fairly low, but that demographic respite is coming to an end. There is an "age bulge" already here, small children now, who will come of age around the turn of the century. This simple fact threatens that even in the absence of anything else, the murder rate, flat so long, with even some signs of declining, may yet soar up again.

4

In any case, after establishing rates and trends, it is necessary at last to begin the much harder job of explaining them, in this and the next several sections. The relevant questions are themselves historical: some of them have been asked for centuries, and H. C. Brearly raised most of them back in 1932, based on research done in the 1920s. The range of possibilities he covered then included the influence of the family and the media, the roles of police, courts, and the death penalty, the impact of poverty and guns, race and ethnicity, regional and national culture. All of these issues are complex, however easy they may seem to politicians and pundits locked into simplistic ideological positions. The answers given here are often different from Brearly's, as conditions have changed and so has the state of our knowledge. They are also controversial, and some of them are still uncertain.

The uncertainty results from the fact that in terms of assigning causes murder is harder to "solve" than any other crime. With rare exceptions women do not rape, the rich do not rob gas stations, the poor do not sell phony stocks. But murder is done by people of every description, for an enormous range of reasons. And none of these reasons are "causes" in the strict sense. All that the historical evidence can offer are such statistical generalizations as that the young, the male, and the poor are more likely to be involved in homicide than the old, the female, and the rich. But of course neither youth nor maleness nor poverty "cause" murder; this is an uncommon crime, and only a small minority of people in any category ever kill another human.

Even in terms of broad statistical generalizations, the example of medieval England, with which this book began, stands as warning to us all. Whatever "caused" the astonishingly high rates of the thirteenth and fourteenth centuries it was not guns or racial differences, not the pressures of city life, not capitalism or socialism, not lack of community or tradition or religious faith, not the absence of the death penalty, not in fact almost any of the usual suspects routinely trotted out in contemporary debate.

But however hard the search, there are clues in the historical evidence that do help explain rates and trends in homicide. It is easiest to begin toward the end, with what has been happening over the past quarter century. This was the subject of the previous section, and at least some of it is widely understood.

Many of the minor ups and downs in recent murder rates are explainable, first, in terms of changes in the drug trade, which has unquestionably grown heavier. Back in 1974 the FBI estimated that felony murders associated with drug trafficking accounted for just 2 percent of the total; by 1994 the rate had quadrupled to 8 percent. The use of cocaine in any form is associated with violent and impulsive behavior, like alcohol and several "designer drugs" and unlike either marijuana or heroin; changes in personal drug use may push rates either up or down. In any case the trade in cocaine and some other drugs is more dangerous than the traffic in illegal alcohol during the Prohibition era of the 1920s. Bulky beer trucks back then delivered to saloons and stores, relatively big retail outlets, in a way that demanded territorial monopoly and thus cooperation; most competition was settled more quickly and peacefully than in the notorious Chicago of Al Capone. The marketing of expensive drugs in small packets, sold by individuals on street corners or indeed anywhere, is inherently more competitive, inviting continual turf wars and wrangling. The marketing problem is not insoluble, but it does mean that occasional dips in local murder rates may mix good news and bad: fewer homicides may simply mean that through superior organization a given drug gang is operating with little interference.

Many of these drug operations involve, use, or spin off gangs of kids. In 1994 the *Uniform Crime Reports* counted 1,157 "juvenile gang killings," a category that did not even exist until the late 1980s. This is a number more than ten times bigger than the 111 (adult) "gangland killings," and accounted for more than 5 percent of all homicides that year.

The fact that drug and other killings are being done by ever younger teenagers suggests another look at two specific issues Brearly looked at nearly three generations ago: the influence of the media and of the family. History offers no direct clues to the impact of either of these, but it does help to put current problems in context.

"Media" is our word; Brearly was concerned with newspapers and movies. The popular press was and is undeniably obsessed with sex and violence. But it always has been—here and in other less murderous nations—as a reflection of a popular appetite for the macabre that extends from the sale of bits of hangman's rope to the bizarre auction of goods belonging to Jeffrey Dahmer. The growth in literacy, and so in readership of crime novels, magazines, and sensational papers, has through most of its history coincided with falling homicide rates, making it hard to establish a clear connection between violent publications and violent behavior.

It is easier to make a case for the impact of modern movies and especially color television on the unsophisticated and semiliterate. The silent black-and-white westerns that alarmed some of Brearly's contemporaries seem today as harmless as Peter Rabbit when compared to either the content or the graphic immediacy of modern cartoons, dramas, and full-length features. The study of moving images and their influence was then in its infancy; it is now an academic industry. Television executives themselves, in accepting the so-called V-chip blocking device early in 1996, have conceded the overwhelming evidence that watching violence tends to beget violence, especially in children. And it would be hard today to duplicate the 1920s finding that what kids remember most is that the bad guys always come to bad ends.

Brearly's concern for the state of the American family is from this vantage even quainter. His major worry was the disruption created by divorce, which resulted in too many kids not "adequately trained for social responsibilities." Divorce at that time ended about one marriage in eight; he used neither the term nor the concept "unmarried motherhood." By the 1990s about one marriage in two was ending in divorce, and nearly one out of three children were being born to single mothers; among big city blacks, the figure reached up to three out of four. And there are many recent studies of the effects of absent fathers. The economic impact is obvious, greatly increasing the chances that a child will grow up in poverty, but in terms of potential violence the psychological or "role modeling" effect may be even greater. With a full-time man in the home a boy learns something of the range of masculine behavior, including compassion and tenderness; with no models but those on the street he is likely to see only the most violently macho end of the spectrum, and to act accordingly.

But if the modest dips and surges in late twentieth-century murder rates may be explained largely in terms of such usual suspects as drugs and kids, the fact that the underlying line has stayed essentially flat since 1974 requires a more fundamental explanation. The bad news that more Americans are being killed by strangers, criminals, and teenagers has been balanced by good news, in that lower percentages are being killed by family, friends, and acquaintances.

The division is not quite that simple: within the family category, falling spousal murders are in part another kind of ironic and complicated good news/bad news story. The women's movement over the past quarter century has finally awakened many Americans to the issue of domestic violence, the fact that historically more of us, especially members of the middle class, have been killed or beaten by family than by strangers. Fears that the movement itself would create bolder and possibly more murderous women have not been borne out in the statistics: proportionally fewer wives are killing husbands than vice versa, as compared to earlier times. But just as the number of reported incidents of domestic assault has been rising, the number of domestic homicides has been falling; that is, Americans have been increasingly willing to call in the police in cases of abuse at a time when truly fatal cases of abuse have been declining. The fact that police take these calls more seriously than in earlier generations may help stop some situations from growing worse and turning lethal. Perhaps, too, the drop in spousal murders has something to do with the growing ease of divorce, as a relatively peaceful means of ending a painful relationship; or (less likely), we have been enjoying happier marriages. But a more easily measured reason why fewer married people of either sex are killing each other is simply that fewer people are getting married in the first place, a trend marked especially among the young, the poor, and the African American, all groups that account for more than their share of homicides.

Whatever its causes, the drop in spousal killings is an important part of the larger picture, which is that over the past several decades homicide rates have been moving in two directions, with the majority of adult Americans committing fewer and fewer and a small minority committing more and more.

It is important to note that this split is not racial. The black share of national homicides has not changed overall since the 1960s. But the African-American community is itself split, as its working and middle classes have moved ahead and a smaller "underclass" has dropped back. And the recent history of black America reflects what has been happening to all of us; we have been drifting apart, essentially along economic lines, in a way that follows a larger historical pattern.

The upward surge in homicide rates that hit the United States beginning in the 1960s was explained, in chapter 8, in terms of the decay of the urban industrial revolution, the transition to postindustrialism. For over a century that revolution and its dual effects on structural employment and social psychology had worked to push rates down. But after the postwar boom of the 1950s the progressive loss of relatively high-paying factory jobs, especially in cities, pushed idle young people into the streets. The institutions of urban-industrial discipline and restraint, above all families, cops, and schools, seemed no longer relevant, as the promise of long-term reward went flat. In a world that stressed consumption over production, the benefits of sober predictable behavior were outweighed by the drive for immediate gratification. The presence of large numbers of young men with drugs in their heads and time on their hands predictably boosted criminal activity of all kinds. And however flat the murder rate has been since 1974, essentially the same forces are still at work.

After the initial, turbulent transition of the 1960s, the working majority has mostly adjusted to the relative loss of manufacturing in favor of office or service employment. During the last quarter of the twentieth century the American economy has continued to generate jobs. But in the postindustrial service-and-computer economy the educational qualifications demanded for good ones have continually been pushed up: once some high school education, then a diploma, then some college, now a degree. Most young Americans have been able to meet the new requirements by doing more time in school, learning to sit still, think ahead, and somehow cope with the sometimes dangerous impulses natural to youth, or at least those that would derail them seriously by leading to crime, pregnancy, or drug addiction. Statistically, people like these, ordinary working- and middle-class people, never got into much serious trouble anyway. Now, whatever their race or ethnicity, they get into even less; given the pressures of time, and of two jobs per family, even the old habit of dropping into a bar after work has fallen into decline.*

But there is another, much smaller but nonetheless too big a group of Americans that has been left behind. While still the envy of the world, the American economy is not as robust as it was during the golden postwar era. As gains in productivity have slipped and the world has grown more competitive, growth rates have slowed. And the price has been paid above all by the undereducated. Once there were factory jobs, good lives, and hope for those who were able to learn the basic rules of regular behavior but balked at spending many frustrating years behind a desk. Now that those jobs are gone, the only alternative for too many is the low-paid service or burger-flipping sector. But there is prosperity enough for all to look at color television, inclusion enough for all to see, hear, and want to taste the delights of consumerism. And for those left behind, delayed gratification, impulse control, and rational behavior seem to make little sense. Told to wait, they do not. Bombarded with thousands of versions of the quintessential advertising message—"Just Do It"—they obey. Told they should have, they reach out and get.

One dramatic illustration of the resulting social psychology is the murderous Los Angeles riots of 1992. Like the urban riots of the 1960s, these were sparked by the police, in this case the widely televised vid-

---

*This, too, has a bad news side. After years of learning to repress impulsive aggressiveness, holding it inward, more working- and middle-class Americans when pushed to the extreme are likely to take out their frustrations on themselves than on others. One result is that the U.S. suicide rate has been creeping upward all these years while, among the majority, the homicide rate has been creeping down, in accord with the theory of the suicide-murder ratio described in chapter 6.

eotape of a group of Los Angeles officers brutally beating a black motorist, Rodney King, arrested after a high-speed chase in March 1991. Four of the policemen were charged with twelve counts of assault. When on April 29 of the following year the officers won acquittal on eleven of these counts, many residents of South Central Los Angeles took to the streets, following a script already prepared by a nervous media. And four days of clashes with police and other citizens left fifty-four dead and over five thousand buildings damaged or destroyed.

This explosion, the biggest since Detroit erupted twenty-six years earlier, was widely interpreted as a kind of revolt by the African-American "underclass" against racism. But while it was clearly *sparked* by anger at racist behavior, the Los Angeles "race riot" of 1992, like many of its predecessors a generation earlier, quickly turned into a "commodities riot," the participants driven less by social rage than by the rage to possess. Social revolutionaries cannot reach city hall, the statehouse, or even the rich white suburbs if they must break into every liquor store and electronics outlet along the way. Even as Rodney King himself pleaded for an end to the shooting and looting, the racial composition of the riot suggested that black protest was not at its heart. A total of 5,438 people were arrested through May 4; some 2,764, or well over half of them, were Hispanic; 568 were white.

The fact that there are large numbers of citizens who somehow share the American Dream but see no legitimate way of making it a reality in their own lives is a deeply disturbing social development. Their violence is far more dangerous to themselves and each other than to the dominant majority. (The one area of family homicide that has been going up, after decades of decline, is infanticide, as always a measure of utter desperation.) People at the very bottom of the social ladder have neither the organization nor the desire to threaten revolution. The media, especially television, with its emphasis on visual crime news, tends to exaggerate the extent of murder, still a rare event, and largely confined within the circle of the most deprived. One result is to frighten the rest of us, helping to dictate where we live and even visit, undermining still-healthy urban neighborhoods as working people leave for the suburbs, condemning the remainder to ever worse conditions.

But increasingly murderous self-destruction among those left behind does sometimes spill over into other lives and places. And if present trends continue, with the postindustrial economy continuing to swell the numbers of these jobless people, the rest of us may have to recognize that we are all in trouble together.

5

Whatever the causes of high murder rates, many Americans, inspired by celebrated cases such as the O. J. Simpson "Trial of the Century," believe that one of them is failure in the justice system. Critics insist that the system is clumsy, full of loopholes that allow too many killers to escape arrest, too many of the arrested to avoid conviction, too many of the convicted to draw light sentences. These are not new complaints, but they have grown louder since the 1960s, as violent crime has become a national issue. Solution is often cast in historical terms: politicians and prosecutors promise a return to "the good old days" when justice was fair but tougher. A historian's response is simply that there was never any such golden age, or none that we would want to return to, and that in fact as we approach the twenty-first century the justice system is working better than ever before.

There is little question, first, that given current conditions the police are operating more efficiently, and fairly, than at any earlier time. The solution of ordinary homicide cases became a clear priority among police departments only during the first half of the twentieth century, and not until well into its second half did the murders of blacks and other marginal citizens get treated seriously all across the country, in part as a result of the growing political power of African Americans and their increased representation within local departments. Not all killings, still, are treated equally, but there is a kind of rough democracy at work in that detectives tend to give the highest priority to cases, such as the murders of children, that most outrage the voting public. It is true that there has been a growing drop in the proportion of cases "cleared by arrest" since the height reached in the 1950s. But as explained earlier, this is a reflection of the rising number of cases, such as murder by strangers, that are by their nature harder to clear. It is hard to deal with homicide in many city neighborhoods; the day of the spontaneous street posse is long over, and potential witnesses are often too terrified, or alienated, to talk. And although some of these problems are related to memories of racism and brutality, too often inflamed by fresh incidents in the 1990s, modern police are far more sensitive on both counts than their predecessors in the past. As one rough index, while the Chicago department alone in the 1920s committed dozens of unprosecuted "justifiable homicides" each year, the annual number now, across this whole nation of over 250 million, is not much over 300. And in a revival of the practice of the previous century, policemen are again, however rarely, at least in some places subject to trial for manslaughter when they kill without compelling reason.

The American federal system, whatever its other virtues, does still handicap much police work. Local, federal, and state agents often fail to cooperate, and while they stumble over and even fight with each other, such desperately poor places as Camden, New Jersey, where gang and drug killings have long been rampant, simply lack the tax base to support effective departments at all. But in the late twentieth century these traditional problems are not as severe as they once were. Communications have greatly improved, making it harder for the likes of H. H. Holmes to slip unnoticed between jurisdictions. One result of making crime a national issue is that the federal government finds ways under both Democratic and Republican administrations to help fund local cops. And the policy of making the resources of the FBI available in high-profile cases has been continually expanded since its origins in the 1930s.

The importance of this and other high-tech aids is easily exaggerated: most homicides are still solved by the same kind of patient questioning of suspects and witnesses as a century ago. Help from the FBI is often slow, as television viewers discovered in 1995 while waiting for the results of lab tests in the Simpson case. It is also too expensive to call on routinely. The bureau is not infallible, either: some of the million man-hours spent on the Unabomber case were spent by experts who drew up a psychological profile showing that the killer was a meticulously neat man, hard to distinguish from his neighbors, in strong contrast to the real Ted Kaczynski, the unwashed, unbarbered, packrat-hermit finally arrested. But there is still no question that continued advances in such areas as forensic pathology, DNA testing, and the psychological profiling of serial and sex killers have lifted the potential in scientific detection up and past the once fanciful exploits of Sherlock Holmes.

There is some advantage in federalism, too, in that each of the thousands of local police departments across the country works differently, and can experiment in what works best. Homicide is the major crime (except for assault) most often "solved," with rates of clearance by arrest far higher than for larceny, burglary, auto theft, robbery, or rape. But the notion that prevention, as distinct from solution, is actually police business is relatively new. The *Uniform Crime Reports* insisted for years that since homicide was mostly a spontaneous affair among family or acquaintances, it was "largely a societal problem beyond the control of the law enforcement community," which could hardly station cops in every bedroom and bar. But that disclaimer was dropped in the late 1980s, as felony murders and killings by strangers increased. Since then several strategies directed at spousal abuse and street crime in general have succeeded, at least in the short run, in cutting local murder rates as well. These range from simply responding faster to "crime in progress" calls and a return to foot patrols and "community policing" to the highly publicized efforts by New York Police Commissioner William J. Bratton, in the mid-1990s, to target areas of high violence by computer and aggressively make arrests for everything from panhandling to public drug use in order to make neighborhoods safer.

Federal funds have sometimes helped these efforts. But the business of making politics out of crime has had negative effects as well. Scholarly research of several kinds, while having no immediate practical value, could eventually help police and others in preventing homicide through better understanding of the causes of violent behavior. But some of that research has been threatened because it offends political interest groups.

One ongoing set of studies, sponsored by the Federal Centers for Disease Control and Prevention, has investigated the effect of gun ownership on homicide, suicide, and accident, viewing deaths from firearms—the second leading cause of death among Americans between the ages of ten and twenty-four—as a problem in public health, in some places a kind of epidemic. Long under fire from the National Rifle Association in alliance with leading Republicans, these studies were cut back in the spring of 1996.

Another line of research, with an old and largely discredited history stretching back to Cesare Lombroso, has attempted to discover whether individual differences in aggressive behavior have some basis in human biology. History aside, there seems some recent evidence that, for example, low levels of the neurotransmitter serotin, which appear to trigger violence in young men, may be affected not only by a stressful environment but by heredity as well. Attempts during the 1990s to investigate a possible link between genetics and homicide have been discouraged by the hostile reaction of minority groups, although all research has centered on purely individual biology, and there has been no hint of any racial differences.

But scholars are only rarely targets of political attack (or indeed attention), and most criticism of the justice system specifically exempts the cops. The usual targets of those who believe that we are too lenient, or "liberal," with killers are rather the courts. The specific complaints include jurors who let their biases interfere with the "duty" to convict, plea bargaining by prosecutors, and legal "technicalities." But in fact courts in the 1990s have been convicting and sentencing at historically high rates. And the issues in practice do not break clearly along "liberal" or "conservative" lines.

Fury was one widespread reaction to the 1995 acquittal of O. J. Simpson for the murder of his wife, Nicole Brown Simpson, and her friend Ronald Goldman. Millions, having followed the trial on television, were resentful of Simpson's expensive team of lawyers. They were even more dismayed by the ultimate action of the largely African-American jury, which apparently ignored much expert testimony and freed a famous black man accused of killing two whites because of suspicion that the Los Angeles police, out of sheer racism, had somehow cooked the evidence. The case against Simpson was powerful. But historically, juries of laypersons have often ignored complex technical evidence when the prosecution cannot produce weapons or witnesses to the crime. The historical record, too, has been all too full of white juries biased in favor of white defendants accused of killing blacks, and even more of white-on-black killings that never came to trial at all. With the recent behavior of the Los Angeles Police Department laid on top of centuries of memory, it may be deplorable but it is hardly surprising that jurors were skeptical of police testimony and gave Simpson the benefit of a "reasonable doubt."

Much public indignation, too, during the 1990s, was aroused by a number of publicized cases in which the issue was not race but gender, as lawyers for wives accused or even convicted of killing their husbands successfully appealed to a "battered woman syndrome" to get their clients freed. In one of these, Florida Governor Lawton Chiles granted clemency to Lynn Kent, who shot her sleeping husband, Lamar, to death and then blamed it on a robber. The action was justified on the basis of psychological testimony that women systematically abused, as she was, are so fearfully traumatized that the normal bounds of "self-defense" must be stretched to accommodate them. This tactic may seem objectionable on several grounds, and a number of feminist observers have complained that it stereotypes women as passive victims. But in fact the "syndrome" only gives a formal name to an ancient prejudice; juries, perhaps especially the all-male juries of history, have always been reluctant to convict women of killing husbands or lovers. In macho Houston, back in 1969, as Henry Lundsgaarde has shown, such women fared very well indeed; one of the rare penalties of any kind was three years probation for shooting a husband as he slept.

The battered woman syndrome looks to laypersons something like the ancient plea of insanity. This has never been a popular defense in high-profile cases, but there is no evidence that it is more common now than in the past, when "temporary insanity" was often a way for jurors to free someone, often abused women, whose plight they found sympathetic. During the late twentieth century many states, or state courts, have abandoned the strict M'Naghten rule in favor of the looser doctrine of "diminished capacity," in which an alleged criminal may escape formal punishment if "as a result of mental disease or defect he lacks substantial capacity either to appreciate the criminality of his conduct or to conform his conduct to the requirements of law." But whatever the rules, when cases get to jurors, or even bench trials by judges, the black letter law has historically been abandoned in favor of their own sense of who or what is or is not "crazy," or blameworthy. And while appeals courts in the past several decades have indeed found technical reasons for throwing out guilty verdicts, usually on the basis of constitutional misconduct by police or prosecutors, the nineteenth century was the real golden age of "technicalities," when cases were routinely overturned on the basis, for example, of misspellings in handwritten indictments.

The larger picture is that while in recent times, as always, there have been many cases in which apparently guilty defendants go free, the overall conviction rate for homicide is higher than at almost any time in the past. Figures from the Justice Department indicate that in the 1990s about half of all those indicted for homicide are found guilty as charged, another 20 percent or so convicted of lesser crimes—manslaughter, for example, in murder cases—for an overall conviction rate of about 70 percent. Only very rarely (as in the midcentury years) has that rate reached over 50 percent anywhere in America, or indeed in medieval England, except in those colonial jurisdictions that also hanged witches and Quakers or condemned African slaves to death by fire.

The basic procedures in homicide cases—inquest, arrest, arraignment, indictment, trial, and sentencing—have evolved slowly over centuries. The trial is at its core, and certainly since the eighteenth century, when the accused were granted lawyers and then allowed to testify for themselves, the trial has been an adversarial contest. And by its nature this Anglo-American adversary system of justice ensures that a number of the accused will go free. Unlike European systems of justice, dominated by judge and prosecution, in ours the parties are not even supposed to be engaged in an impartial search for the truth. The revolutionary tradition reflected in the Bill of Rights is not to trust the state, that is, the prosecution, but to check it through vigorous opposition. And as in any series of real contests, victory may go either way.

From the American beginnings, some of the ancient procedures have been modified: the jury of neighbors and acquaintances replaced with an impartial panel of strangers, public officers taking over the task of prosecution, state and federal constitutions adding protections for the accused. In recent decades and in many states some of the old practices and institutions have been further changed, even abolished. Thus medical examiners have been substituted for coroners, the grand jury, attacked as irrelevant for over a century, abandoned in ordinary criminal proceedings. But the basic adversarial nature of the justice system is too deeply rooted to overturn. Change has always come slowly, conservatively, and some places have found, for example, that the ancient grand jury, with the constitutional American power to grant immunity from prosecution to witnesses who would otherwise claim their Fifth Amendment right to remain silent, is still a powerful investigative tool. The law of unintended consequences, too, is often illustrated by efforts to change "the system." In homicide cases, virtually all of the states during the 1990s have passed laws allowing violent juveniles, some as young as fourteen, to be tried as adults. The intent is to make their records public and to allow longer sentences. But one frequent effect has been that more of them have won acquittal, as defense attorneys have been changed from something like impartial guardians into one-sided advocates.

Prosecutors have been plea-bargaining homicides for well over a century, in large part because they have not been able to predict what twelve citizens in a box will do once cases go to trial. Those citizens have always been the wild cards in the justice system. Even before the American Revolution, John Adams, in defending the British soldiers accused of the Boston Massacre, knew that choosing the right jurors, a key part of the adversary system, was important to his case. Juries have historically freed defendants, and still do, because of a mixture of both "liberal" and "conservative" views. They have been skeptical of the state and its agents, and are in any case supposed not to decide "innocence" but only failure to prove guilt. They have romanticized some kinds of crime, or killers, like the James brothers or even John Dillinger. Long before O. J. Simpson's "dream team" of defense lawyers was assembled, they have been swayed, perhaps too easily, by the eloquence, the legal knowledge, the outside experts provided by high-priced attorneys; the complaint that the rich are better defended than the poor goes back at least to the Age of Jacksonian Democracy. Above all jurors have put themselves in the shoes not of all but of some kinds of defendants.

Juries have never delivered "absolute" justice but have represented, at their best and sometimes worst, the moral sense of their communities. Although often surprisingly fair-minded, historically, in many cases involving unpopular minorities some biases have been too strong to overcome, and they have tended to convict in times of social stress. Otherwise, although contemporary jurors are generally more diverse than those in times past, their prejudices have been quite stable over the centuries. Whatever the law may say they have found it hard, since the Middle Ages, to convict felonious accessories of actual murder: the kid who was there but did not pull the trigger at the convenience store holdup. They have tended to convict, whatever the evidence, the kinds of people accused of crimes they most hate or fear: robbery murder, killing strangers or women, abusing corpses. The Charles Mansons and Jeffrey Dahmers have never had an easy time in court. It is rather the routine manslaughters, the result of sudden fights and quarrels, that have always earned the majority of the acquittals. Americans have generally been inclined to forgive fighters, or those who could arguably plead self-defense. And historically the highest acquittal rates have been registered in what we would now label "conservative" jurisdictions, places where gun ownership is most prized and the macho values most honored, whether the old slave states before the Civil War, South Carolina in the 1920s, or Houston in the 1960s.

But the biggest criminal issue of the late twentieth century has centered not on the conviction rate but on sentencing, above all capital punishment. Here again the historical evidence provides perspective.

Statistics for all fifty states are hard to compile. But as of 1982, just before a major national movement toward more prison construction and longer sentences, a study by the Justice Department figured that the time actually served by those convicted of murder averaged close to seven years. And as of 1987 the department indicated that 17 percent of those convicted of homicide in federal courts (a far smaller number than in the states) were given life in prison, while the rest earned sentences averaging about sixteen years. These are historically high figures, very high. Do such sentences prevent homicide? No, yes, and maybe.

No one has pretended for generations that prisons "reform" their inmates: in recent years attempts at rehabilitation have centered only on the young or the nonviolent. But in the starkest sense, yes, of course, impounding killers helps prevent future homicides; apart from the occasional fellow inmate or guard, those in prison are in no position to kill anyone again. The longer they are in, too, the more they will emerge if not better at least older, and so less inclined to violent behavior. A great upsurge in prison construction during the 1980s, which both encouraged and enabled longer sentences for a variety of crimes, seems also to have had some effect on murder rates—which might otherwise have gone higher—for the same simple reason. While imprisonment is expensive, and arguably wastes potentially productive lives as well as resources, locking up the most "at risk" criminals, such as those convicted of robbery or aggravated assault, means they are not out menacing neighbors or strangers on the street.

But it is not so clear that the threat of prison "deters" those still on the outside. While the justice system nets more criminals than ever before, the pool refills, it seems, immediately. And those who fill it are increasingly younger, poorer, and more alienated from the social mainstream than ever. With less and less to lose, they seem less and less sensitive to the consequences of their actions, either to their victims or themselves.

If not prison, perhaps death? This is an old issue. The actual process of capital punishment, and the publicity surrounding it, is much the same as it has been for many years; the addition of lethal injection to the list of methods has not much changed the ancient death house rituals, although a heightened modern sense of delicacy has in many jurisdictions added the application of a diaper sometime between last meal and final prayer. But some of the arguments in favor of the death penalty have shifted, and so has the legal context.

The U.S. Supreme Court, after having effectively suspended the use of capital punishment from 1966 through its *Furman v. Georgia* decision in 1972, as described in chapter 8, allowed in 1976 in *Gregg v. Georgia* that a new death penalty law might meet the objections it had raised just four years earlier. Ordinary homicides would not call for execution. But if there were particular "aggravating circumstances," spelled out in advance by law, judge or jury might decide on death. Many states followed Georgia, some insisting that after conviction a special hearing must be held to decide the penalty. Most of the "aggravating circumstances" listed in state laws are the ones that have long earned the severest punishment: killing an officer of the law was declared a crime not subject to benefit of clergy way back in Tudor England, and murder for profit, after lying in wait, or through using poison has always been thought especially heinous. More modern concerns are reflected in the listing of race-hate crimes in some states.

A year after *Gregg,* the court in *Coker v. Georgia* struck rape from the list of capital crimes; however terrible the offense, execution was held to be a "grossly disproportionate" punishment. But otherwise the movement has been in the other direction. *McCleskey v. Georgia* in 1987 determined that the pattern of executions in that state was not so racially discriminatory as to invalidate Warren McCleskey's sentence for killing a policeman during a robbery. And *Stanford v. Kentucky,* in 1989, affirmed that death was not too cruel and unusual a punishment for murder committed when the killer was seventeen years old, significantly younger than, for example, either Nathan Leopold or Richard

Loeb, the notorious killers spared the chair on account of their age back in 1924.

In virtually every election year since the mid-1980s, too, the Congress has passed some kind of "crime bill." All of them, after providing more money for state and local law enforcement, have expanded the category of "federal" offenses. Adding dozens to the list of federal crimes deserving death has not yet added to the number of actual executions; all of these "new" measures, except for death for certain kinds of "drug kingpins" (still to be constitutionally tested), have involved actions, such as assassinating the president, that are already defined as first-degree murder in any case and in any state. Conservative partisans of traditional states' rights have not complained about this kind of centralization of power, the effect of which is to further expand the role of the FBI and of federal courts. But liberals have objected on grounds of principle.

The key legal-political issue fought nationally between 1992 and 1996 involved making execution quicker and easier by limiting the right of appeal. Justice is ideally swift as well as sure. And while it may be argued that it is now more fair, in that sense more sure, than ever in the past, as part of the price for that it is certainly slower, at almost every stage. Homicide trials, at the center of the process, take far more time, on average, than they once did: Lizzie Borden's "Trial of the Century" took just two weeks, while O. J. Simpson's stretched out over what seemed interminable months. But what has most maddened supporters of the death penalty is that since *Gregg* repeated appeals, through three tiers of state courts and three tiers of federal courts, have greatly lengthened the passage between sentence of death and its actual execution. In contrast to the Pennsylvania average, a century ago, of less than a year—thought by Robert Ralston, at least, to be too long at the time—the average by the mid-1990s had reached eight years: Warren McCleskey himself was electrocuted only in 1991, after sentencing in 1978. No one is urging a return to the era before the Scottsboro case, in the 1930s, when substantive Supreme Court review was effectively established. But the 1996 edition of biennial crime bills, passed by a Republican Congress and signed by a Democratic president, set deadlines for both prisoners' appeals and judicial decisions, limited inmates to one federal appeal if there is no "clear and convincing" evidence of innocence, and limited the power of federal judges to overturn verdicts unless they are an "unreasonable application of clearly established federal law."

The arguments about capital punishment have changed little since the abolition of public hanging, but the emphasis has. On deterrence the opponents long had the historical and statistical arguments to themselves, although the basic one may be essentially circular: the fact that times, states, and nations with the death penalty usually have higher murder rates than those without may simply reflect that these are the places that have most felt the need for drastic measures. In more recent years proponents have fought back with their own statistical studies, but on the whole the "antis" still have the best of it. In any case deterrence, although it figures in some political debate, is not now the key issue either in popular polls or among opposing theologians or philosophers. Neither is revenge, although if not the key argument this may be the key emotion behind it. The case for death instead now turns on life.

This is an age when Americans fear death and prize life more than in earlier times, perhaps because of a declining faith in life hereafter; modern military policy is often dictated by anxiety over how the public will react to the televised sight of a single body bag. And now that execution is reserved entirely for murder, both sides can insist that theirs is the one that most respects the value of human life, whether of killer or of victim. It is not an easy argument, and does not divide along neat lines: while most of the Roman Catholic hierarchy, for example, opposes the death penalty as a logical extension of its opposition to both abortion and euthanasia, there is no evidence that the laity follows the leadership, and some eminent Catholic philosophers have taken conscientious positions on the other side.

The history suggests that we are still following a trend, now over two centuries old, in which the percentage of condemned killers actually executed has generally if raggedly declined. But except for the period 1966–77 it has not quite receded to the vanishing point. Polls suggest wide support for the death penalty, well over 70 percent in the 1990s, higher among men than women, whites than blacks. But even among African Americans, a substantial minority, and in some years a majority, have favored it, despite their bitter memories. In a democratic nation, divided into fifty states, it is hard to imagine that execution will soon be abolished entirely. There are now several thousand prisoners on death row, with only judicial appeals and executive clemency standing between them and chair or chamber, noose, needle, or firing squad. The first felon executed after *Gregg* was Gary Gilmore in 1977, shot to death in Utah for a robbery murder; since then there have been only a few each year. But while the majority has supported this, the actual business of state-sponsored homicide has always been thought a kind of necessary evil, traditionally as distasteful as the hangman. Even with new limitations on appeals it is hard to imagine a quantum leap in the number, a bloodbath involving all or even most of those currently under condemnation.

No historian doubts, nor should any reader of this book, that many innocent men and women have died at the hands of the state over the past several centuries. While trials on average may now be more fairly conducted than in the past, no one should believe that current procedures have been so perfected that these miscarriages will not happen again. And however refined after *Gregg,* the system cannot be made entirely free of the arbitrary quality that allows one killer to live while it executes another for a nearly identical crime. But these are moral issues, beyond the reach of historical evidence. The majority of Americans clearly have an emotional need to insist on final closure to some kinds of murder. And so the society as a whole will continue each year to choose a few men, rarely women, to help draw moral boundaries, to show in the most solemn fashion that some kinds of murderers are counted as beyond the circle of respect for life because of the ways in which they have taken other lives. All that the history can suggest is that the number of these dismal exemplars has not been and will not be very large, and that their examples have not had and will not have much effect on the murder rate either way.

6

The final issue here is the search to understand why the American murder rate is and so long has been the highest in the developed world. Discussion will begin with two of the more popular suspects, poverty and guns, and move on to culture, the heritage of frontier and slavery.

Although the romantic reformers of the early nineteenth century were the first to use social statistics to establish that the poor are more likely to commit homicide than the rich, this was hardly the first time that the connection was noticed. H. C. Brearly, on the other hand, writing in the 1920s, began his exploration of the causes of homicide in America by arguing against the then-popular notion that excessive rates were somehow the result of evils brought by our excessive riches; his clincher was that the South was both the poorest and the most murderous section of the country. The historical evidence overwhelmingly supports both Brearly and the romantics; poverty is statistically *associated* with homicidal behavior. At the same time the evidence does not suggest that poverty per se is the *cause* of that behavior. Nor is it an explanation either for why American murder rates are higher than those of other nations, or why rates in some past times have been higher than at others.

Absolute poverty, the threat of hunger and cold, is of course not the issue. In the past, as in medieval England, some murders may have been committed out of sheer immediate want, and in the nineteenth century strikers and strikebreakers, among others, fought and killed directly over jobs and livelihoods. But these directly economic issues are not now common. The United States remains the richest of nations. Adult murder rates in contemporary Philadelphia are higher now than they were a century ago, when the population as a whole was far poorer. Married men (and women) with families to support feel the bite of deprivation far more keenly than vigorous young men with no responsibilities, but their rates have always been much lower. And while the long nineteenth- to twentieth-century drop in murder rates coincided with generally rising standards of living, the great upsurge during the 1960s occurred during a time of matchless prosperity, when millions were being lifted up and over the official "poverty line."

But if poverty is no simple answer, the historical evidence does point to related causes for statistical rises and falls in the murder rate. One of them has run through the last half of this book: changes in the structure of employment. There is no clear historical evidence that consistently connects homicide rates after the Middle Ages with changes in short-term economic cycles. Sometimes, as in the 1960s and possibly the 1920s, prosperity and violence have risen together, and there is at least a suspicion that during the previous century good times allowed poor people to buy more alcohol, and so to be in places and do things that were likely to get them into murderous trouble. But if not the short-term cycle, then longer and deeper changes are related to levels of homicide. A good job is more than a source of income; it is a way of life, profoundly shaping personal routines and expectations. The relatively steady and highly paid work offered by the urban industrial revolution, together with all of the institutions, behaviors, and hopes associated with it were as important as anything in our history in driving rates down, just as the transition out of that revolution pushed them up.

And if not absolute want, then "relative deprivation," as explained in this and earlier chapters, is a convincing explanation for much of the upsurge in criminal violence in the late twentieth century. Most Vermonters in the 1820s enjoyed fewer material comforts than contemporary residents of South Central Los Angeles. But they were not continually reminded, in living color, about the lifestyles of the rich and famous, they coped with deprivation in dignity, and they did not watch the majority of their fellow citizens move ahead of them along routes they despaired of following. There is, then, a sense in which Brearly's contemporaries were right to suspect some sort of connection between American riches and American violence. The gap between rich and poor is higher in the United States than in any other developed nation, and has been growing since the early 1970s. And while wealth in itself is even less a "cause" of homicide than poverty is, when the two are bound up close together they do create tensions, temptations, and frustrations that help push up murder rates.

The American gun culture is a much better explanation for our level of homicide than poverty is, but it is still not good enough by itself.

The arguments between supporters of gun control and the National Rifle Association (NRA) are tired now, run off by the numbers. The slogans Guns Kill People and Guns Don't Kill People: People Do are equally correct, and equally half-true. Murder rates are central to the debate: one side points to England and Wales, where private ownership of guns, especially handguns, is very rare and homicide almost equally so; the other counters with Switzerland, Israel, and New Zealand, where ownership is common and homicide almost as rare as in England. Neither side resorts to the historical evidence, although both might score points if they used it selectively. That evidence supports the fans of firearms, to a point, in that widespread use of guns did not by itself push up murder rates in our earliest history. But after that point new weapons did prove more dangerous than those traditionally used when the Constitution was drawn up.

The gun culture in America is as old as the first British settlements. Settlers everywhere found muskets useful in hunting game, protecting property, and making war; so, soon, did the Native Americans. Every government except Quaker Pennsylvania at least theoretically required that able-bodied free men should own them, as members of the militia. While in practice many could not afford or use them, large numbers could and did; colonial history is full not only of war but of riot, rout, tumult, and insurrection among armed rebels. And yet ordinary homicides among white colonists remained relatively uncommon, more so than among their English contemporaries, and there is no evidence that many were committed with the cumbersome muskets of the day.

These low rates continued through the American Revolution and early national periods. Whatever was happening out on the frontiers or down on the plantations, it appears in fact that it was not until the 1840s and 1850s that the American homicide rates in more settled areas, such as New York City, began to soar above those in comparable English places.

The timing is no accident, and if history up to the antebellum decades supports the National Rifle Association, the proponents of gun control can make a stronger case out of what happened after. Small concealable handguns were first mass-produced in the 1840s and 1850s. It was these, not rifles, military pistols, or sporting weapons, that scared middle-class Americans, suggesting that as mobs and immigrants used them they must too, for protection. Among ordinary city dwellers, at the same time, hidden revolvers began to make any routine encounter as potentially deadly as it has been since; the man who carried one into the saloon or on the street was like a booby trap, liable to explode without warning when tripped or bumped. And so it was these "concealed" weapons that were first subject to state regulation and city ordinance.

If the widespread use of firearms has been deeply entrenched in our law and culture, gun control also has a long American history. The targets were those weapons thought most likely to be used for robbery or murder, above all handguns. Beginning in the mid-nineteenth century, state and local legislation in many places required permits, forbade sales to minors and aliens. New York State's Sullivan Law of 1911 tightened the permit procedures and made it a felony to carry a concealable weapon in any village, town, or city, provisions widely copied elsewhere. The apparent "crime wave" of the 1920s inspired the American Bar Association to call for the outright outlawry of pistols not designed for official government use. Even the sportsmen's United States Revolver Association, during the same period, called for a uniform firearms act, which would require a minimum forty-eight-hour waiting period for a permit, with police screening out criminals, aliens, alcoholics, drug addicts, minors, and others thought dangerous as owners.

Several states at that time adopted variations on this model, and also outlawed tommy guns and sawed-off shotguns, the scary new weapons made popular by contemporary gangsters. But while local legislation had earlier been opposed only by a few small arms makers and hardware stores, the scent of absolute prohibition and federal action heated up the debate. The National Rifle Association, formed back in 1871, was greatly expanded during the 1920s, and lobbying Congress became one of its major activities. The mails were effectively closed to pistol sales in 1927, but the Federal Firearms Act of 1938 did no more than charge a token $1 fee to manufacturers and dealers in interstate commerce, who were supposed to keep records and make sure they were not in violation of state permit laws. Thirty years later, during another crime wave, the Gun Control Act of 1968, signed only months after the Kennedy and King assassinations, raised the permit fees to dealers, tightened the requirements for interstate sales, and closed most access to imported heavy weapons.

The arguments have grown hotter with time, which has brought on one side a great growth in NRA membership and on the other the loss, in an increasingly urban nation, of the old tradition of keeping some kind of a musket over the mantle. The constitutional argument has been a standoff; each side has its own interpretation of the Second Amendment, whether the "right to bear arms" was or was not meant to cover only those who served in the militia, with only the kinds of weapons appropriate to individual citizen-soldiers. But otherwise the issues, the arguments, and the politics have all shifted. As recently as 1968 the House of Representatives was divided mostly along geographic lines, with the Northeast and urban areas generally standing for greater control, rural congressmen from the South and West opposed.

Since then the whole matter has been made ideological, pitting liberals and moderates against conservatives. The public, when polled, has long supported control, but the passion and the money have been on the other side, and the battles have gone both ways.

Ten years after an attempt on the life of President Ronald Reagan, by an obviously deranged assassin who severely wounded his press secretary, James Brady, the so-called Brady Bill of 1993 required at the national level the five-day waiting period and background check for handgun permits that several states had long adopted. Beginning in the late 1980s a number of mass murders, together with the increasing firepower of juvenile gangs and drug dealers, suggested the measures included in the crime bill of 1994: outright abolition of assault rifles and other high-tech machines, a general tightening of dealers' licenses and penalties, and abolition of sales to youngsters without parental consent. But these and other control measures are themselves under continuous assault.

The argument for control has changed very little: widespread ownership of guns raises the murder rate, and in the home suicide and accident rates as well. But the argument against control has progressed. Originally the NRA mostly stressed the sporting use of firearms. In the 1990s, when the issue began to center on armor-piercing bullets and assault rifles, it has sometimes taken the extreme position that these killing machines may be needed to protect citizens against agents of their own government. But since the 1920s the basic arguments have been two: one is that gun control does not work, that only honest citizens and not criminals will abide by curbs on sales. The other, related to this, is that gun ownership actually discourages crime by making criminals hesitant to rob, burglarize, or assault people who may have their own defensive weapons. All of these propositions may be subjected to the test of historical experience, which complicates matters by showing some support for both sides.

The NRA is right to point out that state and local curbs on sales have always been evaded, that determined criminals have been able to get whatever they wanted. Given the historic failure of other kinds of prohibition, there is surely little chance that another layer of bureaucratic regulation, especially in a nation as deeply divided as this one, will keep lethal gadgets out of the hands of drug dealers or other professionals. There is evidence, too, for the second point that fear of guns in the home holds down the burglary rate, for example, which is lower here than in contemporary Great Britain. This is an argument with wide popular appeal. The tradition of "justifiable homicide" in this country is an old one, as citizens as well as law officers may legally kill felons in the course of committing crimes such as robbery, rape, or assault. It is quite true that in places like nineteenth-century Bodie, California, where virtually all male citizens went armed, the incidence of robbery and burglary was virtually nil. In the late teens and 1920s, long after the frontier and vigilantism had passed away, Brearly estimated, after surveying big cities like Washington, Detroit, and Chicago, that the number of legally "justified homicides" accounted for over 25 percent of the totals recorded. And it is this heritage that over half the states have recently drawn on, beginning with Florida in 1987, in reversing the legislative trend of three generations by making it easier instead of harder to carry handguns hidden on the person.

But the case of mining towns like Bodie cuts two ways: when every man carried a gun, not many got robbed, but many got killed. While gun control legislation offers no safety from murder committed by calculating professionals, the great majority of homicides have always resulted from near-accidents, sudden flares of temper. Despite the revival of legal gun-toting, according to the *Uniform Crime Reports* "justifiable homicide" by private citizens is now relatively rare, numbering in the 1990s not much more than three hundred killings a year. While this is a substantial figure, roughly equal to the number committed by law enforcement officers, it is by the standards of Brearly's day quite low, accounting for not much over 1 percent of all homicides. Most of them, too, are committed by home owners with weapons legal under any imaginable form of registration. What most gun control proposals might curb is not these but the number of arguments in barrooms and traffic jams that have too often turned suddenly fatal, simply because what would otherwise be no more than a drunken shoving match has been irrevocably transformed by a handgun in easy reach.

If the advocates of control have no clear answer to the problems of enforcement and of professional criminals, they are right on several other points. The high number of gunshot accidents resulting from stashed weapons in the home, many of them fatal to young children, is unique to this country. The growing number of early teenagers with ever-heavier firepower at their fingertips is surely appalling: the ease of killing simply by pulling a trigger, instead of, say, stomping or biting an opponent to death, surely reinforces that psychological failure to understand the real nature of death by violence that is encouraged by graphic pictures on television. And there can be no question that the American ratio of roughly one gun in circulation for every resident is now and has been at least since the mid-nineteenth century a major contributor to our notoriously high homicide rates. That widespread ownership in Israel, New Zealand, and Switzerland does not lead to similar results is explainable in part by the fact that, however big by British standards, the proportion of households with guns in those countries is still not as big as ours and is carefully limited to the kinds of weapons and people that serve in their citizen armies.

Still, there is more to all this than weapons alone. The American love of guns is only part of the explanation for our murder rates: even with all firearms deaths subtracted from the annual totals, we still kill each other at roughly three times the rate of most Western nations. A number of these killings, with or without guns, result from deep psychological problems in the killers, some of them from greed, a few from other carefully calculated motives. But even with these, too, subtracted, we remain a shamefully murderous nation. What must finally and most fundamentally be explained, then, is what it is in our habits, values, and attitudes that makes otherwise quite ordinary Americans more likely to kill people than most other folks are.

Habits, values, and attitudes are components of culture, and culture is the product of history. Americans are a diverse people, with a shared national history but a number of separate histories as well. These separate histories have been very important in shaping homicide rates: for complex historical reasons Irish and Italian immigrants brought violent traditions with them, Jews and Scandinavians did not. And while our shared history has in the long run been even more important, we have shared it unevenly. Two of the most famous and notorious of American experiences, both of them involving racial conflict, are the frontier and slavery. Our several peoples have of course been affected differently by these two, respectively the most famous and the most notorious aspects of our history, and the differences have been reflected in many ways, including regional differences in our murder rates. But in the end all of

us, from Mayflower descendants to Vietnamese refugees, have been affected by both.

The western frontier has long been a favorite suspect among those
trying to explain violence in America, in part because we are proud
of this part of our heritage, and may be willing to admit that there
is a bloody price to pay for those more admirable values and traditions our national mythology has associated with the rugged Indian
fighters, family farmers, miners, and cowboys who populate our historical imagination. But among professional historians it is a cliché
that a frontier experience, as in Canada, need not necessarily leave
a violent heritage. And while from the viewpoint of the dominant
population all of the continent from Maine to California was once
frontier, murder rates have varied enormously across this great stretch,
and there is little correlation between how far a given state is removed
from the excitements of first settlement and its homicide rates: North
Dakota and Utah are far less murderous than North Carolina and
Georgia; and Texas was a sovereign nation half a century before Oklahoma was opened to white residents, and has long been a more violent
place.

While there is something to the "frontier thesis," it has, then, little
to do with recency of settlement. The experience of fighting hostile
Native Americans is more important, but it is not critical either; although it has left permanent scars among surviving Indians, its impact
on later generations of whites has been relatively minor. Minnesota,
ancestral homeland of the formidable Sioux and site of the biggest Indian massacre in our history, has never been known for its violence; nor
has South Dakota, scene of the last encampments of George Armstrong
Custer, Red Cloud, and Sitting Bull.

More important than when a given frontier was settled or how much
fighting it witnessed is the nature of its settlement. In some areas settlement proceeded in orderly, even communal fashion, as in traditionally peaceful New England and the upper Midwest; in others the
outskirts of settlement pushed out past the reach of government. In the
wilder jurisdictions, where a lone man on his place with a gun often
defied the law and made his own, a tradition of prickly armed individualism was born and then honored across the generations, built into the
legal institutions and values of each state. Ranchers and miners were

more likely than farmers to go armed and get into fights, and modern Arizona and Colorado still have higher murder rates than Iowa or Nebraska.

But ultimately the most crucial aspect of a lawless frontier heritage was not direct but indirect: that is, its contribution to the origins of African slavery. It was on the fringes of the Chesapeake, early in the seventeenth century, that isolated tobacco planters, with no effective opposition from government, illegally transformed the institution of indentured servitude into hereditary black slavery. Slavery later rooted elsewhere, too, and left a legacy of racism and tension even after its elimination, in the North, by the revolutionary generation. But it was only in the South that it dominated the economies and social systems of whole colonies, later states. And the most casual glance at the map of murder across modern America will show that, as from the beginnings, the highest rates are those in the South, followed by western places largely settled, often via Texas, by ranchers and other migrants from the Confederacy.

The explanation for the connections among slavery, race, and violence have run throughout this book. An economic system built on the continuous exercise of physical force lasted until the Civil War; after that war a social system built on the subordination of blacks to whites required continual murder, terrorism, and lynching. Until Emancipation the criminal justice systems of the southern colonies and states were built around the maintenance of slavery, with slave owners essentially allowed to make and enforce law as they saw fit, backed by armed civilians on patrol. Other issues, such as interpersonal violence, were neglected. After the war, the traditions of minimal official law enforcement and racially biased justice continued. The effect in both periods was to tolerate and so to encourage murderous behavior, even to "honor" it.

Observers of homicide in any era, including this historian, have always commented on the apparently irrational "causes" of many fatal encounters, unable to decode at a distance the pattern of looks, words, and body language that escalated into fighting and then manslaughter. But they always made a kind of sense to the killer, and often the victim as well. Both were typically young men who shared the same code of values, in which to tolerate any kind of "dishonor" without fighting was to lose the reputation for manhood. These were the values of the bachelor subculture of young and often insecure males, whether on the frontiers of late-eighteenth-century Virginia or the saloons of mid-nineteenth-century Philadelphia. They are still familiar on the streets of Los Angeles, Brooklyn, and Chicago. But observers and historians have always found them especially powerful in the South.

What distinguished the southern code of honor was less its depth than its width. In other places, an evolving sense of middle-class respectability, often sealed by marriage, led young men as they grew older and got steady jobs to abandon physical responses to frustration or insult. In some a sense of personal dignity was deeply engrained by parental or religious training, beyond the reach of sticks and stones as well as words, preventing overreaction to assault from outside the confident inner self. But in the South the daily need to assert personal dominance, first of all over slaves, demanded that even the most successful live by the code and handle their own affairs without calling on the law. Given the examples set by men such as President Andrew Jackson and Senator Ben Tillman, and the historically low rate of conviction for homicide resulting from any kind of quarrel, the need to maintain one's honor with fists, feet, and guns was effectively institutionalized at all levels of southern society.

Black men, and women, made up one of those levels. This book has offered many explanations why homicide among African Americans has long remained at eight to ten times the level among whites. But one of them, at bedrock, has been the southern heritage. Violence directed at whites was punished savagely, violence directed at blacks, by either race, was not. Since the law was no help, disputes must be settled directly, often physically. And with little else to protect, the need to maintain personal respect, even personal safety, through fighting at the slightest provocation became for many the kind of cultural trait it was among the white elite.

The anthropologist Elijah Anderson, analyzing the urban "Code of the Streets" as of 1993, described a set of values and violent responses that are in part specific to the most desperate of poor inner-city blacks. "The frustrations of persistent poverty shorten the fuse"—and so adults beat kids, who remember. Drugs and drug dealers make neighborhoods dangerous. Teenage status rests in part on owning, protecting—often seizing—fashionable shoes, jewelry, jackets. But "the heart of the code is the issue of respect, loosely defined as being . . . granted the deference one deserves." In practice this means that members of this deeply alienated minority must always be ready to counter the most trivial insult by fighting for their reputations or honor, a set of values that any antebellum southern aristocrat would easily recognize.

All of us, in fact, can recognize it: the "code of the streets" is simply an exaggerated version of the code of the schoolyard, of the codes of young men of many races, creeds, and backgrounds, of the free men of medieval villages, Irish immigrants to midcentury America, bachelor workingmen in late-century Philadelphia. It was and is not universally followed among any of these, including traditional southerners and inner-city African Americans. But there is some of it in most men, and it makes us ambivalent about homicide. Southerners, black and white, can on average trace their ancestry in this country longer than any but the original natives, and in good ways and bad they have stamped themselves forcefully onto its culture. Americans condemn the kinds of murderers that all peoples do, Richard Speck and Albert De Salvo. But having long ago abandoned the old medieval insistence on the "duty to retreat" from potentially dangerous situations, we find it hard to draw the line between those who manfully stand up for their rights and outright bullies, even cold-blooded killers, and so we make heroes out of Billy the Kid, Stagolee, even Al Capone. Most of us find ways of outgrowing or transcending this set of values before it pushes us into serious trouble. But wherever it exists it is a recipe for continual and potentially fatal confrontation, as the effort to maintain dominance too often results in losing control.

We misread much about murder, its threat and its origins. In perspective we have been spared more of the worst horrors of homicide than any major nation in the world, last visited by war on our own soil nearly a century and a half ago. But it is still true that murder is a social problem by definition, that every incident leaves scars on the families of both killers and victims, whose number over the last quarter of the twentieth century has reached into the millions. Historically the settled middle class has only at rare times worried about murder, mostly a matter for other folks. But this is one of those times: even as homicides by ordinary adults are falling in number, the most troubling kinds have been rising, from ideological bombings and serial killings to the more common murders by strangers, criminals, and deeply alienated teenagers.

Our reputation for routine daily violence has been well earned. This book has surely shown that the history of homicide is a reflection of history in general. And there is no easy cure for it. Recent changes in the justice system have had only minor effects. Any measures designed to push up the rate at which accused killers are convicted in court—as low, comparatively, as our murder rates are high—would upset centuries of tradition, and win little support among either liberals or conservatives. And the three major reasons for both high American murder rates and low convictions are deeply embedded in our historical experience.

We have been a part of the wider economic world since our seventeenth-century origins, and no country has fully solved the international problems brought by the decay of the urban industrial revolution; while over the past quarter century the United States has generated more new jobs than most others in the West, it has also tolerated a bigger gap between rich and poor. Our love of guns, as old as our origins, is not going to go away. It was in part born of, and long nurtured by, the nearly two centuries of racial warfare that followed European invasion of long-established native peoples. But high murder rates in the United States result above all from the enslavement of Africans, another bloody legacy of the seventeenth century. Slavery and the resulting racial hostilities have encouraged violent confrontation not only in direct and obvious ways but also in others not so easily recognized. We cannot fully escape it, whatever our personal ancestry, wherever we come from or live. Its heritage still lives in habits, values, attitudes, and even institutions that have made Americans historically more likely than other developed peoples to tolerate and even admire the kind of belligerence that leads to violence. It is our version of original sin, and the continual round of killings on the streets, across kitchen tables, in bedrooms, barrooms, playgrounds, and offices is only part of the price that we pay for it.

Select Bibliography

The works below do not include all consulted for this project. The list omits references to many well-known episodes or periods, including the most recent, and citations for familiar or easily found quotations. While including only single sources for all but the most controversial cases or issues, it attempts to suggest books of possible interest to general readers as well as to cite more specialized studies actually quoted or used directly in the text.

Several books have been helpful across the whole of this one, or at least a number of chapters. They range from Lawrence M. Friedman's lively yet scholarly legal history, *Crime and Punishment in American History* (New York, 1993), to Jay Robert Nash's often inaccurate, sensationalized, yet indispensably comprehensive *Bloodletters and Badmen: A Narrative Encyclopedia of American Criminals from the Pilgrims to the Present* (New York, 1995), from which several individual cases have been taken. Two older books by Negley J. Teeters contain lists of executions, useful statistics, and anecdotes: *Scaffold and Chair: A History of Their Use in Pennsylvania, 1682–1962* (Philadelphia, 1963) and *Hang by the Neck: The Legal Use of Scaffold and Noose, Gibbet, Stake, and Firing Squad from Colonial Times to the Present* (Springfield, Ill., 1967). Neither is as scholarly as William J. Bowers, *Legal Homicide: Death as Punishment in America, 1864–1982* (Boston, 1984), which not only summarizes legal arguments but also lists all official executions across several generations, state by state, with crime, method, and race of those executed. David R. Johnson, *American Law Enforcement: A History* (St. Louis, 1981), succinctly covers several centuries of experience at all levels of government.

Modern homicide statistics, since 1933, have been drawn from U.S. Department of Justice, Federal Bureau of Investigation, *Uniform Crime Reports for the United States* (Washington, D.C., 1995), and earlier editions, and U.S. Bureau of the Census, *Statistical Abstract of the United States* (Washington, D.C., 1995) and earlier editions.

355

The differences between American and English law and their effects in practice are described in Richard Maxwell Brown, *No Duty to Retreat: Violence and Values in American History and Society* (New York, 1991). The southern concept of honor is well introduced by Edward Ayers in *Vengeance and Justice: Crime and Punishment in the 19th–Century American South* (New York, 1984); what it has meant to Edgefield County, South Carolina, and its sons and daughters over two full centuries is compellingly described in Fox Butterfield's *All God's Children: The Bosket Family and the American Tradition of Violence* (New York, 1995). The consequences of the opposing concept of dignity (one we know much less about) are suggested by Randolph Roth, "Why Northern New Englanders Seldom Commit Murder," a paper delivered at the meeting of the Society of Historians of the Early American Republic, July 1987. The tensions between slaves and whites and their legal ramifications from the beginnings through the Civil War are sensitively and carefully documented in Philip Schwarz, *Twice Condemned: Slaves and the Criminal Laws of Virginia, 1705–1865* (Baton Rouge, 1988).

Lee Kennett and James Laverne Anderson, in *The Gun in America: The Origins of a National Dilemma* (Westport, Conn., 1975), cover not only the history of the gun culture but also efforts to control it. Homicide in general is the subject of Lt. Col. Dave Grossman's *On Killing: The Psychological Cost of Learning to Kill in War and Society* (Boston, 1995).

Among several useful collections are Roger Lane and John J. Turner Jr., eds., *Riot, Rout, and Tumult: Readings in American Social and Political Violence* (Westport, Conn., 1978), and Ted Robert Gurr, ed., *Violence in America*, vol. 1, *The History of Crime* (Newbury Park, 1989). The former includes Richard Maxwell Brown's survey, "The American Vigilante Tradition." The latter contains important articles on long-term trends in murderous behavior: Ted Robert Gurr, "Historical Trends in Homicide: Europe and the United States," and Roger Lane, "On the Social Meaning of Homicide Trends in America." Two other relevant books by Lane begin in the previous century and move into the twentieth: *Violent Death in the City: Suicide, Accident, and Murder in Nineteenth-Century Philadelphia* (Cambridge, 1979), and *Roots of Violence in Black Philadelphia: 1860–1900* (Cambridge, 1986).

These are not in general cited further, below, under individual chapters, unless they are sources of direct quotation or sustained argument. The books and other works found especially useful for individual chapters include those cited below.

Chapter 1

James Buchanan Given, *Society and Homicide in Thirteenth-Century England* (Palo Alto, 1977), and especially Barbara A. Hanawalt, *Crime and Conflict in English Communities 1300–1348* (Cambridge, 1979), are indispensable, and for early modern England so are the several essays collected in J. S. Cockburn, ed., *Crime in England, 1550–1800* (Princeton, 1977). J. S. Cockburn and Thomas A. Green, eds., *Twelve Good Men and True: The Criminal Trial Jury in England, 1200–1800* (Princeton, 1988), deals with the whole of the period covered. J. M. Kaye, "The Early History of Murder and Manslaughter," pt. 1, *Law Quarterly Review* 83 (July 1967): 365–95, and pt. 2, *Law Quarterly Review* 84 (October 1967): 569–601, explains some of the legal issues in careful detail.

Chapter 2

John Rolfe quotation in Lyon Gardiner Tyler, *Narratives of Early Virginia, 1606–1625* (New York, 1907), "Letter of John Rolfe, 1614," 239–44, quotation on pp. 240–41; quotations on law enforcement from Oscar Handlin, *The Americans* (Boston, 1963), 133; the encounter between West Africans and colonial Americans is well described in John W. Blassingame, *The Slave Community: Plantation Life in the Antebellum South,* rev. ed. (New York, 1979), chaps. 1 and 2; the authority on homicide for the early years is Bradley Chapin, *Criminal Justice in Colonial America, 1606–1660* (Athens, Ga., 1983), quotation on p. 13.

Yasuhide Kawashima, *Puritan Justice and the Indian: White Man's Law in Massachusetts* (Middletown, Conn., 1986), is a good account of legal misunderstandings; King Philip's War in David Horowitz, *The Indian Wars and America's First Frontier, 1607–1776* (New York, 1978).

Moral crimes in Robert Oakes, "Things Fearful to Name: Sodomy and Buggery in Seventeenth-Century New England," *Journal of Social History* 12, no. 2 (Winter 1978): 268–81, Hackett quotation on

p. 274; Puritan justice generally in Daniel A. Cohen, *Pillars of Salt, Monuments of Grace: New England Crime Literature and the Origins of American Popular Culture, 1674–1860* (New York, 1993); infanticide and other capital trials in Peter C. Hoffer and N. E. H. Hull, *Murdering Mothers: Infanticide in England and New England, 1558–1803* (New York, 1993).

The immense literature on the Salem witchcraft trials is neatly summarized in "The Visible and Invisible Worlds of Salem," chap. 2 of James West Davidson and Mark H. Lytle, *After the Fact: The Art of Historical Detection* (New York, 1981); New York justice generally in Julius T. Goebel and T. Raymond Naughton, *Law Enforcement in Colonial New York: A Study in Criminal Procedure, 1664–1776* (New York, 1944), quotation on p. 669.

North Carolina in Donna Spindel and Stuart W. Thomas Jr., "Crime and Society in North Carolina, 1663–1748," *Journal of Southern History* 49, no. 2 (May 1983): 223–44; quotations on proceedings against whites in slave cases in Arthur P. Scott, *Criminal Law in Colonial Virginia* (New York, 1930), 202, 203; arson trials of New York City blacks most conveniently in Winthrop D. Jordan, *White over Black: American Attitudes Towards the Negro, 1550–1812* (Williamsburg, 1968).

Chapter 3

Colonial Mobs in Pauline Maier, "Popular Uprisings and Civil Authority in Eighteenth-Century America," in Lane and Turner, *Riot, Rout, and Tumult;* North Carolina Regulators in Brown, "American Vigilante Tradition"; South Carolina Regulators in Paul David Nelson, *William Tryon and the Course of Empire: A Life in British Imperial Service* (Chapel Hill, 1990); Boston Massacre in John Ferling, *John Adams: A Life* (Knoxville, 1992). The Cherokee in John Phip Reid, *A Law of Blood: The Primitive Law of the Cherokee Nation* (Princeton, 1970), and William C. McLoughlin, *Cherokee Renascence in the New Republic* (Princeton, 1986), quotation on p. 50.

Richmond statistics in Robert M. Saunders, "Crime and Punishment in Early National America: Richmond, Virginia, 1784–1820," *Virginia Magazine of History and Biography* 286, no. 1 (1978): 33–44; Jason Fairbanks in Cohen, *Pillars of Salt,* quotation on p. 25.

Dueling in William Oliver Stevens, *Pistols at Ten Paces: The Story of the Code of Honor in America* (Boston, 1940); Nat Turner in Stephen B. Oates, *The Fires of Jubilee: Nat Turner's Fierce Rebellion* (New York, 1978); quotations on southern character in Ayers, *Vengeance and Justice,* 11–12; Lewis brothers in Boynton Merrill, *Jefferson's Nephews: A Frontier Tragedy* (Princeton, 1976); South Carolina justice in Michael Hindus, *Prison and Plantation: Crime, Justice, and Authority in Massachusetts and South Carolina, 1767–1878* (Chapel Hill, 1980), quotation on p. 130.

Chapter 4

Jewett and Bickford cases in David Ray Papke, *Framing the Criminal: Crime, Cultural Work, and the Loss of Critical Perspective, 1830–1900* (North Haven, Conn., 1987), and Cohen, *Pillars of Salt;* Choate quotation in Cohen, *Pillars of Salt,* 227.

New economy and reform in Roger Lane, "Urbanization and Criminal Violence in the 19th Century: Massachusetts as a Test Case," in Hugh Davis Graham and Ted Robert Gurr, eds., *The History of Violence in America: Historical and Comparative Perspectives* (Washington, D.C., 1969); factory quote in Michael B. Katz, "The Abolition of Beverly High School," in Gary B. Nash and Cynthia J. Shelton, eds., *The Private Side of American History,* vol. 1, 4th ed. (San Diego, 1975), 389–404, quotation on p. 401; attack on capital punishment in David Brion Davis, *From Homicide to Slavery: Studies in American Culture* (New York, 1986), chap. 1, and Louis P. Mazur, *Rites of Execution: Capital Punishment and the Transformation of American Culture, 1776–1865* (New York, 1989).

First police in Roger Lane, *Policing the City: Boston, 1822–1885* (Cambridge, 1967); New York mobs in Paul Gilje, *The Road to Mobocracy: Popular Disorder in New York City, 1763–1834* (Chapel Hill, 1987), quotation on p. 137.

Early police in James F. Richardson, *Urban Police in the United States* (Port Washington, N. Y., 1974), and David Johnson, *Policing the Urban Underworld: The Impact of Crime on the Development of the American Police, 1800–1887* (Philadelphia, 1972); rioting in Paul Gilje, *Rioting in America* (Bloomington, 1996); quotation in J. Thomas Sharf, *History of Baltimore City and County* (Baltimore, 1881), 2:787. Philadelphia homicides in materials collected for Lane, *Violent Death;* new domestic ideals in Carol Z. Stearns and Peter N. Stearns, *Anger: The Struggle for Emotional Control in America's History* (Chicago, 1986); "bachelor subculture" in Elliot Gorn, *The Manly Art: Bareknuckle Prize Fighting in America* (Ithaca, 1986); New York coroners in Eric Monkkonen, "Diverging Homicide Rates: England and the United States, 1850–1875," in Gurr, *Violence in Amerca,* 1:80–101; Prentiss Bishop quoted in Brown, *No Duty to Retreat,* 8; Marion County in David Bodenhamer, "Law and Disorder on the Early Frontier: Marion County, Indiana, 1823–1850," *Western Historical Quarterly* 16, no. 3 (1979): 323–36; vigilantes in Brown, "American Vigilante Tradition"; Joseph Smith in Dallin Oaks and Marvin S. Hill, *Carthage Conspiracy: The Trial of the Accused Assassins of Joseph Smith* (Urbana, 1975). Governor Hammond quotation in Stanley Elkins, *Slavery: A Problem in American Institutional and Intellectual Life* (Chicago, 1976), 219; slave justice and homicide trials in Eugene Genovese, *Roll, Jordan, Roll: The World the Slaves Made* (New York, 1974), bk. 1, pt 2.

John Brown in Stephen Oates, *To Purge This Land with Blood: A Biography of John Brown* (New York, 1970), quotations on pp. 133, 147. Civil War noncombatants in Grossman, *On Killing;* New York Draft Riots in Adrian Cook, *The Armies of the Streets: The New York City Draft Riots of 1863* (Lexington, Ky., 1974), quotation on pp. 198–99; Civil War slave conspiracy in Winthrop D. Jordan, *Tumult and Silence at Second Creek: An Inquiry into a Civil War Slave Conspiracy* (Baton Rouge, 1993). While Otto Eisenschiml's theory of a wider conspiracy to kill Lincoln is dubious, *In the Shadow of Lincoln's Death* (New York, 1940) does have a good account of the trial of Mary Surratt and others.

Chapter 5

New Orleans race riot in Dennis C. Rousey, *Policing the Southern City: New Orleans, 1805–1889* (Baton Rouge, 1996); Kernan in Ayers, *Vengeance and Justice,* 266–67; Horace V. Redfield, *Homicide, North and South: Being a Comparative View of Crime Against the Person in Several Parts of the United States* (Philadelphia, 1880), quotation on p. 10, statistics on pp. 12–13; hill country in William Lynwood Montell, *Killings: Folk Justice in the Upper South* (Lexington, Ky., 1986); Stagolee quotation in Lawrence W. Levine, *Black Culture and Black Consciousness: Afro-American Folk Thought from Slavery to Freedom* (New York, 1977), 418; Edgefield County, Tillman in Butterfield, *All God's Children,* chaps. 3–4; quotations from rape victim, bishop, in Roger Lane, *William Dorsey's Philadelphia and Ours: On the Past and Future of the Black City in America* (New York, 1991), 43, 51; geography of lynching in W. Fitzhugh Brundage, *Lynching in the New South: Georgia and Virginia, 1880–1930* (Urbana, 1993).

Of many histories of Mollies, the one most relied on here is Wayne G. Broehl Jr., *The Mollie Maguires* (Cambridge, 1964); labor violence generally in Philip Taft and Philip Ross, "American Labor Violence: Its Cause, Character, and Outcome," in Lane and Turner, *Riot, Rout, and Tumult,* 218–51; Garfield in Charles Rosenberg, *The Trial of the Assassin Guiteau: Psychiatry and Law in the Gilded Age* (Chicago, 1968); Haymarket in Paul Avrich, *The Haymarket Tragedy* (Princeton, 1984), district attorney quoted on p. 139; Homestead in Paul Krause, *The Battle for Homestead, 1880–1892: Politics, Culture, and Steel,* (Pittsburgh, 1992).

Minnesota massacre, Native Americans, in Robert M. Utley, *The Indian Frontier of the American West, 1846–1890* (Albuquerque, 1984), Sheridan quote on p. 165; western gunfighters in Frank Richard Prassell, *The Western Peace Officer: A Legacy of Law and Order* (Norman, 1972); Cole Younger quote in Nash, *Bloodletters and Badmen,* 334; Bodie, California, in Roger D. McGrath, "Violence and Lawlessness on the Western Frontier," in Gurr, *Violence in America,* 122–46, quotation on p. 124; Rock Springs in W. Eugene Hollon, *Frontier Violence: Another Look* (New York, 1974), quotation on p. 100; vigilante statistics in Brown, "American Vigilante Tradition."

Western Federation of Miners and IWW in Melvin Dubosky, *We Shall Be All: A History of the Industrial Workers of the World* (Urbana, 1988).

Urban violence, suicide-homicide ratio, Philadelphia stories in Lane, *Violent Death, Roots of Violence,* "Social Meaning of Homicide Trends"; professional law enforcement in Susan C. Towne, "The Historical Origins of Bench Trial for Serious Crime," *American Journal of Legal History* 26, no. 2 (1982): 123–59; Mudgett in Harold Schecter, *Depraved: The Shocking History of America's First Serial Killer* (New York,

1994); Oakland in Lawrence Friedman and Robert V. Percival, *The Roots of Justice: Crime and Punishment in Alameda County, California, 1970–1910* (Chapel Hill, 1981).

National executions in Bowers, *Legal Homicide*, and graph in Gurr, "Historical Trends," 36; Judge Gordon quotation in Lane, *William Dorsey's Philadelphia and Ours*, 131.

Forensic medicine and detective work in Jurgen Thorwald, *The Century of the Detective* (New York, 1964), and Julie Johnson-McGrath, "Speaking for the Dead: Forensic Pathologists and Criminal Justice in the United States," *Science, Technology, and Human Values* 20, no. 4 (Autumn 1995): 438–59; Philadelphia detectives in Howard O. Sprogle, *The Philadelphia Police, Past and Present* (Philadelphia, 1887), quotation on p. 298.

Of innumerable Borden books, most persuasive still is Edward Radin, *Lizzie Borden: The Untold Story* (New York, 1961).

Chapter 6

World War I hysteria in H. C. Petersen and Gilbert C. Fite, *Opponents of War, 1917–1918* (Madison, 1957), 203–7; Race riots in Elliot Rudwick, *Race Riot at East St. Louis, July 2, 1917* (Carbondale, Ill., 1964).

Capone in John Kobler, *Capone: The Life and World of Al Capone* (Greenwich, Conn., 1971), Moran quote on p. 235. Possible KKK involvement in Hall-Mills in William M. Kunstler, *The Minister and the Choir Singer: The Hall-Mills Murder Case* (New York, 1964); Ruth Snyder quote in Nash, *Bloodletters and Badmen*, 281; Leopold-Loeb in Arthur Weinberg, ed., *Attorney for the Damned: Clarence Darrow in the Courtroom* (Chicago, 1989), 16–89, quotations on pp. 18, 35, 88; Frances Russell, *Tragedy in Dedham*, 2d ed. (New York, 1971), is the most readable as well as evenhanded account of the Sacco-Vanzetti case, but see the indignant response of Herbert B. Ehrmann, *The Case That Will Not Die: Commonwealth v. Sacco and Vanzetti* (New York, 1969). Homicide statistics 1900–1920s in H. C. Brearly, *Homicide in the United States* (Chapel Hill, 1932), and for an expert modern assessment see Douglas Lee Eckberg, "Estimates of Early Twentieth-Century U.S. Homicide Rates: An Econometric Forecasting Approach," *Demography* 32, no. 1 (February 1995): 1–16. Philadelphia published and unpublished materials from Lane, "Social Meaning of Homicide"; 1895 robbery in Lane, *Roots of Violence,* 104.

FBI story in Don Whitehead's laudatory *The FBI Story: A Report to the People* (New York, 1956), but see Sanford J. Ungar's more critical *FBI* (Boston, 1975).

Chapter 7

Heirens in Lucy Freeman, *Before I Kill Again* (New York, 1955).

Account of the Rosenbergs is taken mostly from Ronald Radosh and Joyce Milton, *The Rosenberg File: A Search for the Truth* (New York, 1983), but see Walter and Miriam Schneir, *Invitation to an Inquest* (Baltimore, 1983).

Philadelphia in Marvin E. Wolfgang, *Patterns in Criminal Homicide* (Philadelphia, 1958).

Mississippi in Charles M. Payne, *I've Got the Light of Freedom: The Organizing Tradition and the Mississippi Freedom Struggle* (Berkeley, 1995), and Maryanne Vollers, *Ghosts of Mississippi: The Murder of Medgar Evers, the Trials of Byron de la Beckwith, and the Haunting of the New South* (Boston, 1995).

International patterns in Gurr, "Historical Trends in Homicide."

Chapter 8

On Kennedy assassination, minute-by-minute account in William R. Manchester, *The Death of a President, November 20–November 23, 1963* (New York, 1967); among saner near-contemporary critiques of Warren Commission, see Brian Jay Epstein, *Inquest: The Warren Commission and the Establishment of Truth* (New York, 1966), and Josiah Thompson, *Six Seconds in Dallas: A Micro-Study of the Kennedy Assassination* (New York, 1967).

Chaney, Goodman, and Schwerner in William Bradford Huie, *Three Lives for Mississippi* (New York, 1965).

Riots in *The Kerner Report: The 1968 Report of the National Advisory Commission on Civil Disorders* (Washington, D.C., 1968).

King and Robert Kennedy assassinations in Janet M. Knight, ed., *Three Assassinations: The Deaths of John and Robert Kennedy and Martin*

Luther King (New York, 1971). Black radicals in August Meier and Elliot Rudwick, eds., *Black Protest in the Sixties* (Chicago, 1970); white radicals in Kirkpatrick Sale, *SDS* (New York, 1973), Allen Matusow, *The Unraveling of America: A History of Liberalism in the 1960s* (New York, 1984), and Edward P. Morgan, *The Sixties Experience: Hard Lessons About Modern America* (Philadelphia, 1991).

Manson in Vincent Bugliosi (with Curt Gentry), *Helter Skelter: The True Story of the Manson Murders* (New York, 1974).

Weatherman quotation in Sale, *SDS,* 628; Boudin and Wilkerson in John Castellucci, *The Big Dance: The Untold Story of Weatherman Kathy Boudin and the Terrorist Family that Committed the Brink's Robbery Murders* (New York, 1986).

Two views of AIM in Russell Means (with Marvin J. Wolf), *Where White Men Fear to Tread: The Autobiography of Russell Means* (New York, 1995), and Stanley David Lyman, *Wounded Knee: A Personal Account* (Lincoln, Neb., 1991); Means quotation in Ward Churchill and Jim Vander Wall, *Agents of Repression: The FBI's Secret War Against the Black Panther Party and the American Indian Movement* (Boston, 1988), 122.

Kent State and Jackson State in William A. Gordon, *The Fourth of May: Killing and Coverup at Kent State* (Buffalo, 1990), and *Report of the President's Commission on Campus Unrest* (Washington, D.C., 1970).

Capital punishment in Bowers, *Legal Homicide.*

International and American murder rates in FBI's *Uniform Crime Reports,* Gurr, "Historical Trends in Homicide," and Lane, "Social Meaning of Homicide"; Houston conviction rates in Henry P. Lundsgaarde, *Murder in Space City: A Cultural Analysis of Houston Homicide Patterns* (New York, 1977), an insightful study of all killings committed in 1969; quotation in Brown, *No Duty to Retreat,* 26; Philadelphia 1972–74 in Lane, *Violent Death,* 137–39.

Chapter 9

Quotations from Sen. Joseph R. Biden Jr., "Combating Violence in America," speech delivered to Wilmington, Delaware, Rotary Club, December 16, 1993, printed in *Vital Speeches of the Day,* March 15, 1994; *Time* January 15, 1996. Some problems in tracing big city homicides in Eric Monkkonen, "New York City Homicides: A Research Note," *Social Science History* 19, no. 2 (Summer 1995): 201–14.

International homicide statistics in World Health Organization, *World Health Statistics Annual* (Geneva, 1995), and earlier editions.

MOVE in Charles W. Bowser, *Let the Bunker Burn: The Final Battle with MOVE* (Philadelphia, 1989).

All modern homicide statistics from *Uniform Crime Reports;* Brearly in *Homicide in the United States.*

Modern big city homicides and detective work in David Simon's highly readable *Homicide: A Year on the Killing Streets* (New York, 1991); FBI in John Douglas and Mark Olshanker, *Mind Hunter: Inside the FBI's Elite Serial Crime Unit* (New York, 1995); state imprisonments in Department of Justice, Bureau of Justice Statistics, *Prison Admissions and Releases, 1982* (Washington, D.C., 1985); recent history of issues in capital punishment in all articles of *Journal of Social Issues* 50, no. 2 (Summer 1994), devoted entirely to "The Death Penalty in the United States."

Early history of gun control in Kennett and Anderson, *The Gun in America.*

State-by-state distribution of homicides in *Statistical Abstract of the United States, 1995;* Elijah Anderson, "The Code of the Streets," *Atlantic Monthly* 273, no. 5 (May 1994): 80–94, quotation on p. 82.

Index

Abdel Rahman, Omar, 318
Abilene, Kans., 171
abjuring the realm, 13
abolitionism, 87, 110, 137
abortion, 119–21, 340
accessories to crime, 26, 336
accidents, 185, 240, 347
Adams, John, 71, 336
Adams, Katherine, 203
Adams County, Miss., 143–44
adoption, 234–35
adultery, 49, 56, 150
adults, juveniles tried as, 336
adversary system of justice, 335
African Americans (blacks): adoption
among, 234; in antebellum homicide cases, 116–19; as armed,
117; black belt, 154; black codes,
147; Black Liberation Army, 286;
Black Muslims, 278, 285; Black
Panthers, 274, 275, 279–80, 284,
286, 301; "Black Power," 274;
black-white murders, 136, 197–
98, 230, 256, 322; blamed for rising murder rate in Sixties, 296;
Brearly on causes of violence
among, 236; chain gangs, 149–
51; citizenship rights revoked,
116; Civil Rights Act of 1964,
271; Civil Rights Movement,
260–65, 272, 279; after Civil
War, 183; in Civil War, 141; class
split in, 327; code of the streets,
352; in contemporary murders,
320–21; conviction rate compared
to whites, 198–99, 257; death

penalty compared to whites, 199,
292; death penalty support by,
340; educational attainments,
187; Farrakhan, 285; in gangs,
117, 302; gun death vulnerability,
230–31; Harlem Renaissance,
218; homicide as leading cause of
death of young males, 321; "hunting the nigs," 118, 183; Irish hostility toward, 105–6; Jackson
State riot, 285; justice system distrusted by, 150, 230; King, 261,
273, 274, 277, 278; leaving the
South for northern cities, 217,
218, 264–66, 273; lynchings in
the South, 151–56, 240; Malcolm X, 278; marriage rate falling
among, 327; miscegenation, 110;
MOVE incident, 315–16; murder identified with, 230; murder
rate after World War II, 257, 265–
66; murder rate in 1960s and
1970s, 302; murder rate increasing in early twentieth century,
242; neighborhoods made red-
light districts, 230; in New York
City Draft Riots, 141–42; norms
of conduct differing in, 266; in
Philadelphia, 116, 198; police distrusted by, 273; in police forces,
330; as professionals, 187; radical
groups of the Sixties, 279–80;
rape of white women, 152, 198;
restrictions on freed people, 64–
65; returning World War II veterans, 250; Scottsboro Boys, 241,

Boston (*continued*)
established, 112; diversity of, 58; domestic violence in 1840s, 126; first regular police patrol, 107; mob violence in antebellum period, 103, 106; murder rate after World War II, 255; *Times,* 93
Boston, Goodwife, 48
Boston Massacre, 70–71, 104, 336
Boston Strangler, 294
Boston Tea Party, 70
Botkin, Cordelia, 202, 203
Boudin, Kathy, 284, 286, 313
Bowen, Dr., 205
boxing, 127–28, 183
Bradshaw, Sir William, 18
Brady Bill of 1993, 346
Bratton, William J., 332
Brearly, H. C.: analysis of U.S. homicide, 235–39, 323; on black death rate from homicide, 230, 231; on the family, 237, 325; *Homicide in the United States,* 229; on infanticide, 234; on justifiable homicide, 347; on killings of police officers, 232; on the media, 235, 325; on poverty and murder, 342
Bridgeman, Laura, 101
Britton, James, 49
Brown, D. Paul, 116, 120
Brown, John, 137–39, 173, 253, 254
Brown, Richard Maxwell, 132–33, 177
Brown, William Hill, 82
Bryant, Carolyn, 262
Bryant, Roy, 262
Buchalter, Louis "Lepke," 246
Buffalo, N.Y., 255
buggery, 49
Bundy, Ted, 319
Bureau of Indian Affairs (BIA), 286–87, 288
burglary, 347

Burns, Anthony, 137
Burr, Aaron, 85
Burton, Mary, 65

Cain and Abel, 1
California: Bodie, 171–72, 347; *Griffin v. California,* 290, 291; as hippie destination, 282; *People v. Anderson,* 293, 295; San Diego, mass murder, 319; vigilantism during gold rush, 133. *See also* Los Angeles; Oakland; San Francisco
Calvinism, 101
Camden, N.J., 331
Capie, John, 129
capital crimes: in antebellum South, 136; in colonial America, 55–56; increase in early modern England, 55–56; in post–World War II America, 253; rape as, 56, 223, 253, 338; robbery as, 56, 80, 223, 253; treason, 24, 28, 55, 79, 253, 254
capital punishment. *See* death penalty
Capone, Alphonse, 220, 231, 236, 242
Carnegie Steel Mill, 164–65
Carr, Thomas, 118
Carter, Bunchy, 280
Case of the Minister and the Choir Singer, 221
Casey, James, 135
Cassidy, Butch, 177
castration, legal, 88
Catholicism. *See* Roman Catholicism
Caverly, John R., 223, 224
Centers for Disease Control study of firearms deaths, 332
Centralia, Wash., 216
Ceylay, Philip, 288
chain gangs, 149–51
Chaney, James, 272, 273
Chapin, Bradley, 54
Chapman, Winifred, 281

The History of Crime and Criminal Justice Series
David R. Johnson and Jeffrey S. Adler, Series Editors

The series explores the history of crime and criminality, violence, criminal justice, and legal systems without restrictions as to chronological scope, geographical focus, or methodological approach.

Murder in America: A History
Roger Lane